AF816814

Reimagineering the Nation

POLITICAL AND SOCIAL CHANGE

Edited by Martin Bak Jørgensen and Óscar García Agustín

VOLUME 4

Zu Qualitätssicherung und Peer Review der vorliegenden Publikation

Die Qualität der in dieser Reihe erscheinenden Arbeiten wird vor der Publikation durch einen Herausgeber der Reihe sowie durch einen externen, von der Herausgeberschaft ernannten Gutachter im Blind-Verfahren geprüft. Dabei ist der Autor der Arbeit dem Gutachter während der Prüfung namentlich nicht bekannt.

Notes on the quality assurance and peer review of this publication

Prior to publication, the quality of the work published in this series is reviewed by one of the editors of the series and blind reviewed by an external referee appointed by the editorship. The referee is not aware of the author's name when performing the review.

Aleksandra Ålund / Carl-Ulrik Schierup / Anders Neergaard (eds.)

Reimagineering the Nation

Essays on Twenty-First-Century Sweden

PETER LANG EDITION

Bibliographic Information published by the Deutsche Nationalbibliothek
The Deutsche Nationalbibliothek lists this publication in the Deutsche Nationalbibliografie; detailed bibliographic data is available in the internet at http://dnb.d-nb.de.

Library of Congress Cataloging-in-Publication Data
Names: Ålund, Aleksandra, 1945- editor. | Schierup, Carl-Ulrik, editor. | Neergaard, Anders, editor.
Title: Reimagineering the nation : essays on twenty-first-century Sweden / Aleksandra Ålund, Carl-Ulrik Schierup, Anders Neergaard (eds.).
Description: Frankfurt am Main ; New York : Peter Lang, [2017] | Series: Political and social change, ISSN 2198-8595 ; Vol. 4
Identifiers: LCCN 2016050418 | ISBN 9783631715185
Subjects: LCSH: Sweden—Social conditions—21st century. | Sweden—Economic conditions—21st century. | Sweden—Politics and government—21st century.| Sweden—History—21st century.
Classification: LCC HN573.5 .R45 2017 | DDC 306.09485—dc23
LC record available at https://lccn.loc.gov/2016050418

Cover Image: "Fragile" by Martin Ålund. Oil on board. ©1996 Martin Ålund

Preparation of this collected volume was funded by FORTE, the Swedish Research Council for Health, Working Life and Welfare [grant number 2006-1524]

ISSN 2198-8595
ISBN 978-3-631-71518-5 (Print)
E-ISBN 978-3-631-71519-2 (E-PDF)
E-ISBN 978-3-631-71520-8 (EPUB)
E-ISBN 978-3-631-71521-5 (MOBI)
DOI 10.3726/b10645

© Peter Lang GmbH
Internationaler Verlag der Wissenschaften
Frankfurt am Main 2017
All rights reserved.
Peter Lang Edition is an Imprint of Peter Lang GmbH.

Peter Lang - Frankfurt am Main · Bern · Bruxelles · New York · Oxford · Warszawa · Wien

All parts of this publication are protected by copyright. Any utilisation outside the strict limits of the copyright law, without the permission of the publisher, is forbidden and liable to prosecution. This applies in particular to reproductions, translations, microfilming, and storage and processing in electronic retrieval systems.

This publication has been peer reviewed.

www.peterlang.com

Table of Contents

Author Bioses

Aleksandra Ålund is professor at REMESO, The Institute for Research on Migration, Ethnicity and Society at Linköping University. She has published widely in Swedish, English and other languages on international migration and ethnicity, identity, culture, gender, youth and social movements.

Magnus Dahlstedt is professor in Social Work at Linköping University. His main research interest concerns constructions of citizenship in the multi-ethnic society with a particular focus on struggles over boundaries of citizenship.

Anna Gavanas is associate professor at Remeso/ Linköping University. Her research covers migration, policy anthropology, gender studies, welfare states, working life and labour studies. Areas of specialization are, among other, domestic services in the EU, privatization of elderly care as well as U.S. fatherhood politics.

Randi Gressgård is professor at Centre for Women's and Gender Research (SKOK), and affiliated with the research unit International Migration and Ethnic Relations (IMER), University of Bergen. Her research interests include migration and minority studies, gender and sexuality studies, and urban studies.

Lisa Kings is senior lecturer at Södertörn University, Sweden. Her research and publications, nationally and internationally, in Swedish and English, are focused on issues on urban theory, social movements, social justice, civil society organization and everyday life.

Åsa Lundqvist is professor in Sociology, Department of Sociology, Lund University. Her main research interests include feminist analysis of the history of the welfare state and welfare policies, especially labour market regulation and family policies.

Vanja Lozic, Ph.D. senior lecturer at the School of Education and Environment, Kristianstad University, Sweden. His research deals with issues in education from the perspectives of ethnicity, multiculturalism, disability and youth cultures. He has published articles on integrated learning and museum-studies.

Diana Mulinari is professor at the Department of Gender Studies, Lund University. Her research focuses on issues of gender and division of labour in a global and intersectional perspective, relating gender and sexuality to issues of social class and ethnicity. She has studied processes of migration and changing ethnic and gender regimes and the mobilisation of new social solidarities.

Paula Mulinari is associate professor at the department of Social Work, at Malmö University. Her main research interest is on labour processes, gender, racialised and class inequalities in the labour market.

Anders Neergaard is associate professor in sociology at REMESO, The Institute for Research on Migration, Ethnicity and Society at Linköping University. His research and publications span issues such as labour migration, racial discrimination, trade union organisation and extreme right-wing/racist parties.

René León Rosales is a postdoctoral researcher at the Child and Youth Studies, Uppsala University. His research focuses on local democracy and policies against discrimination with a focus on ethnic segregation and young people's identification and life strategies in multi-ethnic societies.

Simone Scarpa is a postdoctoral researcher at REMESO, The Institute for Research on Migration, Ethnicity and Society at Linköping University. His research interests are: comparative social policy research, urban studies, poverty and inequality analysis, residential segregation in cities.

Carl-Ulrik Schierup is professor at REMESO, The Institute for Research on Migration, Ethnicity and Society, Linköping University, Sweden. His research and wide range of national and international publications cover issues of international migration, multiculturalism, racism, social-reconstruction in post-communist states, globalisation and the precarization of labour.

Anders Trumberg is a researcher at the Institute for Housing and Urban Research at Uppsala University and affiliated to Centre for Urban and Regional Studies (CUReS) at Örebro University. His work is focused on ethnicity, identity and social segregation within the Swedish schools system.

Viktor Vesterberg is a PhD lecturer at REMESO, the Institute for Research on Migration, Ethnicity and Society at Linköping University. His research focuses on the governance of unemployed migrants.

Carl-Ulrik Schierup, Aleksandra Ålund & Anders Neergaard

1. Reimagineering the Nation: Crisis and Social Transformation in 21st Century Sweden. An Introduction

Abstract: While for long being known as an international role model of tolerant multiculturalism and ethno-national diversity, Sweden is presently characterised by restrictive refuge policies, growing right wing populism but also resistance among civil society actors spearheaded by a variety of social justice movements. This first chapter introduces and contextualises the following 13 chapters of the book. They discuss Sweden's current transformation from varying, but complementary, perspectives. Their authors set focus on the present crossroad in the country's development, in terms of labour, citizenship racism and social exclusion, gender and immigration policy.

The year 2011 will pass into world history as one promising revolutionary change; by many imagined as the dawn of a brighter post-neoliberal future. But numerous manifestations of the hoped-for democratic spring mutated without notice into a reactionary necropolitical fall. In the 'indispensable nation' the Occupy Wall Street Movement, confronting the 'One Percent', was beaten down by the nation's increasingly militarised police force, giving way to a racist neo-conservative tsunami. A much hailed 'Arab Spring' was co-opted or it was smothered in its infancy through 'humanitarian intervention' and covert imperial war games for regime change in dispensable nations across North Africa and the Middle East. Ethno-national fratricide continued to be staged and stepped up by the self-described 'masters of the universe'[1]; the so-called 'international community' of the West.[2]

Yet, the empire was to 'strike back'[3] in the shape of a terrible self-inflicted Jihadist Behemoth, coupled with the so-called 'refugee crisis' of 2015; or more precisely

1 Alluding to Ali (2000).

2 Listen for example to one of the most devastating critiques of 21st century Western interventionism in a lecture on migration and the 'refugee crisis' given by the distinguished US economist, Jeffrey Sachs, at The Institute for Human Sciences, Vienna in March 2016. Available at: <https://www.youtube.com/watch?v=92-E4LYqrpQ> (Accessed April 8, 2016).

3 Alluding to Centre for Contemporary Cultural Studies (1982).

a 'crisis of solidarity' as the UNHCR Regional Coordinator for Europe, Vincent Cochetel (IPI 2015) describes it. This blowback strangely appeared to catch the European Union and its member states by surprise. From an initially bold move by Germany and Sweden, as the number of immigrants seeking shelter in the early autumn of 2015 began to rise things went quickly back to closed borders, barbed wire fences and securitization. Through a Faustian pact with an increasingly authoritarian neo-Ottoman regime, the EU attempted to buy absolution by concentrating its 'refugee problem' into outsourced camps in Turkey, itself riven by civil war (Gelmini 2015). A truly uncomfortable choice. 'Rarely has the EU needed Turkey so badly. And rarely has Turkey looked like such an unattractive partner', concludes Gideon Rachman (2016) in the *Financial Times*. The latest 'formal act of European disintegration', muses Roberto Savio (2016), was the negotiation between 28 European leaders and the Prime Minister of Turkey eventuating in a deal at odds with all international treaties, meaning a total capitulation to 'European values'. The grand European project stands denuded. We see a deformed colossus with feet of clay showing itself utterly incapable of taking responsibility for what amounts to a fraction of the monumental human tragedy, which it has itself been instrumental in bringing about, through colonialism in the past and predatory wars in current times.

'Helping the refugees in their region of origin' – a euphemism for this historical duplicity is indeed an allegedly 'humanitarian' political recipe prescribed by the right extremist *Sweden Democrats* (*Sverigedemokraterna*) as an alternative to Sweden's purportedly 'irresponsible' mass-immigration and asylum policy (99 SD-Problem 2014). Thus, the EU's cynical fix of its 'refugee problem' allows a, for long officially rebuffed, Swedish extreme right party to appear in the guise of the Archangel Gabriel.

The Sweden Democrats is a nationalist and neo-conservative political party with a blatantly racist Nazi past, which has gradually increased the number of its voters in the 2000s and which today holds the balance of power in the Swedish parliament. It is a party which at the time of writing still tends to be morally scorned and which is still to a degree politically boycotted by established parties to the left as well as to the right. But, actually, strategies for breaking the party's advance have, instead of effectively opposing it, lately taken the direction of a panicked step-by-step appropriation of its very agenda, to such a degree that by early 2016 decades of an open and farsighted Swedish asylum and family unification policy have been scrapped in favour of subscribing to many of the extreme right's cardinal positions.

We are thus experiencing a moment of crisis. It is a humanitarian catastrophe, faced by which a vital Swedish civil society has demonstrated strong popular will to welcome and embrace those fleeing from authoritarian regimes and the emergencies produced by imperial intervention and internecine wars. But it is at the same time a moment heavily exploited by an expanding extreme right racist movement. It profits from the propagation of phantasies of invasion by aliens, imagined to import supposedly toxic cultures, beliefs and customs that threaten to infect the life-blood of a noble, yet naïve, Nordic nation. It represents, as defined by Ambavalander Sivanandan (2001), a 'xenoracism' denigrating and reifying 'the displaced, the dispossessed and the uprooted, who are beating at Western Europe's doors, the Europe that helped to displace them in the first place'.[4] Nor is this solely a Swedish phenomenon. It represents a Swedish variety – distinguished by a particularly dramatic, rapid and swift shift – of political perturbations taking place in different forms all across a crisis ridden and increasingly politically fragmenting European Union. Thus '[t]he real crisis is not the influx of refugees to Europe per se', concludes civil society activist and writer, Rajesh Makwana (2016), 'but a toxic combination of destabilising foreign policy agendas, economic austerity and the rise of right-wing nationalism, which is likely to push the world further into social and political chaos'. It is a dire state of the (EU) Union, eventually with even Sweden, for long exemplary with respect to its liberal politics of asylum and refugees, failing to live up to 'humanity's last call for a culture of sharing and cooperation' (Makwana 2016).

Yet, Sweden is no Ireland. No Greece. It is still a country at the top of the international division of labour – a North of the North, but with its reputation for being a 'moral-political great power'[5] and an independent geopolitical actor

4 Sivanandan quoted by Fekete (2001: 23). The full quote is 'a racism that is not just directed at those with darker skins, from the former colonial territories, but at the newer categories of the displaced, the dispossessed and the uprooted, who are beating at western Europe's doors, the Europe that helped to displace them in the first place. It is a racism… that cannot be colour-coded, directed as it is at poor whites as well, and is therefore passed off as xenophobia, a "natural" fear of strangers. But in the way it denigrates and reifies people before segregating and/or expelling them, it is a xenophobia that bears all the marks of the old racism. It is racism in substance, but "xeno" in form. It is a racism that is meted out to impoverished strangers even if they are white. It is xeno-racism.'

5 Deserved or not, depending on your point of view. Sweden's reputation for being an 'exceptional nation' was grounded in the 1970s based on its non-aligned position, aid to third world countries which belonged to the most substantial in the world, its support of national liberation movements and its open refugee policy offering sanc-

gone to a state of vassalage subject to the EU's Common Security and Defence Policy, NATO and the United States. Sweden is, alongside Denmark and the UK, privileged by not being part of the Eurozone. This is one reason why the 2008 economic crisis affected Sweden less than most other European Union member states. It is a country for which a continued open migration and asylum policy would have promised unique opportunities for filling gaps in the labour market, for boosting economic dynamism, for redressing a crisis in an undermanned welfare institutional system, and for successfully combating a looming demographic crisis (Pelling 2015; cf. Scocco and Andersson 2015). The breakdown of the broader solidarities needed for pursuing long term goals of sustainable economic development and resuscitated social welfare resting on broadly-based politics of solidarity scuppered these opportunities. Thus the so-called 'refugee' or 'migration crisis' is rather the symptom of a deeper structurally and institutionally grounded 'crisis of solidarity' – even in Sweden. But the long-looming relapse of the country's welfare system can now be conveniently hidden behind a smokescreen of 'the refugees' (Gemmel 2016).

Sweden is indeed experiencing a deep seated crisis of social solidarity. It is driven by neoliberal politics which since the mid-1990s has made Sweden the OECD member with the fastest growth of social inequality. It has – using a concept coined by the historian Karl Polanyi (2001 [1944]) in his analysis of the economic and political crisis of the 1930s – been driven by a destructive 'commodification' of labour, money and urban and rural environments as they are subjected to a rampant self-regulating market economy. Similar processes today are analysed by David Harvey (2005) in terms of an 'accumulation through dispossession' i.e. looting all that is common. And there was, and in truth still remains a lot common to loot in a Sweden that used to be known as *the* exemplary welfare state. A deepening inequality has been produced through market driven politics of deregulation, privatisation and changes in the taxation regime favouring the well-

tuary for asylum seekers fleering military coups, authoritarian regimes and religious fundamentalism (e.g. Chile, Greece, Iran), South African apartheid, 'humanitarian interventions' and civil wars (e.g. former Yugoslavia, Somalia, Afghanistan, Iraq, Libya, Syria), Yet, this glorious past was accompanied by a more gloomy history represented by a (compared to size of population) huge and advanced military industry geared for export, making Sweden a leading (at times the leading) exporter of arms in the world, measured per capita (Ikegami 2013). Sweden was and is also home to a range of world leading multinational corporations with high percentages of foreign direct investments, but investments which have only rarely lived up to high standards of corporate responsibility (Hakkala and Zimmermann 2005).

off and skinning the already disadvantaged on the margins of the social welfare system. It has produced precarisation of work, citizenship and livelihoods; work and life not only without guarantees, but without predictability. However, this may be far from the end. Seen from the perspective of devoted neoliberals there remains still much to be done in bringing about the Hayekian market society that Polanyi (2001 [1944]: 3) sardonically denounced as a 'stark utopia' in his famous work, *The Great Transformation* (see also Block 2001: xxiv).

Parallel to this there is a crisis of belonging, as the role and function of the nation-state is being remoulded through the covert elite politics of market driven regionalism, internationalisation and globalisation with crucial impacts on the lives of all, but without solid anchorage in democratic processes or a sustainable institutional embeddedness. Taken together, all of this breeds existential insecurity and a crisis of the polity and of identity. It breeds as an adamant twin – similar to the proposition of Polanyi (2001 [1944]) relating to the crisis of the 1930s – contentious 'counter-movements'; yet, as before, these are often met by securitization and a 'state of exception' (Agamben 2005). And some appear to be seen as more 'dangerous' that others and treated accordingly.

The dire state we are in is well illustrated by the fate of an anti-fascist demonstration in the city of Malmö, Sweden, in August 2014, broken by mounted police (who illegally covered the identity tags on their helmets): an armoured brigade ruthlessly charged into a crowd of helpless activists. This could not but call to memory another atrocity: the deadly massacre of demonstrating workers in Ådalen, Northern Sweden in 1931. It was a brutal overture to a great compromise between capital and labour shortly afterwards. This compromise contained a tense class struggle, and it constituted the grounds for the Swedish welfare state until the crucial advance of neoliberal policies from the early 1990s. We have consequently travelled from one Polanyian moment of crisis to another – and from one 'state of exception' to another (Agamben 2005). It corresponds to Antonio Gramsci's famous definition of crisis. We live in a protracted interregnum where 'the old is dying' and where we can only guess what new is yet to come. It is a hiatus that harbours plentiful 'morbid symptoms'.

From this perspective we take as our point of departure in this collection of essays on Sweden's current transformation, the conspicuous crisis and debacle of the proud imagination of the European Union as the apogee of a tolerant multiculturalism and ethno-national diversity. It is a Messianic imaginary for which Sweden and its unique socioeconomic and political model enjoyed the reputation of being the exceptional spearhead (Schierup and Ålund 2011a). However, the EU's complex financial, political and social crisis has given way to despondent imaginaries that depict ethno-cultural diversity produced through immigration as a menace to the social solidarity that supports strong welfare states, and it depicts 'the Other', the migrant, the 'stranger', the 'Muslim', the 'Roma', etc., as the main scapegoats for the crisis. The culminating despondent imagery of the so-called 'refugee crisis' has become the dominant narrative, even in Sweden. Unravelling its causes and consequences is the overall objective of this book.

The book is divided into three main parts.

In Part One, 'The Welfare State in Crisis: Too Much Diversity… or Too Much Austerity?', we turn the conventional populist *and* academic problem of the 'refugee crisis' topsy-turvy. With reference to a changing European context we scrutinize the last quarter of a century's radical neoliberal transformation of the Swedish welfare state. We question the common sense idea that blames migration and increasing cultural diversity for undermining the welfare state and look at the persistent dogma of 'fiscal austerity' as a threat to the solidarity of an integrated multi-ethnic society. We chart the consequences of a deep-seated neoliberal reimagineering of the Swedish labour market and welfare regime, discuss decomposition of the class compromise and the traditionally strong working class organisation on which it rests, and point to the incongruity of a grand narrative of Swedish gender equality as compared with the incapacitating racialisation of migrant and post-migrant women.

In Part Two, 'Neoliberal Imagineering', the notion of *imagineering* is brought into play as a way to capture policies and institutions which have implemented the creative ideas of neoliberal political theory in practical form (Paul 2004). In its five chapters we take a closer look at specific cases of institutional restructuring with a focus on discourses and practices of 'exclusionary labour market inclusion', vagaries of an increasingly commodified school system, an exploitative transnationalised old age care and a securitised management of disadvantaged multi-ethnic urban neighbourhoods with a particular focus on the monitoring of racialised families.

Finally, Part Three, 'Reimagining Community', focuses on the imaginings and agency of upcoming social movements. Its five chapters expose alternative imaginings of societal development and investigate different constellations of actors offering counter-hegemonic prospects. For a start the rise of Sweden's increasingly influential racist-populist movement is discussed in a chapter with a particular focus on the Sweden Democrats. After that the book closes with four chapters focusing on different forms of anti-racist mobilisation. They tell of imaginaries in action and obstacles met by anti-racist workplace mobilization of blue collar workers. They bring into the open the dilemmas of Swedish trade unions and solidarity organisations in civil society confronted with a growing informalisation of the labour market. They discuss urban rebellion and new organisations fighting for 'social justice' and communicate the visions and ordeals of youth in the societal margin of racialised urban neighbourhoods.

PART I: THE WELFARE STATE IN CRISIS. TOO MUCH DIVERSITY… OR TOO MUCH AUSTERITY?

Following the end of the Cold War, 'multiculturalism' and ethno-cultural 'diversity' was propagated as part and parcel of the *credo* of the European Commission. It grounded the commission's self-instated authority to set standards for good governance well beyond the original western core of the EU through its mission to reform a previously 'totalitarian' European East. It has functioned also as a standard discursive weapon legitimising a 'liberal' West's devastating 'humanitarian' crusades across the wastelands of the global Rest's 'failed states'; most notably in Northern Europe's unruly Balkan backyard, in the Middle East and in North Africa. One of its more emphatic manifestations was paraded on the webpage, *Together in Diversity*, designed by the Directory General for Education and Culture in order to promote the *European Year of Intercultural Dialogue* (European Commission 2008) and to set long term processes of 'intercultural dialogue' in motion in the EU's individual member states. Here Europe's great cultural diversity – fusing with neoliberal 'deregulation' – was still represented as a unique comparative advantage. 'The enlargement of the European Union, deregulation of employment laws and globalisation', it asserted, has 'increased the multicultural character of many countries, adding to the number of languages, religions, ethnic and cultural backgrounds found on the continent. As a result,' this manifesto for EU policies on diversity goes on, 'intercultural dialogue has an increasingly important role to play in fostering European identity and citizenship'. Migration is here praised for enriching the continent's culture and 'the intercultural dialogue between the host country society and different migrant communities from other Member States or outside the EU' is seen to have 'a key role to play in strengthening citizenship values and participation for solidarity and cohesion' in European societies.

However, by the second decade of the 21st century, this rhetoric of 'intercultural dialogue' rather abruptly came to sound like an empty and anachronistic moral-political invocation. Speech on good governance in the EU had now become exceedingly dominated by phrases of 'prolonged austerity' (CEO 2011) for which popular support was drummed up through a 'sacralisation' of imagined mono-cultural nations' moral majorities (Houdt, Suvarierol and Schinkel 2011). By 2011 a *tour de force* played out by preeminent custodians of EU neoliberal austerity politics took over the Union's political scene in an apparently synchronised move by heads of government – Angela Merkel in Germany, Nicolas Sarkozy in France and David Cameron in the United Kingdom – to contest a mounting neoconservative nationalism by cannibalising it.[6] In emphatic speeches they all attempted to gain leeway in a tighter battle for political hegemony through scapegoating 'multiculturalism' as a threat to the 'nation's' or its 'people's' cultural unity, social cohesion, core values, equality and progress.

Flying banners of Western liberal democratic 'core values', a good deal of academic and media driven brush-clearing helped to prepare the ideological ground for this new moral-political highway crisscrossing Europe (further in Schierup and Ålund 2011b). It is a common sense and essentially racializing discourse, which in truth has for decades been present as an influential political stratagem in Western European politics (e.g. Schierup 1993). But it has come to increasingly dominate a wide realm of public-political debate across the European Union, especially after the 2008 financial crash underscored a search for legitimacy for neoliberal austerity politics combined with the discriminatory management of migration and race relations. It can lend itself to arguments put forth by certain economists, other social scientists and prominent publicists, warning that a Europe with 'open borders' has become 'too diverse' (Goodhart 2004), thus creating a situation which may putatively undermine the social cohesion and solidarity on which a large welfare state rests, and the willingness of citizens (and of the 'working-class' in particular) to finance comprehensive welfare programmes.

A changing European scene also impacted on Sweden via a growing mainstream media and political discourse urging 'unity' in terms of cultural assimi-

---

6 *Bundeskansler* Angela Merkel attempted to fend off a nostalgic catastrophe-mongering nativism brewing in the ranks of the hegemonic German 'Great Coalition', most dramatically represented by the German Social Democratic politician and former member of the executive council of the Deutsche Bundesbank, Thilo Sarrazin (2010) with the influential immigration-critical book *Deutschland Schafft sich ab* ("Germany Does Itself In"). Through distancing himself from everything multicultural, president Nicolas Sarkozy set out to market himself as more patriotically French than Marine le Pen, who had then taken over her infamous father's leadership of the *Front National*, and who was occasionally rising to first place in the opinion polls during the French presidential election campaign of the time. Premier David Cameron – whose EU friendly policy had become increasingly challenged by the immigration-hostile *United Kingdom Independence Party* (UKIP) under the new dynamic leadership of Nigel Farage (2010), and questioned as well by a national socialist immigration-sceptical discourse looming within the rival *Labour Party* – settled the bill with a long established discourse about 'Multicultural Britain'.

lation. '[I]t is not enough to create similar conditions and possibilities for all people in the economic and social sphere', the Swedish minister for integration warned on the eve of the 2008 depression. In order to secure social cohesion in a democratic society it is 'as important to have [a] shared vision of and emotions of belonging' (Skr. 2008/09:24).[7] At the time of writing (April 2016) this political discourse of 'belonging' has started to increasingly mutate into what used to be seen as distinctive for a despicable populist, xenoracist and Islamophobic regime in neighbouring Denmark, but which could, putatively, never engulf Sweden.

The celebrated (or vilified, depending on your point of view) social-democratic so-called 'Swedish Model' of the welfare state, built during the first four decades after the great depression in the early 1930s, was founded on the World's most distinctive implementation of Keynesian macroeconomics. It rested on two grand historical compacts, one political (the so-called 'cow deal') forging a common block of workers and farmers, and the second concerning industrial relations between capital and labour. It generated decommodification of labour through politics and institutions for labour market regulation, income insurance and social protection. Its ramified institutional structure became for decades following the Second World War geared to facilitating the incorporation of large scale (compared with most other European countries) immigration of labour and asylum seekers, in principle although not always in practice, on equal terms.

Migration has always been a part of Swedish history (Svanberg and Tydén 1998). Yet, prior to World War II Sweden had been a country of high net *emigration*. Sweden figures thus in the classical study of Douglas Massey (1988: 386) among the six countries of the world with the highest rate of emigration, counting 22 percent of the total population between 1846 and 1924. After the war Sweden became, on the contrary, one of the countries with the highest *net-immigration* relative to its population. Post-1945 migration to Sweden resembles that of other parts of North-Western Europe in terms of the shifting national-geographical background of immigrants. First labour migrants came from neighbouring Finland and were joined later by people mainly from Southern Europe (Italy, Greece) and the wider European rim (Yugoslavia, Turkey). During the first three post-war decades, refugee migration was limited and until the late 1960s mainly European, counting 20 000 from German concentration camps and after then refugees fleeing repression in the Soviet satellite states of Hungary (1956), Czechoslovakia (1968) and Poland (1980). After a halt to non-Nordic labour migration, initiated at the behest of the Swedish trade unions, a major shift took place in the early 1970s,

7 For further discussion, see Schierup (2011b).

after which immigrants came mainly as asylum seekers or for family unification. After 1980 – apart from substantial immigration through family unification and a relatively small proportion of labour migrants – most came as refugees from the Western Balkans (the Yugoslav succession wars), or from Asia, Africa, Latin America and the former Soviet sphere of influence. Following Western military interventions, civil wars and state collapse the largest groups of migrants have, after 9/11 2001, come as asylum applicants from Afghanistan, Iraq and Syria. While peaks and slumps have varied in the past due to these external factors – with a maximum of 84 000 asylum seekers in 1992 related largely to the war in Bosnia – the recent immigration of asylum applicants has exceeded all previous high points. Sweden is, thus, the EU member state that received the highest number of asylum applications in the midst of the recent refugee crisis, with 8.4 applicants per thousand inhabitants in 2014 compared with the EU-wide average of 1.2. Eighty thousand applied for asylum in Sweden in 2014, and in 2015 as many as 160 000 (Eurostat 2015).

Until 2015 most migrants have settled permanently. This is an effect of a principled policy of granting permanent residence permits and comparatively easy access to full citizenship. But the 'Swedish Model' has undergone a profound transformation since the early 1980s, in particular through the shift in priority from Keynesian full employment policies to neoliberal fiscal austerity from the early 1990s. This has been paired with sweeping processes of (re)commodification through decomposition of the industrial relations pact, privatisation and outsourcing of public sector services, including transport infrastructure, housing, education, health and care services, labour market management and the social services. Another important aspect of this transformation is a change in discourse and policies on immigration and the incorporation of migrants. In contrast with a predominantly – albeit often contested and compromised (Ålund and Schierup 1991) – positive political discourse that during decades depicted immigration (including that of asylum seekers) as a resource for the Swedish economy and society, the 'immigration is bad for welfare' discourse becoming dominant in the EU of the 2010s has today come to fuel struggles for political hegemony also in Sweden, with 'the refugee crisis' as its central stratagem.

However, are migration and a growing ethnic diversity of the population truly threatening the social solidarity on which a large universal welfare state depends? Or is the solidarity of a universal welfare regime and dynamic multicultural society threatened by fiscal austerity and welfare state retrenchment coming in parallel with the vote-fishing populist strategies of centre-right parties as well as a social democracy void of vision; all in the shadow of the growing strength of right-wing populist extremism?

These are leading questions for the book's Part One, discussed in an overall perspective by Carl-Ulrik Schierup and Simone Scarpa in their contribution, 'How the Swedish Model Was (Almost) Lost. Migration, Welfare and Politics of Solidarity' (Chapter Two). They describe the undermining of rights of social citizenship, the systematic dismantling of the mutually sustaining pillars of the traditional social democratic Swedish welfare state and the profound disarticulation of the Swedish Model, all connected with neoliberal reforms and fiscal austerity implemented during the last quarter of a century.

A new migration law passed in 2008, opening up for temporary labour migration, as well as new austere laws on asylum in 2016 have both broken with the principle of granting permanent residence permits to newcomers and a fast track to full citizenship. We see these changes in migration policy as both related to and in themselves exacerbating deepening and increasingly racializing class divisions and the long-term social exclusion of sizeable population groups from substantial social citizenship rights. In the wake of this development conflicts over redistribution grow callous. At the present time, heartfelt humanitarian appeals (still proclaimed by some political leaders) for solidarity with the wretched of the earth, who are fleeing wars, persecution and complex emergencies, are intractably merged with insistence on fiscal austerity. They thereby turn into a political oxymoron. An emerging blue-brown political hegemony's mediation of its inherent contradiction gives birth to a toxic 'racial austerity' and weeds out, in the same fell swoop, the embryo of a potentially dynamic 'Refugee Keynesianism'[8].

A central pillar of the Swedish Model at its zenith was the hegemony of social democracy supported by a strong labour movement. In Chapter Three, 'The Swedish Model in Transition: Trade Unions and Racialised Workers', Anders Neergaard discusses a current crisis of the Swedish model of industrial relations by focusing on the relationship between Swedish working class trade unions, migrants and racialised workers. In order to capture the dilemmas of worker solidarity, the problem of racialisation of workers within the context of labour unions is at the centre of the analysis. Neergaard connects union organisation and internal political practices with the wider framework of industrial relations as well as the wider societal context of struggles over economic and political development in Sweden. The trade union movement is faced with an increasing number of challenges where all that which was considered a Swedish model of welfare and industrial

8 A phrase coined by Hansen (2016).

relations seems to be breaking down. Few strategies appear to be left for to dealing with the declining strength of an increasingly fragmented working class and a 'subordinated inclusion' of migrants and racialised workers riven with conflicts.

In Chapter Four 'Invisible, Burdensome and Threatening: The Location of Migrant Women in the Swedish Welfare State', Åsa Lundqvist and Diana Mulinari emphasise the gendered character of 'subordinated inclusion'. 'Gender equality' as ideology and institutional practice is a central feature of the Swedish model that has informed policy making for almost half a century. It is supposed to enable both women and men to combine paid work and caring responsibilities, but has been challenged in divisive discourses on migrant and racialised women. In particular, the notion of a 'gender equal family', a central theme in policy making since the 1960s, exposes a doubtful perception of the homogenizing and polarising categories of 'migrant women' (Swedish: *invandrarkvinnor*) and 'Swedish women'. Exploring the location of 'migrant women' within and between work and family life as well as across time, the authors argue that the category of 'migrant women' is perceived as being different from 'Swedish women' in policy discourse, but that the meanings and understandings of the location as 'different' vary over time. They go on to analyse how the category of 'migrant women' has been conceptualised – within and between state policies and discourses on family life on the one hand and labour market participation on the other – from the 1960s in a range of changing and contradictory ways. These variations are related to the successive master narratives of a shifting political hegemony spanning the original social democratic welfare state and its neoliberal transformation. Lundqvist and Mulinari see a shifting location of 'migrant women' as a product of discursive de-personification through successive historical periods, varying between being represented as 'invisible'; 'culturally different', a 'burden', a 'threat to the nation', and finally – within an emerging paradoxical discursive neoliberal-*cum*-neoconservative re-evaluation of the traditional 'migrant women' – as 'care-worker', reborn as a 'resource'. The latter turn up contingent on a prevalent political will to engineer a growing niched, gendered and racialised low wage sector of 'flexible' precarious labour.

PART II: NEOLIBERAL REIMAGINEERING

Subordinated Inclusion or Exclusionary Subordination?

In Part Two, departing from the successful neoliberal project of (re)imagineering the Swedish nation, we turn to the discourses and practices whereby social democratic, but especially right wing governments, have reshaped Sweden since the late 1980s. In doing so, further aspects of a convoluted inclusion-exclusion pairing are discussed, with a focus on three different institutional contexts: the labour market, elderly care, and a fundamentally reshaped public school system.

The new Sweden that began to emerge in the 1990s can be depicted, in a broader perspective, as part of the general transformation of capitalism since the 1970s. From having had the national welfare state as a framework for economic regulation and political governance, Sweden has approached the general model of a neoliberally embedded post-national *workfare* regime (Jessop 2002). This systemic transformation can be summarized in a number of fundamental shifts regarding the relationship between work and welfare – a development that Sweden largely shares with other North Atlantic welfare states. 'Full employment' is redefined as 'full employability,' and unemployment is said primarily to be the result of the individual's (presumably deficient) qualifications. Economic austerity policy gains ground to the cost of social policy, with the aim of creating more flexible labour markets. Thereby social costs are regarded as production costs rather than as a means of redistribution. Socio-political measures are defined less and less as a means to protect citizens from the destructive forces of an unregulated market economy. Transfers to maintain income levels are kept to a minimum in order to drive people into employment and boost an 'entrepreneurial spirit.' Social and employment policies have virtually become a tool for controlling the behaviour of individuals with the purpose of making them adaptable to what corporations and governments regard as the needs of 'the market' (Papadopoulos 2005).

However, the emphasis has increasingly shifted from the nation state to both supranational and a local/regional levels although policies and regulations at the national level remain central. A new control system is emerging, based on a decentralised exercise of power in local, regional, and trans-national development state-business-civil society 'partnerships' (Jessop 2002). In Chapter Five, 'Rationalities of Exclusionary Inclusion: Constructing Others while Combating Social Exclusion', Viktor Vesterberg elaborates a merger of the twin concepts of social exclusion and social inclusion in the context of the Swedish labour force management focused on the European Social Fund's (ESF) program on migrant-integration policies. He argues that a series of projects within the ESF program in Sweden demonstrates a convoluted duality of practices of inclusion and employability embedded in what he defines as 'exclusionary inclusion'. The chapter exposes an inherently contradictory and debilitating governing process. A rationality of exclusionary inclusion is at play when a group or a subject targeted by inclusion measures must first be made *includable* by being positioned as 'excluded' and construed as deviant.

The most fundamental of Swedish social insurances – the pension system – was (in accordance with neoliberal orthodoxy) radically transformed following a severe economic crisis in the early 1990s. This was followed by neoliberal privatization and institutional remoulding of elderly care in Sweden. In Chapter Six, 'Swedish Retirement Migrants and Domestic Services in Spain: Informalisation and Moral Economy in Reimagining Sweden', Anna Gavanas analyses Swedish retirement migrants (IRMs) in Spain. She discusses how the consumption of domestic services (cleaning, care and handyman work) – viewed through the lens of the retiree migrants – resembles the Swedish privatization of elderly care, now outsourced to Spain. Gavanas analyses her informants' perspectives on paid and unpaid as well as formal and informal (regulated and unregulated) arrangements for domestic services, and how this brings out their frustrations in Spain, as well as reflecting the changing welfare state in the Sweden they left behind and to which most eventually intend to return. Caught between collectivism and individualism, Gavanas claims, IRMs are (re-)imagining but also concretely and from below reimagineering Sweden, thereby exposing national discrepancies between welfare states. Analysing solidarity and care among IRMs, as well as relations with informal workers and intermediaries, Gavanas discusses how rationalities of moral economy, prevalent among IRMs, make international discrepancies and inequalities – enmeshed in the wider market of globalized labour – appear more manageable and acceptable, not least when expressed in terms of 'cultural difference'.

In Chapter Seven, 'Towards a New Education Regime: The Neoliberal Turn in Swedish Education Policy', Magnus Dahlstedt and Anders Trumberg scrutinize social and spatial dimensions of a formerly unified Swedish school system which was deeply transformed and fragmented in the wake of radical neoliberal reforms after the end of the 1980s. These were envisaged as liberating reforms to provide space for a plurality of civil society initiatives. But in reality they were engineered chiefly through a sweeping process of privatisation spearheaded by profit maximising (but publicly funded) corporate 'risk capital'; with the brunt of the 'risk' being carried by the state, and in the final instance by ordinary tax-payers. Education has come to be conceptualized as a 'private good' rather than a 'common good'. Dahlstedt and Trumberg argue that this, in particular, has affected the inclusion of migrants.

The priority of 'the market' as the paramount regulatory principle for what has become one of the World's most commodified public school systems has resulted – among other aspects – in deepening divides along intersecting lines of ethnicity-race, gender and social class with respect to schools attended, educational options and educational outcomes for different students. Despite increased opportunities to make individual decisions, following a so-called 'freedom of choice reform' in the early 1990s, intended to increase the plurality of opportunities available to all citizens, actual school achievement and higher education continue to be increasingly distributed along ethno-cultural and socio-economic lines. It has forged a systemically embedded segregation of students in terms of school choice, thus resulting in the production and reproduction of increasingly homogeneous schools in their class and neighbourhood characteristics as well as specific ethnic backgrounds. Consecutive reforms have, consequently, tended to *reinforce* prevailing patterns of differentiation and segregation – particularly in urban areas, where the establishment of an increasing number of independent schools has led to sharper competition for both students and staff. It has caused a growing residential segregation of citizens of migrant background and, consequently, an increasing economic and racialised polarisation of the population, with deeply ingrained spatial dimensions. Seen against this background the dynamics of the deregulated Swedish public school system has become a significant element in the production of increasingly polarised city areas.

'Badlands' of the Kingdom

Residential segregation and the concentration of racialised poverty in disadvantaged neighbourhoods are similar to processes observed in, for example, disadvantaged poly-ethnic suburban environments around Paris and other French cities. Multi-ethnic suburban areas in cities like Stockholm, Malmö, Gothenburg and Uppsala have evolved into territories with the reputation for being 'social problems'. They are, populated largely by marginalised 'majority Swedes' and disadvantaged new ethnic minorities of recent immigrant background (Ålund 1997). These areas are now, due to the (global) economic crisis and neoliberal policies combined with reduced public services investment in the country generally, and multi-ethnic suburbia in particular, exposing a development which may increasingly come to deserve comparison with the 'advanced marginality' (Wacquant 1996) of US urban ghettoes or the 'Badlands of the Republic', a phrase coined by Mustafa Dikeç (2007) to refer to the mainstream political and media image of the racialised French *Banlieus*.

While overexposing crime and violence among migrants and their offspring in these Swedish 'badlands' – 'failed' neighbourhoods 'which Mother Svea[9] appears to have forgotten' (paraphrasing Edling 2015) – the dominant focus in mainstream media and political discourse is on the spectacular, and on culturally-related dif-

9 'Mother Svea' (Swedish: *moder Svea*) is a mythical gestalt symbolising the Swedish nation.

ference and deviance. It veils significant aspects of the social context, most palpably with respect to the conditions under which youths of immigrant background spend their adolescence. A supposedly 'problematic' so-called 'immigrant culture', disconnected from the actually existing social reality, is presented as uniform and collectively shared by ethnic groups or communities. The focus is, in particular, on 'immigrant' gender relations. Violent behaviour is related to the implicitly 'foreign culture' of 'immigrants', which is supposed to collide perilously with that of an imagined (liberal) 'majority society' (Ålund 2003; Ålund and Alinia 2011). Similar to a neo-conservative 'moral underclass discourse' (Levitas 1998), long since established in the US and the UK – exposing cultural 'deviancy', 'dysfunctional' families, and 'deficient parenthood' as root causes of a supposedly evil circle of social exclusion and escalating violence – the most common explanation in public debates about the riots was to declare the parents guilty of inadequate socialising, forcing youth onto the street.

This is the theme of Chapter Eight, 'Problematizing Parents: Representations of Multi-Ethnic Areas, Youth and Urban Unrest,' by Magnus Dahlstedt and Vanja Lozić. In it they scrutinise a persistent institutional polarising and a stigmatising representation of 'Swedes' and immigrants as 'culturally different' in relation to the assumed (liberal) 'core values' of Swedish gender equality, and they criticise a stigmatising representation of migrant woman as culturally conformist and of migrant parents believed inadvertently to reproduce the values of 'cultural traditionalism'. Connecting issues of citizenship, social policy and social cohesion in the Swedish multi-ethnic suburban areas built as part of a large-scale housing project in the 1970s, they argue that the neighbourhoods which from the start were represented in public debate as 'problems', defined in terms of social and/or ethno-cultural Otherness, have now come to be designated as urban 'districts of exclusion'. Addressing wider transformations in welfare policy and governance, Dahlstedt and Lozić discuss this shift of focus as corresponding with changes of social and welfare policy from centralism and social inclusion to 'autonomy' and 'responsibility' with a one-sided and simplifying focus on the individual. They illustrate this change through a critical examination of representations of juvenile delinquency and social unrest among youth in these 'districts of exclusion' during the first decade of the 2000s. Their study is based on interviews with civil servants, the police, individuals in schools and the social services, and personnel from voluntary organizations. This multitude of people involved in work on social inclusion among youth in multi-ethnic suburban areas in Sweden, demonstrate various discursive conceptualizations of the causes of urban unrest and the means to solve them. They share, however, a strong focus on the family and 'migrant' parents as problems in need of being brought into line with supposed Swedish 'core values'. These common sense ideas of problems and solutions correspond to the on-going re-engineering of welfare policy, according to which the main responsibility for the welfare of citizens is put on the individuals themselves rather than on the collective and the state. They are, Dahlstedt and Lozić conclude, related to the dismantling of public welfare services and the consequent unrest among youth.

In Chapter Nine, 'Welfare Policing and the Safety–Security Nexus in Urban Governance: The Expanded Cohesion Agenda in Malmö', Randi Gressgård extends the discussion of a retreating welfare service and issues of securitization, relating them to wider questions of social cohesion, neoliberal economics and welfare institutions. Established welfare state structures and institutions, she argues, form the basis for changing modes of securitisation: more police enforcement in conjunction with more police involvement in 'social' policy interventions. With her empirical focus on urban governance policy and securitization within multi-ethnic urban areas in the city of Malmö, she discusses how partnerships between the police and local authorities intensify and widen the scope of policing in deprived, immigrant-dense areas. As social welfare is conflated with crime prevention and demands for safety and security in a broader political and economic context, she demonstrates how policing, social cohesion and welfare are merged with 'social' crime prevention, amounting to what she calls 'welfare policing'. Her principal argument is that the expanded cohesion agenda, which opens up far-reaching security politics in specific districts, causes entire sub-populations to be labelled as dangerous 'Others', against which 'society', or 'the city', must be defended. Beyond welfare policing's rhetoric about a 'will to empower', an actual 'will to power' expresses the obscure, tough integral character of partnership agreements. Within the limits of the law, albeit in a legal grey zone, welfare policing allows for expanded policy interventions in specific neighbourhoods and domestic domains, which makes it virtually impossible to distinguish between welfare and security politics, Gressgård concludes.

PART III: REIMAGINING COMMUNITY

Time for Backlash: A Populist Neo-Fascism

The chapters in Part Three focus from different angles on Karl Polanyi's (2001 [1944]) prospect of the 'countermovement' briefly mentioned at the beginning of this introductory chapter. It refers to social counterforces that contest a destructive 'commodification' and contra-hegemonic forces aimed at 're-embedding' the market in protective social institutions. We are, however, in a situation where the success of neoliberalism has proceeded so far as almost to annihilate all other political projects that might present economic and social alternatives to a re-regulated 'market society' penetrated by commodification of labour, money (financialisation of the economy) and the environment. It pertains in particular to the social democratic project which in its different forms has almost totally succumbed to and internalised the neoliberal agenda (Schierup, Hansen and Castles 2006). Parties to the left of social democracy, suffering a deep crisis of legitimacy following the collapse of the Soviet Union, could not for long muster much of a countermovement to an increasingly entrenched neoliberalism.

To what extent today's social condition may be captured through a Polanyian frame is still an open question. But in linking countermovements to a rampant commodification (like that implied by today's neoliberal hegemony) Polanyi did not obscure the possibility that counter movements could also take a fascist direction. Today, in many states of Europe represented in the European Parliament, extreme right wing, racist and fascist parties have grown. We have in the beginning of this chapter described how the strategy of Swedish centre-right as well as centre-left parties, facing the increased entry of refugees to Europe and Sweden in 2015, has been to buy into the political agenda of the country's extreme right party, the Sweden Democrats. In the last instance it has resulted in the normalisation of its xenoracist discourse. It has, however, far from broken its ratings in the polls but on the contrary bolstered and legitimised a state of racist normalcy – alluding to Mudde's (2010) concept of 'pathological normalcy' – across most of the political spectrum. Herewith, the fall of 2015 signifies a low point in Swedish Post-Second World War history; a foul spot on our history that we shall never be able to wash off, contends the Swedish writer, Maria-Pia Boëthius (2016). It reminds us, she insists, of 1938, when Sweden together with Switzerland demanded that Nazi Germany should stamp a 'J' in Jewish passports, which was later to bar Jews fleeing persecution in Germany from entry into a multitude of countries.

In Chapter Ten 'From Racial to Racist State? The Sweden Democrats Reimagining the Nation,' Diana Mulinari and Anders Neergaard discuss the political projects of the Sweden Democrats. Using postcolonial, neo-Marxist, and feminist perspectives on the development of racism in Sweden, they argue that the political success of the Sweden Democrats is connected with both the continuity and transformation of racism as an ideology and stratagem in Swedish politics. This development is analysed through elaborating an examination of exclusionary representation and exploitative forms of the subordinated inclusion of migrants. It indicates, Mulinari and Neergaard argue, Sweden's shift from being a 'racial' state to a 'racist' state. They examine, among other matters, the centrality of gender in the political discourse of the Sweden Democrats and combine this with an analysis of the position of migrants within the party. Both cases illustrate a stigmatizing cultural stereotyping and the production of shifting racializing hierarchies dividing the citizenry.

The central interpellation of the extreme right parties (ERP)[10] operates through the construction of racialised or ethnicised 'Others' – the Muslim, the Roma, the Black, or the 'migrant' in general – threatening the nation and the people. A secondary stratagem exposes the image of a betraying elite in politics and in the mass media. Mulinari and Neergaard argue that it was on the societal margins that the seeds of a countermovement began to develop, in the shape of a distorted welfare nostalgia in constellations of populist protest, fascist and racist movements, networks and parties. 'Marginal' refers to the political trajectory, and to an interpellation, in which these were seen and have portrayed themselves as on the outside of the 'establishment' or 'the elite'. However, in tandem with the Sweden Democrats' successive rewriting of its blatantly Nazi and racist past, a growing alliance between the Sweden Democrats and the conservative *cum* neoliberal right is rising, with the result that Sweden's newly transformed migration and refugee policy is evolving into vehicles for the reproduction and proliferation of precarious low wage parts of the labour market. These are politics that will not only affect refugees and racialised citizens, but will further undermine the whole edifice of what is left of the nation's compact between capital and labour. It may appear a paradoxical development given that the success of the Sweden Democrats in acquiring an increasing share of blue collar votes from the traditional, especially Social Democratic left, is supposedly related to the party's appeal to welfare nostalgia.

Workers' Anti-Racism

The development of the Sweden Democrats is, however, confronted by determined resistance among many workers, argues Paula Mulinari in Chapter Eleven. Her chapter, 'Workplaces on the Move: Professional Mobilization against the Extreme Right' is a case study of antiracism focusing on the *exclusionary* racism of the Sweden Democrats a conservative communitarian racism seeking to eliminate the phenotypically or supposedly culturally *different* 'foreigner' from the nation and its territory altogether. Mulinari discusses the anti-racist activism of workers within the Emergency Room at a local hospital in the Swedish city of

10 We use Extreme right as a general term for these parties, as it is most prevalent although there is a plethora of more or less theoretically deduced names (see Table 7.1 in Berggren and Neergaard (2015: 194)).

Malmö, who mobilized to stop visits by Jimmi Åkesson, the leader of the Sweden Democrats and compares this to what takes place among workers in a fire brigade and a police station. She highlights how workers, through their activism, created a new political space that made it possible to mobilize against the extreme right through arguments based on professionalism and care, and explores how workers, by using official documents professing 'core values' relating to the work ethics of welfare professionals, were able to challenge the 'silence' that often normalises racism in the workplace. Mulinari concludes that this form of resistance challenges the boundaries and meaning of racism, since taking a stand against racism was, according to the workers, the 'natural' thing to do from the standpoint of a moral and affective economy that gives meaning to individuals and their work. The article shows that the actions against the Sweden Democrats are related to the workers' understanding of racism as the antithesis of their professional training and work. Thus, connecting the ethical with the political and the emotional, Mulinari envisages patterns of struggle against racism as struggles over what is just, fair and right.

In Chapter Twelve, 'Framing Solidarity through the Unionisation of Undocumented Migrant Workers in Sweden', Nedžad Mešić discusses instances of working class mobilisation. Here the focus of antiracism is rather on mobilisation against the *exploitative* racism of employers; a racism seeking to hyper-exploit the supposedly *inferior* 'Others', deprived of substantiated rights and political impact and inserted into occupational ghettoes[11] of a hierarchic, ethno-racially segmented, labour market.[12] Mešić scrutinises the specific case of an activism targeted at the solidaristic protection and inclusion of *irregular* migrants through an investigation of two Swedish trade union initiatives. He asks what links have forged the solidarity and what lessons can be learned from attempts to mobilise workers whose legal status may be unclear. Forging solidarity between workers, who may have stronger or weaker legal status, depends, he claims, on citizenship conditions and collective bargaining, including attempts to fight 'social dumping'. For more than a decade, particularly since European enlargement in 2004, this challenge has embroiled trade unions and social movements. Illustrated by interviews with both union representatives and migrant activists, Mešić concludes that conflicts between the 'self-interest' of the union (members) and protection of the undocumented workers' interests add further weight to the duality of inclusion

---

11 Here we borrow a notion coined by Stephan Feuchtwang (1982).

12 The dual concept of 'exclusionary' versus 'exploitative' racism is discussed in detail by Mulinari and Neergaard in the book's Chapter Nine.

(right to association), and exclusion (irregularity of work). They erect obstacles for the effective practice of solidarity. Against this background he suggests that the collaboration of unions with civil society solidarity organisations that support undocumented migrants could be an alternative approach. Developing additional forms and ways to extend inclusion to informally employed EU migrants as well as newly arriving undocumented third country migrants – who together share risks of being exploited within the most precarious occupational ghettoes of the informal economy – will be necessary for the development of a more negotiable and transformative character of solidarity and in the long run the sustainability of unions as organisational platforms capable of mobilising all workers against the fragmenting forces of neoliberal austerity politics.

Rebellion from the 'Margin'

Another manifestation of today's counter-movement challenging neoliberal globalisation comes out as violent urban rebellion. It is, using the term of Chatterjee (2002), a 'politics of the governed', in the form of precaritised youth in racialized and socially disadvantaged city regions rioting. It happened in 2009 in the Swedish cities of Malmö, Gothenburg and Uppsala. It happened again in Stockholm in 2013. These violent youth rebellions sprang from disadvantaged districts in large Swedish cities with a high proportion of citizens of migrant background, especially from Africa and the Middle East; visible minorities stigmatised in terms of 'race', 'national origin' or 'migrant background'. They are the offspring of urban transformation and a changing welfare state; a transformation that has affected the institutional landscapes and the redistribution of welfare services, causing disadvantaged districts of large cities to suffer stigmatization, racialization, poverty and long-term unemployment. We see them as a rebellion of what has been called an 'uncivil society' (Bayat 1997) out of the reach of neoliberal governance as opposed to a 'civil society' which has been tamed and disciplined through techniques of governmentality (Neocosmos 2011). It expresses resistance against welfare cuts, privatization, growing unemployment, institutional racism and politics of securitization effected through daily police repression. It is essentially a rebellion confronting a localised 'state of exception' (Agamben 2005) that affect the nation's most disadvantaged neighbourhoods, write Carl-Ulrik Schierup, Aleksandra Ålund and Lisa Kings in Chapter Thirteen, 'Reading the Stockholm Riots: A Moment for Social Justice?'. It pertains to situations marked by the extension of state power through which rights of citizenship can be reduced, overridden or denied by the executive power of government, and through which the boundaries between citizen and non-citizen become increasingly obscured (Nyers 2006).

The riots in Stockholm, 2013, became known worldwide, and were interpreted in the international press as revealing a deep crisis in a 'Swedish model' with growing social inequality polarizing Swedish society along ethnic lines. They could be read against the background of broken promises in a society which refers to itself as the epitome of an inclusionary liberal democracy; a society which has, however, during the last two decades, as contended by the *Financial Times* (2013), mutated into a hazardous neoliberal experiment. Yet, compared with, for example, the London Riots in 2011, the Stockholm riots in 2013 became a moment of truth, an object of critical self-reflection on the highest political level. Could they provide a platform for new political voices, the authors ask. They point to an important difference between the urban rebellion in Sweden 2009 and the 2013 one. It relates to the role that politically articulate new movements of young urban Swedes (predominantly from migrant backgrounds) played in 2013. They exercised their newly built ability to produce an alternative 'reading of the riot' in terms of claims for social justice. In fact, the spectacular urban rebellions ignited the spark which led to the development of new imaginaries of the nation by anti-racist movements with visions of reclaiming an inclusive democratic and equitable society. Out of the boiling cauldron of burning cities we have seen the birth of a new urban justice movement with a range of networks, organisations, and more or less temporary movements, all spearheaded by young racialised people coming out of the nation's most marginalised urban communities. Schierup, Ålund and Kings argue that a changing political landscape of contemporary Sweden – beyond the violence of the riots – brings to light, an autonomous, non-violent and organisationally embedded movement for social justice among young people. It is a movement that resists urban degradation and reclaims the nation for inclusive citizenship, social welfare and democracy.

Along similar lines, René León Rosales and Aleksandra Ålund explore in Chapter Fourteen, 'Renaissance from the Margins: Urban Youth Activism in Sweden', how this new youth-led movement for social justice invents its own spaces for activism, based on educational training, public lectures, interventions in the mass media, and manifestations in public places. They discuss how new learning processes within the movement have functioned as a necessary knowledge base for empowerment aimed at raising emancipatory consciousness and, ultimately, a new political subjectivity. The authors define political subjectivity as the ability to reflect on the limits of the existing public order, as well as to conceive of another order, and in this struggle for meaning, to develop an alternative understanding, gain political voice and related agency for advancing democratic development and socially sustainable cities. They scrutinize in particular the case of the youth organisation *Megafonen*, from Husby, a disadvantaged multi-ethnic Stockholm suburb. This organisation played a central role in shaping public discourse about the Stockholm riots in 2013. *Megafonen* became known worldwide as the mediator of urban justice activists, focusing on the structural reasons for the uprising. In exploring the connection between political subjectivity and agency the authors discuss how young urban-justice activists confront marginalization within the formal context of *invited* spaces for citizenship dialogues and create their own *invented* spaces for public participation. In becoming recognized public voices, young activists from these suburban justice movements position themselves as critical voices against a reductionist Swedish mass media discourse and a general public-political narrative targeting 'criminal youth' rather than focusing on social polarization of the urban space and cultural stigmatisation of those populating the most disadvantaged segregated geographies of social exclusion/inclusion.

With an understanding of being part of Sweden's 'new popular movement' (*den nya folkrörelsen), Megafonen* and similar suburban justice movements seem currently to come closer to established civil society organisations concerned about a looming crisis of democracy and the role of civil society in confronting it. In their conclusion the authors argue that new suburban movements have sprouted in many versions, carrying the seeds of democratic renewal which in the long run can play a fundamental part in institutional transformation towards deeper democracy. Through this they embody an activist citizenship and a vision of society, truly reimagining Sweden.

Democratic Fall or Spring? Imagining a Post-Neoliberal Future

In closing this introductory chapter, we return to the Polanyian problem. Seeing the laissez faire liberalism of the end of the 19th and the beginning of the 20th as unsustainable, he argued that counter-movements would emerge. As we look at a Sweden which has changed exceedingly during the last quarter of a century, two questions arise again and again. The first concern is whether, in the current crisis of the polity, a hegemonic neoliberal reimagineering of economy, nation and society is approaching its end. The second is what will the future be for the incipient popular countermovements of our time.

The current political trajectory in Sweden as well as across most of Europe indicates a possible merger of the neoliberal project of exploitative racism with the extreme right's exclusionary racism. The most damaging response to the deep economic, political and social crisis of the 1930s emerged as Fascism. A projection of this historical trajectory into our time would mean a dire democratic fall. However, it appears too early to assert that our time's neoliberal reimagineering of society has reached its end and it would be premature to conclude that today's

Swedish polity is heading towards a state of Fascism. Inspired by Gramsci's repeated dictum 'I'm a pessimist because of intelligence, but an optimist because of will',[13] we consequently position this book in an epistemological tradition that critically explores the possibilities, the actions of hope and the imaginings of new forms of togetherness.

Whatever the future may hold, Sweden's new justice movement highlights anew Hanna Arendt's (1958) dictum in *The Origins of Totalitarianism* of an equitable 'right to have rights'; a democratic movement from the margin addresses a need for recognition of the excluded as a political voice against the re-emergence of the spectre of totalitarianism in a present turmoil and transformation of democratic frameworks of citizenship. The issues that stand out are whether, and to what extent and in which forms shall we come to see a future that merges the heritage of a seemingly exhausted social democratic project with the incipient movement of young Swedes who cherish the values of people power, social justice and universalist solidarity that once made Sweden enjoy (not always deservedly) the reputation of a moral great power? Could they sprout as the hybrid seeds of a democratic renewal in a time marked by an eruptive 'proliferation of … sites of power and antagonism' (Hall 1987)?

From this overall perspective, two challenging imaginaries exemplify our present time.

One relates to the rise and transmogrification of the Sweden Democrats as well as other extreme right movements across Europe. It represents a dystopian scenario that acknowledges the similarity of the counter-movements of today with the gloomiest instances of a global counter-movement against the disruptive rule of financial capitalism and an unbridled market economy that, in widely different incarnations, swept across Europe and the world in the 1930s. The vast composite counter movement of that period for 're-imbedding' the market in protective social institutions ranged from the New Deal, the Western European welfare state and the developmental state in the global South to the state-totalitarian reactions against economic liberalism represented by Nazism, Fascism and Stalinism. We could in this vein hypothesise, as with what happened in Nazi Germany in the 1930s (after the purging of the proletarian SA wing of the Nazi movement), a neoliberal economic and political hegemony eventually seeking a route for further dominance in a compromise and alliance with a conservative neo-communitarian and xenoracist nationalism. We understand this as a covert stratagem for perpetuating, under

13 Borrowing the phrase from the French writer Romain Rolland, see Santucci (2010: 212).

changing political conditions, hegemonic politics of 'accumulation through dispossession' involving a continued precarisation of labour, livelihoods and citizenship, with migrants (including asylum seekers) as the core of a flexible hyper-exploited precariat[14], yet guaranteeing to the xenoracist extreme right that migrants will never become 'citizens' and gain full membership of the nation.

However, we see a pessimistic one-sided reading of the world as surrendering to global neoliberal elites – a world imprisoned and controlled via technologies of surveillance – as immobilising in that it tends to reproduce 'paradigms of pessimism' to the expense of a 'politics of possibility'.[15] The neoliberal austerity project is slowly being challenged by countermovements, to speak once more with Polanyi. We have seen the growth of inclusive counterhegemonic movements in Spain, Portugal and the UK; not to mention a proliferating coast-to-coast multitude of antiracist grassroots movements in the United States struggling for democratic revival, social justice and custody of the commons. Parallel to, and as part of this, we see a (re)birth of justice movements in the cities of Sweden as well as in the rest of Europe. In consequence we ask whether another spring is breaking through the frozen earth in this kingdom of the North. We ask whether it could be those – represented in the dominant discourse as the 'others', the 'foreign', those 'outside' of our so-called 'society', those depicted as 'not belonging' to the nation – who will be the vanguard in alliances for a renaissance of this nation's historical memory and heritage of human liberation, democracy and social solidarity.

Acknowledgement of Funding

We appreciate generous funding by FORTE, the Swedish Research Council for Health, Working Life and Welfare [grant number 2006–1524].

References

99 SD-Problem. 2014. '11. Hjälp i närområdet,' *99 anledningar att inte rösta på Sverigedemokraterna,* August 20. Accessed March 29, 2016. <http://99sdproblem.blogspot.se/2014/08/11-hjalp-i-naromradet.html>

Agamben, G. 2005. *State of Exception.* Chicago & London: The University of Chicago Press.

Ali, T. (ed.) 2000. *Masters of the Universe? NATO's Balkan Crusade.* London & New York: Verso.

14 Schierup and Bak Jørgensen (2016 [forthcoming])

15 Trimikliniotis et.al (2015) quoting Kyriakides and Torres (2012).

Arendt, H. 1958. *The Origins of Totalitarianism* (Second Enlarged Edition). Cleveland: Meridian Books.

Ålund, A. 1997. *Multikultiungdom. Kön, Etnicitet, identitet.* Lund: Studentlitteratur.

Ålund, A. 2003. 'Etnicity, social subordination and cultural resistence.' In Brochman, Grete (ed) *Comparative Social Research, Special issue on The Multicultural Challenge.* Comparative Social Research 22. Amsterdam: Elsevier, JAI: 245–263.

Ålund, A. and Alinia, M. 2011. 'I skuggan av etno-kulturella stereotypier; genus, aktivism och jämställdhet.' *Sociologisk forskning* 48/2, 43–64.

Ålund, A. and Schierup, C.-U. 1991. *Paradoxes of Multiculturalism. Essays on Swedish Society.* Aldershot: Avebury. Republished 2009 as E-Book on the REMESO home-page, Linköpings University at <http://liu.diva-portal.org/smash/record.jsf?pid=diva2:213706>.

Bayat, A. 1997. 'Un-civil society: the politics of the "informal people".' *Third World Quarterly* 18/1, 53–72.

Berggren, E. and Neergaard, A. 2015. 'Populism – Protest, democratic challenge and right-wing extremism.' In Dahlstedt, Magnus and Anders Neergaard (eds) *International Migration and Ethnic Relations: Critical Perspectives.* London: Routledge, 169–199.

Block, F. 2001. *Introduction. The great transformation.* Boston, MA: Beacon Press.

Boëthius, M.-P. 2016. 'Det spelar roll hur vi gestaltar verkligheten.' *ETC*, January 10. Accessed March 29, 2016. <http://www.etc.se/ledare/det-spelar-roll-hur-vi-gestaltar-verkligheten>

Centre for Contemporary Cultural Studies (ed.) 1982. *The Empire Strikes Back. Race and Racism in 70s Britain.* London: Hutchinson and the Centre for Contemporary Cultural Studies.

CEO (Corporate Europe Observer) 2011. 'Austerity Forever.' *Corporate Europe Observer,* September 22. Accessed March 29, 2016. <http://corporateeurope.org/eu-crisis/2011/09/austerity-forever>

Chatterjee, P. 2002. *The Politics of the Governed.* New York: Columbia University Press.

Dikeç, M. 2007. *Badlands of the republic. Space, politics and urban policy.* Oxford: Blackwell.

Financial Times 2013. 'The challenges of the Swedish model.' *Financial Times,* May 26. Accessed March 29, 2016. <http://www.ft.com/intl/cms/s/0/ba2fb9ee-c47e-11e2-9ac0-00144feab7de.html>

Edling, J. 2015. *Förorterna som Moder Svea glömde.* Stockholm: Verdandi. Accessed March 29, 2016. <http://www.verdandi.se/wp-content/uploads/2015/10/151014-F%C3%B6rorterna-som-Moder-Svea-gl%C3%B6mde.pdf>

European Commission 2008. 'Together in Diversity.' *DG Education and Culture*. Accessed March 29, 2016. <http://www.interculturaldialogue2008.eu/411.0.html?&redirect_url=my-startpage-eyid.html>

Eurostat 2015. 'The number of asylum applicants in the EU jumped to more than 625,000 in 2014.' *Eurostat Newsletter* 53/2015, March 20.

Fekete, L. 2001. 'The emergence of xeno-racism.' *Race & Class* 43/2, 23–40.

Feuchtwang, S. 1982. 'Occupational Ghettos.' *Economy and Society* 11/3, 251–291.

Gelmini, J. 2015. 'Opinion – Merkel seeks Turkey's help over refugee crisis as new migrant bottleneck builds near Slovenia.' *Dr Alf's Blog*, October 20. Accessed March 29, 2016. <http://dralfoldman.com/2015/10/20/merkel-seeks-turkeys-help-over-refugee-crisis-as-new-migrant-bottleneck-builds-near-slovenia-telegraph-john-gelmini/>

Gemmel, L. 2016. 'Välfärdskollapsen göms bakom flyktingarna.' *Dagens Arena*, January 26. Accessed March 29, 2016. <http://www.dagensarena.se/redaktionen/valfardskollapsen-goms-bakom-flyktingarna/>

Goodhart, D. 2004. 'Too Diverse?' *Prospect* 95, February 20. Accessed March 29, 2016. <http://www.prospect-magazine.co.uk/pdfarticle.php?id=5835>

Hakkala, K. and Zimmermann, D. 2005. *Foreign Operations of Swedish Manufacturing Firms. Evidence from the IUI Survey on Multinationals 2003*. Stockholm: Research Institute of Industrial Economics. Accessed July 21, 2016. <http://www.ifn.se/Wfiles/wp/WP650.pdf>

Hall, S. 1987. 'Gramsci and Us.' *Marxism Today* 6/87, 16–21.

Hansen, P. 2016 [forthcoming]. 'Refugee Keynesianism? EU Migration Crises in Times of Fiscal Austerity.' In Jonsson, Stefan and Julia Willén (eds) *Austere Histories in European Societies: Social Exclusion and the Contest of Colonial Memories*. London: Routledge.

Harvey, D. 2005. *A Brief History of Neoliberalism*. Oxford: Oxford University Press.

Houdt, F. van, Suvarierol, S. and Schinkel, W. 2011. 'Neoliberal communitarian citizenship: Current trends towards "earned citizenship" in the United Kingdom, France and the Netherlands.' *International Sociology* 26, 408–431.

Ikegami, M. 2013. 'The End of A "National" Defence Industry?: Impacts of globalization on the Swedish defence industry.' *Scandinavian Journal of History* 38/4, 436.

IPI (International Peace Institute). 2015. 'Cochetel: Migration Causing "Crisis of Solidarity" in Europe.' *International Peace Institute*, October 16. Accessed March 29, 2016. <http://www.ipinst.org/2015/10/todays-refugee-crisis#3>

Jessop, B. 2002. *The Future of the Capitalist State*. Cambridge: Polity Press.

Kyriakides, C. and Torres, R.D. 2012. *Race Defaced: Paradigms of Pessimism, Politics of Possibility.* Stanford, CA: Stanford University Press.

Levitas, R. 1998. *The Inclusive Society? Social Exclusion and New Labour.* London: Macmillan.

Makwana, R. 2016. 'The global refugee crisis: humanity's last call for a culture of sharing and cooperation.' *Share the Worlds Resources,* March 15. Accessed March 29, 2016. <http://www.sharing.org/information-centre/articles/global-refugee-crisis-humanitys-last-call-culture-sharing-and>

Massey, D. S. 1988. 'Economic Development and International Migration in Comparative Perspective.' *Population and Development Review* 14, 383–413.

Mudde, C. 2010. 'The Populist Radical Right: A Pathological Normalcy.' *West European Politics* 33/6, 1167–1186.

Neocosmos, M. 2011. 'Transition, human rights and violence: rethinking a liberal political relationship in the African neo-colony.' *Interface: a journal for and about social movements* 3/2, 359–399.

Nyers, P. 2006. 'The accidental citizen: acts of Sovereignty and (un) making citizenship.' *Economy and Society* 35/1, 22–41.

Papadopoulos, T. 2005. 'The Recommodification of European Labour: Theoretical and Empirical Explorations.' The European Research Institute (ERI) Working Paper Series, No 3. The University of Bath. Accessed March 29, 2016. <http://www.bath.ac.uk/eri/ERI-working-papers/ERI-working-paper-05-03-final.pdf>

Paul, D.E. 2004. 'World cities as hegemonic projects: the politics of global imagineering in Montreal.' *Political Geography* 23/5, 571–596.

Pelling, L. 2015. *Lagliga vägar över Medelhavet. En färdplan*. Stockholm: Arena Idé. Accessed March 29, 2016. <http://www.arenaide.se/rapporter/lagliga-vagar-over-medelhavet/>

Polanyi, K. 2001 [1944]. *The Great Transformation: the Political and Economic Origins of Our Time.* Boston, MA: Beacon Press.

Rachman, G. 2016. 'EU-Turkey summit: high-stakes and unpleasant choices.' *Financial Times*, March 6. Accessed March 29, 2016. <http://blogs.ft.com/the-world/2016/03/eu-turkey-summit-high-stakes-and-unpleasant-choices/>

Santucci, A.A. 2010. *Antonio Gramsci.* New York: Monthly Review Press.

Sarrazin, T. 2010. *Deutschland schafft sich ab. Wie wir unser Land aufs Spiel setzen.* München: Deutsche Verlags-Anstalt (DVA).

Savio, R. 2016. 'Can Europe Survive – Back to a Better Yesterday?'. *IPS,* March 11. Accessed March 29, 2016. <http://www.ipsnews.net/2016/03/can-europe-survive-back-to-a-better-yesterday/>

Schierup, C.-U. 1993. *På kulturens slagmark: mindretal og størretal taler om Danmark.* Esbjerg: Southern Jutland University Press.

Schierup, C.-U. and Bak Jørgensen, M. (eds.) 2016 [forthcoming]. *Politics of Precarity: Migrant conditions, struggles and experiences.* Leiden: Brill.

Schierup, C.-U., Hansen, P. and Castles, S. 2006. *Migration, Citizenship and the European Welfare State. A European Dilemma.* Oxford: Oxford University Press.

Schierup, C.-U. and Ålund, A. 2011a. 'The End of Swedish Exceptionalism? Citizenship, neoliberalism and politics of exclusion.' *Race & Class* 53/1, 45–64.

Schierup, C.-U. and Ålund, A. 2011b. 'From Paradoxes of Multiculturalism to Paradoxes of Liberalism.' *Journal for Critical Education Policy Studies* 9/2, 125–142. Accessed March 29, 2016. <http://www.jceps.com/?pageID=article&articleID=228>

Scocco, S. and Andersson, L.F. 2015. *900 Miljarder skäl att uppskatta invandring. En analys av invandringens effekter på de offentliga finanserna i Sverige 1950–2014.* Stockholm: Arenaidé.

Sivanandan, A. 2001. 'Poverty is the New Black.' *Race & Class* 43/2, 1–5.

Skr. 2008. *Egenmakt mot utanförskap – regeringens strategi för integration.* Skr. 2008/09:24. Stockholm: Arbetsmarknadsdepartementet.

Svanberg, I. and Tydén, M. 1998. *Tusen år av invandring: en svensk kulturhistoria.* 2nd Edition. Stockholm: Gidlund.

Trimikliniotis, N., Parsanoglou, D. and Tsianos, V.S. 2015. 'Mobile Commons and/in Precarious Spaces: Mapping Migrant Struggles and Social Resistance.' *Critical Sociology*, 1–15.

Wacquant, L. 1996. 'The rise of advanced marginality: notes on its nature and implications.' *Acta Sociologica* 39/2, 121–139.

PART I: THE WELFARE STATE IN CRISIS. TOO MUCH DIVERSITY… OR TOO MUCH AUSTERITY?

Carl-Ulrik Schierup & Simone Scarpa

2. How the Swedish Model Was (Almost) Lost. Migration, Welfare and the Politics of Solidarity

Abstract: This chapter analyses the shift from an expansive Swedish welfare state with full employment as its paramount priority to an austerity-driven neoliberal model subordinating social and employment policies to the goals of inflation control and debt reduction. The authors discuss implications of this for rising inequality and social exclusion, with a focus on the Swedish welfare state in general and immigration and integration policies in particular.

A Self-Fulfilling Prophecy

'Open your hearts!' appealed former Premier, Fredrik Reinfeldt in a stirring speech to the Swedish people. He was kicking off his conservative party's[1] campaign before the parliamentary elections scheduled for September 2014. It was at a moment when an ever-growing flight from the Middle East via the Mediterranean was becoming a top political issue labelled 'the EU's refugee problem'.[2] The premier pleaded passionately for solidarity in welcoming the wretched who had been expelled by wars, outrageous atrocities and complex emergencies from less fortunate parts of the world. Among this multitude fleeing violence, death and destruction, large numbers would, he anticipated, seek protection in Sweden during the coming years. They would eventually, like numerous refugees and other immigrants to Sweden before them, become integrated as fellow citizens, enter the labour market, continue to build the country and consolidate its cherished openness and freedoms. Yet, Reinfeldt earnestly appealed at the same time to the

1 The *Moderaterna* has long been the largest and most important party on the right of the Swedish political spectrum. As leader, Reinfeldt was responsible for changing the party's earlier, overtly neoliberal, profile into an avowedly welfare state-friendly one. It maintained the rhetoric of the cherished values of 'the Swedish Model' (e.g. collective agreements for regulating the labour market), yet pursued a factual neoliberal reform agenda premised on fiscal austerity, tax reductions, welfare state retrenchment, public service privatization, denigration of the unions' role, etc.

2 Reinfeldt's speech is available at: <https://www.youtube.com/watch?v=iChPRQCVLio> (Accessed March 17, 2016).

population to be 'patient'. This tremendous humanitarian task and exercise in solidarity, he stated, would be an exceedingly costly venture and it would preclude any build-up of welfare during the coming years. A grand humanitarian motion, yet wrapped in a 'There Is No Alternative' (TINA) message.[3] It conveyed to the people that the austerity over which consecutive Swedish governments had presided since the mid-1990s, in particular Reinfeldt's own centre-right alliance during two consecutive electoral periods (2006–2014), was inevitable. It is a politics that has accomplished a ground-shattering reimagineering of the nation, of the welfare state and of the political economy on which it rests.

Reinfeldt's message has been taken to heart by many Swedes, but often in a twisted form. His oxymoronic opposition of 'immigration' and 'welfare' has been taken as authoritative evidence of the long since propagated dogma of the populist radical right; i.e. that 'welfare' and 'immigration' are mutually antagonistic and that immigration should therefore be damned. For existing immigrants within the nation's border certain rules must prevail. 'Deserving' citizens must be treated differently from 'non-deserving' foreigners, in order to protect the claims of the former to the scarce resources of a crisis-ridden welfare state in a hardening globalised world. These are common sense populist axioms that seem to have progressively colonised much of the Swedish political spectrum from the right to centre-left. They come habitually merged with another common sense belief: that ethnic diversity, produced by immigration, will weaken the nation's solidarity.

This common sense credo could indeed strengthen its authority by reference to academic research.

One of the most influential interventions in an ongoing debate about migration and welfare was made by the economists Alberto Alesina and Edward Glaeser (2004) in their widely quoted comparative study on combating poverty in the US and Europe. In it, they made the prediction that in the long term increasing immigration will force European countries to respond to decreasing support for the welfare state by cutting social expenditure and thus edge towards the US residual welfare model. A premise of their argument is that large-scale immigration and concomitant ethnic diversity may become detrimental to the formation of collective solidarity by undermining the willingness of citizens (and of the working-class in particular) to finance comprehensive welfare programmes. It is a controversial argument that has been widely circulated in economics[4] and in

3 'There is no alternative' (the famous TINA assertion) remains forever associated with Margaret Thatcher and the neoliberal ideology that has overwhelmed most of the world since the beginning of the 1980s.

4 E.g. Stichnoth and van der Straeten (2013).

other social sciences[5]. However, it has also been fundamentally challenged,[6] both by questioning the basis of its theoretical and analytical premises, and by putting the validity of its empirical evidence in doubt.

Thus, based on results from a comprehensive cross-national study, Peter Taylor-Gooby (2005) argues that the alleged negative effect of ethno-racial diversity on collective solidarity and welfare expenditure may be confined to the United States. Will Kymlicka and Keith Banting (2006) maintain that whether ethno-racial diversity and high immigration induce a retraction of welfare expenditure or not is politically determined, and that politics combating the social stigma attached to migrants and ethno-racial minorities increase collective motivation for social solidarity and nation building. Steffen Mau and Christoph Bukhardt (2007; see also Mau 2009) argue that public values and attitudes are no simple reflex reaction to the degree of ethno-racial 'fractionalization' nor to the level of immigration into a country. Values and attitudes are mediated by welfare state structures. They depend on how inclusion/exclusion is institutionally organized and on whether social policy programmes have been constructed in ways that reinforce or weaken conflicts over redistribution.[7]

Nevertheless, the basic argument that increasing ethnic diversity produced by immigration tends to erode the basis of support for the welfare state and constrain the actual magnitude of redistribution that can be achieved in a country has continued to circulate as a recurrent perspective. In real life politics, this perspective has, as argued in the introduction to this book (Chapter One. See also further Chapter Ten), been taken to heart by several of Europe's xenoracist extreme right parties, among them France's *Front National*, and the Nordic extreme right parties, including the Sweden Democrats (*Sverigedemokraterna*). It has moreover been an impetus for the formation of a contemporary neoliberal-neoconservative hegemony across the European political mainstream. Not least because of this development, which has had a crucial impact on shaping the European and Swedish present, it continues to be pertinent to subject the negative diversity-equality equation (NDE) to critical theoretical and empirical scrutiny.

Taylor-Gooby (2005), among others, has argued that the NDE prediction has long been challenged empirically as well as theoretically by the capacity of the so-called Swedish model to combine a very liberal immigration policy with a

5 E.g. Eger (2010); Larsen (2011); Dahlberg, Edmark and Lundqvist (2012); Finseraas (2012); Lentin and Titley (2011); Hooijer and Picot (2015); Koopmans (2010).

6 Overview in Wagle (2013).

7 Elsewhere we have discussed these controversies and propositions in detail with reference to the Swedish case (Scarpa 2015a).

comparatively generous, highly decommodifying and universal welfare state. The Swedish model, Taylor-Gooby contends, refutes the postulated inevitable trade-off between ethnic diversity and social cohesion. Its generous and inclusive policies demonstrate effectively the power of social-democratically inspired politics to mediate, or reverse, the allegedly negative effect of ethnic fractionalization on welfare state development, which thus falsifies the NDE thesis.

Having been a high emigration country at the beginning of the 19th century Sweden became, relative to its population, one of the most important immigration countries in the North Atlantic world after the end of the Second World War. It is today one of the OECD member states with the highest proportion of foreign born in its population – 16 percent or 1.6 million in a total population of 10 million. Approximately 30 percent of all children currently born in Sweden have one or two parents born abroad.[8] Immigration is, accordingly, a major reason that the country experiences a looming 'demographic' crisis to a lesser degree than most other European countries, and immigration has contributed, and continues to contribute immensely, to Sweden's economic growth (Scocco and Andersson 2015).

The fundamental premises of the Swedish immigration policy regime were formulated by the mid-1970s in the heyday of the 'Swedish Model' of the social democratic welfare state. In spite of ever-present paradoxes, resting on often startling discrepancies between theory and practice (Ålund and Schierup 1991), the model had for long confronted positively – compared with most other European states – the challenge of merging extended civil, political, and social rights of citizenship with a political framework divorced from 'nativist' conceptions of 'belonging' (Ryner 2000: 68). This has depended on upholding a broadly principled consensus supported by all mainstream political parties, left and right, not to exploit issues of migration, ethnicity, race or nation as populist political stratagems. It is a consensus on a liberal asylum policy, on liberal rules for family unification, on quick access to permanent residence and full social citizenship for migrants, and on the importance for a democratic society of supporting the political empowerment of migrants and their descendants. It is a consensus that has repeatedly been challenged and partially restored in the context of recurrent crises and reforms of the Swedish model (Ålund and Schierup 1991; Schierup and Ålund 2011a). However, with the winds of xenophobia and neo-fascism currently sweeping over today's Europe and Sweden, we have seen the authorised disposal of the original Swedish model's moral political foundations in the dustbin of history

8 Raneke (2013).

and experienced the transmogrification of a still prevalent right-left consensus into its apparently mirror opposite (see Chapter One).

It is the aim of the present chapter to transcend – in order to complement – a critically countervailing moral-political discourse that insists on respecting 'human rights' through retrieving a historical-structural explanation of this historical *volte face* with the focus on the deep-seated transformation of the political economy and institutional bearings of 'the Swedish model'.

The shift in the political climate and subsequent institutional changes that have taken place in the Swedish welfare state do not seem to have affected the popularity of the current Swedish *economic* model, domestically and internationally. On the contrary the capacity of the Swedish economy to recover quickly from the downturn caused by the global financial crisis that began in the latter half of 2007 has repeatedly been held up as an example that could be followed by other EU countries (Schnyder 2012; Steinmo 2013; Scarpa 2015a). However, the recognition of the international competitiveness of the Swedish economy has increasingly tended to be accompanied by critical comments focusing on the allegedly sub-optimal achievements of the Swedish immigration policy regime, which is often regarded as some sort of faulty cog in an otherwise well-oiled machine. Sweden ranks first in the latest (2015) MIPEX ranking of integration policies and is perceived as one of the countries with the most humane and generous immigration policy.[9] Despite the resources devoted to integration policies, the outcomes are nevertheless pointed out as remarkably inferior to those in other countries which according to the same criteria are ranked lower, particularly considering the differences in employment and poverty levels between immigrants and natives (Wiesbrock 2011; OECD 2014; Hooijer and Picot 2015). Hence, a growing number of commentators interpret the mismatch between the intentions of policies and their actual outcomes, together with recent trends in Swedish attitudes towards immigration, as further evidence of an inevitable trade-off between ethnic diversity and welfare state sustainability.

The present chapter challenges this axiomatic assumption, which seems to have become a self-fulfilling prophecy. The crisis of the Swedish model has somehow haunted Swedish domestic politics for several decades and nowadays seems to have become an added 'recited truth' in the ubiquitous narrative of liberal migration and diversity policy as a failed experiment (Lentin and Titley 2011: 11). Our argument is that neoliberal and austerity-oriented reforms of the Swedish welfare

9 The MIPEX ranking can be found at this link: <http://www.mipex.eu/key-findings> (Accessed August 4, 2016).

state since the early 1990s have progressively eroded the integration potential of social policies and have thus been a major factor in shaping the current reality of deepening, and increasingly ethnically tinged, class divisions and long-term social exclusion of sizeable population groups from substantial citizenship rights.

Against this background, the chapter seeks to explain how welfare reforms implemented in the last quarter of a century resulted in an overturning of the Swedish model and have been crucial in the subsequent redefinition and reconfiguration of citizenship rights. In the following section, we assess essential features of the Swedish model during its 'Golden Age'. Then we describe the systematic dismantling, since the early 1990s, of its mutually sustaining pillars. We focus in particular on the shift from an expansive Keynesian welfare state with full employment as its paramount priority to an austerity-driven neoliberal model subordinating social and employment policies to the goals of inflation control and debt reduction. We discuss implications of this for rising inequality and social exclusion, with a focus on the Swedish welfare state in general and immigration and integration policies in particular. We go in conclusion back to the paradox embedded in the heartfelt humanitarian politics for solidarity by Sweden's former premier, Fredrik Reinfeldt. We raise the question of possible alternative futures that emerges dimly out of a sharpening contest for political hegemony, with the rising populist xenoracism as a central actor. In this battle, the central stratagem is who will command the power to fill a floating signifier of 'solidarity' with legitimate truth.

Pillars of the Swedish Model

The foundation of the emergence of social citizenship rights and the North Atlantic welfare states in the 20th century was the so-called 'decommodification' of labour, i.e. the extent to which benefits and transfers are guaranteed by the welfare state irrespective of labour market participation and earnings. In Gøsta Esping-Andersen's memorable definition, which has been highly influential in comparative welfare state research, '[t]he outstanding criterion for social rights must be the degree to which they permit people to make their living standards independent of pure market forces. It is in this sense that social rights diminish citizens' status as commodities' (Esping-Andersen 1990: 21). The roots of this concept can be traced to the sociologist Thomas Humphrey Marshall's (1992 [1950]) theory of citizenship, according to which the irreversible three-step progression of civil, political and social rights would have led to a decline of class inequality or even to 'class abatement' (Marshall 1992 [1950]: 47).

Marshall saw the development of the welfare state as the solution to an inherent contradiction between *democracy* and *capitalism*. According to Marshall, it would be possible to realize fully the tripartite model of citizenship, based on its civil, political and social dimensions, only by ensuring a minimum standard of material well-being to every citizen. Hence, the level of expansion of social rights constituted a crucial element in the realization of the conjunction of the three aforementioned dimensions. In fact, a fair and non-discriminatory access to the labour market, together with the establishment of a minimum level of social and economic security, should be ensured by the provision of income protection in the event of old-age, sickness, disability, and unemployment, as well as of basic social services such as health and education. This would provide grounds for the engagement of the working-class in political life and, therefore, for initiating a process of bottom-up mobilization able to transform modern nation-states into advanced welfare states.

However, the neoliberal turn in Western politics since the early 1980s has proved that the process of expansion of citizenship rights of which Marshall spoke is far from being unidirectional. It can be reversed when there is a change in the balance of power.

In recent decades, the neoliberal restructuring of welfare states, in combination with the increase in international immigration from the global South, resulted in the exacerbation of class inequalities and in the subsequent growth of the segment of the population that is excluded from citizenship. The rolling back of the welfare state seems to have called into question Marshall-inspired accounts of social citizenship, such as those that have dominated comparative welfare state research, for their lack of consideration of the differentiation of social rights between immigrants and native-born populations across countries. As explained in more detail below, the Swedish example illustrates well the limits of mainstream comparative welfare state research in deciphering the causes and patterns of such differentiation in social rights by immigrant or native backgrounds.

Probably the most influential account of the cross-national differences in decommodification levels is the one establishing a causal relationship between the forms of political hegemony and the institutional trajectories of welfare state development. In the Scandinavian countries, the political influence of certain class-based organizations – such as labour unions but also small farmers' organizations – has been stronger than in other Western countries (Therborn 1984; Nordheim Nielsen 1988). They are deemed to have played a unique role in organizing political demands 'from below', as well as in establishing the institutions of the welfare state with its redistributive and population-wide policies (Mann 1987). The universal welfare states of these countries have traditionally de-commodified labour to the highest degree, compared with the 'conservative' welfare states of continental Europe and 'liberal' (or residual) welfare states of Anglo-Saxon countries such as the US and the UK (Esping-Andersen 1990).

Sweden is generally recognized as the ideal example of the universal welfare state typology on account of the long period of the political hegemony of the Swedish Social Democratic Party (*Sveriges socialdemokratiska arbetareparti*, henceforth SAP) – which can be regarded as the first pillar of the model. Traditionally, the political strength of the SAP rested on class-based 'popular movements' (*folkrörelser* in Swedish), which were centred on strong labour unions with high membership rates. In a context of long-standing political stability, the SAP played the role of guarantor of labour rights and used its undisputed dominance for establishing a strong collective regulation of pay and employment conditions, together with the right to co-determination in the workplace. Social democracy managed to maintain its hegemony by forming cross-class alliances with common social policy goals. Thus the original Swedish Model stemming from the early 1930s rested on two grand historical compacts: a political agreement (the so-called 'Cow Deal') between the SAP and the Farmers League (*Bondeförbundet*), which represented small farmers, and the so-called Saltsjöbaden agreement on industrial relations between the Trade Union Confederation (LO) and the Employers' Federation (SAF).

The second pillar of the Swedish model can be identified in the Rehn-Meidner model, which was introduced in the 1950s and the 1960s. It was based on the combination of a commitment to full employment, 'solidaristic' wage policy and a restrictive fiscal policy. Sweden has historically had one of the highest degrees of centralization in wage bargaining negotiations, which made it possible to implement a solidaristic wage policy where workers remained committed to wage moderation by agreeing to receive the same pay for the same job, regardless of the profitability of their firms. A consequence of this solidaristic wage policy was the strong compression of the wage structure, which ensured one of the lowest levels of income inequality in the OECD area (Rueda and Pontusson 2000). Another consequence was the creation of a dynamic economic environment in which allowing wage levels to rise in less competitive firms would result in shutdowns and bankruptcies but also in a continuous upgrading of the industrial structure. At the same time, wage moderation ensured high profits in more competitive and export-oriented firms. The aim of active labour market policy was to secure full employment by providing retraining and upgrading for displaced workers from less competitive firms and favouring their reemployment in more competitive ones or in other geographical areas (Scarpa 2013). Hence, the Rehn-Meidner model was geared to keeping unemployment at a minimum and to guaranteeing full employment.

The third pillar of the Swedish model was the principle of the universalism of the welfare state. A generous and all-encompassing social policy was also an instrument for generating loyalty to the Swedish model among all classes and protecting the welfare state against 'backlash sentiments' (Esping-Andersen 1990: 69).

A universal coverage of social insurances has traditionally been maintained by a combination of basic security entitlements and supplementary earning-related benefits. Basic security entitlements (in the form of flat-rate benefits) were offered to all citizens, aimed at eradicating poverty. These basic entitlements were topped by earning-related measures with an income-maintenance function to safeguard standards of living in case of employment interruption. This two-tier structure of social security institutions aimed at the inclusion of all social groups within the same welfare programmes in order to allow the formation of a broad pro-welfare coalition between workers and a growing white collar middle class (Esping-Andersen 1990: 67–69).

A universalistic welfare state also required the development of a large social service infrastructure, which in turn was able to absorb a substantial share of the labour force. The creation of these welfare state jobs, together with the centralized bargaining system, is deemed to have brought about the (virtual) 'suppression' of segmentation in the Swedish labour market (Swenson 1991) – i.e. the abolition of the distinctions between primary and secondary employment sectors, each with its own pay and working conditions. Public welfare services with universal coverage – including all levels of education, child and elderly care, health services, etc. – appealed, and still do appeal, to both traditional and new professional middle class groups.

The welfare state's social basis and public legitimacy were strengthened by the large-scale incorporation of women in the labour market and their inclusion in the welfare system on at least formally, if not substantially, equal terms, while the comprehensive public social service system was supposed to substitute for their domestic care work.[10] Similarly, in the 1960s and 1970s, Sweden's immigrant workers were incorporated on terms of 'subordinated inclusion' (Mulinari and Neergaard 2005). Labour migrants used for managing peaks of economic cycles and temporary labour shortages were often exposed to discrimination (Rauhut 2010) so that an unequal ethnic division of labour emerged (Persson 1972; Ålund 1985; Schierup and Paulson 1994). However, migrants were not, as in central and southern Europe, exploited as disposable guest workers without essential rights

10 However, notwithstanding its high rate of female employment, the Swedish labour market has remained one of Europe's most gender-segregated (EGGE 2009).

of citizenship or as clandestine workers in an irregular labour market. They were soon acknowledged as permanently resident 'denizens', enjoying—in principle if not always in practice—full access to the welfare system (see Hammar 1990).

A batch of socially inclusive legal-institutional measures by the mid-1970s summarised the intentions of Swedish immigration and integration policy through the formula 'Equality, Partnership, Freedom of Choice' (Ålund and Schierup 1991). The measures aimed at securing unconditional access for migrants to the entire complex of rights of citizenship in the advanced Swedish welfare state. They reinstated fast tracks to permanent residence permits, naturalisation and family unification, which had been instituted earlier and were targeted at facilitating political participation and the empowerment of migrants. They paid, at least in principle, respect to rights for retaining and mobilising migrants and their descendants' unique resources of culture and identity (Ålund and Schierup 1991; Schierup and Ålund 2011b. See also Chapter One). Of particular interest for our analysis in this chapter is the almost full incorporation of working migrants as members of trade unions and through this into the system of collective bargaining (Details in Chapter Three, this volume). This, in combination with regulated migration and an orderly process of asylum and integration of refugees in the labour market and the industrial relations system, was supposed to prevent wage dumping, to help combat ethno-racial segmentation and thereby to safeguard solidarity within the working class as a whole.

From the Swedish Model to the Swedish Consolidation State

In the mid-1980s, the second pillar of the Swedish model, namely the Rehn-Meidner Model, began to face structural problems due to the steady fragmentation of collective bargaining structures, which led to a sectorial dispersion of wage growth and to higher-than-average increases in most competitive export-oriented firms (Ryner 2002). Decreasing coordination of wage negotiations resulted in rising inflation rates, while credit liberalization contributed to a consumption boom that was financed to a great extent by loans from international financial markets (Englund 1999). The overheating of the domestic economy was aggravated by the decision of the central government to keep interest rates high in order to defend the Swedish krona, by adopting a fixed rate of exchange linked to the European Currency Unit (ECU). The country was then forced to undertake a devaluation in order to avoid speculative attacks against the (overpriced) national currency; this decision put the banking system under strain, due to the increase in the repayment costs of foreign loans. The crisis of the banking sector escalated rapidly into a more general financial crisis that had a far-reaching impact on all the sectors of the economy, with a unique fall in GPD and a significant number of bankruptcies.

The eruption of the financial crisis was also associated with the apparent demise of the first pillar of the Swedish model, i.e. the political hegemony of the SAP. The symbolic dates of this demise are usually identified by the results in the national elections of 1991 and more recently in those of 2006 and 2010, which were won by a centre-right alliance of four parties. This interrupted an otherwise stable period of social democratic and social democratic/green government[11]. However, accounts that are more recent suggest that in Sweden, as in other European countries, the crisis of support for left-wing parties had begun earlier and their hegemony had remained uncontested only until the end of the 1960s. 'The period thereafter', argues Jenny Andersson (2015: 568), 'has been one of increasing electoral competition and political uncertainty, characterized not only by social democracy's increasing dependence on alliances, but also by increasing tensions within the labour movement itself'. A formerly unified union policy and the centralized wage bargaining system had, by the 1990s, both been thoroughly dismantled in favour of decentralized bargaining and collective union-employer agreements at branch and enterprise levels.

The financial crisis under the short-lived centre-right Bildt government (1991–94) is habitually understood to have opened the gates to a neoliberal austerity regime.[12] Yet, already in its financial plan for 1989–90 a social de Social Democratic government had discarded an already questioned Keynesian macroeconomic policy to history's litter bin in order to follow neoliberal policy prescriptions (Ryner 2002). A new social democratic government, ruling from 1994 to 2006, shared ideological premises with Britain's *New Labour* and its 'Third Way' and it continued to subordinate its reiterated promises to guarantee full employment to anti-inflation measures. This contributed to placing Sweden among the OECD countries with the fastest-growing income inequality, albeit starting from a very low level (Björklund and Jäntti 2011), thus reversing an unbroken decades-long trend of declining inequality.

An emerging 'new' Swedish Model – was, as it were, approaching the ideals of the 'embedded neoliberalism' prescribed by current European Union policies (discussed in Chapter Three), but sharing also their inherent social hazards. Put

---

11 Conditionally supported by the Swedish Left Party (*Vänsterpartiet*), heir to the old Swedish communist party.

12 See further the detailed discussion in Schierup, Hansen and Castles (2006).

differently: a transformative programme indeed but one in imminent danger of selling out social citizenship and distributive justice.

The financial crisis of the early 1990s resulted in unemployment soaring to levels not seen since the 1930s. The overall rate went up abruptly from 1.5 per cent in 1989 to 8.1 in 1994. Rising costs of the welfare benefit system, combined with the fall in tax revenues, forced the central government to adopt cost-containment measures, as public debt almost doubled from about 45 percent of GDP in 1990 to over 80 percent in 1995 (Haffert and Mehrtens 2015: 134). Ultimately, the financial crisis resulted in the beginning of the retrenchment phase of the Swedish welfare state and, therefore, in the undermining of the third pillar of the Swedish model, i.e. the principle of universalism.

As mentioned, the financial crisis of the early 1990s is generally recognized as the event that triggered welfare state retrenchment in Sweden. Though its dramatic impact on the Swedish economy is undeniable, that crisis nevertheless does not explain why the retrenchment was not reversed when the economy improved and a new Social Democratic government took office from the mid-1990s until 2006. Tentatively, an explanation may be derived from social theories linking the reduction of the financial autonomy of national governments to the pressures arising from European integration and (relatedly) from the imposition of austerity as the 'default' macroeconomic policy.

Wolfgang Streeck (2014), for one, has described the role of the European Union as that of a 'liberalization machine' that, by imposing flexibilization, deregularization and privatization on member states, steadily but irrevocably reduced the ability of national governments to intervene in the economy and engage in welfare state activities. The endpoint of this restructuring process was what Streeck defined as the 'consolidation state', i.e. a multilevel governance regime dedicated to continuing austerity politics and based on a double process of 'de-politicization of economics' and 'de-democratization of politics'. The consolidation state represents an antithesis of the Keynesian welfare state. It emerged in response to the shift of the power balance towards the financial markets, which have become the most powerful political constituency in EU member states. Austerity-based fiscal consolidation measures operate as instruments by which the governments of consolidation states demonstrate their willingness to match the expectations of financial markets, to the detriment of those of other constituencies represented by the labour movement and civil society organizations. The vain hope of the governments in charge of consolidation states is that, by 'buying time' with austerity measures (Streeck 2014), they may eventually be able to reintroduce expansive and demand-side policies which would lead to sustained economic growth, increased employment the decreasing social inequality.

The Swedish example, however, shows that this expectation did not materialize when the economy recovered from the recession and became one of the fastest growing in Europe even though the Eurozone's fiscal austerity pact is not binding for Sweden as a non-member. In a recent study Lukas Haffert and Philip Mehrtens (2015) made the argument that the adoption of an austere fiscal regime in Sweden in the aftermath of the crisis of the early 1990s had the effect of reorienting the debate on fiscal policy towards a wide and entrenched consensus on the need to keep public spending under control. 'All parties', they contend (Haffert and Mehrtens 2015: 136), 'try hard to avoid the impression of behaving financially irresponsibly. Government and opposition are outbidding each other in a race to see who can spend less public money'. This cross-party realignment in favour of austerity resulted from the introduction of automatic fiscal stabilizers in 1997, which have obliged the central government to preserve a budget surplus target of 1 percent of GDP over every business cycle in order to bring down the accumulated public debt. Since that year, every Swedish government has in practice been forced to comply with this target and avoid deficits, while keeping inflation down. Furthermore, the introduction of an expenditure ceiling (also from 1997) has drastically reduced the room for expansionary pro-welfare policies, even though budget surpluses can still be used for cutting taxes 'as the ceiling affects expenditure but not revenue' (Haffert and Mehrtens 2015: 137). In turn, tax cuts financed from surpluses have generated pressures for additional cutbacks in social expenditure, together with a general restraint on public sector expenditure.

By 1998, the previous budget deficit was turned into a budget surplus. From that year until the beginning of the global financial crisis of 2007–2008, Sweden always achieved the targeted budget surpluses. None of the main political parties publicly questioned the pursuit of austerity nor attempted to modify the overall framework of public expenditure control, even marginally. For instance, once back in power (in 1995 and 2014), the SAP committed itself to maintaining most of the changes in the tax and benefit system that had been introduced by previous right-wing governments.

The most visible consequence of the transformation of the Swedish model from a thoroughly institutionalised welfare state into 'the most advanced case of a consolidation state with a firmly established austerity regime' (Streeck 2015: 23) has been a sharp decline in public revenue and public expenditure. The decline was about ten percentage points of GDP between 1990 and 2012 for both public expenditure and public revenue, although the former decreased faster than the latter, hence ensuring the required budget surpluses (Haffert and Mehrtens 2015: 139). The cuts in public expenditure led to various kinds of adjustment to the Swedish welfare state, involving all policy domains and all types of service and income provision.

In this respect, an official investigation prepared for the Swedish parliament by a group of leading policy analysts has shown that, since the early 1990s, Sweden has lost its leading position with regard to the relative generosity of many welfare benefits compared with other OECD countries (Palme et al. 2012).

In particular, the unemployment insurance system has undergone significant reforms on both the financing and benefit sides. These reforms concerned the replacement level of benefits but also the maximum income level for replacement and the costs of the membership fees. The aforementioned study estimated that until 2005 the Swedish unemployment insurance system was the second most generous in the OECD (after Switzerland) but, in a five-year span until 2010, the average amount of benefits became lower than that of twelve comparable countries (Palme et al. 2012: 32). The lowering in the replacement rate in 2007 was only partly responsible for this reduction in benefit generosity. Another reason can be found in the implicit decision not to adjust the maximum income level to inflation and wage developments since 2002 (Leijon et al. 2013). Whereas in that year 80 percent of the (eligible) full-time workers who became unemployed received benefits equivalent to the legislated replacement rate, this proportion declined to 10 percent in 2015 (Arbetslöshetskassornas Samorganisation 2015). Part of the explanation for this is the fact that membership fees of union-controlled unemployment insurance funds were extremely low until 2007 and were tax deductible. In that year, the right-wing government decided to shift a greater share of the financing burden of the unemployment insurance system from general taxation to the union-controlled funds and to abolish the tax deductions on membership fees. The effect of this reform was a general increase in individual membership fees, which led about 400,000 people to abandon the unemployment funds and about 250,000 workers to opt out of the unions (Kjellberg 2011: 90). The decline in union membership was particularly large in the employment sectors with the largest shares of foreign-born workers (Kjellberg 2011: 84). Ultimately, the reduction in unemployment insurance fund membership resulted in a parallel increase in the number of unemployed individuals who did not qualify for insurance-based unemployment benefits and were forced to rely on municipal social assistance.

The reform of the sickness insurance system was another factor contributing to the growth in social assistance caseloads. The duration of sickness benefit was virtually unlimited until 2008 but in that year a maximum duration was set at one year, after which time an assessment is made of whether the beneficiary meets the requirements for an extension of eligibility (although at a lower replacement rate) (Ulmestig 2013). There is evidence that a growing proportion of individuals with long-term health problems and disabilities are forced to apply for social assistance benefits after their sick leave runs out (Leijon et al. 2013: 42).

In sum, social assistance shifted from being the last resort of income security for people experiencing temporary economic difficulties, to being 'a permanent source of income in circumstances where unemployment and sickness insurance cover people increasingly insufficiently' (Angelin, Johansson and Koch 2014: 173). The growth in importance of social assistance within the Swedish income security system occurred nevertheless in the context of its declining effectiveness in alleviating poverty. In 1990, social assistance benefits were, on average, more generous in Sweden than in the Netherlands, Germany and the UK, but in 2009 Sweden provided less generous benefits than these three countries (Kuivalainen and Nelson 2010: 22). As a consequence of the insufficient adjustment of benefit levels to the cost of living during the period in question, Sweden changed from being one of the few European countries with social assistance benefits above the at-risk-of-poverty threshold (i.e. below 60 percent of median income), to joining the other European countries providing benefits below that level (Kuivalainen and Nelson 2010: 22).

Along with the general trend towards declining generosity, income protection against unemployment became conditional on job-seeking efforts, with a constant monitoring of recipients' cases and the imposition of sanctions in the event of non-compliance with eligibility rules. The current Swedish model has become reminiscent of the disciplining *workfare* programmes originally introduced in Anglo-Saxon countries and then implemented in the European context (Peck 2001; Lødemel and Trickey 2001; Schierup, Hansen and Castles 2006). Instead of upgrading the skills of the unemployed through education and training, the function of labour market policy has more and more become a matter of keeping presumptive welfare clients 'active' and ready to accept any available job, even those for which they are overqualified. The focus has been increasingly placed on the improvement of the self-promotion skills of unemployed recipients of welfare benefits, who tend to be held responsible for their labour market reintegration as well as for their own economic situation (Bengtsson 2014). This normative shift in social policy orientation signalled an interruption and, to a certain extent, even a reversal of the long-run process of increasing decommodification that characterised the previous phases of development of the Swedish model. In line with political developments in the EU as a whole, the tendency since the early 1990s has been a sharp trend towards the recommodification of labour. In other words, deregulation and new institutional forms of control are (re)connecting people's welfare more directly with the market value of their labour.

Finally, it is important to mention the reform of the pension system in 1998, with the shift from a 'defined benefit' to a 'defined contribution' approach linking benefit levels to individual contributions but also to financial market performance, as workers have been obliged to divert part of their contributions to private funds (Belfrage and Ryner 2009). Moreover, the replacement of the universal pension scheme (*folkpension*) by a means-tested benefit ('guarantee pension', or *garantipension*), to be received only by those who do not qualify for a contributory pension, indicate a radical overhauling of the previous system based on cross-class solidarity and universal entitlements.

The budget surpluses achieved through cuts in welfare state expenditure have been used to finance a series of tax breaks and reductions. In fact, as mentioned, the establishment of the expenditure ceiling has not limited the capacity of the central government to intervene on the revenue side. Some examples of these initiatives included: the reduction of the marginal rate of tax on capital income and interest deductions (1991), the abolition of inheritance taxes (2004), the abolition of the wealth tax (2007), and the replacement of the national property tax on dwellings with a lower municipal fee (2008). Clearly, high-income groups gained the most from these fiscal reforms. Indeed, since the 1980s, the contribution of capital gains and stock option revenues to the incomes of individuals at the top of the distribution has been unparalleled in the history of the country, following a development similar to that in the US, even if in a more limited fashion (Roine and Waldenström 2012). Another tax reform contributing to rising inequality was the introduction of a form of earned income tax credit (*jobbskatteavdrag* in Swedish) in 2007, a measure that has been expanded five times since then. Because welfare benefits do not qualify for this tax credit, its introduction resulted in a widening of the income gap between individuals in employment and those out of work (Fritzell et al. 2014: 647).

Until the mid-1980s, the expansion of the Swedish welfare state was associated with a steady decline in income inequality, which reached the lowest level ever, with a Gini coefficient of about 0.200 (Björklund and Jäntti 2011: 31). From the mid-1980s onwards, the retrenchment of the welfare state resulted in the reversal of the long-running trend of decreasing inequality. In fact, Sweden recorded the fastest income inequality increase (in percentage points) among OECD countries, with a rise in the Gini coefficient by almost one third from the mid-1980s, up to 0.259 in 2008 (OECD 2011).

Income inequality continued to rise even after the beginning of the global financial crisis. A report by Statistics Sweden showed that Sweden experienced the highest increase in disposable income (+26 percent) among Northern and Western European countries between 2005 and 2010 (SCB 2012: 26). However, during this period the poverty level remained stable at about 6 percent for individuals in employment but it increased from 26 percent to 36 percent among those out of work (SCB 2012: 38). The growth of the poverty gap between these two groups reflected the widening income differentials, which were accentuated by the introduction of the aforementioned reforms of the tax and benefit systems.

Hence, not all social groups benefited equally from the general improvement of the economic situation in the country since the late 1990s, as well as from the more recent (and unequalled in Northern and Western Europe) increase in average income in the aftermath of the global financial crisis. Immigrants, and in particular those who arrived in the last two decades, were especially badly affected by welfare state retrenchment and rising inequality.

The Impact of Austerity on Immigration and Integration Policy

Like other policy areas, the Swedish immigration policy regime developed as a constituent and integral part of the Swedish model. Therefore, as the Swedish model began to accumulate problems after the mid-1980s, immigration policy began showing signs of a looming crisis in its capacity to incorporate newly arrived immigrants (Ålund and Schierup 1991; Schierup, Hansen and Castles 2006). The economic crisis of the early 1990s, and the subsequent restructuring of the welfare state, had negative impacts on the integration of immigrants. The groups that were most affected by these developments were those who, in those years, came as asylum seekers from war-torn countries in the Middle East and the Balkans. When the crisis was at its peak, Sweden received the second highest number of asylum applications per capita in Europe (after Switzerland) from these geographical areas, which continued to be the main sources of non-labour migration to the country, culminating with the present refugee crisis in the Middle East.

In the period 1993–1995, the increase in unemployment was much higher among foreign-born than among native-born. Thus, the overall rate of open unemployment in Sweden (as a percentage of the active labour force) went up abruptly from 1.5 per cent in 1989 to 8.2 per cent in 1993, but among foreign-born from 3.5 per cent to 24 per cent during the same period (SCB 2004).

Even after the Swedish economy fully recovered from the recession, the employment gap between foreign and native born stabilized at a higher level than pre-crisis (Schierup, Hansen and Castles 2006; Bevelander 2009). A recent study has found that notwithstanding the improvement in the employment performance of immigrants from the global south in the period from 1998 to 2008, the gap from natives remained substantial and was larger for women than men (Bevelander 2013). For instance, considering women separately, the gap for those from Iran and Vietnam was 20 percent higher and for those from Somalia it was 55 percent higher than the average for women overall. For men, the gap was, for instance, 10 percent for those from Turkey and 40 percent for those from Iraq and Pakistan compared with *the overall men's average.*

However, the aggregate employment rate of foreign-born is remarkably higher in Sweden than in many other OECD countries (OECD 2015: 83). Indeed, the latest MIPEX report[13] gave Sweden the highest score for immigrant labour market integration among the thirty-eight countries considered (EU-28 plus Norway, Canada, South Korea, New Zealand, USA, Japan, Switzerland, Australia, Iceland, Turkey). Moreover, the Swedish welfare state seems to be more successful than those of six comparable countries in lifting immigrants out of poverty (Sainsbury 2012: 121). That the Swedish welfare state is more effective in reducing poverty is attributed to the higher degree of inclusiveness of social policies because legally resident immigrants enjoy similar social rights to native-born citizens.

Against this background, it can be argued that, in absolute terms, immigrants in Sweden fare better than their counterparts living in other European countries. At the same time, according to some socio-economic indicators, the gap in living conditions from native-born seems to be worse in Sweden than in other countries where redistribution is lower. This comparatively higher level of inter-ethnic inequality clearly points to a structural problem of the Swedish welfare state in levelling out the opportunities between those of immigrant and non-immigrant backgrounds.

Long-term redundancy and a changing labour market policy are presumed to have caused large groups of foreign-born to become increasingly dependent on means-tested, residual social welfare or low second-rate, unemployment compensation (discussed by, among other, Lundh et al. 2002: 58). While the proportion of households of foreign-born receiving means-tested social welfare allowances (not including unemployment insurance payments) corresponded, largely, to the Swedish average in the 1970s, it had gone way above it in the 1990s (Franzén 2001). By the mid-1990s people born in 'former Yugoslavia', 'the Middle East', and Africa were receiving means-tested social security payments over ten times

13 See footnote 9.

more often than Swedish-born (Vogel 2002: 54).[14] This was an important factor behind the widening of the poverty gap between natives and foreign-born, as only 20 percent of working-age natives experienced poverty at least once in the period 1996–2007 compared with 45 percent of immigrants (Obućina 2014: 8). A recent study estimated that, in the period 2007–2008, the percentage difference in poverty rates between non-EU immigrants and native-born in Sweden was the fourth largest (after Belgium, Finland and Ireland) when sixteen EU countries were compared (Hooijer and Picot 2015: 9). The existence of a higher risk of poverty for immigrants is explained by the specific labour market barriers they face: 'Even the very effective Swedish welfare state cannot totally make up for the severe disadvantages that immigrants face in the Swedish labour market', concludes Christel Kesler (2014: 55).

The overrepresentation of immigrants among welfare recipients, and with less access to income related social insurances, provides a partial explanation for their higher risk of poverty. As seen in the previous section, the period from the early 1990s onwards was characterized by a stagnating or declining generosity of welfare benefits; accordingly, disparities in income and poverty levels increased considerably between individuals in and out of employment. Also newly arrived asylum seekers were to experience more precarious conditions. In fact, in 1994 the reduction of the amount of the daily allowance for asylum seekers waiting for a decision on their application (*dagersättning*) contributed to the deterioration of their economic situation. The benefit has not been adjusted for inflation since that year: the amount is currently SEK 71[15] for single adults, SEK 61 for cohabiting partners, and between SEK 37–50 for minor children, depending on their age. When asylum seekers are accommodated in a reception centre these levels are reduced to SEK 24, SEK 19, and SEK 12 respectively (www.migrationsverket.se).

Additionally, since the early 1990s, integration policies have been affected by the general 'workfarist' reorientation of Swedish labour market policy, which has led to an increased emphasis on the need to accelerate immigrants' economic self-sufficiency (as well as to reduce the overall costs of the immigrant reception system). Municipalities have been given freedom to implement introductory programmes for newly arrived immigrants and to provide economic incentives in return for participation – the so-called introductory allowance (*introduktionsersättning för nyanlända*). Although participation was voluntary, the municipalities could impose economic sanctions (including the reduction or withdrawal of

14 Aggregated survey data from the period 1993–2000.

15 Corresponding to approximately 7.6 Euro.

the introductory allowance) if migrants refused to accept a job offer or to participate in educational or vocational training (Borevi 2012: 84; Sainsbury 2012: 92).

A major change occurred in 1997 when integration policy was separated from that of migration-related issues by the creation of two government authorities, i.e. the Migration Board (*Migrationsverket*, founded in 2000) and the Integration Board (*Integrationsverket*, instituted in 1998). The separation aimed at expanding the scope of integration from an issue concerning only the foreign-born subpopulation group to one concerning the whole Swedish population and, therefore, all citizens irrespective of their ethnic or cultural backgrounds (Schierup and Ålund 2011b: 49; Sainsbury 2012: 91). The purpose was to challenge the stereotypical representation of immigrants as a homogeneous group sharing specific needs and facing disproportionate disadvantages compared with the rest of the population. Immigrants were expected to participate in the introductory programmes only in the early period after their arrival and to achieve economic self-sufficiency as quickly as possible, in order to become eligible for the non-targeted and population-wide integration policy.

The new integration policy was in line with the social inclusion, employment and social cohesion objectives of the emerging European social agenda (Schierup, Hansen and Castles 2006: 48–80). In fact, the buzzwords of this policy were 'employability', 'entrepreneurship' (with a focus on small ethnic businesses), immigration as a factor contributing to regional growth, 'diversity management' as a value-adding measure for firms, etc.

The change in the scope of integration policies also affected the role of ethnic associations. While in the 1970s the emphasis was on the political participation and representation of ethnic groups, at the end of the 1990s the focus of public funding bodies began to turn to the involvement of ethnic associations in projects favouring the integration of their members, with an eye to enhancing their long-term 'employability'. The priorities of public funding for ethnic associations have thus changed. After having been regarded as relatively independent civil society actors in the framework of corporatist interest intermediation (Soininen 1999), ethnic associations have more and more been assigned the role of ancillary stakeholders in the development of employment-oriented projects and in the achievement of economic growth-centred objectives.

One of the major political objectives of the right-wing government that came to office in 2006 was to reorganize the reception system, with the purpose of reducing the existing inter-municipal variation in the implementation of immigrant-targeted introductory programmes. Formally, the aim of the right-wing government was to speed up the labour market integration of immigrants by modifying the administrative structure of the reception system, while preserving its basic institutional framework.

In this regard, one of the first acts of the government was to close the Integration Board and transfer its responsibilities for the reception and integration of newly arrived immigrants to the Migration Board and to the County Administrative Boards, which in Sweden function as regional branches of the central government (Bevelander 2013: 202). However, the subsequent 'Establishment Reform' (*etableringsreformen*), launched in 2010, went beyond a merely administrative reorganization and implicitly resulted in the strengthening of the work-related conditions attached to immigrants' participation in introductory programmes (Larsson 2015; Qvist 2016).

The Establishment Reform transferred the coordinating responsibilities for the introductory programmes from the municipalities to the state-controlled public employment office system (*Arbetsförmedlingen*). At the same time, private providers were allowed to work on commission for the public employment offices as 'Pilots' (*etableringslotsar*) for newly arrived immigrants. The new reception procedure allows eligible immigrants (those aged 20–64 with a residence permit for humanitarian reasons) to choose their Pilot among different private providers. This measure was supposed to support immigrants during the introductory period and assist them to become economically self-sufficient. While participation in the introductory programmes is still voluntary, immigrants who choose to participate are entitled to a new type of benefit, the so-called Establishment Allowance (*etableringsersättning*), which is more than the social assistance to which they would be virtually entitled in case of non-participation in the programme. In practice, though, municipalities can reject claims for social assistance when immigrants refuse to participate in the Establishment activities (Larsson 2015: 46). At the same time, the amount of economic compensation for the Establishment Pilots has depended upon a results-based remuneration system rewarding the rapid integration of immigrants into the labour market, irrespective of the quality and the security of employment, rather than their participation in long-term skill-upgrading programmes (Larsson 2015: 124–30).

The decision to involve private providers in the organization of introductory programmes for newly arrived immigrants was linked to the general trend of New Public Management reforms. Since the early 1990s it brought market-based solutions into the public sector as a way to improve its economic efficiency and its (alleged) responsiveness to the needs and demands of citizens (Blomqvist 2004).

The drive for privatization in the welfare sector accelerated at the turn of the millennium and especially after the election of the right-wing government in

2006, which enacted a new Public Purchasing Act (*Lagen om offentlig upphandling*, LOU), coming into effect in 2008 and thereby implementing a previous EU directive (Directive 2004/18/EC). This new Act allowed private providers to compete on equal terms and conditions with public sector organizations for the provision of services, as well as to extract profits from the welfare sector. Competition among all providers was supposed to have beneficial effects in terms of cost savings and quality gains, but there is no evidence suggesting that these objectives have been achieved (Hartman 2011a). Hence, while the Swedish welfare state has maintained its financing functions, the social service sector has at the same time become increasingly privatized. Between 2002 and 2010, the proportion of workers in this sector who are employed in private firms has in fact risen from about one-tenth to about one-fifth of the total (Hartman 2011b: 23).

The subsequent Freedom of Choice Act (*Lagen om valfrihet*, LOV), passed in 2009, introduced a licensing model by which all providers meeting the requirements defined by the central government were allowed to operate as contractors for public services. The effect, in practice, was to redefine the role of citizens from passive recipients of social services and benefits to active consumers capable of making conscious and informed choices reflecting their preferences, while actively taking responsibility for their own well-being. Indeed, the Government Bill that launched the Establishment Reform referred explicitly to the Freedom of Choice Act. It thus set out that '[u]sing a free-choice system is a part of the effort to shift the focus on the user, transferring power from politicians and civil servants to the individual, to provide an increased freedom of choice, together with more providers and greater variety' (Arbetsmarknadsdepartementet 2009: 76).

Still, a recent study has provided evidence that the choices of newly arrived immigrants participating in the Establishment initiatives are far from being free and unconstrained, primarily due to the lack of interpreters who can assist them in overcoming the language barriers in the public employment offices (Larsson 2015). Furthermore, according to the same study, the results-based remuneration system created incentives for the Pilots to pressure their 'clients' to accept any kind of job, either in the formal or informal sector. Hence, it has been argued that the Swedish reform has been essentially inspired by a neoliberal notion of empowerment, expecting immigrants and refugees to take the initiative for their own integration 'without taking into consideration the structural barriers in society that exclude [them] from entering the labour market' (Fernandes 2015: 258).

Perhaps the indicator that best provides a sense of the scale of these 'structural barriers' is given by the degree of exclusion of foreign-born from the labour market, relative to native-born. According to the latest OECD figures, Sweden has the largest unemployment gap between native- and foreign-born of the 38 countries covered by the comparison. Only Greece, Spain and Belgium ranked higher (OECD 2015: 89). According to another report by Statistics Sweden, although Sweden is the country with the third lowest share of long-term unemployed (six months or more) in total unemployment in the EU28, it is also the country with the largest difference in long-term unemployment between native- and foreign-born (SCB 2013).

At the same time, immigrants who succeed in obtaining employment are often found at the bottom of the labour market and in low paying jobs that are not commensurate with their skills and/or work experience before immigrating. This problem concerns particularly immigrants with education obtained outside of Sweden, as their credentials are often not recognized and therefore they are forced either to pursue further education (or even to restart it from scratch), or to accept jobs for which they are overqualified (Alatalo and Ostapenko 2014). There is vast empirical evidence that similar mechanisms of exclusion operate even against first generation immigrants, who made investments in acquiring specifically Swedish human capital (e.g. through long-term education), as well as against children of immigrants who were born in Sweden (Rydgren 2004). Both groups tend in fact to be hindered by institutionally grounded discriminatory practices from entering into the protected 'core' of the labour market.

These changes have taken place in the context of the general shift from a Keynesian welfare state that was committed to full employment, and succeeded in preventing the bifurcation of the labour market into low-wage and high-wage sectors, to a neoliberal consolidation state. The latter is characterised by higher unemployment rates, particularly among migrants and their descendants, but also by the emergence of a low-wage secondary labour market, where informal work arrangements are increasingly common. Foreign-born are overrepresented in this secondary labour market and especially in the restaurant, cleaning, transport and caretaking private service industries (De los Reyes and Wingborg 2002; Slavnic and Urban 2008; Gavanas 2010; Urban 2013). In line with the recent trend towards tax reduction, a series of cuts have been instituted in order to stimulate job creation in some of these industries and create employment opportunities that were explicitly conceived as 'well-suited' for unemployed immigrants. The initiatives include lowering VAT on restaurant and catering services in 2012 (Urban 2013) and the introduction of tax deductions for households purchasing domestic services or home repair services in 2007 (Nyberg 2015).

The combined effect of the central government's interventions on the supply side (with the enforcement of activation requirements) and on the demand side (with tax reductions for job creation in low-skilled private services) has been an intensification of existing labour market inequalities along ethnic lines. A growing proportion of foreign-born, as well as children of foreign born, suffers from unemployment and social assistance receipt and periods of intermittent employment in low-paying occupations, which means they do not qualify for unemployment benefits. In this respect, the latest report by the Swedish Agency for Youth and Civil Society (MUCF 2016) showed that differences between native- and foreign-born young adults have become dramatic in all aspects of social life, from education to the labour market, to participation in political or cultural activities. In 2015, 90 percent of native-born lower-secondary level students were eligible to continue to the upper secondary level, while the corresponding percentage was 57 percent among foreign-born. In that same year, the unemployment rate was 11 percent among natives aged 16–24 and 35 percent among foreign-born in the same age group. Moreover, foreign born and the offspring of foreign born were also less likely to be politically active than native born and children of native born (MUCF 2016).

Thus, for migrants and racialised groups, as argued by Anders Neergaard (2009), the shift from a full employment regime to one where unemployment becomes a driving force for a disciplinary recommodification of labour means, at the same time, a shift from 'subordinated inclusion' to 'subordinated exclusion'. It links racialised labour to either a desired wage-depressing reserve army and/or precarious work in low-wage occupational ghettoes, which is in turn linked with inferior access to collective organisation and political resources.[16]

Since the 1990s, the general rise of inequality has also become more visible in the Swedish urban landscape, with a growing socio-spatial polarisation along ethnic and income lines in cities (Scarpa 2015b). This socio-spatial polarization has been due to both 'gentrification' and 'filtering' processes (Hedin et al. 2012). Gentrification has mainly taken the form of 'super-gentrification', due to the inflow of high-income households into already rich neighbourhoods, dominated by single-family owner-occupied housing. Instead, low-income filtering involved especially poorer neighbourhoods dominated by rental multifamily housing, which experienced a further decrease in average income.

Migration reforms during the 2000s have added new aspects to this ongoing precarisation of work and livelihoods and to a deepening racialisation of inequality. A new law on labour migration passed by parliament in 2008 (Regeringen

16 The notion of 'occupational ghetto' was coined by Stephan Feuchtwang (1982) in a study of discrimination and racialisation of the UK labour market.

2008) made the duration of residence permits, and eventually access to full formal citizenship, conditional upon the duration of employment contracts. Its opening up for an, in principle unlimited, employer-driven temporary migrant workers' scheme has been characterised as 'a slight revolution' (Cerna 2009) in a country with a longstanding and ramified edifice of inclusive citizenship subject to democratic guarantees, perhaps more inclusive than anywhere else (Sainsbury 2006). Fear among trade unions that the new temporary migrants' dependence on particular employers, together with an ever present danger of losing employment and a work permit, would lead to an exceedingly weak bargaining position and exposure to excessive exploitation (Davidsson 2008; Hjärtberg 2008) has proved to be grounded (e.g. Calleman and Herzfeld Olsson 2015).

The 2008 law opened up, in consequence, a *third* – disadvantaged and precarious – status, alongside the long established dual statuses of (full) *citizen* and *denizen*. Through its insistence on making residence dependent on employment status, the law, in effect, extended the range of the increasingly implacable insistence on a disciplinary labour flexibility. However, it shifted the driving force of a move from subordinated inclusion to subordinated exclusion to the realm of immigration control and an increasingly discriminatory citizenship law. Thus Sweden has been a latecomer to the emerging Europe-wide practices of so-called 'managed migration', which have become more stringently monitored than the guest worker systems of *Middeleuropa* (German, Austrian, Swiss) ever were (e.g. Guild, Carrera and Atger 2009; Guiraudon 1998). Étienne Balibar (2004) sees this as an emerging legally sanctioned European Apartheid. It guarantees employers long term access to an abundant cheap and readily disposable global labour force which is excluded from the privileges of citizenship yet in the same fell swoop it appeases the extreme right with guarantees that only a few of these new precarious workers will gain access to full citizenship and membership of the nation.

This is a development of precarisation and a political co-opting of the extreme right that has become extended and deepened in tandem with the unfolding of the present 'refugee crisis.' It is tightly interwoven with the contest for power between the left and right at a moment marked by political turmoil with the 'refugee crisis' tactically posited as a loaded stratagem at the centre of the political debate and media discourse.

Between 'Refugee Keynesianism' and Racial Austerity

The ruling centre-right alliance lost the Swedish general election of 2014. A minority government of social democrats and the Swedish Green Party (*Miljöpartiet*), with parliamentary support by the Left Party (*Vänsterpartiet*), took over.

Even so the populist Sweden Democrats held a solid balance in parliament and promised to turn down any overall budget that did *not* include a halt to a generous asylum policy and further immigration. Political panic and disarray ensued, but collapse was averted in December 2014 by a re-forged grand left-right compact (*Decemberöverenskommelsen*) with the explicit purpose of blocking the Sweden Democrats from political influence. The 'December Compact' was supposed to last for two consecutive electoral periods (eight years). On this foundation the new left-green government ventured to put forward a budget proposing public investments connected with a continued liberal asylum policy as well as general investments in new de-commodifying labour market, education and welfare policy reforms. It looked, argues Peo Hansen (2016) in a critical study of Europe's 'immigration crisis', as though a new 'refugee Keynesianism' would be on the advance, by which spending on refugee reception would boost economic dynamism and growth with the capacity to invest in welfare reforms rather than necessitating incremental fiscal austerity.

Initially, argues Hansen, neither Sweden nor Germany succumbed to outright 'racial austerity'. On the contrary an initially bold move to handle the 'refugee crisis' through a necessary increase in public sector spending provided an opportunity for a 'rare Keynesian laboratory environment' (Hansen 2016: 33). '[N] umerous reports corroborate this picture', he contends, 'with … refugee related spending impacting positively on economic growth in the EU in general, and with a more significant mid- and long-term impact predicted for those countries' (Hansen 2016: 33).[17] It indicated a scenario which – as developed in Lisa Pelling's (2015b) report, *Legal Passages over the Mediterranean* – suggests a realistic synergy between an open and liberal immigration and asylum policy and a sustainable economic and demographic development. The workability of such a scenario is amply supported by the dynamic impact on the Swedish public finances which migration effected throughout the entire post Second World War Period (Scocco and Andersson 2015). However, for this effect to be sustainable a catalytic interplay between two levels of public policy would be crucial, argue Sandro Scocco and Lars Fredrik Andersson (2015: 7). The 'little policy of integration', targeted directly at forward looking policies for migration management and immigrant integration and the 'big policy of integration', entailing 'a well-functioning economy, with a high level of employment, low unemployment, good provision of housing in strong labour market regions, coupled with a well-functioning educational system marked by high quality and equity' would need to come together. It is

17 Referring to, among others, IMF (2016) and Statistics Sweden (SCB 2016).

a scenario supported by a major recent comparative study which documents a general positive correlation between strong welfare regimes and 'generous' politics of asylum (Boräng 2013). Reception and integration of refugees at a grand scale is 'a humanitarian investment that yields economic dividends' argues more recently political economist Phillippe Legrain (2016) in a major report.

Yet the window of opportunity for an immigration-driven Keynesian integration scenario closed abruptly: in Germany, in Sweden and in the EU in general. In the cases of Germany and Sweden, argues Hansen (2016), attempts to explain this 'with a simple caving in to racial austerity à la Denmark or Hungary' are unsatisfactory. An 'abrupt shift', he contends, 'from a policy of 'welcome' to one of rejection, from a policy designating refugees as a demographic-economic necessity to one branding refugees as a societal peril', needs a more complex explanation. 'In order to challenge refugee austerity in today's EU this necessarily also implies challenging the EU's master regime of fiscal austerity. Otherwise the first will only go as far as the latter allows' (Hansen 2016: 29–30). This argument points to the Eurozone's persisting regressive dynamics. Yet it needs to be qualified further with reference to the differential conditions and relations of power in struggles for hegemony in Germany compared with Sweden. Germany is the mastermind and the fervent guardian of the Eurozone's austere financial regime, the rules of which do not in principle bind Sweden as a non-member. In Sweden a populist extreme right party holds the balance in parliament, which is not the case in Germany. Sweden in the 2010s had a huge surplus in its public finances. The country would have had extremely favourable conditions for cheap public borrowing. It had a real economic capacity for, potentially, making vast public investments in infrastructure, housing, education and for including a broad and sustained societal incorporation of large numbers of newcomers driven by a forward looking and sustained 'refugee Keynesianism' with full employment as a principal goal.

In Sweden fiscal austerity was originally instituted at a moment of deep recession by a social democratic government but is today heavily questioned by large swaths of the party's constituency and a still powerful labour movement. Several motions by the post-2014 left-green minority government have indeed started to probe fiscal austerity. The past decades' dismantling of the public sector, disruptive tax reforms and politics forging a growing low wage precarious labour market with substantial unemployment guaranteeing 'morale' and discipline are examples. Almost any initiative in this direction has provoked vehement reactions from the parliamentary right, which is potentially capable of blocking any motion through a covert alliance with the Sweden Democrats. This party appears, besides being heavily lobbied by organisations of employers, ready to support any parliamentary motion from the political right in return for a halt to further immigration. Our view is therefore that the upholding of a stringent fiscal austerity regime is politically over-determined by a looming coalition between the racist-populist extreme right and the mainstream neoliberal right.

Impressed by a vast, seldom seen, mobilisation of Swedish civil society stirred by the globally publicised image of the dead body of three-year-old Alan Kurdi from Syria washed onto a beach in Turkey, social democratic premier, Stefan Löfven, as late as September 2015 still spoke with confidence of Sweden as 'a country carrying solidarity as our greatest pride'. However, following an apparent flow of votes in consecutive opinion polls from the largest party in the conservative block (*Moderaterna*) to the Sweden Democrats, and a rebellion within the ranks of the centre-right opposition, the tactical December Compact crashed after only nine months. It appears (as argued in Chapter One and Ten) as a moment of crisis when the neoliberal right starts to realise that in order to repair its hegemony it needs to revitalise its own conservative nationalist roots and with one accord co-opt the expanding populist extreme right. This suggests a looming blue-brown pre-Second World War scenario of racial austerity but with novel features.

This new-old bid for hegemony by the parliamentary right, as argued in the introduction (Chapter One. See also Chapter Ten), precipitated a rapid race to the bottom in a regressive competition for the pragmatic appropriation of the fundamentals of the extreme right agenda between the two major political blocks, with the Sweden Democrats applauding this development on one side and the Left Party isolated in defence of the earlier liberal refugee policy. The fall of the left-right December Compact was followed in October 2015 by a new, fundamentally altered, right-left compact. It was to turn the overall anti-populist consensus, which had been the principled ground for incorporating immigration, asylum and integration policy into the Swedish welfare state model for decades, into its mirror image, reflecting a clear shift in the power balance. It involves a landslide concession to – as well as an implicit legitimation of – the extreme populist right. It includes, as well, the cheap sale of cherished standards and electoral promises by the red-green government coalition, yielding to long-standing claims for labour market restructuring by the political right.

In November 2015, the red-green minority government decided effectively to block the admission of refugees and reduce the intake to the EU-imposed minimum quota, while instating ID-controls at the border with Denmark, in what corresponded to a de facto rupture with the 1951 Geneva Convention relating to refugees, as well as a partial interruption of the country's Schengen membership. Trafficking of refugees has become increasingly criminalised with even individuals who help refugees with an obviously humanitarian purpose being targeted. What is of particular importance with reference to the focus of the present chapter is, however, that a re-forged right-centre-left political compact[18] managed in one fell swoop to opt for dismantling cardinal principles which for decades had functioned as warrants of social solidarity and the basis of the Swedish model.[19] The central principle of permanent residence permits targeted at far-sighted integrating of refugees has been sacrificed in favour of making the granting of temporary residence the main rule (with the manifest intention of deterring refugees from seeking asylum in Sweden).[20] For most, temporary protection means a short period of thirteen months – with three years for only the rather few who receive protection due to their UN Convention status. Moreover, refugees with temporary protection are bereft of family unification rights. These rights, which used to be among the most liberal, will conceivably become the most restrictive in the whole of the EU (passed through parliament in June 2016, but retroactively applied on refugee applicants from November 2015).

The only way to access family unification and to change temporary protection into permanent residence will be through obtaining a taxable income deemed adequate for 'self-sufficiency'; in effect this would mean securing employment quickly. It looks like an extension of the austerity-driven neoliberal axiom of 'employability' to the realm of refugee and asylum policy. It puts an immense pressure on refugees to accept immediately any available employment, without being able to wait for a validation of their professional qualifications or to learn Swedish in order to be able to apply for more qualified jobs (Pelling 2015a). It tends to equalise the status of refugees and that of temporary labour migrants, who do not have the security of an extended citizenship. It reduces opportunities to pursue a long-term integration and professional development project, and – with employers capable of playing the deportation card at any time – jeopardises prospects for unionisation and political empowerment. However, what distinguishes the situation of refugees as job seekers from circulant labour migrants, and which makes them particularly vulnerable, is that employers must (in principle if often not in practice) offer the circulant labour migrants wage, working conditions and social security according to the normal standards of collective agreements in any relevant branch. Despite being formally acknowledged in the new law, this

18 Again with the exception of the Left Party.

19 Manifestly aimed at organising an 'orderly' asylum and refugee reception policy and at 'bringing down increasing costs'. See Regeringskansliet (2015).

20 Except for unaccompanied minors, refugees in resettlement schemes, and families with children.

labour market security does, according to the new refugee-compact, not apply to so-called 'introductory jobs' (*introduktionsjobb*) for refugees. It puts these in a position where they are even more likely to be exposed to the whims of the most predacious employers in the occupational ghettoes of an ethnically divided cutthroat labour market. This exemption from collective agreement coverage has until now been unthinkable in the Swedish context. It represents in fact a concession from the social democrats to the most keenly neoliberal factions in the political alliance on the right and a hard blow to the Swedish model. This implicit perception of the temporarily protected as a precarious reserve army of labour for low wage sectors was further affirmed by taking another concession from the left and a heartfelt issue for the right into the new 'Refugee Compact'. It relates to an extension of the reach of tax exemptions for household services in order to stimulate refugees' employment in this low wage and precarious 'immigrant' occupational ghetto.

Although the current amendments have been presented as temporary in nature, and as motivated by exceptional circumstances, they are perceived – domestically and internationally – as providing (further) support for the tenet that, beyond a certain threshold, immigration compromises the structural integrity of any welfare state, including the highly developed Swedish one. This view was echoed by the minister of foreign affairs, Margot Wallström, in a widely-discussed interview with *Dagens Nyheter*, Sweden's leading newspaper, just a few weeks prior to the aforementioned U-turn in asylum policy. She argued that the country could not cope with a refugee load of that magnitude without causing the system to 'collapse' (Stenberg 2015). 'System collapse' was almost immediately thereafter adopted as a mantra echoed throughout most of the Swedish political establishment; whether self-ascribed 'left' or 'right', 'liberal' or 'conservative'. It was put to work as a saluted common sense ideological trope and discharge from liability that could conveniently push the blame for two and a half decades of systematic mismanagement and demolition of Swedish public institutions (the financial system, the housing market,[21] the railroad system, primary and secondary education,[22] the

21 See e.g. Christophers (2013).
22 See Dahlstedt and Trumberg Chapter Seven, this volume.

police organisation[23], employment offices,[24] the social services[25], the public health system[26]) onto the victims fleeing the burning 'belt of ruins' that was once projected to become the EU's 'stable and prosperous neighbourhood' (Hemicker 2016).

Politics of Solidarity in an Age of Austerity. A Contradiction in Terms?

As argued in the book's introductory Chapter One, rather than speaking of a 'refugee crisis' as the true cause of the EU's and Sweden's current political malaise, we need to speak of a 'crisis of solidarity'; and from more than one perspective. With reference to the general argument discussed at the beginning of the present chapter, we do agree that 'the Swedish Model' of the welfare state, or what remains of it, suffers from a crisis of solidarity. However, to explain this crisis, which has long been looming, in terms of a negative 'diversity-welfare equation' is to turn the order of things topsy-turvy. We need to build on the principled arguments of scholars such as Kymlicka and Banting (2006), Taylor-Gooby (2005) and Mau and Bukhardt (2007; see also Mau, 2009), referred to in our introduction, who believe that public values are politically moulded and institutionally mediated. The social solidarity, on which any universal welfare regime needs to rest, is dependent on whether politics, policies and institutional practices either *reinforce or weaken* conflicts over redistribution.

Our argument here indicates at the same time that two and a half decades of politically driven politics of austerity and welfare institutional fragmentation have managed finally to tip the balance in favour of the former (reinforcement of distributive conflicts). This has driven fast-rising inequality and social and ethno-racial segregation, and with migration, 'too much diversity' and the 'refugee crisis' as ideological battering rams in struggles for hegemony (Schierup and Ålund 2011b).

---

23 In a fuming critique of government policies, akin to New Public Management, Lena Nitz (2013), chair of the union of Swedish police employees *(Polisförbundet)* argues that 'democracy, the rule of law and ethics, fundamental for police work… has been put on the backburner as government policies have been one-sidedly focused on efficiency… [Q]uantative demands on the police', she argues, 'have not taken into account that dubious methods of operation undermine the population's trust in the police as well as the propensity to cooperate with the police. Seen in a wider perspective', Nitz argues, 'this will negatively influence the capacity of the police to carry out its main tasks – to uphold the rule of law, combat crime and increase safety and security'.

24 E.g. Larsson (2015).

25 E.g. Blomqvist (2004).

26 E.g. Hartman (2011a).

At the time of writing, the Sweden Democrats' divisive and segregating welfare chauvinist discourse – opposing deserving Swedish citizens, seen for generations to have 'earned' the rights and privileges of the welfare state, with migrants, the allegedly 'undeserved' social privileges of whom are supposed to 'undermine' the welfare state – appears to have become a political game changer, adopted by a widening political spectrum (Osman 2016). Conservative-cum-neoliberal 'mainstream parties', in particular, seem to be stumbling over their feet in a race to outbid each other in advocating the reduction of long established rights (health services and access to de-commodifying social benefits) for migrants. Indeed, the optimistic projection of the Sweden Democrats' leader (Karlsson 2016) – that his party will soon rule in coalition with Sweden's largest neoliberal-conservative party – appears indeed likely.

Our analysis exposes the eschewed character of an increasingly mainstreamed imagination that feeds this ideo-political *volte face*, pitching 'undeserving foreigners' and 'deserving natives' against each other in a zero-sum game for supposedly scarce resources in a crisis-ridden welfare state, purportedly undermined by immigration. We have demonstrated that the socially integrative capacities of the Swedish welfare model were compromised, without any connection with 'immigration' or 'ethnic diversity', well before the start of the recent refugee crisis. Consequently, it is not the scale of immigration or increasing 'ethnic diversity', which threaten to make the Swedish welfare state unsustainable. It is austerity politics and neoliberal restructuring of Swedish public institutions, which, during the past quarter of century, have undermined a deeply transmuted welfare state's capacity to offer emancipatory and non-discriminatory pathways of incorporation to immigrant newcomers as well as to many others among Sweden's disadvantaged.

The Swedish model's basic features were its commitment to full employment (in the context of high levels of trade union membership), an overall compression of the wage structure (associated with a low level of segmentation in the labour market), and an extensive development of social citizenship rights. These features, in the heyday of the model, constituted the basis for achieving an unmatched degree of decommodification. The institutional arrangements of labour market regulation were geared to ensure the long-term competitiveness of the country rather than adapted to temporary fluctuations in global markets. The functioning of the Swedish model required a great effort in terms of resources devoted to income security schemes and active labour market policies, but its neoliberal transformation has given rise to a new political economy that is geared towards the creation of low-wage ghettoes on the margins of the labour market.

With the abandonment of full employment as the main policy goal, and the gradual dismantling of the institutional framework that had historically sustained it, the vision of the Swedish model as a universalistic and egalitarian welfare state has become more and more a fiction. Latter-day restructuring processes resulted in a remarkable erosion of welfare provision, with a parallel intensification of exploitation in the low-skilled sectors of the labour market. The diminishing 'core' of the labour market continues to be regulated and protected but is changing in character from being the standard for all workers to being a privileged position in society, something which has become increasingly inaccessible for foreign-born. To be sure, selective and conditional recruitment under the banner of 'diversity' helps a certain number of racialised 'others' to overcome these barriers and be co-opted into the core. But a growing proportion of those who are excluded from this core are individuals with an immigrant background who often – irrespective of their education, qualifications, and previous work experience – continue to find themselves stuck at the margins. For them, the ongoing reorganization of employment relations in the Swedish labour market risks puncturing, or setting aside, their social citizenship.

The social polarization associated with the fragmentation of the Swedish labour market into privileged and increasingly marginalized sectors has been further exacerbated by the increase in income inequality caused by the reduced redistributive capacity of the tax and benefit system. The driving force behind the rolling back of the Swedish welfare state has been the shift to austerity politics since the outbreak of the economic crisis of the early 1990s and later due to the obligations related to EU membership. However, the austerity agenda was not reversed even when the Swedish economy recovered after the crisis and became one of the fastest growing in the EU.

It is essential to realize that the new institutional landscape that is emerging from these restructuring processes marks a significant turning away from the traditionally de-commodifying Swedish model. What is described as the Swedish version of a 'consolidation state' (Streeck 2014, 2015) epitomizes, in a very advanced form, a general EU-wide trend towards austerity, privatization and radical recommodification of labour. The decommodification of labour was a key demand of the traditional labour movement and a foundation of the political power of wage earners and the comprehensive welfare reforms of the 20th century. The recommodification that is taking place today is eroding both the social and ultimately the civil and political rights of the welfare state. With ever more circumscribed social rights, subordinated groups are having difficulty availing themselves of their civil and political rights. The ongoing transformations of the welfare state therefore entail far-reaching consequences for the ideals of a vital, functioning democracy and distributive justice. All over Europe, immigrants and their children are hit particularly hard. An uncompromising duty to work at any price, elevated over rights of citizenship, decent work and sustainable livelihoods, has now also come to dominate the management of migration and the system of asylum and refugee reception. Temporariness, insecurity and unpredictability increases the pressure on the individual to accept whatever terms of work and employment are offered.

This poses the immanent need to venture beyond a despondent image of 'system collapse' and confront the challenge of rebuilding sustainable institutions for social solidarity. But a humanitarian vision of solidarity, void of criticism of the last twenty years of fiscal austerity and political economy of dispossession, goes only half way and ends up being self-defeated. 'If Sweden is in collapse and nothing functions, which words do we have left to describe what now happens in Syria?' former Premier Fredrik Reinfeldt[27] exclaimed in March 2016 in a renewed heartfelt appeal for solidarity, wrapped in an implicit critique of the course on which a new leadership of his own political party – as well as most of the rest of the Swedish polity – has now embarked. Yet, as contended by our scrutiny in this chapter, it is the contingent premise of Reinfeldt's emphatic 'Open your hearts!' speech – that large-scale immigration and welcoming the world's wretched entails politics of fiscal austerity – which undermines the very humanitarian solidarity the former Premier appealed for, in favour of the dismal politics of racial austerity. It will more firmly set in concrete a fragmented labour market, segregated cities and a society already heavily divided along lines of 'origin', 'ethnicity' or 'race'.

Thus, 'solidarity' is a floating signifier in an ongoing political struggle for hegemony. One vista professes a neoliberal politics of humanitarian solidarity with open borders, but with social security at a minimum for newly arrived, and with a crackled social citizenship even for 'deserving Swedes'. A morally induced solidarity with those fleeing wars and persecution is essential, but becomes a self-defeating position if associated with austere politics that produce systemic injustice and an ever-deeper social inequality. It is a position now apparently abandoned by Reinfeldt's own dominant party on the right, but still pursued by the Centre Party (*Centerpartiet*), the most neoliberal among all parties in the Swedish parliament. However, the dilemma posed by its binary opposition between migration and welfare has been taken by the horns by the Sweden Democrats. This second

27 Available at: <https://www.youtube.com/watch?v=ItaaM3v-fCA> (Accessed March 24, 2016).

political option presents us with a scenario of a shrunken xenoracist solidarity paired with a populist welfare nostalgia – yet yielding to a rational marriage with most of a neoliberal-neoconservative mainstream political right – playing the race card – and big capital. It promises to combine privileges of citizenship for narrowly defined 'deserving' insiders with extensive hyper-exploitation of precarious circulant 'aliens'. If coupled with continuing austerity it could, however, be just another scenario through which at the end of the day a nationalist welfare politics may be realised as incremental exclusion from established rights of citizenship, also for a supposedly 'deserving' majority. The question remains whether, in the ongoing cynical game of thrones, the 'Swedish Model' will be finally lost, or whether we – under circumstances where neoliberal austerity politics appears everywhere to be challenged – could still come to see a third option coming to the fore in order to bring proof to arguments positing a positive correlation between strong and inclusive welfare regimes and an open and 'generous' refugee policy. It would be a policy promising to mediate the postulated antagonism of migration and welfare in favour of a Keynesian style renaissance of a more inclusive solidarity with immigration as a powerful locomotive.

Acknowledgement of Funding

We appreciate generous funding by FORTE, the Swedish Research Council for Health, Working Life and Welfare [grant number 2006-1524].

References

Alatalo, J.M. and Ostapenko, O.V. 2014. 'The Swedish system: The image cracking when taking a closer look.' *Geoforum* 53/5, 82–83.

Alesina, A. and Glaeser, E.L. 2004. *Fighting Poverty in the US and Europe.* Oxford: Oxford University Press.

Andersson, J. 2015. 'A Model of Welfare Capitalism? Perspectives on the Swedish Model, Then and Now.' In Pierre, Jon (ed.) *The Oxford Handbook of Swedish Politics.* Oxford: Oxford University Press, 563–77.

Angelin, A., Johansson, H. and Koch, M. 2014. 'Patterns of institutional change in minimum income protection in Sweden and Germany.' *Journal of International and Comparative Social Policy* 30/2, 165–79.

Arbetslöshetskassornas Samorganisation 2015. *Rapport över kompensationsgrad vecka 6/2015.* Stockholm: Arbetslöshetskassornas Samorganisation.

Arbetsmarknadsdepartementet 2009. *Nyanlända invandrares arbetsmarknadsetablering – egenansvar med professionellt stöd*. Regeringens Proposition 2009/10:60. Stockholm: Arbetsmarknadsdepartementet.

Ålund, A. 1985. *Skyddsmurar. Etnicitet och klass in invandrarsammanhang*. Stockholm: Liber.

Ålund, A. and Schierup, C.-U. 1991. *Paradoxes of Multiculturalism. Essays on Swedish Society*. Aldershot: Avebury. Republished 2009 as E-Book on the REMESO home-page, Linköpings University as: <http://liu.diva-portal.org/smash/record.jsf?pid=diva2:213706>

Balibar, É. 2004. *We, the People of Europe? Reflections on Transnational Citizenship*. Princeton, NJ & Oxford: Princeton University Press.

Belfrage, C. and Ryner, M. 2009. 'Renegotiating the Swedish Social Democratic Settlement: From Pension Fund Socialism to Neoliberalization.' *Politics & Society* 37/2, 257–87.

Bengtsson, M. 2014. 'Towards Standby-ability: Swedish and Danish Activation Policies in Flux.' *International Journal of Social Welfare* 23/1, 54–70.

Bevelander, P. 2009. 'The immigration and integration experience: The case of Sweden.' In Segal, Uma A., Doreen Elliott and Nazneen S. Mayadas (eds.) *Immigration Worldwide: Policies, Practices, and Trends*. Oxford: Oxford University Press, 286–302.

Bevelander, P. 2013. *Scandinavia's Population Groups Originating from developing Countries: Change and Integration*. Nordic Council of Ministers.

Björklund, A. and Jäntti, M. 2011. *SNS Välfärdsrapport 2011. Inkomstfördelningen i Sverige*. Stockholm: SNS förlag.

Blomqvist, P. 2004. 'The choice revolution: privatization of Swedish welfare services in the 1990s.' *Social Policy & Administration* 38/2, 139–55.

Boräng, F. 2013. 'National Institutions – International Migration. Labour Markets, Welfare States and Immigration Policy.' PhD diss., Department of Political Science, Gothenburg University.

Borevi, K. 2012. 'Sweden: The flagship of multiculturalism.' In Brochmann, G. and Anniken Hagelund (eds.) *Immigration Policy and the Scandinavian Welfare State, 1945–2010*. London: Palgrave Macmillan, 25–96.

Calleman, C. and Herzfeld Olsson, P. 2015. *Arbetskraft från hela världen. Hur blev det med 2008 års reform?* Stockholm: Statens Offentliga Utredningar. Accessed March 29, 2016. <https://vimeo.com/149006506>

Cerna, L. 2009. *Changes in Swedish Labour Immigration Policy: A Slight Revolution?* Stockholm: SULCIS.

Christophers, B. 2013. 'A monstrous hybrid: The political economy of housing in early twenty-first century Sweden.' *New Political Economy* 18/6, 885–911.

Dahlberg, M., Edmark, K. and Lundqvist, H. 2012. 'Ethnic diversity and preferences for redistribution.' *Journal of Political Economy* 120/1, 41–76.

Davidsson, M. 2008. 'Nya regler för arbetskraftsinvandring.' *Lag & Avtal*, November 12. Accessed March 29, 2016. <http://www.lag-avtal.se/nyheter/article58337.ece>

De los Reyes, P. and Wingborg, M. 2002. *Vardagsdiskriminering och rasism i Sverige. En kunskapsöversikt*. Integrationsverkets Rapportserie 2002: 13. Norrköping: Integrationsverket.

Eger, M.A. 2010. 'Even in Sweden: the effect of immigration on support for welfare state spending.' *European Sociological Review* 26/2, 203–17.

EGGE (European Commission's Expert Group on Gender and Employment) 2009. *Gender segregation in the labour market. Root causes, implications and policy responses in the EU*. Brussels: EGGE.

Englund, P. 1999. 'The Swedish Banking Crisis: Roots and Consequences.' *Oxford Review of Economic Policy* 15/3, 80–97.

Esping-Andersen, G. 1990. *The Three Worlds of Welfare Capitalism*. Oxford: Polity Press.

Fernandes, A.G. 2015. '(Dis) Empowering New Immigrants and Refugees through their Participation in Introduction Programs in Sweden, Denmark, and Norway.' *Journal of Immigrant & Refugee Studies* 13/3, 245–64.

Feuchtwang, S. 1982. 'Occupational Ghettos.' *Economy and Society* 11/3, 251–91.

Finseraas, H. 2012. 'Anti-immigration attitudes, support for redistribution and party choice in Europe.' In Kvist, Jon, Johan Fritzell, Bjørn Hvinden and Olli Kangas (eds.) *Changing Social Equality. The Nordic Welfare Model in the 21st Century*. Chicago: The University of Chicago Press, 23–44.

Franzén, E. 2001. 'Socialbidrag bland invandrare: erfarenheter från Sverige.' *Sociologisk Forskning* 38/3–4, 9–39.

Fritzell, J., Bacchus Hertzman, J., Bäckman, O., Borg, I., Ferrarini, T. and Nelson, K. 2014. 'Sweden: increasing income inequalities and changing social relations.' In Nolan, Brian, Wiemer Salverda, Danielle Checchi, Ive Marx, Abigail McKnight, István György Tóth and Herman van de Werfhorst (eds.) *Changing Inequalities and Societal Impacts in Rich Countries. Thirty Countries' Experiences*. Oxford: Oxford University Press, 641–65.

Gavanas, A. 2010. *Who Cleans the Welfare State? Migration, Informalization, Social Exclusion and Domestic Services in Stockholm*. Research Report 2010/3. Stockholm: Institute for Future Studies.

Guild, E., Carrera, S. and Atger, A.F. 2009. *Challenges and Prospects for the EU's Area of Freedom, Security and Justice: Recommendations to the European Commission for the Stockholm Programme*. Brussels: Centre for European Policy Studies. Accessed March 29, 2016. <http://aei.pitt.edu/10762/01/1830.pdf>

Guiraudon, V. 1998. 'Third country nationals and European law: obstacles to rights' expansion.' *Journal of Ethnic and Migration Studies* 24/4, 657–74.

Haffert, L. and Mehrtens, P. 2015. 'From Austerity to Expansion? Consolidation, Budget Surpluses, and the Decline of Fiscal Capacity.' *Politics & Society* 43/1, 119–48.

Hammar, T. 1990. *Democracy and the Nation-State: Aliens, Denizens and Citizens in a World of International Migration*. Aldershot: Avebury.

Hansen, P. 2016. 'Refugee Keynesianism? EU Migration Crises in Times of Fiscal Austerity.' In Jonsson, Stefan and Julia Willén (eds.) *Austere Histories in European Societies: Social Exclusion and the Contest of Colonial Memories*. London: Routledge.

Hartman, L. (ed.) 2011a. *Konkurrensens konsekvenser. Vad händer med svensk välfärd?* Stockholm: SNS.

Hartman, L. 2011b. 'Inledning.' In Hartman, Laura (ed.) *Konkurrensens konsekvenser. Vad händer med svensk välfärd*? Stockholm: SNS Förlag, 9–31.

Hedin, K., Clark, E., Lundholm, E. and Malmberg, G. 2012. 'Neoliberalization of housing in Sweden: Gentrification, filtering, and social polarization.' *Annals of the Association of American Geographers* 102/2, 443–63.

Hemicker, L. 2016 'Eine Ära der Instabilität ist angebrochen.' *Frankfurter Allgemeine*, January 21. Accessed March 29, 2016. <http://www.faz.net/aktuell/politik/ausland/naher-osten/muenchner-sicherheitsreport-ueber-kriege-krisen-und-konflikte-14031523.html>

Hjärtberg, E. 2008. 'Kommunal kritiska till en ny lag om arbetskraftsinvandring.' *Kommunalarbetaren*, November 13. Accessed August 2, 2016. <http://www.ka.se/kommunal-kritiska-till-en-ny-lag-om-arbetskraftsinvandring>

Hooijer, G. and Picot, G. 2015. 'European Welfare States and Migrant Poverty. The Institutional Determinants of Disadvantage.' *Comparative Political Studies*. IMF (International Monetary Fund) 2016. *The Refugee Surge in Europe: Economic Challenges*. IMF Staff Discussion, SDN/16/02.

Karlsson, P. 2016. 'Åkesson: Jag sitter i tio år till.' *Aftonbladet*, August 3. Accessed March 29, 2016. <http://www.aftonbladet.se/nyheter/samhalle/article22610588.ab>

Kesler, C. 2014. 'Welfare states and immigrant poverty Germany, Sweden, and the United Kingdom in comparative perspective.' *Acta Sociologica* 58/1, 39–61.

Kjellberg, A. 2011. 'The decline in Swedish union density since 2007.' *Nordic Journal of Working Life Studies* 1/1, 67–93.

Koopmans, R. 2010. 'Trade-offs between equality and difference: Immigrant integration, multiculturalism and the welfare state in cross-national perspective.' *Journal of Ethnic and Migration Studies* 36/1, 1–26.

Kuivalainen, S. and Nelson, K. 2010. *The Nordic welfare model in a European perspective*. Research Report 2010/11. Stockholm: Institute for Future Studies.

Kymlicka, W. and Banting, K.G. 2006. 'Immigration, Multiculturalism, and the Welfare State.' *Ethics & International Affairs* 20/3, 281–304.

Larsen, C.A. 2011. 'Ethnic heterogeneity and public support for welfare: Is the American experience replicated in Britain, Sweden and Denmark?' *Scandinavian Political Studies* 34/4, 332–53.

Larsson, J.K. 2015. *Integrationen och arbetets marknad: hur jämställdhet, arbete och annat "svenskt" görs av arbetsförmedlare och privata aktörer*. Stockholm: Atlas Akademi.

Legrain, Phillippe 2016. *Refugees Work: A Humanitarian Investment that Yields Economic Dividends*: Tent.

Leijon, O., Häkkinen Skans, I., Lindblad, J., Persson, H. and Söder, M. 2013. *Personer som uppnår maximal tid i sjukförsäkringen. Vilka är de och vad händer efteråt?* Report 2013:6. Stockholm: Swedish Social Insurance Inspectorate.

Lentin, A. and Titley, G. 2011. *The crises of multiculturalism: Racism in a neoliberal age*. London: Zed Books Ltd.

Lundh, C., Ohlon, R., Rooth, D.-O., Bennich-Björkman, L. and Pedersen, P.J. 2002. *Arbete? Var god dröj! Invandrare in välfärdssamhället*. Stockholm: SNS.

Lødemel, I. and Trickey, H. 2001 *'An offer you can't refuse': Workfare in international perspective*. Bristol: Policy Press.

Mann, M. 1987. 'Ruling class strategies and citizenship.' *Sociology* 21/3, 339–54.

Marshall, T.H. 1992 [1950]. *Citizenship and Social Class*. Cambridge: Cambridge University Press.

Mau, S. 2009. 'Migration and welfare state solidarity in Western Europe.' *Journal of European Social Policy* 19/3, 213–29.

Mau, S. and Bukhardt, C. 2007. 'Ethnic diversity and welfare state solidarity in Europe.' Paper presented at the AGF midpoint Conference, Berlin, Germany, November 29–30.

MUCF (Myndigheten för ungdoms- och civilsamhällesfrågor) 2016. *Ung idag 2016. En beskrivning av ungas levnadsvillkor*. Stockholm: Myndigheten för ungdoms- och civilsamhällesfrågor.

Mulinari, D. and Neergaard, A. 2005. 'A "black skull" consciousness. Narratives of the new Swedish working class.' *Race & Class* 46/3, 55–71.

Neergaard, A. 2009. 'Racialisation in the Labour Market: In Search of a Theoretical Understanding.' In Neergaard, Anders (ed.) *European Perspectives on Exclusion and Subordination: The Political Economy of Migration*. Maastricht: Shaker Publishing BV, 201–22.

Nitz, L. 2013. 'Polisförbundet: Jakten på effektivitet får aldrig gå ut över rättssäkerheten.' *Dagens Arena*, March 1. Accessed March 29, 2016. <http://www.dagensarena.se/opinion/polisforbundet-jakten-pa-effektivitet-far-aldrig-ga-ut-over-rattssakerheten/>

Nordheim Nielsen, F. (ed.) 1988. *The Welfare State Projects of the Scandinavian Labour Movements – Models for a reformist Road to Socialism or Dead End Streets?* Copenhagen: Forlaget Sociologi, Sociologisk Institut.

Nyberg, A. 2015. 'The Swedish RUT Reduction – Subsidy of Formal Employment or of High-Income Earners' Leisure Time?' In Morel, Nathalie and Clément Carbonnier (eds.) *The Political Economy of Household Services in Europe*. London: Palgrave Macmillan, 221–41.

Obućina, O. 2014. 'Paths into and out of poverty among immigrants in Sweden.' *Acta Sociologica* 57/1, 5–23.

OECD 2011. *Divided We Stand: Why Inequality Keeps Rising*. OECD. Accessed March 29, 2016. <http://www.oecd.org/els/soc/dividedwestandwhyinequalitykeepsrising.htm>

OECD 2014. *Finding the Way: A discussion of the Swedish Migrant Integration System*. Paris: OECD publishing. Accessed March 29, 2016. <http://www.oecd.org/migration/swedish-migrant-intergation-system.pdf>

OECD 2015. *Indicators of Immigrant Integration 2015: Settling in*. Paris: OECD publishing.

Osman, B. 2016. 'Välfärdschauvinismen anammas av allt fler och det är farligt.' *Expressen*, April 19. Accessed March 29, 2016. <http://www.expressen.se/kronikorer/bilan-osman/valfardschauvinismen-anammas-av-allt-fler-och-det-ar-farligt/>

Palme, J., Ferrarini, T., Nelson, K. and Sjöberg, O. 2012. *Sveriges socialförsäkringar i jämförande perspektiv En institutionell analys av sjuk-, arbetsskade-och arbetslöshetsförsäkringarna i 18 OECD-länder 1930 till 2010*. Parlamentariska socialförsäkringsutredningen, S 2010:04. Uppsala University, Department of Economics.

Peck, J. 2001. *Workfare States*. New York, NY: Guilford Press.

Pelling, L. 2015a. 'Fristad Sverige? Om skyddssökande arbetskraftsinvandrares villkor.' In Calleman, Catharina and Petra Herzfeld Olsson (eds.) *Arbetskraft från hela världen. Hur blev det med 2008 års reform?* Stockholm: DELMI, 244–89.

Pelling, L. 2015b. *Lagliga vägar över Medelhavet. En färdplan*. Stockholm: Arena Idé. Accessed March 29, 2016. <http://www.arenaide.se/rapporter/lagliga-vagar-over-medelhavet/>

Persson, G. 1972. 'Invandrarna och arbetarklassen i Sverige.' *Zenit* 27, 4–14.

Qvist, M. 2016. 'Activation Reform and Inter-Agency Co-operation – Local Consequences of Mixed Modes of Governance in Sweden.' *Social Policy & Administration* 50/1, 19–38.

Raneke, A. 2013. 'Vart femte barn har utländsk bakgrund.' *SCB (Statistics Sweden)*. Accessed March 29, 2016. <http://www.scb.se/sv_/Hitta-statistik/Artiklar/Vart-femte-barn-har-utlandsk-bakgrund/>

Rauhut D. 2010. 'Integration of Immigrants in Sweden 1945–1975.' *Finnish Yearbook of Population Research* 45, 103–22.

Regeringen 2008. 'New rules for labour immigration.' *Government Offices of Sweden*. Accessed March 29, 2016. <http://www.regeringen.se/content/1/c6/10/72/00/2a13eb93.pdf>

Regeringskansliet 2015. *Insatser med anledning av flyktingkrisen*. Stockholm: Regeringskansliet.

Roine, J. and Waldenström, D. 2012. 'On the role of capital gains in Swedish income inequality.' *Review of Income and Wealth* 58/3, 569–87.

Rueda, D. and Pontusson, J. 2000. 'Wage inequality and varieties of capitalism.' *World Politics* 52/3, 350–83.

Rydgren, J. 2004. 'Mechanisms of exclusion: ethnic discrimination in the Swedish labour market.' *Journal of Ethnic and Migration Studies* 30/4, 697–717.

Ryner, J.M. 2002. *Capitalist restructuring, globalization and the third way: Lessons from the Swedish model.* Abingdon: Routledge.

Ryner, M. 2000. 'European welfare state transformation and migration.' In Bommes, Michael and Andrew Geddes (eds.) *Immigration and Welfare: Challenging the Borders of the Welfare State*. London and New York, NY: Routledge, 51–72.

Sainsbury, D. 2006. 'Immigrants' Social Rights in Comparative Perspective: Welfare Regimes, Forms in Immigration and Immigration Policy Regimes.' *Journal of European Social Policy* 16/3, 229–244.

Sainsbury, D. 2012. *Welfare states and immigrant rights: The politics of inclusion and exclusion.* Oxford: Oxford University Press.

Scarpa, S. 2013. 'New Geographically Differentiated Configurations of Social Risks: Labour Market Policy Developments in Sweden and Finland.' In Harsløf,

Ivan and Rickard Ulmestig (eds.) *Changing social risks and social policy responses in the Nordic welfare states*. London: Palgrave Macmillan, 220–44.

Scarpa, S. 2015a. 'The Swedish Model during the International Financial Crisis: Institutional Resilience or Structural Change?' In Romano, Serena and Gabriella Punziano (eds.) *The European Social Model Adrift: Europe, Social Cohesion and the Economic Crisis*. Abingdon: Ashgate, 107–26.

Scarpa, S. 2015b. 'The Spatial Manifestation of Inequality.' PhD diss., Department of Social Work, Linneaus University.

SCB (Statistics Sweden) 2004. Sysselsättning och arbetslöshet 1975–2003. Stockholm: Statistics Sweden.

SCB 2012. Levnadsstandard i Europa. Levnadsförhållanden rapport 124. Stockholm: Statistics Sweden.

SCB 2013. Arbetskraftsundersökningarna (AKU) tredje kvartalet 2013 – Tema: Risker för långtidsarbetslöshet. Stockholm: Statistics Sweden.

SCB 2016. *Sveriges ekonomi*. Första kvartalet 2016. Stockholm: Statistics Sweden.

Schierup, C.-U. and Ålund, A. 2011a. 'From Paradoxes of Multiculturalism to Paradoxes of Liberalism.' *Journal for Critical Education Policy Studies* 9/2, 125–142.

Schierup, C.-U. and Ålund, A. 2011b. 'The End of Swedish Exceptionalism? Citizenship, neo-liberalism and politics of exclusion.' *Race & Class* 53/1, 45–64.

Schierup, C.-U., Hansen, P. and Castles, S. 2006. *Migration, Citizenship and the European Welfare State. A European Dilemma*. Oxford: Oxford University Press.

Schierup, C.-U. and Paulson, S. 1994. *Arbetets etniska delning. Studier från en svensk bilfabrik*. Stockholm: Carlssons.

Schnyder, G. 2012. 'Like a phoenix from the ashes? Reassessing the transformation of the Swedish political economy since the 1970s.' *Journal of European Public Policy* 19/8, 1126–45.

Scocco, S. and Andersson, L.F. 2015. *900 Miljarder skäl att uppskatta invandring. En analys av invandringens effekter på de offentliga finanserna i Sverige 1950–2014*. Stockholm: Arenaidé.

Slavnic, Z. and Urban, S. 2008. 'Socio-Economic Trends in the Swedish Taxi Sector -Deregulation, Recommodification, Ethnification.' *International journal on multicultural societies* 10/1, 76–94.

Soininen, M. 1999. 'The "Swedish model" as an institutional framework for immigrant membership rights.' *Journal of Ethnic and Migration Studies* 25/4, 685–702.

Steinmo, S. 2013. 'Governing as an engineering problem: the political economy of Swedish success.' In Schäfer, A. and Wolfgang S. (eds.) *Politics in the Age of Austerity*, Cambridge: Polity Press, 84–108.

Stenberg, E. 2015. 'Margot Wallström om bränderna: SD har ett ansvar.' *Dagens Nyheter*, October 30. Accessed August 2, 2016. <http://www.dn.se/nyheter/sverige/margot-wallstrom-om-branderna-sd-har-ett-ansvar/>

Stichnoth, H. and van der Straeten, K. 2013. 'Ethnic diversity, public spending, and individual support for the welfare state: A review of the empirical literature.' *Journal of Economic Surveys* 27/2, 364–89.

Streeck, W. 2014. *Buying time: The delayed crisis of democratic capitalism*. Verso Books.

Streeck, W. 2015. *The rise of the European consolidation state*. MPIfG Discussion Paper.

Swenson, P. 1991. 'Managing the managers: The Swedish employers' confederation, labor scarcity, and the suppression of labor market segmentation.' *Scandinavian Journal of History* 16/4, 335–56.

Taylor-Gooby, P. 2005. 'Is the future American? Or, can left politics preserve European welfare states from erosion through 'racial' diversity?' *Journal of Social Policy* 34/4, 661–72.

Therborn, G. 1984. 'The Coming of Swedish Social Democracy.' *Annali della Fondazione Giangiacomo Feltrinelli* 1983/84, 527–93.

Ulmestig, R. 2013. 'Incapacity Benefits – Change and Continuity in the Swedish Welfare State.' In Lindsay, Colin and Donald Houston (eds.) *Disability benefits, welfare reform and employment policy*. London: Palgrave Macmillan, 178–98.

Urban, S. 2013. 'Restaurant Work Experience as Stepping Stone to the Rest of Labour Market.' *Nordic Journal of Migration Research* 3/2, 100–09.

Vogel, J. 2002. 'Inkomst och fattigdom.' In Vogel, Joachim, Mikael Hjerm and Sven-Erik Johansson (eds.) *Integration till svensk välfärd? Om invandrares välfärd på 90-talet*. Stockholm: Statistics Sweden and the National Institute for Working Life, 35–56.

Wagle, U. 2013. *The Heterogeneity Link of the Welfare State and Redistribution*. Berlin: Springer International Publishing AG.

Wiesbrock, A. 2011. 'The Integration of Immigrants in Sweden: A Model for the European Union?' *International Migration* 49/4, 48–66.

Anders Neergaard

3. The Swedish Model in Transition: Trade Unions and Racialised Workers

Abstract: The chapter analyses working class trade union policies and practices relating to migrants and racialised workers in Sweden in order to assess the capacity for action in an acute moment of crisis and transformation of the welfare state, the labour market and the country's unique industrial relations system. The argument is that the Swedish blue collar trade union movement, facing the declining strength of an increasingly fragmented working class, is without any clear strategies of facing these challenges.

Introduction

At the time of writing this chapter dramatic changes in the Swedish political landscape are occurring. Facing a large increase in refugees seeking asylum in Sweden the Social Democratic and Green party government has with support from three of the four established right-wing parties in opposition implemented exceptional reforms. The aim as formulated by the government is for a limited time to adapt the Swedish regulations to the EU minimum level, restricting and limiting access to apply for asylum, shifting from permanent to temporary residence permits for refugees, and significantly curtailed the possibilities for family reunification. Parallel to this, and partially using refugees as the reason, right-wing parties and the private employers association are actively arguing for creating low-paid employment with 75% of the accorded minimum wage of the collective agreements. The three smallest of the right-wing parties argue that this could be legislated against the principle of collective agreements. This would most likely constitute the hitherto greatest threat to the traditional model of Swedish industrial relations, whilst at the same time become a cornerstone in the racialisation of the Swedish labour market; producing a racialised fraction of the working class characterised as the working poor.

It appears in this background more important than ever before to discuss trade union policies and practices relating to migrants and racialised workers in Sweden, in order to assess the capacity for action. This is especially paramount in an acute moment of crisis and transformation of the welfare state, the Swedish labour market, as well as the country's distinctive industrial relations system.

It is a commonly held point of departure that trade unions are negative to labour migration[1]. This idea is indeed not without substance, yet there are numerous cases that bear witness to the opposite[2]. A growing volume of research, often influenced by the recognition of the increasing porousness of borders (Sassen 1999), document that trade unions have increasingly become both strategically and rhetorically less negative to labour migration, and especially migrants, than they may have been in the past (Watts 1998; Haus 2002). At the same time, and despite formal declarations on international solidarity, the dominant frame of reference of trade unions (Sweden being no exception) remains that of the (nation-) state and the national arena[3]. This chapter attempts to situate these issues of borders and the politics of solidarity in an analysis of the Swedish working class trade union confederation '*Landsorganisationen*' (LO).

While varying over time and space, trade unions can be seen as organisations spanning at least three different, but interconnected, fields of action. In the most restricted sense, they are an *organisation of members* that through statutes, practices and discourse, organise and represent the interests of their members. This internal dimension of trade unions focuses on those who are organised, under which circumstances they form, and how any conflicting interests of the members are negotiated. The organisation of trade unions is a precondition for acting within the wider field of the industrial relations' system, whereby the *interests of the organisation in relation to employers* are pursued, yet also in relation to other unions. Finally, trade unions are also *actors in a wider societal arena,* beyond the organisation of its members and the field of industrial relations, as unions pursue self-interests, as well as those of their members across the wider political system. Theorising trade unions in this complex three-pronged perspective locates them as central actors in capitalist social formations. As the organisers and mobilisers of workers, trade unions build different collectives and solidarities, spanning across class, gender and ethnicity. Secondly, within the industrial relations system, unions represent, and struggle for, their members, constructing solidarities within the labour market and in workplaces. They relate to employers, but also to other trade unions and trade union confederations, locally, nationally and internationally. Finally, as political actors in the wider societal arena, trade unions influence politics and facilitate the aims of the organisations in ways contingent on the politics and practices in the first two arenas.

1 Penninx and Roosblad 2000.
2 Schierup et al. 2015.
3 Gumbrell-McCormick and Hyman 2013.

One particular issue, which is however, rather under-researched, concerns trade unions' relation to *racialised workers*. In this chapter the central concern is to analyse the relationship between Swedish working class trade unions and racialised workers, who to a large extent, may be captured as a racialised fraction of the working class[4]. The term 'racialisation' is accordingly central to the argument. It has most coherently and productively been theorised by the sociologist Robert Miles (1993). While the use of racialisation has increased lately, references to Miles' understanding are mainly applied within labour market and trade union research (Mulinari and Neergaard 2004; Frank 2005; Johansson 2008)[5].

Miles argues that 'in certain historical conjunctures and under specific material conditions, human beings attribute certain biological characteristics with meaning in order to differentiate, to exclude and to dominate: reproducing the idea of "race"' (Miles 1993: 44). Thus, he concludes, 'they create a racialised Other and simultaneously they racialise themselves' (Miles 1993: 44). He links further the processes of racialisation to the situation of migrants, arguing that they have come to 'occupy a structurally distinct position in the economic, political and ideological relations of … capitalism, but within the boundary of the working class' (Miles 1982: 165). Migrants, Miles concludes, 'therefore constitute a faction of the working class, one that can be identified as a racialised faction' (Miles 1982: 165).

Influenced by Miles, the term 'racialised workers' will be used to refer to those, with or without migrant background, who are subordinated within hierarchical divisions of labour, with ascribed stereotypical identities in terms of skin colour, culture, religion etc. This is based on assumed ethnic and racial differences, which, as negative attributes, affect their working conditions, professional mobility and public representation. Based on this definition, 'migrants' and 'racialised workers' are distinguished between as the latter category includes workers without themselves being migrants, as for example the children of migrants and later generations, born in Sweden, but still positioned as racialised. Central to the argument is that the problem analysis of the racialisation of workers within the context of labour unions, needs to interconnect unions' internal political practices with the spectrum of industrial relations and political struggles, with the relations of power in wider societal contexts.

The chapter starts with a short theoretical introduction, situating trade unions in neo-Marxist, post-colonial/antiracist perspectives on worker solidarity

---

4 For a discussion of this aspect see Miles 1982: 169.

5 In Sweden it was introduced in quite different contexts by sociologist Aleksandra Ålund (1995, 1999), the historian of ideas Bernt Skovdahl (1996) and the cultural geographer Irene Molina (1997).

and trade unions. Following the theoretical frame, the subsequent section introduces briefly the origin, core and crisis of the Swedish model of industrial relations. The central part of the chapter focuses on the evolving positions and practices of LO, the Swedish blue-collar trade union federation, and its member organisations in relation to migration, especially racialised workers. The argument is thus structured into three interconnected parts. The first discusses the LO labour movement within the wider political and societal frame, with a focus on citizenship issues. The second deals with the core site of industrial relations and the position of racialised workers. Finally, the third section concentrates on the LO and its unions as membership organisations, and the representation of racialised workers therein.[6] Each of the sections are structured along lines emphasising the difference between a 'Keynesian' and 'neoliberal' industrial relations systems. In conclusion, it is contended that the Swedish LO trade union movement is faced with an increasing number of challenges which all need to be discussed in the more general context of a 'Swedish model' of welfare, and of industrial relations that currently appears to be disintegrating. Ultimately, it is argued that so far there seems to exist only few strategies with the capacity to deal effectively with social problems represented by the declining strength of an increasingly fragmented working class.

Building solidarities across three arenas: organisation, production and society

In Marxist understandings, trade unions are often seen as the concrete manifestation of the working class. Departing from a materialist analysis of workers as forced (free) to sell their labour, the central idea is that this produces a common reality, which is conducive in creating a consciousness leading to collective organisation. While this is an important point of departure, subsequent research has in a number of ways problematised, or critically qualified, the Marxist scheme along at least four dimensions:

6 The chapter is based on two interviews studies, analysis of trade union documents and trade union newspapers, as well as secondary literature. The first interview study was from the early 2000s, focussing on migrant trade union activists (for more information see Mulinari and Neergaard 2004). The second interview study took place 2014 and 2015 with twelve officials of LO and its trade union engaged in issues of migration, antidiscrimination and membership issues (for more information see Neergaard 2015a, 2015b).

1. The common material reality is always relative and with large variations.
2. The consciousness of wage workers is not only affected by the material reality in production, but furthermore from other social relations (i.e. gender, racialisation).
3. Consciousness can never be directly deduced from the location in social relations as it is always shaped by contentious processes of articulation.
4. Collective organisation is always partial and institutionally fractured by internal struggles.

Each of these dimensions bears directly on the topic of trade unions and racialised workers. Weberian influenced trade union research has, in addition, focused on boundary making, and how organisations not only include, but at the same time exclude (Parkin 1974). Boundary making through processes of inclusion and exclusion has been further developed by, in particular, feminist and antiracist scholars arguing that trade unions are shaped by their social embeddedness that includes gendered and racial structures (Cockburn 1991; Sivanandan 1982).

In classical Marxist research there has been a tendency to deduce solidarity from structural location (Hyman 1971). While research has shown that structural location may (but at best partially) designate a basis for solidarity, the theoretical traditions inspired by a cultural turn in Marxism have emphasised the importance of culture, identity and subjectivity for class based politics and working class organisation (Fantasia 1989; Wills 2001). This is a central argument already in the classic work by EP Thompson (1963), *The Making of the English Working Class*. Richard Hyman (1999) for one – rephrasing Benedict Anderson's (1991) classic concept of the 'imagined community' – emphasises mutuality, accountability and the recognition of common interests as the basis for relationships among diverse communities. In a similar vein, labour studies scholar Richard Hyman's (1999) arguments use the concept of 'imagined solidarity' (see also Simms 2012). According to Hyman (2001), the challenge of labour movements today lies in the exhaustion of their old model of collectivism that was connected to a concept of a working class that did not recognise differentiations by gender, ethnicity, age, etc. A similar position is taken by Rick Fantasia (1989), who uses the concept of 'cultures of solidarity' in a study of US unions to name the forms of class consciousness that workers develop in their everyday struggles. Fantasia argues that these spaces of solidarity often occur outside the unions or rather, in the name of union struggles, but in the absence of formal unions. In criticising a one-sided structural perspective, Wrench (2004) cautions against a tendency to read too much from structural factors such as union strength or systems of regulation. Instead, he argues that the impact of political discourse and social struggles are central in configuring union orientations. What is more, Wrench contends from a scholar perspective there is a need to be alert to critical incidents and moments when trade union strategies and perspectives begin to shift.

The neoliberal onslaught in the Swedish industrial relations model

The Swedish model of industrial relations has been extensively researched (Kjellberg 2001; Korpi and Shalev 1979; Nycander 2002), including its evolution and change during the last couple of decades (Sandberg 2013). The origin of the industrial relations model may be traced back to three central moments: the 1906 December compromise; the 1928 law on collective agreements; and the 1938 Saltsjöbads-deal. The first and third were agreements between the Swedish Employers' Association and the blue-collar trade union LO (Nycander 2002). These created a framework in which the labour market actors agreed on the right of unions to organise, the right of employers to direct and manage work, and the ambition of both 'social partners' to organise the labour market through joint negotiations – resulting in binding collective agreements, at least in terms of careful delimitation of the scope for industrial action. This position was based on both employers and unions being negative towards state intervention and preferring instead a form of 'self-regulation' to secure industrial peace. Thus, in contrast to many other countries, there are no formal legislative minimum wages in Sweden. Instead, wages are set through collective agreements that the employers' associations and trade unions have to actively negotiate. The role of the state within industrial relations was marginal, although the development of the welfare regime was central in shaping the balance of power between employers and workers. This was especially paramount through the actively pursued goal of full employment from the 1930s, and the subsequent use and expansion of social insurance for de-commodification.

On an organisational level, this has been characterised by a strong working class trade union movement and a robust organisation of private employers. With time, the public sector employers became organised. On the wage earner side, organisations evolved into a class, or stratified trade union movement, with three separate confederations: a) based on the blue-collar working class (LO); b) The Swedish Confederation of Professional Employees (TCO), and c) the more academic Swedish Confederation of Professional Associations (SACO) (Bruhn, Kjellberg and Sandberg 2013; Kjellberg 2015).

In negotiating collective agreements, the trade unions and employers associations are, in essence, free to invoke industrial conflict through strikes and lockouts, even in support of other trade unions and employers. However, this very wide scope of freedom is with a signed collective agreement, converted into a peace obligation. In addition, there is a labour court for strong adjudicating conflicts between organised employers and trade unions (Öberg and Svensson 2002).

In explaining the strength of Swedish (especially working class) trade unions, Kjellberg (2011) argues that the combination of workplace presence by strong central trade unions, and cross trade union coordination through confederations, are central. In addition, the Ghent model of unemployment insurance, where insurance funds are organised and administered by trade unions, is also recognised as important for high union density (Kjellberg 2009; Scruggs 2002).

During the era of the Keynesian welfare regime, the Swedish model of industrial relations was geared towards enhancing gradual structural change of the economy. The implementation of the Rehn-Meidner model (see also Chapter 2) steered capital-labour agreements on wages that would put inefficient industries out of business, but also create wealth among efficient companies. An effect of this became, denoted by the LO notion of 'the solidaristic wage policy', decreasing income differences, within and between different groups of salaried workers. Notwithstanding, women and workers of foreign background still earned less[7]. This period was also marked by the changing balance between profits and wages, as the wage share continuously increased (Lindberg and Bengtsson 2013).

While the state has played a marginal role as direct actor in the field of industrial relations, the role of the state has been important for two reasons. Firstly, through general macroeconomic and welfare policies the state has – to borrow the concept from Jessop (1999) – created a strategic selectivity in shaping the balance of power between capital and labour, but also between different fractions of capital and labour. In addition, at times the state has intervened directly in industrial relations. A central example is when the social democratic government, following the radicalisation of trade unions in the early 1970s, passed legislation in areas such as codetermination and employment security. The most radical reform – the wage earners' funds – was also a proposal of this time. Albeit, due to Social Democratic electoral losses in 1976 and 1979, it became first implemented (but in a substantially more modestform) in 1982 when the Social Democrats returned to government (Meidner 1994; Pontusson and Kuruvilla 1992).

Towards the mid-1980s, the industrial relations system was increasingly challenged by a number of factors. Seen from a macroeconomic perspective,

7 Squeezed between women often understood as native (or 'white') and workers of foreign background (or racialised) often understood as men; migrant women often experience the double discriminatory effect (Knocke 2011).

the internationalisation of the economy and increasing stagflation was met by a Social Democratic government that successively dismantled some of the key Keynesian institutions. The dominant private employers organisation (*Svenska Arbetsgivareföreningen*)[8] campaigned against wage earners funds and challenged, together with the public employers' organisation, centralised wage bargaining. While the trade unions in the 1970s had driven the Social Democratic Party towards the left, the party itself was now pushing trade unions towards the right. This produced tensions within the broader labour movement, the so called 'War of Roses' (Korpi 1993). The professional and academic trade union confederations were increasingly challenging the position of the LO and solidaristic wage policies. Within LO increasing tensions grew forth, especially between the municipal unions dominated by women arguing for more influence within, but who were met with resistance by the dominant industrial trade union LO. An example of this was a speech by the chairman of the metalworker trade union at the 1986 LO congress claiming that the members of the municipal union were 'cuckoo eggs in the nest,' arguing that 'when one has nursed them, they will even eat up mom'[9].

As the Keynesian institutional framework was dismantled and an increasingly global economic exposure prevailed in the 1980s, a reversal of this development began, with the successive trend of a falling wage share (Lindberg and Bengtsson 2013) and increasing wage dispersion among LO members. Before the social democratic government, for the second time since it took power in 1932, was ousted in the 1991 general election, it had changed the overarching macroeconomic policy priority from full employment to price stability, as well as applied for EU membership. In early 1992, a deep economic crisis broke producing unemployment unheard of since the 1929 depression. While average unemployment from 1970 to 1991 was 2.9%, never exceeding 4.5%, it increased in the period 1992–2015 to 8.0%, never falling below 6.6%[10].

The right-wing government coalitions have at times intervened in industrial relations, often reflecting directly or indirectly the strategic selectivity of private employers. Following their electoral victory in 1994, the wage earners' funds were abolished. Regaining government again in 2006, the right-wing rule immediately implemented reforms of unemployment insurance, dramatically increasing monthly fees in addition to a sharp drop in unemployment insurance coverage

8 In 2001 *Svenska Arbetsgivareföreningen* was reorganised into *Svenskt Näringsliv* (SN) together with *Sveriges Industriförbund*.

9 Available at <http://wwwc.aftonbladet.se/nyheter/9803/02/blom10.html> (Accessed July 31, 2016).

10 Calculations based on SCB labour force survey (SCB.se).

(Kjellberg 2015). This thus produced the largest decline in trade union density since the failed general strike of 1909. The effect was strongest among the youth and foreign born, especially in the private service sector. If one in addition takes into account the ratio of unemployment, then the concrete effect was an increasing number of foreign born without income related unemployment insurance.

Despite decreasing unionisation, especially concerning the LO unions, the coverage of collective bargaining is currently still very high and fairly stable. Including so-called 'associated agreements' (in which unorganised employers individually agree with trade unions to follow the collective agreement), collective bargaining coverage for 2013 is estimated as 89% of the workforce (Kjellberg 2015). In this sense, employers have wider degrees of organisation than the trade unions.

Studies of the employment structure in recent decades have emphasised that the Swedish development is in line with the global polarisation theory (Autor, Katz and Kearney 2006; Goos, Manning and Salomons 2009). Accordingly, employment in the middle of the job hierarchy, both defined by wages and by qualifications, is decreasing, while employment in the upper parts of the labour hierarchy, and particularly in the lower parts, is increasing (Åberg 2013). Thus, concerning employment patterns, there is a structural decline within manufacturing, mining, energy and environment, and a substantial increase in service employment. This also accounts for a bifurcated development of service employment, both linked to work with high-skill and low-skill requirements. In addition, consumer demand for service work has increased. A general demand for service provision accelerates as income rises, increasing income inequality stimulates service provision for high income households and, at the same time, state interventions aim to reduce the price of service consumption by tax reforms, and especially tax deductions. In addition, there has been a shift from public to private service provision following privatisation reforms based on public tax finance of welfare services, which has opened for private enterprises in different forms to compete in providing these. While part-time and time-limited employment became partially a characteristic of the feminised parts of the labour market, typical informal work has been increasing during the last decades. Outsourcing and subcontracting in both private manufacturing and service have been an important structural change (Håkansson and Isidorsson 2014), although probably even more so within the public sector (Thörnquist and Engstrand 2011).

Researchers have been reluctant to argue that the model is in dissolution. The basic architecture of the Swedish model of industrial relations seems to have muddled through, although in a changing and increasingly contested context, in which the established neo-corporatist regime of labour relations was continuously challenged. This was confronted from many different directions, gradually being transformed into what Bob Jessop (2004) has termed a Schumpeterian workfare post-national regime (see also Schierup, Hansen and Castles 2006). While differentiating in estimating to what extent this represents a systemic shift, there is wide agreement that substantial changes have occurred in Swedish industrial relations. Here, three central features are important to emphasise: a marked decrease in the degree of working class unionisation; a shift from a low to high unemployment economy; and, the informalisation of a previously regulated Fordist economy (Slavnic 2010). This latter affects women and youth, but in particular, racialised workers with respect to deteriorating wages, degraded working conditions and growing unemployment. Current unemployment among the foreign born is well above that of native born (see Table 1 below). In a study taking individual characteristics into account, the unemployment risk of foreign born citizens was estimated, sharing with Norway and Switzerland, the highest inequality ratio in 2013 (OECD 2015).

Table 1: Unemployment rates for domestic and foreign born Swedes

	2006	2007	2008	2009	2010	2011	2012	2013	2014	2015
Foreign born	13,2%	12,1%	8,8%	15,2%	16,4%	16,2%	16,0%	16,3%	16,3%	16,1%
Swedish born	6,1%	5,4%	5,1%	7,1%	7,2%	6,2%	6,4%	6,4%	6,1%	5,4%
Total	7,1%	6,2%	6,1%	8,4%	8,7%	7,6%	7,9%	8,1%	8,0%	7,5%
Ratio	2,2	2,2	1,7	2,1	2,3	2,6	2,5	2,5	2,7	3

Source: Kjellberg 2015; AKU SCB

With this short overview of Swedish industrial relations, the central topic of the LO and its trade unions' politics and practices towards migration and racialised workers will now be addressed.

LO and migration – citizenship rights of racialised workers

The Swedish state of the early 19th century has been described as an employer-friendly, but not generally anti-labour, state (Nycander 2002); or relatively neutrally placed between labour and capital (Crouch 1994). With ascendancy of the Social Democratic government in 1932, the working-class trade union movement became increasingly orientated towards the nation-state context (Neergaard 2000). A consequence of this has been that the successive debates on labour migration over the years have focused *more* on protecting industrial relations, and less on restricting migration.

To grasp the trade unions positions towards migration in Sweden, different forms of migration will be differentiated between. Roughly outlined from a trade union perspective, it is possible to discern four administrative forms which potentially, and in different ways, impact trade union policy. These are: free movement across borders; labour migration; refugee and family reunification; and irregular migration.

Concerning migration as the 'free movement' across borders, it is possible to discern four different phases over time. Sweden until the 1920s, had for centuries been mainly an emigrant country. At this time, borders were in principle open with little regulation of immigration until World War I (Svanberg and Tydén 1998). The second phase of free movement came with the creation of the Nordic countries passport union in the early 1950s. This regional mobility space was created with the basic support of the trade unions which saw it as offering employment opportunities and higher wages in other Nordic countries, during a time in which there was a strong labour demand with Finnish migrants composing the largest group (Frank 2005; Yalcin 2010). Sweden's 1995 membership into the European Union by contrast, provoked some resistance from the trade unions, but focused less on migration, and more on the general implications for the welfare regime, and to a certain degree, the Swedish system of industrial relations (Meidner 1999).

Initially, it was the expansion of the European Union towards Eastern Europe that free movement became an issue. A few LO trade unions argued for invoking the right to transitional restrictions. The LO central board unanimously voted however, against the implementation of transitional arrangements. As the European Union expanded its membership in 2004, Sweden became, together with Ireland and UK, one of only three older member states that did not restrict immigration from the new members (Krings 2009). Despite concerns among the trade unions, the result was a modest number of East European migrants to Sweden, in contrast to Ireland and especially the UK. Tamas and Münz (2006: 72) argue that their low numbers in Sweden may be explained by a combination of strong labour market regulation, the wide scope and inclusion of collective agreements and 'general jobless growth'. Despite the limited impact in numbers, it has had large institutional effects on Swedish industrial relations, discussed below.

The second form, labour migration, defined through state regulation tying residence permits to labour permits, has historically been at the centre of attention for Swedish trade unions. Bucken-Knapp (2009) argues that the Swedish trade union movement has been fairly positive to labour migration, although strongly engaged in formulating labour migration legislation that is compatible with the core aspects, what they see as the Swedish model of industrial relations. The first and major phase of post-World War II labour migration was structured through corporatist demand-based regulations. This phase ended in the early 1970s in a context of economic crisis, growing unemployment, increasingly negative LO trade union declarations, and with state authorities hesitant to grant labour permissions (Frank 2005). From this period, labour migration was rather limited, linked to shortages and mainly focussed on experts to be recruited from abroad for particular demands, often through a long administrative process. In 2008, this relatively restrictive migration policy changed through a new labour migration reform regime enacted by the right-wing government together with the Green Party. This reform, according to the Organisation for Economic Cooperation and Development (OECD), could be seen as the most liberal (employer) driven labour migration scheme among OECD members (OECD 2011). It was actively and positively greeted by the academic union confederation SACO, and basically well-received by the professional TCO confederation, but staunchly opposed by the LO, together with the Social Democratic and Left Parties (Bucken-Knapp 2009).

Swedish trade unions have been fairly inactive in trying to influence migration legislation concerning the third form; refugee and family reunification migration. This has basically been considered as outside the scope of trade union politics. Notwithstanding, the extent to which trade unions have been engaged has generally been concerned as securing conditions for refugees and family reunification migrants, with the aim of preventing the development of migrants' exclusions, to the extent that they would challenge the unions and their members, as well as the industrial relation model.

The fourth and final form, irregular migration, became increasingly a concern for the LO and its trade unions during the 2000s. With a strong position on regulated migration, the basic principle of the LO was that such migrants should not be in Sweden. At the same time, the irregular migrants with very few rights, also in comparison with other OECD countries, were working in the labour market. Their weak bargaining position made them vulnerable to informalised super exploitation which will be discussed more thoroughly below (see also Chapter 12). Therefore, this became a difficult and contentious issue for the LO and its trade unions.

Consequently, LO's position on migration may be framed as a question, pertaining basically to the particular industrial relations of the Swedish model. In this sense, labour migration has been at the core, centred on the need for state regulation linked to labour market demand. Concerning free movement, the trade unions have been more positive in the times of labour demand (the Nordic passport union), cautious in a context in which they did not expect much migration (membership in European Union), and sceptical but accepting in the context of expecting more migration (EU enlargement and the EU Service Directive). The point has less been to prevent migrants from coming to Sweden, but more to secure that migration did not negatively affect the strength of trade unions and the functioning of the industrial relations' system. The central tenet of the unions' cautiousness, but overall positive approach to migration, has been to safeguard influence on and support for government policies that would guarantee 'citizenship' rights for migrant workers.

Racialised workers and citizenship rights

The LO trade unions have been in favour of regulated migration, especially neo-corporatist arrangements concerning labour migrants as broadly defined. The central idea has been to maintain the strength of trade unions within industrial relations, which has been promoted by advocating expanding rights for migrants more generally. This was however not self-evident from the beginning. The neo-corporatist arrangements concerning labour migration were characterised by a modest degree of unfree wage labour[11] as in many other Western European countries, which did not end until 1967/8 (Frank 2005). Initially, trade unions did accept and support aspects of unfree wage labour but departed from that position during the 1950s (Yalcin 2010). From this period on, the LO pursued an inclusive immigrant and integration policy. This entailed support for permanent residence permissions that would ensure that unemployment would not lead to expulsion, nor force migrants to take whatever available job offer, even outside of collective agreements. What would become an inclusionary immigrant policy became even more important as labour migration in the 1970s declined, partially due to the LO's view that it was not conducive to rising unemployment (Mulinari and Neergaard 2004). It was instead replaced by increasing family reunification and refugee migration in which LO was, as discussed above, fairly neutral (Schierup 1991). The trade union strategies and proposals, focussing on the inclusion of migrants and migrant workers, centred on different approaches, although connected. At the core was to secure that migrant workers were covered by the Swedish collective agreements, and thus in principle, ensure they received the same working conditions and salaries as domestic workers. However, parallel to this, LO was active in supporting government proposals that removed differentiations between migrants and natives concerning welfare rights, furthermore targeting policies aimed at strengthening migrants' positions. An example of this, based on a 1968 resolution in the Council of Europe recommending language education for migrant workers, was how the LO secured an agreement with the SAF employers' association on Swedish language education. In this agreement, the employers organised a minor

11 Unfree labour is used to emphasise how migrant and racialised workers are denied rights enjoyed by other (free) workers, and thus cannot compete under equal conditions due to institutional and informal discrimination (Brass 2015; Cohen 1987; Miles 1987; Schierup et al. 2015).

part of language training in work time, paid salaries for migrants to take additional hours of instruction, and agreed to unpaid leave for yet more hours of education financed by the state. This was complemented with legislation allowing migrants without work to avail themselves of free Swedish language education for a total of 240 hours (SOU 2003: 77, 62–63). Furthermore, issues that only indirectly affected the trade unions and their positions within the industrial relations, concerned the political and legal status of migrants, advocating rights for voting in local and regional elections linked to residence and not citizenship. The trade unions were also positive to facilitate naturalisation of migrants.

With a clear strategy of avoiding an ethnically or racialised split labour market, and in a context in which LO had substantial political clout with social democratic governments, the trade union movement developed a general strategy of inclusion towards migrants and migrant workers. This strategy focused on welfare regime inclusion and the equality in formal rights, but also supported multiculturalist policies as well as municipal and regional voting rights. It could be argued that this strategy included aspects of co-optation, and within the social democratic labour movement (Ålund and Schierup 1991; Yalcin 2010). Yet, at the same time it was a project of expanding substantial rights to racialised workers in various domains of society.

Landsorganisationen: racialised workers and industrial relations

While acknowledging and supporting multiculturalism and diversity in the wider societal field, and actively participating in abolishing formal discrimination concerning the right of migrants and racialised workers, there was little interest at this time to analyse structural foundations of racism, and embedded racialised discrimination in the labour market, or wider society in general (Johansson 2008). While the trade union movement had knowledge of the situation of racialised workers in working life, it was generally viewed as caused by human capital variances, especially Swedish language deficits, ethnicised cultural differences and lack of knowledge about the Swedish society.

Beside Swedish language education, and minor interventions as securing employment safety for migrants called to do military service in birth countries, there was very little trade union action within industrial relations focused on improving the situation of racialised workers. This is interesting in that industrial relations and collective agreements are probably the core areas of trade union activity; the core rarely mobilised to improve the situation of racialised workers. One explanation that links with locating deficiencies with migrants as racialised workers is to see them as a reserve army of labour. Thus, in advancing general improvements in working conditions and wages, this would also spill over into racialised workers. In following the employment pattern of racialised workers, the thesis of a reserve army of labour finds support. In the 1950s, and especially the 1960s and 1970s, they were to be found in the labour intensive industry that slowly was rationalised away (Lundh and Ohlsson 1999; Leiniö 1988), and migrant women also in the declining domestic work sector (de los Reyes 1998). Subsequently, racialised workers increased their share of private service employment within the hospitality and building maintenance sectors:

> We are creating a society where it is not about immigrants' getting the worst jobs, but rather that they do not even get those jobs. We in the labour movement cannot see this happen… To succeed, we must have the union's help' (Falk 1995).

> It is only to acknowledge that this is so. We have not spent the immigrants and segregation tendencies the attention needed. We have not in time seen the alarming trends in discrimination against immigrants in the workplace … (Falk 1995)

The first quote by the Social Democratic immigrant minister Blomberg marks – as argued – the first systematic acknowledgment that the trade union movement has to actively combat an increasingly racialised labour market. The quote is from a period in the aftermath of the 1992 depression as the economic crisis in which unemployment for the first time after WWII could be compared to the 1930s. It was a period with around 8% general unemployment and, depending on how one operationalises racialised workers not born in a Nordic country, it was 40% (newly arrived), 30% (non-Nordic citizens), 19% (longer than 5 years) and 14% (naturalised non-Nordic). The quote from the minister reinforces what was mentioned above, that the concern is not of racialised workers having the worst jobs – this in a sense is the normality that was captured in subordinated inclusion (Neergaard 2009). The shock that is expressed concerns what could be called subordinated exclusion, a situation in which racialised workers are outside of the labour market, unemployed and at best in the margins of employment.

The second quote above, by Jan Edling, immigrant responsible at LO, is important because it now shifts (or complements) the deficit argument with highlighting both segregation and discrimination as causes for the subordinated exclusion of racialised workers. It is also important in that it locates the dynamics of these processes too within the workplaces, thereby making it an issue of industrial relations. However, while it was a breakthrough on a symbolic level, in many ways shifting the rhetoric emphasising discrimination, and later on racism, in the working life, there were few institutional interventions. Through agreements with employers, the benefits of diversity were emphasised, as well as the willingness to combat discrimination. While Sweden from 1986 had legislation against discrimination, it was extremely weak and focussed on a soft law approach, it was not until 1999 that a more robust antidiscrimination law was enacted into working life. It had long been counteracted by both trade unions and employers as being outside the tradition of Swedish industrial relations. When implemented, it emphasised the role of trade unions as advocates for employees being discriminated against (Soininen 2002); a role that the trade unions were not enthusiastic about.

During recent decades, there has been an increasing fragmentation of the legal status of migrants that together with a growing racialisation and racism, are creating complex and dynamic realities affecting the labour market, the trade unions and other forms of organisations, in a number of different ways (Mesic and Ålund 2011). Concerning the legal status of migrants, there is a hierarchy of formal entitlements in which naturalised migrants are the most privileged, generally only possible after five years of regular living in Sweden (although shorter exceptions exist). While there exist some important formal differences, mainly concerning the right to vote in national elections and risking expulsion if convicted of a crime with prison sentence, the second category of permanent residency enjoys almost the same rights as full citizens. A third category is comprised of migrants with other Nordic citizenship that through the wider passport union basically have the same rights as those with a permanent residence permit. A fourth category is 'mobile workers' who as intra-EU migrants have the right to stay in Sweden without limit of time, that is, as long as they can economically provide for themselves, including through social insurance. This right is – as in many other countries – becoming increasingly circumscribed however, especially in relation to access to welfare services. In Sweden, it has recently been brought into light in public debate the particular case of the apparent sudden arrival of indigent Roma from Romania, who as EU-citizens are attempting to provide for themselves by begging (but also availing themselves of legitimate rights to social support). So-called 'third country' (non-EU) temporary labour migrants, comprise a fifth category. They are in a particularly vulnerable position, as their right to reside and work is tied to maintaining an employment relationship with a particular employer, or to find another employer within three months, and reapplying for residence. Asylum applicants are yet another category, pending final decision by authorities and courts on the approval or rejection of their application. As this process can take years, legislation has been passed allowing for some rights to seek and take employment. In line with an increasing shift towards what has been called the 'work line' by the right wing parties – fundamentally a neoliberal labour supply-side ideology, increasingly the link of employment status to rights – the possibility for those receiving asylum application rejection to "switch track" and apply for a labour migration permit from within Sweden (the normal process from abroad) has been opened. Still, this is a complicated administrative task and is based on being able to show that one has worked in accordance to collective agreements, paying income and payroll taxes equivalent to at least a 13,600 SEK per month salary (approximately 1,400 Euros) from the same employer for a period of two years. There are extremely few cases resulting in residence permits secured by asylum seekers through "switching track". The final, seventh, category is the undocumented migrant. There are large variations in the estimate of how many irregular migrants there are in Sweden, most of whom are rejected refugee applicants, but some enter Sweden on tourism visas or with the purpose to work, and thereafter become undocumented migrants. This variation in forms, and subsequent legal status of different categories of migrants, create challenges for individual Swedish trade unions and their broader confederations concerning strategies and policies.

While there has been limited interest among trade unions to develop industrial relation policies aimed at improving the particular subordinate inclusion, or exclusionary subordination, of racialised workers, this is not the case concerning racialised workers in the context of the 2008 labour migration reform, as well as to European Union and posted workers, and to a smaller extent, irregular migrants (Neergaard 2015b). The 2008 labour migration reform could be seen as the most liberal (employer) driven labour migration scheme among the OECD members (OECD 2011). From a LO perspective, the reform has forced the trade unions to become more involved in the industrial relations of the berry industry, developing and securing collective agreements with employers that employ seasonal migrant workers, especially from Thailand. As berry picking has generally not been regarded as wage labour, the trade unions' engagement was an effect of overexploitation, protests by labour migrants and media exposure (Neergaard 2015a). In contrast, the major focus and interest by the trade unions have focused on labour migration in the private service sectors within the hospitality and building maintenance industries respectively. While the legislation prior to the 2008 reform was neo-corporatist with the government in the centre, the new legislation concentrates on employers' needs. The Swedish Migration Board's task is to grant the employers' applications, not to question whether the employer or the offer of employment is genuine.

> The union's task is simply to provide their opinion about if the working conditions are comparable to those in the collective agreement or not? We have no possibilities, nor any mandate, to check the authenticity of the conditions that are described in the employers' application. This mandate does not, in actuality, rest with anyone currently (Lundby-Wedin et al. 2010).

Although the legislation and the governments rhetoric maintains that work permits are only approved when the applicant conforms to the conditions of the labour market in general, laid down in collective agreements, it is asserted in the above statement that neither the authorities, nor the unions, have the actual opportunity to secure that; once approved, the conditions of work permits are fulfilled. That the LO unions argue in this way could be interpreted as a one-sided account, however, similar arguments have been heard from the Swedish Association of Graduate Engineers (who had been in favour of the law), and from the Swedish Migration Board.

On closer inspection of the occupational categories which have been granted in the work permits under the new legislation, it is hard not to think that the wage question and, more generally, working conditions constitute the main factors in the employers' demand for migrant workers. There are two characteristics which these sectors share; they are very labour-intensive, and they are relatively immobile. This means that the issue of the provision of labour is central, and it is in this context that migration and unfree labour may become an important part of a cost-cutting strategy.

It is however, not only through the labour migration reform that the trade unions feel that the established industrial relations are being challenged. The free movement and posted workers within the European Union are especially affecting the construction sector through 'bogus self-employment' (Thörnquist 2013) and stationed workers; both participating to the process of informalisation. Additionally, within the cross-border transportation sector, trade unions have argued that cabotage[12] in various regular and irregular forms is also producing informalisation, making it difficult for trade unions to maintain the collective agreements.

Free movement within the EU has heightened the debate to which extent it is producing a race to the bottom, in which national industrial relations are squeezed by EU free market regulations. In a Swedish context, the emblematic case is that of Laval. In 2004, the Latvian company *Laval un Partneri Ltd* won a contract for school renovation in the Vaxholm municipality near Stockholm. It was put under blockade by the Swedish Building Workers' Union in a struggle to pressure the company into accepting a Swedish collective agreement. The Swedish labour court asked the European Court of Justice for a ruling of the legitimacy of the blockade. The 2007, ECJ Laval judgment came as a shock for the Swedish trade union movement, as it challenged a central pillar staunchly defended by the trade unions; the right to use

---

12 Cabotage is the transport of passengers or goods within the borders of one country, performed by a company that is registered outside the country's borders (Sternberg et al. 2015).

collective action to pressure employers into signing collective agreements (Woolfson, Thörnqvist and Sommers 2010).

In the overall labour market perspective, the numbers that these examples represent are quite limited, although within certain subsectors of industries are of substantial importance. Moreover, the direction and application of regulation seem to be going against the trade unions, indicating a substantial shift in the balance of power between labour and capital in Swedish industrial relations.

The trade unions are maintaining that their struggle is about workers' rights, defending that collective agreements should cover the whole labour market, and arguing that changes are exposing migrants and racialised workers to risk of heightened exploitation. The employers as well as the right-wing parties, with a hegemonic position in the debate, are instead arguing that it is the trade unions' protectionism, discrimination against migrants, and basically an insider-outsider struggle in which the unions are defending their privileged position.

A final aspect in analysing the LO and its trade unions in relation to racialised workers, is to study the priorities on the agenda. As aforementioned, LO is a trade union confederation attempting to coordinate a heterogeneous group of working class trade unions. In March 2015, there was an agreement among those unions within LO concerning a "Future programme", in which 14 aims would steer the negotiations of the LO and its unions until 2028 (LO 2015). It is interesting to note that despite the knowledge of the situation of racialised workers in the labour market, noted above as developing from subordinated inclusion towards subordinated exclusion, they are not mentioned as a group or category at all. Clearly, a number of the goals would improve the situation for all workers, and some would relatively improve racialised workers' situations more. While women workers' struggles within the trade union have been tough, the document reflects substantial programmatic advances. Although the central category of it is the worker, in a number of points the struggle against the subordination of women workers have been presented as a priority to consider.

In the autumn of 2015, when the LO was attempting to coordinate its trade union for the collective agreement bargaining with employers' associations during 2016, the interpretation of how to use the strategic document was ridden with conflicts. On the 21st of October 2015, the LO decided to not enter the large wage bargaining round with a concerted approach among its trade unions. This failure was based on resistance by some of the major trade unions to a proposal for an approach prioritising wage increases for low paid workers. One has to go back more than two decades to find a similar situation in which the LO trade unions entered a collective agreement bargaining round without organised concertation. While there are different interpretations concerning the reasons for not agreeing on a concerted approach, there are grounds to link it to an intersectional analysis of conflicts within the LO. The proposal would relatively have benefited both the women dominated unions, and also the unions with most racialised workers in the private service sector. The official in charge of collective agreements of the powerful industrial trade union *IF Metall* argued that while they could agree on wage increases above the average for the nurse aids of the municipal union, they were against a general approach on raising those of low-paid workers[13]. The argument being that not all low-paid workers are value-discriminated, and that such an approach would give the nurse aids a lesser increase. In doing so, it seems a more nuanced approached compared to the example above from 1986 with the 'cuckoo eggs in the nest' metaphor. The target this time was not the women dominated municipal union, but instead other low-paid workers, a group strongly dominated by a racialised workforce.

The 'Future programme' document, and the breakdown of concerted LO collective agreements bargaining, reflect the general position of the LO and its trade unions in relation to racialised workers; they do not really exist when it comes to probably the most central aspects in the Swedish model of industrial relations – that of collective agreements. This does however not mean that they are always made invisible. There are a number of projects, policies and rhetoric concerning racialised workers, but they are almost always in the periphery of what LO and its trade unions consider the core work. The next section will turn to the trade unions as organisations in which struggles over distribution, recognition and representation occur.

The trade unions and racialised workers as members

In the early 1970s, there was for a number of reasons a window that opened for racialised workers within the trade union movement. Prior to this, racialised workers were expected to join the unions but there was very little space for them within the unions more generally, or in relation to the experiences that reflected their subordinated insertion within wider society. The position of racialised workers served as a reserve army of labour, or in the periphery of the trade union movement. Some of the explanation for this window is linked to the general radicalisation within the working class with 'wild cat strikes', and which there seems to have been an overrepresentation of racialised workers (Korpi 1981). This was also a period in which the LO was developing policies more generally

13 Available at <http://arbetet.se/2015/10/21/de-kan-ha-sprackt-lo-samordningen> (Accessed Feb 12, 2016).

towards migrants, where the proposals for migrants to be able to participate in municipal and regional elections were being developed (Yalcin 2010). Furthermore, migrant or ethnic associations were becoming more established in line with a neo-corporatist frame (see Ålund and Schierup 1991). This became the time of local immigrant committees linked to the local organisation of LO, and on the national level the immigrant council of the LO. Until the end of the 1980s, this institutional setup channelled issues concerning immigrants. According to Yalcin (2010), the dominant role of this institutional arrangement was on the one hand to ground the LO's development of immigrant policies, and even more so to socialise racialised workers into the LO tradition, linking them to social democratic mobilisation. Central here was control and information from above. In contrast to focussing on how LO mobilised through the immigrant committee and council, on the other hand, other scholars argued that while these organisations took some of the challenges that migrant and racialised workers experienced, the major problem was that they were peripheral to the core activities of local trade unions, and even counteracted or marginalised (Knocke 2000; Johansson 2008).

In the mid-1990s, the situation of racialised workers, as noted above, is increasingly highlighted within the trade union movement, both from the central leadership of the LO as the following quote shows, and from racialised workers.

> Everybody should be organised in unions and covered by agreement. If any group is left out, there is a risk that they take jobs below the negotiated wages, says Bertil Jonsson. LO and other trade union organisations – central and local – have awakened late (LO magazine, 1995).

From this period until the electoral defeat of the Social Democratic government in 2006, there were a number of government initiatives attempting to understand, and to some extent address, the racialised character of the Swedish labour market and society in general (including research and government inquiries). Moreover, as framed in the quote above, it is also a period in which the LO and trade unions start to take these issues into account. For one thing, they began publishing a number of reports, adding:

> A new dimension of class and gender analysis. For some time LO in the analysis brought in another dimension, if you are born in Sweden or any other country, while maintaining the division of class and gender (Nelander, Acchiardo and Goding 2006: 2).

However, for the trade union leadership the point of departure seems less to be a concern with racialised workers – although that is also an aspect – and more how the increasingly subordinated exclusion of racialised workers affects the position of the trade unions within industrial relations. Thus, in extension, the need to organise them to prevent a development in which they sell labour below the level of the collective agreements.

It was in this context that the network of immigrant union activists, FAI, was formed with the purpose of fighting discrimination within and out with the trade unions (Mulinari and Neergaard 2004, 2005). One of the key people in building FAI expresses the context of the organisation's aim in the following quote:

> The union runs in our veins. It is hot. Many of us have been involved in agitation campaigns, union organisation, demonstrations, strikes, experienced the police, prison and exile. But also joy, friendship, solidarity, identity and dignity. FAI believes in the union as we believe in the sun: we firmly believe although it does not always shine. Today the sun is not shining. The union isn't shining for us immigrants either… We do not want to take over … we want to be a part ([Chairman of FAI] Nuñez n.d.).

FAI was interesting in a number of ways. It was an initiative by racialised workers, but with formal support from the LO leadership (Yalcin 2010). On the one side, FAI was very clear in presenting itself as a part of the trade union movement, trying to avoid the suspicion that they were attempting to divide the movement with loyalties outside, as illustrated by the following informant:

> There are serious problems but we should not 'break' the unions. I do not believe (as others do) that we have the right to divide the working-class movement. That is why FAI will only be needed for some years in order to strengthen immigrants' position within the unions. We do not want a separate organisation. If the Swedish unions did their work, if they stopped working only for Swedes, I do not believe we would need FAI (Informant 23).

At the same time it was critical for the trade union policies in not taking seriously the racialised character of the labour market in their industrial relation policies, and not the least marginalising the voices of racialised workers. Issues of discrimination and even racism were highlighted, and it tried to distance itself from the traditional way of linking migrants and racialised workers to the Social Democratic party and the trade union through national/immigrant or ethnic associations. It was in that sense, an attempt to forge a pan-ethnic or a collective network of racialised workers within the trade union movement. This highlighted both the discrimination and racism in the labour market and the trade unions, and hence by offering to actively participate in the trade union struggle for all of its members:

> We are all black skulls … it does not matter where we come from, what we have in common, is that we understand each other, we have the same experience, the same bloody work, the same suspicion when we go shopping, the same problem with the children … Many say that we are not, but I say, as things are, we are all black skulls (Informant 9).

As with the immigrant committees, while receiving support from the central hierarchies of the trade union confederations, and to some extent trade unions, it proved difficult to convert the engagement and support into concrete local trade union practices or to include these issues within the trade union collective agreement agenda. In 2010, the central network was closed, although some local networks tried to continue.

One of the aims of the FAI, as well as at times expressed by the LO leadership, is to increase the number of elected and employed officials with foreign backgrounds, with the rhetoric of reflecting the members. This has however been at best a very slow process. There are few systematic surveys of the representation of racialised workers within the trade unions, all focussing on foreign born (for an overview see Yalcin 2010).

Despite a lower degree of unionisation, the increasing number of racialised migrants and post-migrant generations, becoming union members, in combination with racialised segmentation of the labour market – both sectorial and workplace (Aslund and Nordström Skans 2005) – has created trade unions in which the majority are racialised workers (see Table 2 below). While this has increased prospects for them to be elected as representatives, so far it is still a marginal phenomenon.

Table 2: Percentage of foreign-born members in blue collar trade unions

	2004	**2014**
The Swedish Construction Workers' Union	6	11
Elektrikerförbundet	5	9
The Swedish Building Maintenance Workers' Union	36	43
GS, The Swedish Union of Forestry, Wood and Graphical Workers	9	12
The Commercial Employees' Union	12	16
The Hotel & Restaurant Workers' Union	34	45
IF-Metall, Industry and Metal Workers' Union	23	21
The Swedish Municipal Workers' Union	15	23
The Swedish Food Workers' Union	22	30
The Union of Service and Communication Employees	7	10
The Swedish Transport Workers Union	9	17
Landsorganisationen TUC	14	22

Source: Nelander and Goding 2006; Correspondence with LO 2015.

All members of the trade union confederation LO board are Swedish born. In the boards of the LO trade unions, the number of foreign born has been slightly above 5 percent in the last decade (2004, 11 of 198, 5.5%; 2008, 10 of 196, 5.1%; 2012, 10 of 153, 6.5%)[14]. Racialised trade union activists often present nuanced accounts for this strong underrepresentation. These span everything from language issues, historical trade union experiences, the structural marginalisation within the labour market, bad conditions, discrimination issues, as well as Swedish recruitment networks (Mulinari and Neergaard 2004)[15]. In contrast, trade union leaders often emphasise a low interest, that it is a question of time, or that it is not an issue if in democratic membership organisations, as the following quote illustrates:

> Well, maybe we discuss gender more, to get the women in. The union is not unaware of the problem of few board members with a foreign background. But I must admit that it may not top the agenda (Gravlund 2009).

While there seems to have been an increasing awareness within the LO concerning the importance of trade unions in struggling against ethnic and racial discrimination, as well as improved representation, there are still few concrete manifestations that the trade unions are becoming more diverse, and representative among the elected officials. Furthermore, while part of this change is probably an effect of migrant and racialised trade union activists with support from LO leadership, it is also perhaps explained by the general crisis of the trade unions in a new neoliberal social formation, with declining strength in relation to employers, as well as professional and academic trade unions. It is known from international research that a partial explanation for trade unions' interest in organising and mobilising racialised workers is linked to declining unionisation, as well as trade union activity (Schierup et al. 2015).

At the same time as the LO is representing a working class that is increasingly racialised and feminised, the interpellation of the racist extreme-right party – the Sweden Democrats (SD, see chapter 10 for more information) – is rapidly increasing its support among working class, mainly white, men. The Swedish Transport Workers' Union has the most restrictive rules concerning the SD of all the LO unions. However, most of the unions have rules aimed at restricting active SD from holding positions within the trade unions, linking it to the unions' values or statutes on human rights. These decisions reflect a general tendency among unions

---

14 Available at <http://arbetet.se/2008/10/17/svenska-mn-styr-i-lo-frbunden/> (Accessed July 28, 2016).

15 For a recent example expressing this difference see <https://www.transport.se/Transportarbetaren/Start/Nyheter1/Fa-utlandsfodda-i-Transports-topp/> (Accessed July 28, 2016).

to face the growing strength of politically articulated racism and its manifestation in the everyday workings of trade unions. However, despite this the support of the SD has been growing, especially among some unions – the construction and transport workers – where the percentage in opinion polls seems to be way above the national average. While other trade unions, especially those with high percentages of racialised workers, seem to have relatively few members supporting the SD. The extent to which these numbers stabilise, will give the LO and its trade unions a number of significant problems to deal with. The stratification within the working class that is strongly gendered and racialised will with this additional development become political. Furthermore, there is no clear political trade union strategy on how to handle this manifestation. While trade unions have had a rhetoric of human rights, international solidarity and diversity, there are also trade union leaders arguing that the trade union movement has to take the SD sympathising trade union members' concerns more seriously[16]. Having become the most politicised and central issue in Sweden today, it is really challenging the unions.

In summarising the LO analysis and its trade unions in relation to racialised workers, one may discern different and partially conflicting perceptions. The most central understanding of racialised workers is of silent and passive members. However, the linkage between the LO and the Social Democratic Party has also meant that the trade unions view the migrant and racialised worker as a probable voter of the Social Democrats, but also in extension, a channel into migrant communities and as advocates of the reformist labour movement. Conversely, the dominant threat has always been, but increasingly so, that the racialised workers would be unorganised, and therefore prepared to sell their labour below the collective agreement. In addition, and partially in conflict with this perception, is the threat of racialised workers supporting factions within the trade union linked to parties left of the Social Democratic. The suspicion towards racialised workers has at time also been linked to the threat of self-organising, outside of the LO unions.

Conclusion

This chapter has focussed on the working class trade union movement and racialised workers in Sweden, situated in three central arenas: socio-politically, industrial relations and membership organisation. In doing so, the discussion has been structured by a gradual transformation of both the welfare regime, and the industrial relations system, from a Keynesian towards a neoliberal frame.

16 Available at <http://sverigesradio.se/sida/artikel.aspx?programid=3071&artikel=6377855> (Accessed July 28, 2016).

Analysing the wider societal and political arena, it is argued that the central dynamic guiding the LO and its trade unions was to maintain and defend the industrial relation system. As a consequence, whilst focussing on migration, it has been the regulation of labour migration that has been most central. In this sense, the 2008 labour migration reform, at least in principle, challenged the traditional setup of industrial relations, and thus it is understandable why the LO has been negative. In the case of 'free movement', the trade unions, with some exceptions concerning EU enlargement, have generally seen them as compatible with the industrial relations, although posted workers and service directives are viewed as problematic, and the Laval case was seen as threatening. Concerning refugee and family reunification migration, trade unions have basically viewed this as outside of their area. In all cases, the central aspect has been to support and even initiate reforms that have given racialised workers' rights. It is difficult to assess the balance between solidarity and citizenship rights, and defending industrial relations in these policies.

Concerning trade unions' politics and practices towards racialised workers within the sphere of industrial relations, the picture is partially different. With the exception of supporting some few restrictions in the decade following WWII, the central practice has been to a formal equality. There have been few trade union initiatives within industrial relations particularly targeting the subordinated inclusion or exclusion that racialised workers face in working life. Here, it seems probable that as long as it was a question of subordinated inclusion, the interest from the trade unions has been low, whereas the subordinated exclusion that increasingly characterises racialised workers in the labour market, has produced more interest for action as it threatens the industrial relations in the long run. However, agreeing among the LO trade unions on concerted negotiations with employers failed in 2015, and while there were no discussions concerning the situation of racialised workers, the proposal on the table would have improved not only women workers, but even more so racialised workers.

Finally, as organisations of members, there has been very little interest and work to come to grips with the limited space for, and the under-representation of, racialised workers as trade union representatives. With few exceptions, mostly coming from racialised activists within the trade union, but at time others as well, the trade union has emphasised the formal equality of all members, arguing that these aspects are more explained by different characteristics of racialised workers, than by structural and institutional practices within the unions. Few would argue that better representation is bad, but there is no systematic interest in prioritising these issues.

It is thus tempting to conclude that the LO and its trade unions have in general seen the situation of racialised workers as a peripheral issue; the exceptions being either when migration legislation or the situation of racialised workers were deemed as threats to industrial relations, or when they could be mobilised either as social democratic voters, or members of trade unions. The LO and its unions are interest based, and to more profoundly change these practices, racialised workers together with other trade union members, would need to mobilise around their interests and put their issues at the top of the trade union agenda. This has thus far not happened.

However, June 21 2016 the parties of the Swedish Parliament, with the exception of the small neoliberal Centre Party (*Centerpartiet*) and the Left Party (*Vänsterpartiet*), voted through a three year temporary legislation on migration (see further Chapter 2. It was ironic that the second vice speaker of the parliament, Björn Söder of the Sweden Democrats, was presiding the decision and that the SD parliamentary representatives were applauding and cheering the decision (see Chapters 10 and 11). While there had been strong critique from civil society organisations of the enacted legislation this critique had mainly focussed on humanitarian, legal and practical issues. While some (especially trade unions) noted in passing that the proposed legislation would affect industrial relations, this was not brought up as a major issue.

This lack of systematic critique is, however, highly problematic in a situation with more than 150,000 new applicants for asylum. The new legislation and changing institutional following in its wake may have deep seated implications for an already declining or even dissolving Swedish model of industrial relations. The new policies and the sheer number of refugee applicants will mean the entry of thousands of new unfree workers into the Swedish labour market. It is calculated that half of the applicants will be rejected[17] providing a possible large irregular workforce with no means of subsistence prepared to take jobs at any cost (see Chapter 2 for further points). What is likely to ensue is an informalisation of blue collar jobs in general. This will conceivably force blue collar trade unions to quickly adopt new strategies. It remains to be seen which strategic choices will be taken. We hypothesise that three major options will be in play: unions continuing to stick their head in the sand, waiting for supposedly better times to come; new inclusive struggles for informalised and racialised labour, or a shift to exclusionary and racialised strategies.

17 Available at <http://www.svt.se/nyheter/inrikes/fler-asylsokande-tvingas-atervanda> (Accessed July 28, 2016).

Acknowledgement of funding

We appreciate generous funding by FORTE, the Swedish Research Council for Health, Working Life and Welfare [grant number 2006-1524, and the network grants, numbers 2008-1451 and 2012-1443].

References

Anderson, B. 1991. *Imagined Communities. Reflections of the Origin and Spread of Nationalities*. London: Verso.

Aslund, O. and Nordström Skans, O. 2005. *Will I see you at work? Ethnic workplace segregation in Sweden 1985–2002*. Working Paper 2005:24. Uppsala: Institutet för arbetsmarknadspolitisk utvärdering (IFAU).

Autor, D. H., Katz, L. F. and Kearney, M. S. 2006. 'The Polarization of the U.S. Labor Market.' *American Economic Review* 96/2, 189–194.

Brass, T. 2015. *Towards a Comparative Political Economy of Unfree Labour: Case Studies and Debates*. New York: Routledge.

Bruhn, A., Kjellberg, A. and Sandberg, Å. 2013. 'A New World of Work Challenging Swedish Unions.' In Sandberg, Åke (ed.) *Nordic Lights. Work, Management and Welfare in Scandinavia*. Stockholm: SNS, 126–186.

Bucken-Knapp, G. 2009. *Defending the Swedish Model: Social Democrats, Trade Unions, and Labor Migration Policy Reform*. Rowman & Littlefield.

Cockburn, C. 1991. *In the Way of Women. Men's Resistance to Sex Equality in Organisations*. London: Macmillan.

Cohen, R. 1987. *The New Helots: Migrants in the International Division of Labour*. Aldershot: Avebury.

Crouch, C. 1994. *Industrial Relations and European State Traditions*. Oxford: Oxford University Press.

de los Reyes, P. 1998. 'I skärningspunkten mellan genus och etnicitet. Ett ekonomiskt-historiskt perspektiv på invandrarkvinnor i svenskt arbetsliv.' *Arbetsmarknad Och Arbetsliv* 4/1, 13–33.

Nuñez, C No date. Folder of Fackligt aktiva Invandrare. Stockholm: FAI

Falk, L-Å (1995) 'Blomman vädjar till facket om hjälp', LO-tidningen, Dec 1, 1995. Stockholm: LO.

Fantasia, R. 1989. *Cultures of Solidarity: Consciousness, Action, and Contemporary American Workers*. Berkeley: University of California Press.

Frank, D. 2005. 'Staten, företagen och arbetskraftsinvandringen: en studie av invandringspolitiken i Sverige och rekryteringen av utländska arbetare 1960–1972.' PhD diss., Växjö University.

Goos, M., Manning, A. and Salomons, A. 2009. 'Job polarization in Europe.' *The American Economic Review* 99/2, 58–63.

Gravlund, W. 2009. 'Dåligt ställt med invandrare i facktoppen.' *Helsingborgs Dagblad,* January 3. Accessed July 31, 2016. <http://www.hd.se/lokalt/helsingborg/2009/01/03/daligt-stallt-med-invandrare-i-facktoppen/>

Gumbrell-McCormick, R. and Hyman, R. 2013. *Trade unions in Western Europe : hard times, hard choices.* Oxford: Oxford University Press.

Haus, L. A. 2002. *Unions, immigration, and internationalization: New challenges and changing coalitions in the United States and France.* New York ; Palgrave Macmillan.

Hyman, R. 1971. *Marxism and the Sociology of Trade Unionism.* London: Pluto Press.

Hyman, R. 1999. 'Imagined Solidarities: Can Trade Unions Resist Globalization?' In Leisink, Peter (ed.) *Globalization and labour relations.* Cheltenham: Edward Elgar, 94–115.

Hyman, R. 2001. *Understanding European Trade Unionism: Between Market, Class and Society.* London: SAGE.

Håkansson, K. and Isidorsson, T. 2014. 'The trade union response to agency labour in Sweden.' *Industrial Relations Journal* 45/1, 22–38.

Jessop, B. 1999. 'The strategic selectivity of the state: reflections on a theme of Poulantzas.' *Journal of the Hellenic Diaspora* 25/1–2, 1–37.

Jessop, B. 2004. 'Multi-level governance and multi-level meta-governance.' In Bache, Ian and Matthew Flinders (eds.) *Multi-Level Governance.* Oxford: Oxford University Press, 49–74.

Johansson, J. 2008. 'Så gör vi inte här i Sverige. Vi brukar göra så här.' : retorik och praktik i LO:s invandrarpolitik 1945–1981.' PhD diss., Växjö University.

Kjellberg, A. 2001. 'Klass, etnicitet och facklig organisering.' In Holmgren, Anna (ed.) *Klassamhället – förändring, splittring och facklig vanmakt.* Stockholm: LO, 76–103.

Kjellberg, A. 2009. 'The Swedish Ghent system and trade unions under pressure.' *Transfer: European Review of Labour and Research* 15/3–4, 481–504.

Kjellberg, A. 2011. 'Trade Unions and Collective Agreements in a Changing World.' In Thörnquist, Annette and Åsa-Karin Engstrand (eds.) *Precarious Employment in Perspective. Old and New Challenges to Working Conditions in Sweden.* Bruxelles: Peter Lang, 47–100.

Kjellberg, A. 2015. *Kollektivavtalens täckningsgrad samt organisationsgraden hos arbetsgivarförbund och fackförbund.* Research Reports No. 2013:1, Updated May 8, 2015. Department of Sociology, Lund University.

Knocke, W. 2000. 'Sweden: Insiders Outside the Trade-Union Mainstream.' In Penninx, Rinus and Judith Roosblad (eds.) *Trade Unions, Immigration and Immigrants in Europe 1960–1993. A comparative Study of the Actions of Trade Unions in Seven West European Countries*. New York and Oxford: Berghahn Books, 157–183.

Knocke, W. 2011. 'Osynliggjorda och "fragmenterade" - Invandrade kvinnor i arbetslivet.' In Mulinari, Paula and Rebecca Selberg (eds.) *Arbete – Intersektionella perspektiv*. Stockholm: Gleerups, 211–227.

Korpi, W. 1981. 'Unofficial Strikes in Sweden.' *British Journal of Industrial Relations* 19/1, 66–87.

Korpi, W. 1993. 'Politik och väljare bakom valutgången 1991 / Politics, issues and voters in the Swedish 1991 election.' *Sociologisk Forskning* 30/1, 3–28.

Korpi, W. and Shalev, M. 1979. 'Strikes, Industrial Relations and Class Conflict in Capitalist Societies.' *The British Journal of Sociology* 30/2, 164–187.

Krings, T. 2009. 'A Race to the Bottom? Trade Unions, EU Enlargement and the Free Movement of Labour.' *European Journal of Industrial Relations* 15/1, 49–69.

Leiniö, T.-L. 1988. 'Sex and ethnic segregation in the 1980 Swedish labour market.' *Economic and Industrial Democracy* 9/1, 99–120.

Lindberg, I. and Bengtsson, E. (eds.) 2013. *Den sänkta löneandelen: Orsaker, konsekvenser och handlingsalternativ*. Stockholm: Premiss.

LO 2015. *Gemensamma långsiktiga mål för tre kongressperioder*. Stockholm: LO.

Lundby-Wedin, W., Bardh, P., Nordström, A., Tilly, H., Lindgren, L., Sjöö, P.-O., … Öhlund, H. 2010. 'Stoppa rovdriften på arbetskraft'. *Svenska Dagbladet*, Nov. 21, 2010.

Lundh, C. and Ohlsson, R. 1999. *Från arbetskraftsimport till flyktinginvandring*. Stockholm: SNS.

Meidner, R. 1994. 'The rise and fall of the Swedish model.' In Clement, Wallace and Rianne Mahon (eds) *Swedish Social Democracy: A Model in Transition*. Toronto: Canadian Scholars' Press, 337–346.

Meidner, R. 1999. *Manifest för full sysselsättning*. Stockholm: Atlas.

Mesic, N. and Ålund, A. 2011. 'Asymmetric Partnership: Migrant organisations, trade unions and equality Ombudsman.' *Revija Za Sociologiju* 41/1, 51–76.

Miles, R. 1982. *Racism and migrant labour*. London: Routledge & Kegan Paul.

Miles, R. 1987. *Capitalism and unfree labour: Anomaly or necessity?* London: Tavistock.

Miles, R. 1993. *Racism after 'race relations'*. London: Routledge.

Molina, I. 1997. 'Stadens rasifiering. Etnisk boendesegregation i folkhemmet.' PhD diss., Department of Social and Economic Geography, Uppsala University.

Mulinari, D. and Neergaard, A. 2004. *Den nya svenska arbetarklassen: rasifierade arbetares kamp inom facket*. Umeå: Boréa.

Mulinari, D. and Neergaard, A. 2005. 'Black skull' consciousness: the new Swedish working class. *Race & Class*, 46/3, 55–71.

Neergaard, A. 2000. 'Fackföreningsrörelsen: mellan "globalisering" och "individualisering".' In Neergaard, Anders and Ylva Stubbegaard (eds.) *Politiskt inflytande*. Lund: Studentlitteratur, 159–189.

Neergaard, A. 2009. 'Racialisation in the Labour Market: In Search of a Theoretical Understanding.' In Neergaard, Anders (ed.) *European Perspectives on Exclusion and Subordination: The Political Economy of Migration*. Maastricht: Shaker, 201–221.

Neergaard, A. 2015a. 'Migration, racialisation and forms of unfree labour – Dilemmas of union solidarity in Sweden.' In Schierup, Carl-Ulrik, Ronaldo Munck, Branka Likić-Brborić and Anders Neergaard (eds.) *Migration, Precarity and Global Governance: Challenges for Labour*. Oxford: Oxford University Press, 139–159.

Neergaard, A. 2015b. '"Det fackliga löftet": Solidaritet, fackföreningsrörelse och arbetskraftsinvandring.' In Calleman, Catharina and Petra Herzfeld Olsson (eds.) *Hur har det det och varför? En antologi om villkoren för arbetskraftsinvandrare i Sverige*. Report 2015:9. Stockholm: Delmi, 200–243.

Nelander, S., Acchiardo, M.-P. and Goding, I. 2006. *Facklig organisationsgrad bland utlandsfödda*. Stockholm: Löne- och välfärdsenheten, LO.

Nelander, S. and Goding, I. 2006. *Andelen medlemmar i facket med utländsk bakgrund*. Stockholm: Löne- och välfärdsenheten, LO.

Nycander, S. 2002. *Makten över arbetsmarknaden rbett perspektiv på Sveriges 1900-tal*. Stockholm: SNS.

OECD 2011. *Recruiting Immigrant Workers, Sweden*. Paris: OECD Publishing.

OECD 2015. *Migration. Permanent immigrant inflows*. Accessed July 31, 2016. <https://data.oecd.org/migration/permanent-immigrant-inflows.htm#indicator-chart>

Parkin, F. 1974. 'Strategies of Social Closure in Class Formation.' In Parkin, Frank (ed.) *The Social Analysis of Class Structure*. London: Tavistock, 1–19.

Penninx, R. and Roosblad, J. (eds.) 2000. *Trade Unions, Immigration and Immigrants in Europe 1960–1993. A Comparative Study of the Actions of Trade Unions in Seven West European Countries*. Oxford & New York: Berghahn Books.

Pontusson, J. and Kuruvilla, S. 1992. 'Swedish Wage-Earner Funds: An Experiment in Economic Democracy.' *Industrial & Labor Relations Review* 45/4, 779–791.

Sandberg, Å. (ed.) 2013. *Nordic Lights: Work, Management and Welfare in Scandinavia*. Stockholm: SNS.

Sassen, S. 1999. *Globalization and its Discontents. Essays on the New Mobility of People and Money*. New York: New Press.

Schierup, C. U. 1991. '"The duty to work": the theory and practice of Swedish refugee policy.' In Ålund, Aleksandra and Carl-Ulrik Schierup (eds.) *Paradoxes of Multiculturalism: Essays on Swedish society*. Aldershot: Avebury, 21–47.

Schierup, C.-U., Hansen, P. and Castles, S. 2006. *Migration, Citizenship, and the European Welfare State: A European Dilemma*. Oxford: Oxford University Press.

Schierup, C.-U., Munck, R., Likic-Brboric, B. and Neergaard, A. 2015. *Migration, Precarity, and Global Governance: Challenges and Opportunities for Labour*. Oxford: Oxford University Press.

Scruggs, L. 2002. 'The Ghent System and Union Membership in Europe, 1970–1996.' *Political Research Quarterly* 55/2, 275–297.

Simms, M. 2012. 'Imagined solidarities: Where is class in union organising?' *Capital & Class* 36/1, 97–115.

Sivanandan, A. 1982. *A different hunger: Writings on Black Resistance*. London: Pluto Press.

Skovdahl, B. 1996. *Skeletten i garderoben. Om rasismens idéhistoriska rötter*. Tumba: Mångkulturellt centrum.

Slavnic, Z. 2010. 'The Political Economy of Informalization.' *European Societies*, 12/1, 3–24.

Soininen, M. 2002. 'Exploring EU ethnic diversity and antidiscrimination: A Swedish perspective.' Paper presented at the Immigration Politics: Between Centre and Periphery. National States and the EU, Turin, Italy, March 22–27.

SOU 2003:77. 2003. *Vidare vägar och vägen vidare : svenska som andraspråk för samhälls- och arbetsliv : betänkande*. Stockholm: Fritzes offentliga publikationer. Accessed July 31, 2016. <http://www.regeringen.se/sb/d/108/a/925>

Sternberg, H., Filipiak, M., Hofmann, E. and Hellström, D. 2015. *Cabotagestudien: A study on trucking deregulation and cabotage in Scandinavia and beyond*. Lund: Lund University.

Svanberg, I. and Tydén, M. 1998. *Tusen år av invandring: en svensk kulturhistoria*. 2nd edition. Stockholm: Gidlund.

Tamas, K. and Münz, R. 2006. *Labour Migrants Unbound? EU Enlargement, Transitional Measures and Labour Market Effects*. Stockholm: Institute for Future Studies.

Thompson, E. P. 1963. *The making of the English working class*. London: Gollancz.

Thörnquist, A. 2013. 'False (Bogus) Self-Employment in East-West Labour Migration: Recent trends in the Swedish construction and road haulage industries.' *TheMES (Themes on Migration and Ethnic Studies)* 41, 1–43.

Thörnquist, A. and Engstrand, Å.-K. (eds.) 2011. *Precarious Employment in Perspective: Old and New Challenges to Working Conditions in Sweden*. Bruxelles & New York: P.I.E. Peter Lang.

Watts, J. R. 1998. 'Italian and Spanish Labour Leaders' Unconventional Immigration Policy Preferences.' *South European Society and Politics* 3/3, 129–148.

Wills, J. 2001. 'Community Unionism and Trade Union Renewal in the UK: Moving beyond the Fragments at Last?' *Transactions of the Institute of British Geographers* 26/4, 465–483.

Woolfson, C., Thörnqvist, C. and Sommers, J. 2010. 'The Swedish model and the future of labour standards after *Laval*.' *Industrial Relations Journal* 41/4, 333–350.

Wrench, J. 2004. 'Trade Union Responses to Immigrants and Ethnic Inequality in Denmark and the UK: The Context of Consensus and Conflict.' *European Journal of Industrial Relations* 10/1, 7–30.

Yalcin, Z. 2010. 'Facklig gränspolitik: Landsorganisationens invandrings- och invandrarpolitik 1946–2009'. PhD diss., Örebro Studies in History, Örebro University.

Åberg, R. 2013. 'Tjugohundratalets arbetsmarknad : fortsatt uppkvalificering eller jobbpolarisering?' *Ekonomisk Debatt* 41/2, 6–15.

Ålund, A. 1995. 'Ungdomar, gränser och nya rörelser.' In Statens Invandrarverk (ed.) *Rasismens varp och trasor. En antologi om främlingsfientlighet och rasism*. Norrköping: Statens Invandrarverk, 54–75.

Ålund, A. 1999. 'Feminism, Multiculturalism, Essentialism.' In Werbner, Pnina and Nira Yuval-Davis (eds.) *Women, Citizenship and Difference*. London: Zed Books Ltd.

Ålund, A. and Schierup, C.-U. 1991. *Paradoxes of Multiculturalism: Essays on Swedish society*. Aldershot: Avebury.

Öberg, P. and Svensson, T. 2002. 'Power, Trust and Deliberation in Swedish Labour Market Politics.' *Economic and Industrial Democracy* 23/4, 451–490.

Diana Mulinari & Åsa Lundqvist

4. Invisible, Burdensome and Threatening: The Location of Migrant Women in the Swedish Welfare State

Abstract: Gender equality is a hallmark for the Nordic welfare states. The chapter discusses how the category of migrant women has been conceptualised from the 1960s onwards. It relates to the connection between state policies and public-political discourses on family life on the one hand, and labour market participation on the other.

Introduction

Gender equality as ideology and practice has informed policies in Sweden for almost half a century, especially by facilitating women and men to combine paid work and caring responsibilities. Thus, the notion of a 'gender equal family' has been a central theme in policy making from the 1960s onwards (Ellingsæter and Leira 2006; Nyberg 2012).

Gender equality policies, as first introduced, built upon a theoretical understanding of gender as a central principle of a hierarchical social organisation in which women and men were assumed to have unequal access to social and economic power – both in the labour market and the family (Leira 2002; Liljeström 1978). To change such inequities, policy reforms were implemented early on to level unequal gender relations, mainly through the individualisation of the welfare system and the inclusion of men in care work (Lundqvist 2011).

The outcomes of gender equality policies were however already critically examined by the 1970s and 1980s. Despite reforms, feminist scholars argued that hierarchies remained between women and men, both at work and at home (Hirdman 1989; Widerberg 1986)[1]. Moreover, scholars in the field of migration and ethnic relations argued early on that advocates of the gender equality ideology, when discussing migration, departed both theoretically, and in its operationalisation, from a perspective marginalising other forms of discrimination (cf. Knocke 1986; Ålund 1991a, 1991b).

1 Later analyses also pointed to the normative regulation of not only heterosexuality but also family forms evolving from these policies (Martinsson 2000; Dahl 2004).

Hence, racialised forms of discrimination, including hierarchical differences in access to both material and symbolic resources between various groups of women (and men) have been ignored in the development of gender equality policies. Moreover, the notion of gender equality policies has been identified as a specifically 'Swedish' or 'Nordic' cultural quality, resulting in the construction of migrant women and men as outside its scope (de los Reyes 1998; Knocke 1991; Mulinari 2008; Squires 2007; Ålund 1999). Annika Olsson has recently described this development in terms of 'conditional gender equality policy':

> [...] gender equality policies have not even on an ideal level included all Swedish citizens or people resident in Sweden. Only certain citizens and others who define Sweden as their home are included (in the gender equality ambition, author's remark). This is true especially regarding gender equality in working life, a central arena for gender equality reforms (2014: 90, authors' translation).

Departing from such perspectives and debates, this essay discusses how the category of migrant women has been conceptualised within and between state policies and discourses on family life on the one hand and labour market participation on the other, from the 1960s onwards. The main purpose is thus to explore the location of the category of migrant women[2] within and between work and family life, across time. The argument rests on the assumption that the category of migrant women is constructed as different from 'Swedish women' in policy discourse, but that the meanings and understandings of their location as varying over time. To exemplify these variations, how migrant women are constructed within family and labour market policy discourses between the 1960s and 2015 will be analysed.

Three periods in which the understanding of migrant women changed are identified. The emergence and establishment of gender equality policies in the beginning of the 1960s represents the first period. The main assumption in politics at the time departed from the idea that gender equality was (to become) a general and central feature of modern Sweden (Melby, Ravn and Wetterberg 2008). Migrant women however, especially as articulated in labour market policies, tended to be categorised not only as culturally different from 'Swedish women', and therefore difficult to include in a gender equal project, but also as an *invisible* category in the migration process, often described as merely a family member (de los Reyes 1998, 2000).

---

2 The analysis only includes migrant women with permanent or temporary residence permit or who are Swedish citizens. Thus migrant women lacking residence permits are outside the scope of our analysis.

The second period of analysis covers the development in the 1990s. Marked by retrenchment and major restructuring processes, the gender equality ideology changed, with the structural analysis of gender inequities becoming blurred by neoliberal notions of 'freedom to choose' and 'flexibility'. The economic crisis of the 1990s, resulted in increasing unemployment among migrant women that stayed at relatively high levels, despite the recovering of the economy, towards the end of the decade, resulting in new ways of positioning migrant women. She was no longer only constructed as culturally different, but also seen as a victim – as a homogeneous collective burdened with patriarchal tradition – and thereafter, as a *burden* for the welfare state. This discursive shift has to do with increased sickness rates among immigrant women, which in turn followed the heavy employment among labour migrants, in particular, migrant women working in greater occurrences than ethnic Swedish women in the male-dominated industrial manufacturing. Moreover, an increasingly dominant orientalist public discourse came during the 1980s to stigmatise migrant women from the Middle East in particular, exacerbating their disadvantage in an increasingly exclusivist labour market and welfare state (Ålund and Schierup 1991).

The third period follows from the development in the new millennium. During the 2000s, notions on gender equality in the Swedish context still loomed over the policies directed towards families with children, while at the same time unemployment figures decreased rapidly for a majority of the population. However, this development, as aforementioned, did not include migrant women[3]. The post 9/11 era moved the location of migrant women into a much more precarious position than before (cf. Butler 2003). If migrant women in the 1990s were constructed as a burden in the Swedish welfare state, migrant women in the new millennium were created as a *threat* to the wellbeing of the (welfare) state, and the assumed core values of Swedish society such as gender equality. However, migrant women were not only constructed as a threat. In the wake of a number of welfare reforms by the end of the 2000s, including tax deduction on household services, a rather different discourse also emerged. Closely connected to the increasing number of migrant women working within the household sector, they were additionally

3 There are however considerable variations between migrants' participation in the labour market, especially in relation to country of origin and to how long they have been in Sweden. Migrants from Latin America and the EU15 exhibit about the same employment rates as Swedish born citizens, while citizens from Asia and Africa have much lower employment rates than other groups. In 2012, unemployment among women born outside Sweden was 15 percent while only 6 percent of women born in Sweden were unemployed (Petersson 2015).

perceived as 'specifically suitable' care-workers. This development is explored in the last section of this chapter.

The analysis in this chapter is inspired by the 'what's the problem represented to be' approach, developed by Carol Bacchi (2009), especially the assumption that governments do not react to pre-existing assumed 'problems' – they are instead active in creating 'problems' of various kinds. The analysis builds primarily upon previous research, but also the examination of policy documents, mainly published as governmental commission reports. The chapter is explorative in nature, aiming to contribute to critical debates on the role of gender equality in the construction of the migrant as the Other – and ultimately, as the racialised Other. It is argued that different but complementary discursive constructions of migrant women have contributed to the development of contemporary contradictions within discourses on the Swedish gender equality policy regime.

The chapter is structured as follows: First, the early gender equality policy regime and its consequences for women in the family and the labour market are explored. The location of migrant women herein follows this presentation. Second, changes within the 1990s are highlighted and discussed with special focus on increasing unemployment and the emergence of migrant women as a burden to the welfare state. Finally, the limelight is placed upon the new millennium, in which continuously high unemployment figures are investigated, together with how increasing islamophobia, and the success of right wing xenophobic parties throughout Europe have contributed to construct migrant women as a threat to the Swedish nation.

The Swedish Gender Equality Regime

The establishment of public policies facilitating women to combine paid labour with family life are deeply embedded in the history of the Swedish welfare state. As a response to decreasing fertility rates and alarming poverty levels among families with children, a number of policy reforms were already enacted by the 1930s, such as the means-tested maternity leave, the introduction of free maternity and child welfare centres, as well as sexual education. A decade later in 1948, the universal childcare allowance was introduced, and maternity insurance became widespread in the 1950s (Lundqvist 2011).

All of these reforms were directed towards women as mothers. The 1960s however, marked the beginning of a new era: It was a time when traditional values and ideas surrounding the concept and social practice of the nuclear family were questioned and redefined in policymaking. New actors became involved in the growing debate on women's and men's roles in society, and the discourse of the 'gender equal family' emerged. Academic scholars in the field of so-called sex-role research argued that sex/gender and gender relations were socially constructed, and they strongly opposed any tendencies to confuse women's reproductive capacity with the care for children (Baude 1992; Dahlström et al. 1962; Liljeström 1978). In parallel, an increased labour market shortage, the demands from the nascent women's movement, and the emerging gender equality policy discourse in politics, all marked the way for the entrance of women into the labour market, as well as the expansion of childcare (Florin and Nilsson 2000).

To lower women's thresholds into the labour market, a series of political initiatives were implemented, including massive investments in public childcare, and the introduction of a gender-neutral parental insurance in 1974. Other elements included individual taxation (1971) and the legalisation of abortion (1975), crowned with the emergence of gender-equality policy (1978) as a political realm in itself. As a result, the number of women entering the labour force increased rapidly from around 30 percent of the total applicable female force in the beginning of the 1950s, to about 60 percent in 1970, and further to 82 percent in the 1980s (SOU 1984:31; SCB 2014). This trend continued until the early 1990s when about 83 percent of all women between 20 and 64 participated in paid labour (SCB 2014). The family thus, became an early public concern, with the individual was at the centre of reform efforts, rather than the (heterosexual) family as such (Lundqvist 2011; Nyberg 2012).

This development has come to be characterised as a transition from 'familisation' to 'de-familisation' (or 'individualisation'); that is, an evolution from a male-breadwinner family model to a policy that emphasises the right of all individuals to do paid work, while at the same time encouraging shared responsibility for the family in combination with publicly funded childcare: a 'dual earner/dual carer family model' (Daly 2011, Ellingsæter and Leira 2006; Leira 2002; Lewis 1992).

Interestingly, and of course rather disturbingly, the development presented above tended to exclude migrant women. Instead of being included in the political ambition of gender equality, migrant women became an invisible category due to the total neglect of their existence in the labour market and as individuals within the homes. This development is further explored in the next section in which the location of the migrant woman in the early Swedish model of gender equality will be returned to. Special emphasis is made on how migrant women have been constructed within the realm of labour market policies.

Subordinated Inclusion: Migrant Women as Invisible and as a Problem

In the context of a growing labour shortage, labour migration increased from the 1950s onwards[4] where not only men migrated to Sweden. Women from various parts of Europe also migrated during the 1950s and 1960s: many of them together with their families, others by themselves, resulting in high levels of employment for this particular group (Knocke 1986; Leiniö 1984; SOU 1997: 137). In contrast to women born in Sweden who, if employed, mainly worked in the public or service sectors, most migrant women were employed in the industrial sectors, such as textile and clothing production, but also in manufacturing and chemical industries (de los Reyes 1998; Knocke 1991). Additionally, in comparison to Swedish born women, the employment rate among migrant women was higher during the 1960s and the 1970s.

However, even if migrant women were highly active both in the migration process and in their labour market strategies, labour and migration policies coded the term immigrant (*invandrare)* as male; defined by state authorities as accompanying family members, as 'only adult males were counted in relation to Sweden's labour force needs' (SOU 1974: 53). Migrant women were thus located as an *invisible category* in labour market policy discourse (de los Reyes 1998). Their role as workers was obscured, while they simultaneously participated in the labour force (Ålund 1985; Knocke 2006).

This specific period of time may be conceptualised in terms of *subordinated inclusion*, grasping the establishment and development of what was emerging as a Swedish racialised working class (Mulinari and Neergaard 2004). While migrant women had access to formal citizenship rights, they were located in subordinated positions in all spheres of life (Ålund and Schierup 1991).

The location of migrant women in this first period, classified as the concept of subordinated inclusion, added to the analysis of understanding the exclusion of migrant women from the 'gender equal family': migrant women were indeed included in the labour market, but their autonomy never recognised. The definition of a migrant woman as a family member also excluded her from the 'gender equal family': she was in policy discourse never de-familised or individualised as in the construction of the Swedish born women.

---

4 It is important to note that in contrast to Germany, the 'guest worker system' was never introduced in Sweden, and the fundamental right for families to be together was taken for granted within Swedish migration policies. Women (even when they came with their husbands) were provided of their own legal status and work permit.

Migrant women were at the same time not only defined as a 'family member' and invisible as workers, they were also powerfully presented as different; represented as uneducated, religious and carriers of traditional family values. The construction of the migrant woman as *culturally different* can be found in a government commission report in 1979, investing the future immigration policies:

> The collision between on the one hand the immigrant woman's upbringing and background, and the norms and values of Swedish society on the other, make it very difficult for her to function as mother and wife. While she is tied to her own tradition and role as a woman, she is also asked to meet the change demands of her children's faces in school and through friends. Moreover, her husband demands her to maintain the permanence of traditional female roles (quoted in Knocke 1991: 3, authors' translation).

Note how she is constructed (despite her experience of migration and active labour market participation) as a passive object, acting upon external demands, from both her children and husband. Note also how the binary opposition between tradition and modernity locates her outside the realm of the gender equality discourse; not only does it obscure her skills as a worker, but also stigmatises her as a mother. The 'culturalisation' of migrant women was analysed by sociologist Aleksandra Ålund:

> Debates on immigrant women's problems however contain ideological undertones which do not benefit the women themselves. Immigrant women are gradually being lulled into picturing themselves as vulnerable, in need of help as undermined by their inferior position in the labour market, by their outmoded traditions, cultural heritage, husbands, large families, life-styles and values. In short they are developing a negative self-image. A wall of problem centred ideologies has been erected which prevents them from seeing themselves clearly from recognising not only their genuine limitations but also their opportunities and resources (Ålund 1991a: 48).

According to Ålund, these representations were created and reproduced within gender scholarship, which in turn over-focused on migrant women's patriarchal cultures, resulting in a marginalisation of their cultural skills to resist. She also argued for the need of a shift from:

> [...] stereotyped culturalist interpretations of subordination towards a more comprehensive recognition of their own historical experience and present situation. The meaning of a cultural background as a history and as a culture of rebellion ought to be included in Scandinavian feminist analysis (Ålund 1991a: 67).

To summarise, in a context in which family and gender equality policies emphasised the importance of placing the individual at the centre of reform, rather than the (heterosexual) family as such, migrant women were on the one hand made invisible as an employee, and located within the realm of the 'traditional' family, thereby constructed as problematic on the other, reinforcing the boundaries between the category of 'Swedish women' and that of migrant ones.

Unemployed, Sick and Burdensome: The Location of Migrant Women in the Neoliberal Era

The transformation of the Swedish welfare state during the 1990s is remarkable. In international comparison, the level of employment by the end of the 1980s was very high and the number of unemployed was historically low. This all changed rapidly over the coming years, and previous characteristics inscribed in the Swedish model such as the idea that public benefits should be instituted as a social rights to high-level benefits were abandoned[5].

In 1991, a centre-right wing government took power, (re)affirming neoliberal concepts such as 'freedom to choose' and 'flexibility' in the Swedish context (as opposed to the alleged rigidity of welfare service provision hitherto), most obvious in the provision of social services, for example the voucher system in schools and hospitals (Boréus 1994, 1997). At the same time, the centre-right wing government continued the hard currency policy, which was met with massive currency speculation at the beginning of 1992, resulting in a de facto 20 percent devaluation. When the hard currency policy failed and unemployment increased from 1.5 percent to 9 percent in just a few years, the government instead aimed at reducing the public deficit and lowering inflation. As a result, compensation rates and sickness, parental and unemployment insurance were reduced to 80 percent (from 90 percent) (Palme 2002)[6].

Cutbacks in the welfare provision system were accompanied by the introduction of a workfare ideology: a 'duty to work in return for benefits in the lowest tier of the income maintenance system' (Kildal 2001: 28) became a central ideology in labour market policy making.

In parallel to the cutbacks in the replacement levels, the dramatic development of the labour market also affected the 'dual-earner/dual-carer family model' (cf. Sainsbury 2000). For example, the increase in women's labour market participation was

---

5 This development had already started in the 1980s when the Social Democrats decided to leave the previous corporatist model and introduced the so-called 'third way model'.

6 For example, parental insurance was affected by changes in the health insurance system. The level of compensation was 90 percent between 1974 and 1995. The percentage was lowered however, just as in the case of unemployment insurance, to 80 percent in 1995, and – when the Social Democrats were in power – to 75 percent in 1996. It was restored to 80 percent in 1998, owing to the economic recovery (Duvander et al. 2015).

broken in the 1990s and changed into a rapid decrease in the female labour force, from about 85 percent in the early 1990s to 73.9 percent in 1998. Thus, differences in labour market participation between women and men, which had narrowed in the preceding decades, again increased. While men's unemployment stabilised around 1994, female unemployment continued to increase until 1997 as an effect of the gender-segregated labour market, where male-dominated sectors were hit before those dominated by women (Stanfors 2007: 82–83).

Interestingly, migrant women were affected before majority women. A telling example is the women from the former Yugoslavia. They had, in 1988, an unemployment rate of 0.8 percent. In 1992, before the refugees from the civil war were present in the labour market, unemployment rates within this group had increased to slightly more than 12 percent. The drastic deterioration of the labour situation can be explained by the fact that the recession first impacted industrial employment, and thus reinforced earlier processes of discrimination regarding migrant women's locations within the labour market. Migrant women had been concentrated in manufacturing jobs, which made them a particularly vulnerable group (Knocke 2006: 59–60).

The welfare systems were partly reset after the crisis ebbed and female labour market participation returned to pre-crisis levels. However, economic growth in the late 1990s did not improve the social and economic conditions of all groups. Instead, the marginalisation of a number of segments in the labour market continued, making the level of living considerably worse than that of others in society, both in terms of income and poverty levels (Hammarstedt 2008). Two groups were noted as particularly vulnerable: lone-parent families and citizens born outside Sweden, especially those born outside Europe. Among lone mothers and non-European migrants, unemployment rose by 56 percent and 39 percent respectively between 1992 and 1997 (Ds 2002: 82). Hence, the economic and political shift in the 1990s provided a new understanding of difference, towards a focus on it as a burden for the welfare state, and 'immigrant women' (*invandrarkvinnor*) were created as those with problematic levels of sick leave, often understood in terms of their culture and not related to difficult working conditions' (SOU 2005:56, cf. de los Reyes 1998; Knocke 1991).

In parallel to this development, conflicts over the meaning of culture and nationhood increased in policy debates, with larger groups of racialised citizens facing unemployment and discrimination in the labour market (Arai, Regner and Schröder 1999). To this analysis, the emergence of the notion of *cultural distance* must be added. The concept was used both within the public debate and in research, suggesting that migrants (particularly migrants from outside Europe) were in need of the kind of social and cultural skills that the restructuring of the welfare state, as well as the alleged emergence of new forms of working place cultures, demanded (Mattsson 2005). This is articulated within one of the reports from the Committee of Immigration Policies from 1995:

> Just like demands on social competence, demands on language competence can of course function as a cover-up for discrimination. Increasing demands regarding social competence in today's corporations, i.e. despite if the employees are Swedish or immigrants, means that they must comply with the working culture and function as a team member. Knowledge about, and experience of, working within a Swedish environment can be considered to be an important competence. It means that an employer can balance objective aspects when hiring new employees, disqualifying cultural difference (SOU 1995: 23, authors' translation).

The concept of *cultural distance* marginalised the sociological explanations that emphasised ethnic discrimination in the labour market. Instead, the concept re-inscribed and explained processes of exclusion (and discrimination) through migrant's lack of cultural and social skills. Aleksandra Ålund and Carl-Ulrik Schierup (1991: 3) use the term prescribed multiculturalism to grasp these policies, or rather the tensions of these multicultural policies based in the denial of power relations between different citizens' groups, often reinforcing fixed and essentialist notions of culture.

To this end, another powerful discourse emerged, stating that the (previous) paternalistic welfare state – in which migrants were conceptualised as victims – destroyed the creative capacity of migrants through 'clientelistic' forms that not only passivised them, but did not respect their cultures, particularly their desire to care for their children and elders (Johansson and Molina 2002).

The solution presented – to the crisis of the welfare state and to migrants' rising unemployment levels – was the creation of migrants' small businesses, or what has been conceptualised as the 'ethnic economy'. Thus, to overcome unemployment, the migrant was to become an entrepreneur. Zoran Slavnic (2013) argues that immigrants' small businesses have been expected both to reduce unemployment among immigrants and to help integrate them into Swedish society in general. The argument that discrimination was outside the diverse policies targeting migrants as entrepreneurs is also present in Oscar Pripp's (2001) study on migrants' efforts to establish a business.

However, while the notion of 'migrant as entrepreneurs' is neutral, the subtext is coded as male; or rather, the point of departure for migrant entrepreneurs is often that of migrant families, one that obscures power relations among its members.

In her analysis of entrepreneurship for migrant women, Suzanne Mason (2003) describes the projects she has studied (a Turkish restaurant and a catering firm) as initiated from the top-down and excluding and marginalising migrant women's professional skills. She argues that women with very different professional and educational backgrounds are brought together to start cooperatives, suggesting that state policies are based on a narrow definition of migrant women's skills towards what is historically coded female work (cleaning, cooking, caring).

Once again, labour market policies introduce or reinforce patriarchal relations within migrant communities, and migrant women are left outside gender equality policies. In a context of welfare retrenchment, unemployment and increasing social polarisation, the location of migrant women thus changed, and the representation of them as marginal, different and in need of education was complemented with that of them as burdensome, with lasting sick leave periods. Hence, the economic and political shift in the 1990s provided a new understanding of difference, towards a focus on difference as a burden for the welfare state.

A Threat to the Nation? The Location of the Category of Migrant Woman in the Securitisation State

> Those who gain representation, especially self-representation, have a better chance of being humanized, and those who have no chance to represent themselves run a greater risk of being treated as less human, regarded as less human, or indeed, not regarded at all (Butler 2003: 141).

In Judith Butler's appraisal of how representations of the Other have been dislocated and transformed in post-9/11 America, she identifies a paradox in the construction of who is being treated as human, or, regarded as less human. Through the lens of Emmanuel Levinas' concept of the 'face', she argues that humanisation is constructed through the personification of the Other, but at the same time, dehumanisation processes occur through representations of the 'evil face', illustrated by for example media's coverage of the enemies of the US such as Saddam Hussein and Yaser Arafat (Butler 2003).

In the Swedish context, the development in the aftermath of 9/11 has, as elsewhere, changed the location of migrant women. The paradox developed in Butler's analysis can be used to explore how migrant women on the one hand are represented primarily as according to their position in the labour market, portrayed as 'specifically suited' to do care work, but also as traditional and (still) affixed in patriarchal family patterns, and therefore potentially dangerous, or even a threat, to an alleged 'Swedish gender equality culture'.

The discussion will begin by describing the economic and social conditions of the new millennium. The economy for many families with two incomes improved rapidly in the beginning of the 2000s, and disposable income increased for two-parent families with children. Employment rates also improved, cutbacks in the welfare system were to a certain degree reversed, and several family-policy reforms were introduced, such as a maximum fee for childcare enabling families with children to improve their living standard (Försäkringskassan 2009).

Even if the situation among migrant men and women did not improve as rapidly as for those Swedish born, employment rates did increase slowly during the new millennium. However, the period reveals a shift in the location of where migrant women and their daughters worked: as still employed in precarious branches, but also in the expanding forms of domestic/household services (Gavanas and Calleman 2013); a growing sector especially after the 2006 election.

The Social Democratic government fared badly in the 2006 election, and a centre-right wing government gained power, under the name of *Alliansen*. The Alliance government campaigned on the basis of the 'work line' – a classical social democratic theme, reinvented by the centre-right parties in the mid-2000s. The most significant feature of the work line, as championed by the Alliance government, was the supply-push measures of labour market policy, to reduce marginalisation (*utanförskap*), as well as to facilitate and enhance labour market participation, also for groups with weak or uneven interaction with the labour market. Family policy was also drawn into this reinvention of the work line, and again, after a long interlude of relative political independence, gender equality was subsumed under labour market policy in a very clear way.

In addition to a number of family policy reforms such as the gender equality bonus and the (re)introduction of the cash-for-care scheme, the Alliance government also introduced a strategy to combat gender inequities in the labour market. The aim of this strategy was to facilitate female self-employment, which in turn was supposed to propel gender equality in the private sector. A number of measures were enacted, including the cancellation of wealth taxation, reduced corporate taxation, lowered payroll taxes *and* the tax deduction for household services:

> The tax deduction for household work will lead to more equal conditions for women and men to combine family life and working life. Women reduce their working hours to do household work to a greater extent than men. If women are given better possibilities to reallocate their time from household work to market-based work, their likelihood of earning higher incomes and participating on the labour market on equal terms will increase (Skr. 2008/08: 39).

The introduction of tax deduction for household services has resulted in a growing sector for migrant women who do household work in the homes of Swedish born families. Anna Gavanas (2013) asserts that in addition to the tax deduction, the Swedish market for domestic service is expanding as a result of welfare state cutbacks, as well as the privatisation of public care, deregulation, internationalisation and the flexibility of labour markets; in turn creating precarious conditions for migrant women employed as domestic workers. This discourse follows according to Emilia Roig's (2014) analysis of the German situation in relation to European Commission directives, where besides job creation and responding to care needs, the aim is at 'freeing' the productive potential of the more highly skilled women.

Through the practices of household services, difference is thus understood via assumed positive qualities of migrant women as care workers (Gavanas and Calleman 2013). However, at the same time, difference in the new millennium is also read as a threat to the wellbeing of the welfare state and the core values of the Swedish society. Among other things, the emergence of the notion of 'dangerous neighbourhoods' has triggered new debates and practices, among others increasing policing (Ericsson, Molina and Ristilammi 2002; Brune 2004; Razack 2004).

One of the spaces through which the category of migrant women was translated into a field of struggle between the civilised Sweden and the backward others was the public debate around demands for the prohibition of the hijab as a symbol of women's subordination. Carina Listerborn (2015) uses the notion of an economy of hate to grasp the experience of everyday violence for the Muslim women who wear the hijab. Hanna Wikström (2007) arrives to similar conclusions suggesting that the location of migrant families is highly restrained by hegemonic discourses that link 'Swedishness' to modernity and democracy.

The argument that migrant cultures were not only traditional and backwards, but also dangerous was early on articulated in relation to what was popularly termed 'honour killing'. When so called 'honour-related violence' became the subject of heated debates in the early and mid-2000s, the Social Democratic Minister of Gender Equality, Margareta Winberg, argued that this violence could only be halted if men from cultures accepting this type of violence learned to respect the ruling gender equality ideals in Sweden (Lundqvist 2011).

In their analysis, Linnea Littmann and Jenny Höglund (2012) demonstrate how political discourse on violence against women both include migrant women through the category of women, but also exclude them through an understanding violence against Swedish women as structural, and a conceptualisation of violence against migrant women as cultural. The culturalist discourse, these scholars argue, constructs 'migrants' as an undifferentiated whole in terms of assumed uniform 'cultural' traits that distinguish the 'west' from the 'rest', and 'them' from 'us'. These policies not only increase the criminalisation of racialised men, but silence issues of poverty, institutional racism and exclusion.

When the discourses of migration, as the major cause of social problems and a threat to the wellbeing of European citizens, shift from the margins to mainstream public discourse, and when the discourses on migrant families as culturally different are transformed into discourses on migrant cultures as a threat, migration becomes a security issue. This is followed by the increase of genetic testing for defining family ties (Ilpo 2014) and the use of bon-scanning for documenting the age of undocumented children and adolescents[7]. This is a development now being witnessed, too in the context of the Swedish welfare state.

When individual traits have been taken away, the representation of migrant women as a culturally threating collective clearly transforms individuals into a de-personalised mass, and, following Butler (2003), even can be read as the dehumanised process of becoming an 'evil face'. How to change this development is one of the most important social questions of today.

Concluding Remarks

In this chapter it has been argued that despite gender equality intentions aiming to decrease inequalities between women and men in the home and at work, policies and discourses tend to reinforce group inequalities within and among the category of women.

While difference has been fundamental in the inscription of the category of migrant women within welfare policies, the meaning of difference has changed in the three periods discussed in this chapter. In the first one, within a regime of social democratic subordinated inclusion, migrant women were made *invisible* as workers and understood as *problematic,* in need of education and support within the sphere of the family. While Swedish gender equality policies developed from the understanding that women's subordinated positions in the home and labour market were effects of structural processes, migrant woman's societal position was thus explained through her own deficiencies located in her traditionalist culture. Consequently, migrant women were conceptualised and analysed as already being different in the early stage of the gender equality policy regime.

7 For a criticism see: http://www.lakartidningen.se/Klinik-och-vetenskap/Kommentar/2015/10/Svart-att-sakert-faststalla-alder-hos-asylsokande-barn/ (Accessed August 4, 2016).

In the second period, both unemployment and the levels of sick leave among migrant women increased rapidly. This development was a consequence of the economic crisis, yet too the ethnically segregated labour market in which migrant women had traditionally been employed in manufacturing jobs, and at the time faced severe physical injuries. Nevertheless, instead of interpreting migrant women's situation as a result of poor working conditions, their situation was understood in terms of their culture. In this context, the concept of *cultural distance* was used in policy documents to explain increasing unemployment and sick leave among migrant women, especially by emphasising migrant's lack of social and cultural skills. To overcome such difficulties, migrant women were encouraged to become entrepreneurs, especially focussing on traditionally female tasks such as cooking and cleaning. During this period, migrant women were again marginalised in relation to the gender equality regime: the analysis of her as culturally different (as a worker and as a mother) and a burden (especially in the labour market) to the welfare state placed her outside the realm of the 'dual-earner – dual-carer family model'.

The development after 9/11 changed the location of migrant women once again. Even if she was still portrayed as traditional, and fixed in patriarchal family patterns, her position was now seen as a potential threat to the Swedish gender equality regime. This was especially the case when debates on so-called 'honour killings' emerged in the early 2000s. At the same time, it is important to highlight the fact that migrant women's position in the labour market also changed, which in turn, affected their location. She (and now her daughters) was still employed in precarious branches, but in the aftermath of the tax-deduction introduction on domestic/household services, the expansion of migrant women employed as such increased rapidly, resulting in the construction of migrant women as particularly suited to perform domestic work. Thus, migrant women were created as a cultural threat to core Swedish values and social cohesion, but also as specifically suited care-givers, embodying assumed positive qualities as care–workers. This duality exposes paradoxes of the Swedish gender equality policy regime: gender equality policies are built upon ideals on a de-familised (or individualised) family model, including the right of all adults to paid work and to share caring responsibilities within the family. However, as this chapter has shown, the construction of migrant women as invisible, burdensome or threatening makes it difficult to include them in the alleged Swedish family model. As invisible, she was never individualised; as a burden, she never belonged to the same cultural practice as 'Swedish women'; and as a threat, but potentially a well-suited domestic worker, she became object of the anti-thesis of the gender equality regime – she was locked into traditional familial values, embodying the skills of the domestic worker.

The location of migrant women in the Swedish welfare state is, on that background, a product of discursive de-personification. Through successive historical periods, their location has shifted from being invisible, through time becoming represented as an assumed cultural collective – in terms of cultural difference – as a burden, as a threat to the nation, and finally, as an option for the 're-traditionalisation' of gender with migrant women as care-workers. However, while there is no doubt that emerging forms of racism will blame them for the changing conditions of the Swedish welfare state, it is clear that on-going activities and struggles for social rights among various social movements across the country, will create spaces of conviviality, challenging essentialist understanding of ethnic and national belonging.

References

Arai, M., Regner, H. and Schröder, L. 1999. 'Är arbetsmarknaden öppen för alla?', Appendix 6 till *Långtidsutredningen 1999/2000*, SOU 2000: 7. Stockholm: Fritzes.

Ålund, A. 1985. *Skyddsmurar; Etnicitet och klass i invandrarsammanhang*. Stockholm: Liber.

Ålund, A. 1991a. 'The power of definition.' In Ålund, Aleksandra and Carl-Ulrik Schierup (eds.) *Paradoxes of Multiculturalism. Essays on Swedish Society*. Aldershot: Avebury, 47–69.

Ålund, A. 1991b. *Lilla Juga; Etnicitet, familj och kvinnliga nätverk*. Stockholm: Carlssons.

Ålund, A. 1999. 'Feminism, Multiculturalism, Essentialism.' In Nira Yuval-Davis and Pnina Werbner (eds.) *Women, Citizenship and Difference*. London: Zed Books, 147–161.

Ålund, A. and Schierup, C.U. 1991. *Paradoxes of Multiculturalism. Essays on Swedish Society*. Aldershot: Avebury.

Bacchi, C. L. 2009. *Analysing Policy. What's the problem represented to be?* Pearson: French Forest.

Baude, A. (ed.) 1992. *Visionen om jämställdhet*. Stockholm: SNS förlag.

Boréus, K. 1994. *Högervåg. Nyliberalismen och kampen om språket i svensk debatt 1969–1989*. Stockholm: Tidens förlag.

Boréus, K. 1997. 'The shift to the right: Neo-liberalism in argumentation and language in the Swedish public debate since 1969.' *European Journal of Political Research* 31/3, 257–286.

Brune, Y. 2004. *Nyheter från gränsen – tre studier i nyhetsjournalistik om 'invandrare', flyktingar och rasistiskt våld*. Göteborg: Göteborg Universitet.

Butler, J. 2003. *Precarious Lives. The Powers of Mourning and Violence*. London: Verso.

Dahl, U. 2004. *Progressive Women, Traditional Men: The Politics of 'Knowledge' and Gendered Stories of 'Development' in the Northern Periphery of the EU*. PhD diss., University of California, Santa Cruz.

Dahlström, E, Brun-Gullbrandsen, Dahlström, G., Holter, H., Thyberg, S., Tille, P-O. 1962. *Kvinnors liv och arbete: Svenska och norska studier av ett aktuellt samhällsproblem*. Stockholm: Prisma.

Daly, M. 2011. 'What Adult Worker Model? A Critical Look at Recent Social Policy Reform in Europe from a Gender and Family Perspective.' *Social Politics* 18/1, 1–23.

de los Reyes, P. 1998. 'I skärningspunkten mellan genus och etnicitet. Ett ekonomiskt historiskt perspektiv på invandrarkvinnor i svenskt arbetsliv.' *Arbetsmarknad & Arbetsliv*, 4/1, 13–31.

de los Reyes, P. 2000. 'Folkhemmets Paradoxer. Genus och etnicitet i den svenska modellen', *Kvinnovetenskaplig Tidskrift*, (2): 27–46.

Ds 2002. *Welfare in Sweden: The Balance Sheet for the 1990s*. Ds 2002: 32. Stockholm: Socialdepartementet.

Duvander, A-Z., Ferrarini, T and Johansson, M. 2015. *Familjepolitik för alla? En ESO-rapport om föräldrapenning och jämställdhet*. Stockholm: Finansdepartementet.

Ellingsæter, A-L. and Leira, A. 2006. *Politicizing Parenthood in Scandinavia*. Bristol: Policy Press.

Ericsson, U., Molina, I. and Ristilammi, P.M. 2002. *Miljonprogram och media. Föreställningar om människor och förorter*. Stockholm: Riksantikvarieämbetet & Integrationsverket.

Florin, C. and Nilsson, B. (eds.) 2000. Någonting som liknar en oblodig revolution. jämställdhetens politisering under 1960- och 1970-talen. Umeå: Umeå University.

Försäkringskassan 2009. *Ensamstående föräldrars ekonomiska situation*. Socialförsäkringsrapport 2009:4. Stockholm: Försäkringskassan.

Gavanas, A. 2013. 'Gender, Culture and Work in Global Cities.' *Women's Studies International Forum* 36, 54–64.

Gavanas, A. and Callemann, C. (eds.) 2013. *Rena hem på smutsiga villkor? Hushållstjänster, migration och globalisering*. Göteborg: Makadam.

Hammarstedt, M. 2008. 'Assimilation and participation in social assistance among immigrants.' *International Journal of Social Welfare* 18/1, 85–94.

Hirdman, Y. 1989. *Med kluven tunga. LO och genusordningen*. Stockholm: Atlas.

Ilpo, H. 2014. 'Biological citizenship across the borders: politics of DNA profiling for family reunification.' *Scandinavian Journal of Social Theory* 15/3, 343–360.

Johansson, S. and Molina, I. 2002. 'Kön och ras i rumsliga identitetskonstruktioner.' In de los Reyes, Paulina, Irene Molina and Diana Mulinari (eds) *Maktens (o) lika förklädnader. Kön, klass & etnicitet i det postkoloniala Sverige*. Stockholm: Arbetslivsinstitutet.

Kildal, N. 2001. *Workfare Tendencies in Scandinavian Welfare Policies*. Geneva: ILO.

Knocke, W. 1986. *Invandrade kvinnor i lönearbete och fack. En studie om kvinnor från fyra länder inom Kommunal- och Fabriksarbetareförbundets avtalsområde*. Stockholm: Arbetslivscentrum.

Knocke, W. 1991. 'Invandrade kvinnor – vad är 'problemet'?' *Kvinnovetenskaplig tidskrift* 3, 4–15.

Knocke, W. 2006. 'Den strukturella diskrimineringens försåtlighet – Ett historiskt och nutida perspektiv.' In SOU *På tröskeln till lönearbete,* SOU 2006:60. Stockholm: Kulturdepartementet.

Leiniö, T-L. 1984. 'Inte lika men jämlika? Om finländska invandrares levnadsförhållanden enligt Levnadsnivåundersökningarna 1968, 1974 och 1981.' Report from *Levnadsnivåundersökningen* 1981: 6. Stockholm: Institutet för social forskning.

Leira, A. 2002. *Working Parents and the Welfare State. Family Change and Policy Reform in Scandinavia*. Cambridge: Cambridge University Press.

Lewis, J. 1992. 'Gender and the Development of Welfare regimes.' *Journal of European Social Policy* 2/3, 159–73.

Lewis, J. 1997. 'Gender and Welfare Regimes. Further Thoughts.' *Social Politics* 4/2, 160–177.

Liljeström, R. 1978. 'Sweden.' In Kamerman, Sheila B. and Kahn, Alfred J. (eds.) *Family Policy: Government and Families in Fourteen Countries*, New York: Columbia University Press.

Listerborn, C. 2015. 'Geographies of the veil: Violent encounters in urban public spaces in Malmö, Sweden.' *Social and Cultural Geography* 16/1, 95–115.

Littmann, L. and Höglund, J. 2012. *Different Strokes for Different Folks: An intersectional analysis of the political discourse concerning migrant women exposed to domestic violence in Sweden*. Department of Sociology: Stockholm.

Lundqvist, Å. 2011. *Family Policy Paradoxes. Gender Equality and Labour Market Regulation in Sweden 1930–2010*. Bristol: Policy Press.

Martinsson, L. 2000. 'Annorlundahet som fetisch.' In Hagström, Ylva (ed.) *Porträtt utan ram. Kön och sexualitet bortom strukturalismen*. Lund: Studentlitteratur.

Mason, S. 2003. 'Self-employment policies from the perspective of citizenship, gender, and ethnicity.' *International Review of Sociology – Revue Internationale de Sociologie* 13/1, 219–234.'

Mattsson, K. 2005. 'Diskrimineringens andra ansikte – svenskhet och "det vita västerländska".' In de los Reyes, Paulina and Masoud Khamali (eds.) *Bortom Vi och Dom. Teoretiska reflektioner om makt, integration och strukturell diskriminering*, SOU 2005: 41. Stockholm: Fritzes, 139–159.

Melby, K., Ravn, A.-B. and Wetterberg, C.C. (eds.) 2008. *Gender Equality and Welfare Politics in Scandinavia: The Limits of Political Ambition?* Bristol: Policy Press.

Mulinari, D. 2008. 'Women friendly? Understanding gendered racism in Sweden.' In Melby, Kari, Anna-Birte Ravn and Christina Carlsson Wetterberg (eds.) *Gender Equality and Welfare Politics in Scandinavia: The Limits of Political Ambition?* Bristol: Policy Press, 167–183.

Mulinari, D. and Neergaard, A. 2004. *Den nya svenska arbetarklassen*. Umeå: Boréa.

Nyberg, A. 2012. 'Gender Equality Policy in Sweden: 1970s–2010s.' *Nordic Journal of Working Life Studies* 2/4, 67–84.

Olsson, A. 2014. 'Arbetslivets villkorade jämställdhet: Varför jämställdhetsarbete och intersektionalitet hör ihop.' In de los Reyes, Paulina. 2014. 'Introduktion.' In SOU, *Inte bara jämställdhet. Intersektionella perspektiv på hinder och möjligheter i arbetslivet*. SOU: 2014: 34. Stockholm: Fritzes.

Palme, J. 2002. *Welfare in Sweden: The balance sheet for the 1990s*. Stockholm: Socialdepartementet.

Petersson, S. 2015. *Utrikes födda på arbetsmarknaden. En forskningsöversikt*. Stockholm: Regeringskansliet.

Pripp, O. 2001. *Företagande i minoritet – Om etnicitet, strategier och resurser bland assyrier och syrianer i Södertälje*. Stockholm: Mångkulturellt Centrum.

Razack, S. 2004. 'Imperilled Muslim Women. Dangerous Muslim men and Civilised Europeans Legal and Social Responses to Forced Marriages.' *Feminist Legal Studies* 12/2, 129–174.

Roig, E. 2014. *Care Crisis: Racialised Women at the Crossroads of Migration, Labour Market and Family Policies*. Berlin: Heinrich-Böll-Stiftung.

Sainsbury, D. 2000. 'Välfärdsutvecklingen för kvinnor och män på 1990-talet.' In Bergmark, Åke (ed.) *Välfärd och försörjning*, SOU 2000:40. Stockholm: Fritzes, 87–128.

SCB (Statistics Sweden). 2014. *På tal om kvinnor och män. Lathund om jämställdhet 2014*. SCB: Örebro.

Skr. 2009. *En jämställd arbetsmarknad – regeringens strategi för jämställdhet på arbetsmarknaden och i näringslivet*. Skr. 2008/09:198. Stockholm: Näringsdepartementet.

Slavnic, Z. 2013. 'Immigrant Small Business in Sweden: A Critical Review of a Research Field.' *Journal of Business Administration Research* 2/1, 29–42.

SOU 1974. *Invandrarna och minoriteterna*. SOU 1974: 69. Stockholm: Fritzes.

SOU 1982. *Förvärvsarbete och föräldraskap. Åtgärdsförslag från jämställdhetskommittén. Betänkande avgivet av Jämställdhetskommittén*. SOU 1982:18. Stockholm: Fritzes.

SOU 1984. *Arbetsmarknadspolitik under omprövning. Betänkande av delegationen för arbetsmarknadspolitisk forskning*. SOU 1984: 31. Stockholm: Fritzes.

SOU 1995. *Delbetänkande av Invandrarpolitiska kommittén*. SOU 1995: 76. Stockholm: Fritzes.

SOU 1996. *Sver§ige, framtiden och mångfalden: slutbetänkande från Invandrarpolitiska kommittén*. SOU 1996:55. Stockholm: Fritzes.

SOU 1997. *Glastak och glasväggar. Den könssegregerade arbetsmarknaden*. SOU 1997: 137. Stockholm: Fritzes.

SOU 2005. *Det blågula glashuset. Strukturell diskriminering i Sverige*. SOU 2005:56. Stockholm: Fritzes.

Squires, J. 2007. *The New Politics of Gender Equality*. Basingstoke: Palgrave Macmillan.

Stanfors, M. 2007. *Mellan arbete och familj: Ett dilemma för kvinnor i Sverige. 1900–2000*. Stockholm: SNS.

Widerberg, K. 1986. 'Har kvinnoforskning med jämställdhetspolitik att göra?' *Kvinnovetenskaplig tidskrift* 6/3, 36–47.

Wikström, H. 2007. *(Im)possible Positions. Families from Iran & Postcolonial Reflections*. PhD diss., Göteborg University, Department of Social Work.

PART II: NEOLIBERAL REIMAGINEERING

Viktor Vesterberg

5. Rationalities of Exclusionary Inclusion: Constructing Others while Combating Social Exclusion

Abstract: This chapter analyzes labour market projects targeting unemployed migrants in Sweden. The goal of these projects is to increase employability and generate social inclusion among the targeted populations. The results of the chapter reveal a rationality that constructs exclusion of the targeted groups as essential for working with social inclusion – a rationality of *exclusionary inclusion*.

Introduction

The twin concepts of social exclusion and social inclusion are pivotal in the political discourse about the labour market and migrant-integration policies in the European Union (EU) as well as in Sweden (Schierup, Krifors and Slavnic 2015). In Swedish politics, the inclusion of migrants has, since 2010 when the Swedish Public Employment Service took responsibility for integration politics, been more tightly tied to participation in the labour market (Larsson 2015). From an EU perspective, social inclusion generally entails making citizens economically self-sufficient by preparing the populations for participation in the labour market (de la Porte and Jacobsson 2012). The European Commission's recommendation (2008: 3) regarding the social inclusion of excluded people explicitly states that national inclusion strategies should 'address the needs of people excluded from the labour market [...] and enhance their employability'. Further, the Commission prescribes

> [...] active and preventive labour market measures, including tailored, personalized, responsive services and support involving early identification of needs, job-search assistance, guidance and training, and motivation to seek a job actively (European Commission 2008: 3).

This chapter examines labour market projects co-financed by the European Social Fund (ESF), which target unemployed migrants in Sweden.[1] These projects are

1 The analyzed projects were active during the programme period 2007–2013. During this programme period the ESF in Sweden co-financed 2 335 projects. The ESF's

relevant to study since the ESF seeks to finance 'innovative and experimental methods of working' with social inclusion and employability (Swedish ESF Council 2007).

Although the projects strive to create social inclusion of unemployed migrants, they seem to simultaneously construct the targeted subjects[2] through exclusionary discourses, identifying them as 'Others', and thus contributing to what I have chosen to call 'exclusionary inclusion'.

The terminology of exclusionary inclusion has similarities to Giorgio Agamben's (1998) discussion about *Homo Sacer*, a specific subject trapped in a paradoxical state of *inclusionary exclusion* and *exclusionary inclusion.* Agamben argued that a fundamental conceptual divide in Western politics is that of 'the political existence' (bios) and 'bare life' (zoe), or in other terms between exclusion and inclusion. In contemporary Western politics, the boundaries of inclusion and exclusion are becoming increasingly blurred, not least exemplified by the figure of 'the refugee'. Elaborating on Agamben's thoughts, Bülent Diken argues that

> [...] an exclusionary inclusion politicizes the subject, in our case the refugee. Thus, every time the refugee is 'excluded' we should be looking for the inclusive gesture that follows it, which is part and parcel of the social bond between 'us' and 'them' (2004: 85).

When analyzing a specific case I will in the following apply this understanding to illustrate how rationalities of exclusionary inclusion operate when targeting unemployed migrants. Rationalities of exclusionary inclusion are at play when a group or a subject targeted by inclusion measures must first be made *includable* by being positioned as excluded and constructed as deviant. This rationality – this specific way of understanding and governing – does not stand unchallenged, but is repeatedly contested by those who participate in the projects.

The aim of this chapter is to demonstrate dualities of contemporary practices of inclusion and employability through rationalities of exclusion of unemployed migrants in Sweden. The governing of unemployed migrants take place through the 'games of truth' played by project employees and by the targeted subjects (i.e.,

---

budget for the whole of the EU was approximately SEK 750 billions, of which the ESF in Sweden was allocated SEK 6.2 billions. The ESF projects in Sweden had approximately 439 000 participants during this programme period (Swedish ESF Council, 2014). In relation to the overall public spending on measures of integration and labour market politics in Sweden, which amounted to approximately SEK 85 billion in 2015 (Ministry of Employment, 2015), the ESF-funded projects only represented a small part.

2 The subject position that I refer to as *targeted groups*, *targeted subjects*, or *participants* comprises the unemployed migrants who are the target of each project's activities. I use *employees* to refer to the staff of professionals tasked with educating the unemployed migrants who participate in the projects.

the project participants); games in which exclusionary discourses of inclusion and employability are constructed as well as contested. In this study, I pose the following analytical questions: How is exclusion produced when one seeks to create social inclusion through enhanced employability? What rationalities and truths underlie the practices of exclusionary inclusion? What opposition to dominant discourses on employability can be found in the practices that seek to create social inclusion? The dominant discourses are never fixed; there are always alternative ways of thinking about inclusion and subjectivities among both the targeted migrants and the employees engaged in practices of migrant inclusion (cf. Cruikshank, 1999).

Although great efforts have been made to facilitate social inclusion in the Swedish labour market, an ethnicised social exclusion still poses a tangible social and political problem. Previous research on ESF projects targeting unemployed migrants (Vesterberg 2013, 2015) has indicated a rationality that links the inclusive and empowering ambitions of the projects to the exclusionary ethnicisation of migrants as culturally Others. This rationality produces ethnic differentiation and builds on exclusion as a prerequisite for inclusionary work (cf. Tesfahuney and Grip 2007). Such construction of subjectivities, manifest power relationships within practices for inclusion.

As will be shown, initiatives that target migrants are inevitably embedded in powerful historical discourses, ethnicising the targeted groups and producing Otherness (Said 1978). These discourses remain prevalent and affect the social exclusion and inclusion of migrants.

Various social problems are constructed as being related to particular target groups. Many groups, apart from migrants, are constructed as deviant. For instance, criminal offenders are targeted by techniques of moral engineering and responsibilization, which is meant to facilitate their adaptation to societal normality (Kemshall 2002). The poor constitute another targeted group to be disciplined into normality in neoliberal regimes (Soss, Fording and Schram 2011). Mikael Holmqvist (2009) has shown how impaired people are rehabilitated to normality through labour market programmes, which involve stigmatized work tasks. Unemployed youth, dropouts, and at-risk youngsters compose a group that is often targeted when the governing task is to 'civilize the rabble' (Kivinen and Rinne 1998; Kelly 2007). These heterogeneous groups exemplify what John Welshman (2006) refers to as the political problem posed by 'the unemployable'.

As a specific target group, migrants have been persistently problematized as being in need of certain interventions and specific measures for normalization (Anderson 2013; Inda 2006). The projects for inclusion analyzed in this chapter illustrate how long-term unemployed migrants become a target for practices of normalization (Wright Nielsen 2015). These practices of normalization – what they do, what they create, how they include and exclude, and how they might be contested – need to be analyzed in their concrete forms (cf. Wright Nielsen 2015).

Analytical Perspective

The empirical scope of this chapter encompasses both the projects in which the inclusion of migrants is practised and ESF policies for social inclusion and employability. In order to shed light on the discourses and practices concerned with including migrants through employability measures, I use previous ethnographic fieldwork from labour market projects co-financed by the ESF to illustrate rationalities of exclusionary inclusion.[3] Interviews and ethnographic fieldwork can problematize rationalities of social inclusion in ways that empirical material which is focused solely on policies and documents cannot, since the opposition, counter-conduct, and struggles around 'truths' are not visible in such material. In the practices of labour market projects, counter-conduct becomes visible as a refusal to engage in, or as simple opposition to, the conduct encouraged by the project employees (cf. Foucault 2004b).

The analytical perspective applied here is inspired by the concept of governmentality, as elaborated by Michel Foucault and other scholars (Foucault 1991; Rose 1999; Dean 2010). This perspective views liberalism as a political rationality and an art of government that seeks to conduct the conduct of the governed, in contrast to classic political philosophy, which focuses on a coherent power emanating from the state. In this chapter, *rationality* refers to more or less calculative ways of governing that involve certain techniques for achieving what is the goal of governing (Rose 1999). Nikolas Rose (1999) further argues that governing always operates according to certain rationalities, which seek to construct specific ways of understanding the task at hand. Mitchell Dean (2010) discusses the rationalities of governing in relation to specific forms of truth, which seek to render particular problems and issues governable.

---

3 I conducted the fieldwork in 2009 and 2010. It consisted of interviews with unemployed people participating in labour market projects and with staff working on those projects, as well as participant observations in several ESF projects. The ethnographic fieldwork was carried out with the aim of observing the practices of the ESF projects and of interviewing project participants and employees in order to compile detailed descriptions of everyday life and practices.

In governmentality studies, the focus has often been on neoliberalism and/or on advanced liberal governing[4] which encompass various rationalities and techniques that are crucial components in the practices of normalization. Thus, the focus is on the modes of regulation and governing activities directed at fostering employable and includable subjects (Miller and Rose 2008). When analyzing practices of social inclusion from a governmentality perspective, the focus is how the will to include delineates both what is 'normal' and what falls outside that category ... [of] what is excluded (Popkewitz and Lindblad 2000). Thus, projects that seek to foster social inclusion are analyzed as practices of normalizing the unemployed migrants who are constructed as deviant and excluded – as a kind of governmentality of normalization.

As Dean (2010: 195) argues, the whole population is the primary object of government, but there are always 'sub-populations to be targeted', and specific populations are constructed as requiring particular interventions. This is precisely what is being done in labour market projects, which target unemployed people with foreign backgrounds – a segment of the population is pinpointed, problematized, and targeted by governing techniques of inclusion and normalization.

Anne Schneider and Helen Ingram (1993) argue for the importance of analyzing the construction of target groups since different groups tend to be constructed in different ways, whereas some are portrayed more positively than others are. Whether a specific group is constructed as hard working and deserving, or lazy and unmotivated, affects how problems are associated with the group as well as how the policies and practices are received by the targeted group itself. This is important since policy constructs the problems to be solved, as well as suitable ways of solving problems associated with specific groups. As Schneider and Ingram (1993) argue, the actual construction of the target groups is an empirical issue, which I analyze through both policy discourse and ethnographic empirical material.

One crucial aspect of making specific populations governable is to define and name the groups that are to be governed (Gordon 1980). Rendering specific segments of the population governable requires that they first be known, named, and classified – a rationality deployed by the ESF when it finances projects that specifically target 'unemployed people with a foreign background'. Thus, unemployed migrants tend to be constructed as in need of some sort of intervention and transformation if they are to become well-adapted subjects in their 'new homes'.

4 The concepts of *neoliberalism* and *advanced liberal governing* are used interchangeably in this chapter. For a discussion of the relationship between the two concepts, see for instance Rose (1996).

Following this logic, advanced liberal societies, such as contemporary Sweden, are in need of what one might call 'advanced liberal subjects' (Vesterberg 2013) who align themselves with the prevailing norms of Western advanced liberal governing. According to Rose (1999), a society that is governed through advanced liberal rationalities has economic growth as its main organizing principle, and is characterized by competition, entrepreneurship, and a will to foster human behaviour that fits the norms of a market economy. Thus, the advanced liberal subject meets these normative standards and thrives in marketized discourses, which are characterized by competition and entrepreneurial spirit.

Further, an analysis of advanced liberal governing can focus on a broad range of practices that seek to direct the conduct of those targeted by governmental aspirations (Rose 1996). Rose (1996) argues that advanced liberal governing depends on experts of different kinds, and that the authority of expertise arises from a claim to knowledge and truth. Thus, the ability to govern properly becomes related to knowledge in a specific area of a person's expertise. In the case of the ESF projects the experts focus on knowledge about how people can become employable and integrated into society. This is what Rose (1999: 92) has called an 'expertise of subjectivity'. In this regard, I view project employees as experts on employability and inclusion.

Studies of governmentality has been criticized for failing to analyze opposition and struggle in power relationships and in the governing of populations (Bröckling, Krasmann and Lemke 2011; Brady 2014). How opposition and counter-conduct is enacted can be difficult to make visible and analyzable in the documented, polished government programmes that are often analyzed in studies of governmentality. Since counter-conduct and opposition are often played out in spontaneous and unpredictable ways (Bröckling, Krasmann and Lemke 2011) it is easier to capture through ethnographic fieldwork. It is crucial to analyze opposition to government because opposition is always a part of any power relationship and shapes the ways in which power can be exercised (Foucault 1997a). One strategy for analyzing counter-conduct is to engage in an ethnographic approach that focuses on ways of thinking, acting, intervening, directing, and forming subjects, thus highlighting the dynamics of power struggles in the relationships between the ESF project employees and the targeted subjects (cf. Brady 2014). In this way, an ethnography of governmentalities blurs the boundaries between political programmes or schemes and the everyday practices of governing.

In the following, I discuss power struggles and counter-conduct in several labour market projects. Specific events in the projects are analysed as 'games of truth' (Foucault 1997b) – that is, as language games concerned with how labour market projects are understood and thought about. Foucault suggests that there is 'an entire ethnology of truth-telling to be pursued' (Foucault 2014: 14). Some truths have a broad consensus among those who are involved in the projects, while others are highly contested. Such 'games of truth' and dynamic power struggles of everyday life can be captured through ethnographic research that explores governing in practice (Brady 2014).

To summarise this analytical perspective, I analyze the rationalities of government and the governing techniques that seek to guide the conduct of the targeted subjects, as well as analyze how such rationalities are opposed.

Neoliberalism, the EU, and Sweden

Contemporary neoliberal politics targeting migrants contain traces of past practices embedded in rationalities, which seek to make the problem of unemployed migrants understandable in specific ways (cf. Dean 2010). The ESF projects are embedded in a long history and in a continuous discursive nexus of ethnicity and poverty-relief that to some extent has always had the goal of transforming and normalizing ethnicised Others (cf. Soss, Fording and Schram 2011; see also Chapter Three in this volume). In this way, the governmentality of normalization transforms ethnically problematized Others into subjects who are deemed employable according to contemporary Western norms (Vesterberg 2013). The global neoliberal economic development that facilitates the marketization, individualization, and responsibilization of citizens has also affected Sweden (See also Chapter Two in this volume). In recent years, the country's integration and migration politics have merged with neoliberal economic discourses, constructing migrants as a potential 'flexible resource for local and regional economic growth' (Schierup and Ålund 2011: 130).

Neoliberalism is one of the most popular concepts in contemporary social sciences, including governmentality studies (Brady 2014). Peo Hansen and Sandy B. Hager (2010: 62) argue that the EU is embedded in neoliberal politics, and that a neoliberal European 'policy consensus' was established during the 1980s and 1990s. Neoliberalism in the EU should not be understood as classic laissez-faire politics promoting 'less governing'; rather, it is a politics in which the state is a very active player and in which the main objective is to support the market economy (Foucault 2004a).

Neoliberalism saw an upswing in the 1980s and 1990s, but the rationalities of the market economy have guided the EU since its beginning, albeit embedded in different regimes. Until the 1980s, the EU was heavily influenced by social-democratic politics, which focused on European citizenship and substantial social rights (Hansen and Hager 2010). Nevertheless, Williams Walters and Jens Henrik

Haahr (2005) argue that the EU's social policy has always been embedded in a market rationality that promotes competition within an expanding market economy. The overarching goal of the ESF has always been to increase workers' mobility in order to strengthen the European market economy. An important step towards a neoliberal governmentality was taken with the launch of the single market project in 1985 (Hansen and Hager 2010).

According to Gøsta Esping-Andersen's (1990) typology of welfare state regimes, Sweden is traditionally described as a typical social-democratic welfare regime. Social-democratic hegemony started to shift towards a governmentality more influenced by neoliberalism in the 1980s, and the economic crisis that hit Sweden in the 1990s delivered what has been described as 'the final blow to Swedish welfare policies as we once knew them' (Larsson, Letell and Thörn 2012: 3). The categorization of Swedish welfare as the epitome of a classic, social-democratic welfare state has thus been challenged, not least owing to the influence of the EU and of general global trends of neoliberalism such as individualization, marketization, decentralization, and privatization (see further Chapter Two in this volume). As the ESF is one of the EU's main instruments for influencing national policy, with a focus on employment and reducing social exclusion (European Commission 2015), it is also an important way by which the EU's discourse on labour guides Swedish politics. Through the ESF, the EU's discourse, on social exclusion, has gained influence in Swedish labour market politics (Fauerbæk 2004) with strengthened neoliberal rationalities of flexibilization and individualization.

Creating Inclusion through Employability Measures

Policies governing the distribution of the ESF's billions of Euros across member states have long been devoted to the task of promoting social inclusion and social cohesion, as well as combating discrimination and social exclusion.

The ESF was initiated at the same time as the European Coal and Steel Community (ECSC) was founded in 1951. In its early years, the fund was primarily engaged in upgrading the skills of workers in core industries, such as coal and steel, and in increasing workers' mobility. Migrating workers could, for instance, receive language education subsidized by the fund. During the 1980s and 1990s, the fund focused to a large extent on adapting the labour force to new technology and high-skilled jobs in the service sector. In addition to these efforts, the fund has always, contends Julian Hale (2007: 3–4), 'looked out for the more vulnerable in society who may be socially excluded'. One group positioned as being at risk of exclusion has, he contends, been described as comprising 'people of different origins and ethnic groups'.

The ESF programme period 2000–2006, dubbed Equal, rested on the five goals of 'increasing employability, encouraging inclusive entrepreneurship, facilitating adaptability, promoting gender equality, and integrating asylum seekers' (European Commission 2011). The Lisbon Agenda and the European Employment Strategy (EES), both of which focused on increasing the population's employability, as well as on strengthening social cohesion and inclusion, inspired the subsequent programme period (2007–2013). In the policies for the current programme period (2014–2020), the focus on social inclusion has been strengthened further:

> [A]t least 20% of the Fund [is allocated] to social inclusion [so that] people in difficulties and those from disadvantaged groups will get more support to have the same opportunities as others to integrate into society (European Commission 2014).

All these initiatives have focused on migrants as a specific target group, constructing them as needing particular assistive measures. In ESF policy, one prominent approach for including migrants is to focus on increasing their employability. Thus, there is a rationality involving certain techniques and specific ways of understanding the task at hand (Rose 1999) that links social inclusion to employability, not least in the case of 'disadvantaged groups' such as migrants.

This rationality is also visible in the policy of the Swedish ESF Council (2007) which states that 'routes to integration [...] into working life for disadvantaged persons' are to be facilitated through 'measures that increase employability'. This is understood as 'contributing to greater social cohesion and inclusive working life, focusing on persons who today are currently far from the labour market'. Further, 'special priority will be given to making it easier for persons with a foreign background [...] to establish themselves on the labour market'. Techniques deployed for reaching these strategic goals include 'intensive job searching, counselling, education and coaching' (Swedish ESF Council 2007: 41).

In the policy discourse of the Swedish ESF, the targeted subjects are positioned as 'far from the labour market', 'disadvantaged', 'vulnerable', and having a 'foreign background' – in other words, as will be shown, they are being problematized, ethnicised, and excluded from normality.

Swedishness and Otherness

An Ethnography of Governmentality

My studies (Vesterberg 2013, 2015) of ESF projects targeting unemployed migrants have shown that the targeted groups tend to be constructed as bearers of 'cultural codes' that contradict the codes of normality in Swedish society. As I have argued, the targeted subjects in these projects are constructed, both in policy and by employees, as requiring interventions in order to gain the competence and characteristics deemed valuable in advanced liberal societies. For instance, gender equality operates as a marker of Swedishness (cf. Bredström 2005; de los Reyes, Molina and Mulinari 2006), and the targeted subjects are positioned in the project discourse as deviant in relation to the norms of Swedish gender equality (see further Chapter Four in this volume). Further, the targeted migrants are constructed as different from employable 'Swedes' or even as embodying the very opposite of Swedishness – for instance, in terms of social competence, idleness, motivation, and health (Vesterberg 2013, 2015).

Given these findings, I seek to capture the 'multiplicity and dynamics of everyday social life' through ethnographic fieldwork and to highlight the often contested construction of subjects that is taking place in the governing of unemployed migrants (cf. Brady 2014: 13).

The rationality of exclusionary inclusion can be illustrated by an interview in which one project employee discusses the inclusion of migrants in terms of breaking up groups: 'We [the employees] have to work to break up Arabic-speaking groups [of participants] that sit by themselves, so that we can meet'. The rationality underpinning this quote constructs the group as more or less self-segregating, and implies that the project's task is to actively interfere with this voluntary segregation in order to create social inclusion through interaction with 'us'. The 'Arabic-speaking groups' sitting by themselves become objects for inclusion when they are positioned as excluded and in need of integration into the larger group.

When discussing gender equality as a marker of Swedishness, another project employee first mentioned encouraging project participants to develop a clear idea about what field they wanted to find work in; something deemed necessary in order to strengthen their employability. The interviewed project employee then gendered this rationality in a way that positioned unemployed migrant women as passive victims:

> Many [participants] come from cultures where, mostly, the women are not used to thinking for themselves because they are used to being told what to do; used to following. This can be a bit tricky.

This quote positions unemployed migrant women within a patriarchal discourse, and migrant men are, by implication, the ones in charge and doing the thinking. As an effect of this, unemployed migrant women are problematized as lacking the ability to visualize a realistic future for themselves as working citizens because they 'are not used to thinking for themselves'. A similar rationality also appears in a written summary of the project's first year describing the characteristics of project participants. According to this summary, the target group consisted of:

> [...] a group of new Swedes who has not entered the labour market at all. There are those who are illiterate and have weak skills in Swedish. [...] There are also women who, because of religious and cultural traditions, do not reach a position in working life. (Project summary)

Here, unemployed migrant women are constructed as passive bearers of problematic religious and cultural traditions, something that in contemporary Sweden apparently hinders them from becoming employable. Through a discourse of 'foreignness', these women are positioned as culturally deviant Others (cf. Ålund and Minoo 2011) who need to reshape their religious and cultural traditions if they are to become employable and included in society.

Another instance of this rationality comes from a project employee who was discussing a particular project participant as a 'successful example'. The participant was a migrant woman who, when she first began participating in the project, had been shy and withdrawn, and wore a veil, and who was thus problematized through ethnicised discourses. After some time in the labour market project, however, she had discarded her veil and divorced her husband. In the discourse of the project employee, this woman had liberated herself from her patriarchal culture and was now empowered, standing on the threshold of Swedish gender equality (see further Chapter Four). In relation to such rationalities, such ways of gendering and ethnicising the unemployability of the targeted subject, the decision to persistently hold to one's religious and cultural traditions, can be interpreted as a form of active opposition to the dominant norms of the majority society, which constantly encourages individuals to transform themselves to align with it.

During a participant observation of one project, I asked one unemployed participant, a woman in her sixties who spoke fluent Swedish, how she liked the activities. She answered that it felt like a kindergarten, and that 'a bunch of Arabs chattering' gave her a headache. She pointed out that 'they should speak Swedish here'. Another unemployed participant, a man in his forties, also fluent in Swedish, discussed the issue of language in a similar way:

> Many don't even want to try to speak Swedish. They know some, but they don't want to do it. Then comes this cackle; they sit there and translate for each other, and we sit here like fools, those of us who speak Swedish.

When participants enrol in this project, they sign a contract which regulates behaviour in terms such as: 'We will respect each other'; 'We take off our outdoor clothing when we are indoors'; 'We do not use alcohol or drugs during project hours'; 'We arrive on time for meetings'; 'We clean the premises every day', and '*We speak Swedish to one another*'. When I asked one project employee about the language rule, she answered that it was very important 'that no one feel excluded'. But while conducting observations and speaking to project participants, I gained the impression that many participants spoke their first language as a way to help their fellow participants understand what the project employee said, since not all of them understood Swedish well enough to follow. In other words, they were interpreting for each other precisely *so that no one would feel excluded*. The complexity of the language issue makes visible a paradoxical aspect of the rationalities of exclusionary inclusion: everyone will speak Swedish in order to foster inclusion, but speaking Swedish excludes those with insufficient skills in that language. This particular project focused especially on unemployed people with a 'foreign background' but was also open to persons born in Sweden. Its target group was formulated in the project application as 'all those who live in exclusion'. As this incident shows, however, the linguistic issue created some tensions that could hardly be said to strengthen social inclusion; instead, they drew boundaries between 'us,' who speak Swedish, and 'them', who do not.

Regarding the position of project employees, one of them described their professional role as 'life-coaches who work with the whole participant: self-esteem, therapy, health, and job coaching' (Vesterberg 2011a: 16). This understanding of one's professional role reveals something about the position of the 'experts of subjectivity' (Rose 1999) who facilitate the transformation of problematized subjects into employable and included citizens. The project employee thus not only engages in improving skills deemed important for specific jobs but also works with nearly every aspect of the unemployed migrant's life, from fostering a positive self-image through therapy to improving their physique through health coaching. In this rationality, a reciprocity in the relationship between experts and targeted subjects becomes apparent. The project employees construct participants as unemployable and excluded in order to identify them as targets for their own expertise and knowhow. Simultaneously, project participants are constructed as needing the employees' knowledge in order to be included and become employable. In this way, the experts of subjectivity construct a demand for their skills and thus for their own employability. The same project employee gave a lecture focused on job searching that provided some additional indications of how an employable individual is defined in the project:

> We are selling a commodity when we look for a job. That's why it's important that we believe in this commodity – that is, in yourself, your ability, and your competence. Who wants to buy a commodity that not even the seller believes in?

The project employee here encourages the targeted subjects to embrace an understanding of themselves as confident and competitive – as market-oriented subjects. This kind of subject formation produces what Jason Read (2009) calls the subject of neoliberalism, *Homo economicus*, or what I have called advanced liberal subjects (Vesterberg 2013). Through this market rationality, citizens are encouraged to adapt their subjectivity to the norms of capitalism and entrepreneurship – to see themselves as commodities competing for job opportunities with other citizens.

Work Placement and Entrepreneurship as Games of Truth

During my ethnographic fieldwork in ESF projects, two particular and contested techniques for employability distinguished themselves as arenas for struggles over truth, as 'games of truth' – namely, work placement and entrepreneurship.

Work placement as a technique for enhancing the employability of ESF project participants (Vesterberg 2011b), was a recurring topic in my observations and interviews with participants. Together with education and job coaching, work placement was one of the most frequently deployed techniques in the ESF projects that targeted unemployed migrants (Engstrand, Andersson and Vesterberg 2010).

When work placement was discussed in the project, one participant claimed that 'work placement is work for slave pay'. The project employee responded that work placement should not be seen as or compared to 'real wage-labour'. The participant maintained that working eight hours per day for little or no money was tantamount to slavery. The project employee tried to stop this game and end the discussion by saying, 'But that's the way it works; you do work placement in order to get a job!' The issue became even more complex when it was discussed in relation to migration and ethnicity, as one participant indicated:

> Swedes do work placement once, and then they get a job. I do work placement after work placement after work placement, but I don't get a job. I don't want it to be like this anymore!

Work placement as a technique for inclusion and employability may thus operate in a way that strengthens the targeted subject's experience of exclusion from the labour market. This interview quote illustrates a feeling for migrants of being caught in an inescapable circle of work placements. In this way, the rationality of exclusionary inclusion becomes ethnicised when the measures for inclusion construct an experience of exclusion along ethnic lines. This experience is not unique, as research shows that migrants often have a precarious foothold in the labour market; whether they are excluded or included, they often find themselves in a position subordinate to the majority of the population (Neergaard 2006). The conclusion of the project participant – 'I don't want it to be like this anymore!' – clearly illustrates a critical attitude towards the rationality of work placements targeting migrants, and harbours the potential to counter the imposed measures.

Another field note records that one participant came to the project on his first day, and in a positive spirit said, 'All I want is a job!' But the project employee told him that he first needed to practise his language skills, then go to work placement, and *then* he would be ready to take on a regular job. The employee's rationality constructs the unemployed migrant's route to employment as a path consisting of several steps towards employability and inclusion. These steps – learning the Swedish language, going to work placement, and then seeking regular-wage work – are clearly contested as a truth. Ethnicised project participants conceptualized work placement as an inescapable circle of unpaid work rather than as a fruitful path to regular employment.

During an interview with a project employee who was responsible for one project's work placements, I, as an interviewer, initiated a game of truth. This particular project's target group was newly arrived, unemployed migrants. I asked this project employee whether the 'real problem' was that there simply were not enough jobs available, and that is why they had to send so many of the participants to work placement. The project employee then expressed concern about the attitude of many of the unemployed migrants. She stated that many project participants said, 'There are no jobs for me'. The project employee clearly disliked this attitude, contending that 'There are always jobs for those who want them, *if you really want to work*' (Vesterberg 2011b: 23f).

In the same interview, the project employee also raised critical concerns that nuanced the dominant discourse about work placement as something that is always desirable and positive for the unemployed migrants. When she talked about how the project had been implemented before she joined its staff, she said that many migrants had been exploited, and that participants were sent to work placements that were unrelated to their career development. However, her approach was different:

> I don't just send them [project participants] to send them somewhere. They used to send them anywhere, and I think that could be very humiliating for the participants. It has to be fair. […] So I listen to them [and learn] what they really want to do. Before, they were exploited; they sent participants to help renovate [a project employee's] terrace. […] So I put an end to that when I started here. It did not make me popular. […] It makes me furious. (Interview with project employee responsible for work placements)

This quote demonstrates that the position of experts is not necessarily tied to the dominant discourse on work placement as an indisputable 'natural path' to regular employment. Instead, the project employee raised a concern about, and was opposed, to what she perceived as specifically ethnicised exploitation (See further Chapter Three).

The truth game around work placement concerns how and whether it is to be seen as a desired and effective technique for creating inclusion through enhanced employability, as well as how unemployed persons of an ethnicised group are encouraged by project employees to avoid negative or critical thoughts and boost their positive thinking and self-confidence. The analysis also shows that the dominant discourse (e.g., that the 'natural path' to work for migrants is language skills, work placement, and finally regular employment) does not always stand unchallenged. When the participant is encouraged to think of work placement as a positive way of enhancing his or her employability, the counter-move is not to uncritically accept this truth but to challenge it and deliver an alternative truth regarding how one's relationship to the labour market should be understood.

The two subject positions, speaking and struggling over truth, are also relevant here. The project employees occupy the position of 'experts' – their professional task is to deliver a discourse officially sanctioned by the EU and the ESF, and in many ways they are obliged to construct the discourse of work placement as a rational and desirable way of tackling exclusion and unemployment among migrants. Rose (1996) argues that the authority of experts arises from their claim to knowledge and truth, and that expertise is given a prominent position in governing advanced liberal societies. The targeted subjects, on the other hand, may attempt to oppose and change the 'truths' of the experts, and their counter-conduct is fuelled by the first-hand experience of being unemployed migrants, an experience that might not have been shared by the experts.

A similar struggle over truth and meaning took place in another project when entrepreneurship as a remedy to unemployment among migrants was discussed. The project participants, a vast majority of whom were migrants, were encouraged to start businesses in order to combat their social exclusion. The kind of businesses the project focused on were in domestic services and the cleaning industry – two highly ethnicised industries (Gavanas 2013).

The following section builds on field notes from a project event at which a lecturer from Almega[5] was invited to speak about entrepreneurship and opportunities for starting a business in domestic services or in the cleaning industry. One project participant objected to the positive discourse on self-employment presented by the lecturer, claiming that she was living on welfare and could barely afford food for her children – a situation that made her afraid to borrow money to start a business. Neither did she want to experience the economic insecurity that starting a business can entail.

5 Almega is the employers' organization for the Swedish service sector.

A project employee entered the discussion and said that there were not enough jobs for everyone in Sweden, but if one started a business, one could create one's own job. 'You've got to keep on fighting; you can hire yourself and be your own boss' was the message the project employee conveyed. The sceptical participant refuted these 'truths' by claiming that no one would lend her money because she lived on welfare. This answer did not satisfy the project employee, who continued the truth game by telling the participant that she was approaching the question from 'the wrong end' and that she should focus on the opportunities of entrepreneurship instead. The participant was told not to talk about problems or about the economy, but to believe in herself and her ideas, to try her idea out and deal with the problems later.

This did not put an end to the game. The participant answered that she had never had a real job but had only held work placements, and that this would be a disadvantage when starting a business. The project employee answered by telling her, 'You've got to fight; nothing comes for free'. The game of truth ended with the participant claiming that she 'fights all the time' and that her situation was making her depressed (Vesterberg 2011b: 16f).

These games of truth can be interpreted as a kind of opposition to particular techniques deployed when promoting social inclusion and employability for ethnicised target groups – as 'specific instances of counter-conduct', something often neglected in studies of governmentality (Bevir 2010: 425). The project employees present work placement as a necessary step towards finding a permanent, full-time job, making unemployed migrants more employable in the eyes of employers. Encouragement to try entrepreneurship and self-employment operates through a, somewhat contradictory, but simultaneously similar rationality. There are paradoxical aspects of work placement versus entrepreneurship as measures for improving employability. In the exchange cited earlier, a project employee argued that there are jobs for everyone, if they really want to work. This contradicts another employee's 'truth', that there are not enough jobs for everyone in Sweden and that entrepreneurship presents a solution to this dilemma. Similarities in the rationalities include a focus on boosting the project participants' confidence and encouraging positive thinking as crucial for combating one's own social exclusion. This game of truth is played out between, on one hand, a sceptical project participant who expresses great reservations about whether she could truly overcome her exclusion and unemployment by starting a business and, on the other hand, the lecturer from Almega and a project employee, who are interested in shaping entrepreneurial subjects who are eager to start their own businesses and become self-employed.

Both these techniques for improving inclusion through employability are constructed as desirable ways of combating unemployment. This in turn breaks the exclusion of the unemployed migrants, since, according to this rationality, self-sufficiency seems to be equivalent to social inclusion. Clearly, these are contested truths – the targeted subjects do not necessarily share the same view as the experts on these matters. The project participants want to be included in society and wish to participate in the labour market, but not necessarily under the conditions or in the ways that are offered to them. They want to work, but not to do 'work placement after work placement' just because they are migrants. They want to be employable, but not if that means being stuck in a circle of unpaid work. They want to be self-sufficient, but not if they must take great economic risks by starting a business and becoming self-employed. Through an ethnography of governmentality focused on truth games, I have shown that the formation of the employable self is contested in language games, and that the 'truths' delivered by project employees are sometimes opposed by the targeted subjects themselves.

Concluding Reflections

How is exclusion produced when one seeks to create social inclusion through enhanced employability? As I have discussed, the construction of deviance and ethnicised 'difference' always relates to 'normality' in inclusion practices such as the ESF projects targeting unemployed migrants. These constructions of normality and difference occur in ESF policy, as well as in the everyday practice of the projects. To make the targeted subjects includable and employable, they are first ethnicised as different and then positioned as excluded. Though inclusion practices seek to normalize unemployed migrants, the boundary around those who are understood as different is constantly created through constructions of cultural differences (Tesfahuney and Grip 2007). Regarding work placement as a regularly used technique for addressing social inclusion and employability, my analysis has illustrated that work placement can foster a feeling of exclusion when it does not lead to regular employment. Feelings of exclusion and ethnicised Otherness can be evoked, particularly when the view is that work placement leads to regular jobs for indigenous Swedes but not for migrants.

What rationalities and truths underlie the practices of exclusionary inclusion? As the analysis has shown, rationalities of exclusionary inclusion target subjects who first need to be constructed as excluded and deviant, so that they can then become included and normalized; in other words, normality presupposes deviance. Otherwise, measures seeking to achieve social inclusion through enhanced employability would appear irrational or at least rather pointless. In the particular case of the labour market projects that target unemployed migrants, this rationality becomes ethnicised when, for instance the issues of insufficient skills in the Swedish language or the wearing of a veil, are problematized as markers of unemployability and deviance.

My analysis also identifies a rationality consisting of a kind of discursive commodification of the self as saleable. Project employees proclaimed this viewpoint when they encouraged the targeted subjects to think of themselves as commodities competing in a market. This rationality is an illustrative example of fostering advanced liberal subjects constructed through market economy norms, such as entrepreneurial spirit and competition. These norms and 'truths' construct the unemployed migrants as ethnicised and unemployable, thus making them governable (cf. Dean 2010).

What opposition to dominant discourses on employability can be found in the practices that seek to create social inclusion? I have demonstrated that governing unemployed migrants takes place through games of truth played between project employees and the targeted subjects. The analysis has also shown that the labour market projects are spaces for counter-conduct and opposition to the dominant discourse that enhanced employability automatically leads to inclusion. Project participants can, and do, oppose the 'truths' delivered by project employees by staging counter-conduct and by refusing to become employable or to be included in the ways that are imposed on them. Struggles over meaning concerning the techniques of inclusion through employability are played out in games of truth, and dominant discourses can in this way be opposed when the targeted subjects act and speak in ways that declare: 'We do not want this truth' (Foucault 2004b: 201). In this way, the everyday governing of unemployed migrants in labour market projects can be disrupted and disturbed. The ethnographic approach taken here shows that the construction of subjects as employable is not a simple, neat, top-down process. Rather, it emerges in power relationships that consist of both the employees' attempts to direct the behaviour of the targeted subjects and the counter-conduct of project participants who contest the 'truths' of inclusion and employability. The analysis has also illustrated that project employees do not always uncritically support dominant discourses but may also reject certain aspects of the measures for employability.

This illustrates Foucault's (2002) argument that power is never a one-way relationship, and that wherever there is power, there is resistance. On one hand, the analysis indicates that activities that focus on employability through inclusion risk strengthening the divide between 'us' and 'them', thus producing ethnicised Otherness when trying to create a more inclusive society and to combat exclusion. On the other hand, the analysis also shows that no truth is absolute; there is always room for opposition and contestation in the discursive language games in the everyday practices of social inclusion. Truths are never permanent but are always contingent, and the practices of inclusion are never totally closed to new interventions. New ways of thinking about inclusion and subjectivities are always possible (cf. Cruikshank 1999) – for the targeted migrants themselves, as well as for the experts engaged in the crucial issues of migrant inclusion. Like the unemployed migrants, they can also contest the discourses within which they practice their profession.

Funding Acknowledgement

This work was supported by the Swedish Research Council for Health, Working Life and Welfare [Grant number 2006–1524].

References

Agamben, G. 1998. *Homo Sacer: Sovereign Power and Bare Life*. Stanford: Stanford University Press.

Anderson, B. 2013. *Us & Them? The Dangerous Politics of Immigration Control*. Oxford: Oxford University Press.

Ålund, A. and Minoo, A. 2011. 'I skuggan av etno-kulturella stereotypier; Perspektiv på forskning om genus, jämställdhet och etniska relationer i Sverige.' *Sociologisk forskning* 2, 43–64.

Bevir, M. 2010. 'Rethinking governmentality: Towards genealogies of governance.' *European Journal of Social Theory* 13/4, 423–441.

Brady, M. 2014. 'Ethnographies of neoliberal governmentalities: From the neoliberal apparatus to neoliberalism and governmental assemblages.' *Foucault Studies* 18, 11–33.

Bredström, A. 2005. '"Love in another country": "Race," gender and sexuality in sexual education material targeting migrants in Sweden.' *Sexualities* 8/4, 517–535.

Bröckling, U., Krasmann, S. and Lemke, T. 2011. 'An introduction.' In Bröckling, Ulrich, Susanne Krasmann and Thomas Lemke (eds.) *Governmentality. Current Issues and Future Challenges*. London: Routledge.

Cruikshank, B. 1999. *The Will to Empower: Democratic Citizens and Other Subjects*. Cornell: Cornell University Press.

de la Porte, C. and Jacobsson, K. 2012. 'Social investment or recommodification?' In Morel, Nathalie, Bruno Palier and Joakim Palme (eds.) *Towards a Social Investment Welfare State?* Bristol: Policy Press.

de los Reyes, P., Molina, I. and Mulinari, D. (eds.) 2006. *Maktens (o)lika förklädnader. Kön, Klass & Etnicitet i det postkoloniala Sverige.* Stockholm: Atlas.

Dean, M. 2010. *Governmentality: Power and Rule in Modern Society.* London: Sage.

Diken, B. 2004. 'From refugee camps to gated communities: Biopolitics and the end of the city.' *Citizenship Studies* 8/1, 83–106.

Engstrand, Å-K., Andersson, J. and Vesterberg, V. 2010. *Bortom Lissabonstrategin: Om projektarbetares erfarenheter av inkluderingsarbete.* Linköping: Linköping University.

Esping-Andersen, G. 1990. *The Three Worlds of Welfare Capitalism.* Oxford: Polity Press.

European Commission 2008. *European Commission recommendation (2008) of 3 October 2008 on the active inclusion of people excluded from the labour market.* Official Journal of the European Union L 307/11.

European Commission 2011. 'Equal: Welcome to Equal.' Archived March 23, 2011. Accessed March 10, 2016. <http://ec.europa.eu/employment_social/equal_consolidated/>

European Commission 2014. 'European Social Fund 2014–2020.' Last modified September 15, 2014. Accessed March 10, 2016. <http://ec.europa.eu/esf/main.jsp?catId=62&langId=en>

European Commission 2015. 'Glossary: European Social Fund'. Last modified January 10, 2015. Accessed March 10, 2016. <http://ec.europa.eu/regional_policy/en/policy/what/glossary/e/european-social-fund>

Fauerbæk, L. 2004. 'Competition versus regulation: Swedish articulations on the EU labour market discourse.' In Garsten, Christina and Kerstin Jacobsson (eds.) *Learning to be Employable: New Agendas on Work, Responsibility and Learning in a Globalizing World.* Basingstoke: Palgrave Macmillan, 63–83.

Foucault, M. 1991. 'Governmentality.' In Burchell, Graham, Colin Gordon and Peter Miller (eds.) *The Foucault Effect: Studies in Governmentality.* Chicago: University of Chicago Press, 87–105.

Foucault, M. 1997a. 'Sex, power and the politics of identity.' In Rabinow, Paul (ed.) *Ethics Subjectivity and Truth.* New York: The New Press, 163–175.

Foucault, M. 1997b. 'The ethics of the concern for self as a practice of freedom.' In Rabinow, Paul (ed.) *Ethics, Subjectivity, and Truth.* New York: The New Press, 281–303.

Foucault, M. 2002. *The History of Sexuality. Vol. 1. The Will to Knowledge*. Harmondsworth: Penguin.

Foucault, M. 2004a. *The birth of Biopolitics: Lectures at the Collége de France 1978—1979*. New York: Palgrave Macmillan.

Foucault, M. 2004b. *Security, Territory, Population: Lectures at the Collège de France 1977–1978*. New York: Palgrave Macmillan.

Foucault, M. 2014. 'Inaugural lecture.' In Brion, Fabienne and Bernard E. Harcourt (eds.) *Wrong-Doing, Truth-Telling: The Function of Avowal in Justice*. Chicago: The University of Chicago Press, 11–27.

Gavanas, A. 2013. 'Migrant domestic workers, social network strategies and informal markets for domestic services in Sweden.' *Women's Studies International Forum* 36, 54–64.

Gordon, C. 1980. 'Afterword.' In Michel, Foucault. *Power/Knowledge*. New York: Pantheon Books, 229–261.

Hale, J. 2007. *European Social Fund: 50 Years of Investing in People*. Luxembourg: Office for Official publications of the European Communities.

Hansen, P. and Hager, S.B. 2010. *The Politics of European Citizenship: Deepening Contradictions in Social Rights and Migration Politics*. New York: Berghahn Books.

Holmqvist, M. 2009. 'Disabled people and dirty work.' *Disability and Society* 24/7, 869–882.

Inda, J.X. 2006. *Targeting Immigrants*. Oxford: Blackwell Publishing.

Kelly, P. 2007. 'Governing individualized risk biographies: New class intellectuals and the problem of youth at risk.' *British Journal of Sociology of Education* 28/1, 39–53.

Kemshall, H. 2002. 'Effective practice in probation: An example of "advanced liberal" responsibilisation.' *The Howard Journal* 41/1, 41–58.

Kivinen, O. and Rinne, R. 1998. 'State, governmentality and education: The Nordic experience.' *British Journal of Sociology of Education* 19/1, 39–52.

Larsson, J.K. 2015. *Integrationen och arbetets marknad*. Stockholm: Atlas.

Larsson, B., Letell, M. and Thörn, H. 2012. 'Transformations of the Swedish welfare state: Social engineering, governance and governmentality – An introduction.' In Larsson, Bengt, Martin Letell and Håkan Thörn (eds.) *Transformations of the Swedish Welfare State: From Social Engineering to Governance?* Basingstoke: Palgrave Macmillan, 3–23.

Miller, P. and Rose, N. 2008. *Governing the Present*. Cambridge: Polity Press.

Ministry of Employment 2015. 'Statens budget 2015 i siffror.' Last modified May 5, 2015. Accessed March 10, 2016. <http://www.regeringen.se/artiklar/2015/04/statens-budget-2015-i-siffror>

Neergaard, A. 2006. 'Rasifierad rekrytering i storstadskommunen: Mellan exkluderad och inkluderad underordning.' In Neergaard, Anders, Arne Nilsson and Ewa Gunnarsson (eds.) *Kors & tvärs: intersektionalitet och makt i storstadens arbetsliv*. Stockholm: Normal, 164–184.

Popkewitz, T. and Lindblad, S. 2000. 'Educational governance and social inclusion and exclusion.' *Discourse: Studies in Cultural Politics of Education* 21/1, 5–44.

Read, J. 2009. 'A genealogy of homo-economicus.' *Foucault Studies* 6, 25–36.

Rose, N. 1996. 'Governing "advanced" liberal democracies.' In Barry, Andrew, Thomas Osborne and Nikolas Rose (eds.) *Foucault and Political Reason. Liberalism, neo-liberalism and rationalities of government*. London: University of Chicago Press, 37–65.

Rose, N. 1999. *Powers of Freedom: Reframing Political Thought*. Cambridge: Cambridge University Press.

Said, E.W. 1978. *Orientalism*. New York: Pantheon Books.

Schierup, C-U., Krifors, K. and Slavnic, Z. 2015. 'Social exclusion.' In Dahlstedt. Magnus. and Anders Neergaard (eds.) *International Migration and Ethnic Relations: Critical Perspectives*. New York: Routledge, 200–227.

Schierup, C-U. and Ålund, A. 2011. 'From paradoxes of multiculturalism to paradoxes of liberalism: Sweden and the European neoliberal hegemony.' *Journal for Critical Education Studies* 9/2, 125–142.

Schneider, A. and Ingram, H. 1993. 'Social construction of target populations: Implications for politics and policy.' *The American political science review* 87/2, 334–347.

Soss, J., Fording, R.C. and Schram, S.F. 2011. *Disciplining the Poor: Neoliberal Paternalism and the Persistent Power of Race*. Chicago: University of Chicago Press.

Swedish ESF Council 2007. *National Structural Fund Programme for Regional Competitiveness and employment (ESF) 2007–2013*. CCI number 2007SE-052PO001.

Swedish ESF Council 2014. *Socialfonden i siffror. Projektens deltagare och nytta*. Örebro: Apel.

Tesfahuney, M. and Grip, L. 2007. 'Integrationism: Viljan till detsamma.' *Nordisk Samhällsgeografisk Tidskrift* 43, 61–91.

Vesterberg, V. 2011a. *(O)likheter och egen makt. Om ett Socialfondsprojekt för Ökat Arbetskraftsutbud*. Linköping: Linköping University.

Vesterberg V. 2011b. *Alla ska ju ut på praktik. Möjligheter, begränsningar och problem med praktik i arbetslivet som medel för integration.* Linköping: Linköping University.

Vesterberg, V. 2013. 'Ethnicised un/employability: Problematized Others and the shaping of advanced liberal subjects.' *Ephemera. Theory & politics in organization* 13/4, 737–757.

Vesterberg, V. 2015. 'Learning to be Swedish: Governing migrants in labour market projects.' *Studies in Continuing Education* 37/3, 302–316.

Walters, W. and Haahr, J.H. 2005. *Governing Europe: Discourse, Governmentality and European Integration.* London: Routledge.

Welshman, J. 2006. 'The Concept of the unemployable.' *The Economic History Review, New series* 59/3, 578–606.

Wright Nielsen, T. 2015. 'Empowerment och normalisering.' In Montesino, Norma and Erica Righard (eds.) *Socialt arbete och migration.* Malmö: Gleerups.

Anna Gavanas

6. Swedish Retirement Migrants and Domestic Services in Spain: Informalisation and Moral Economy in Reimagining Sweden[1]

Abstract: This chapter analyses Swedish international retirement migrants (IRMs) in Spain and their privatised consumption of domestic services (cleaning, care and domestic work). Between themselves, as well as in relations with workers and intermediaries, IRMs are part of a moral economy where increasing international gaps and inequalities appear more manageable, while enmeshed in the wider market of globalised labour. Through collective and individual strategies, IRMs' moral economies mitigate the changing conditions of family and transnational gaps between welfare states.

There is a hand written note on the wall of a Swedish grocery store in Becenil[2], the Canary Islands: 'Are you looking for cleaning help? My name is Paula and I'm from South America looking for extra work here in Becenil. I only speak Spanish, am just over 50 years old, well behaved, honest and meticulous'.

Paula provides domestic services informally for a network of Swedish retirement migrants in Becenil, charging ten Euros per hour. She used to be a teacher in Bogota but moved to Spain looking for work when she became unemployed in 2008.

> Today I work more and more because the Swedes recommend me to each other. I do well because I do a good job and I have talked to many who prefer Latinos and Latinas for cleaning, because we do it better than Spaniards, because we are good at cleaning. We are organised, clean and honest, and I think that's important.

Paula works approximately twelve hours per day, seven days per week. She sends money to her daughter and relatives in Colombia, as well as saves for a house:

---

1 Acknowledgements: This chapter is based on a project funded in 2013–2015 by two agencies: the Swedish Research Council (VR) Dnr 421-2012-675; and the Swedish Research Council for Health, Working Life and Welfare (FORTE) FAS Dnr 2012-0223. Project members were Associate Professor Anna Gavanas (PI), Dr Ines Calzada and research assistant Virginia Paez.

2 To preserve the anonymity of interviewees, all names of islands, villages and towns are pseudonyms.

she plans to retire and return to Colombia in seven years. She prefers Swedish customers because she thinks they treat her more respectfully than those from other nations, such as the Spaniards. It is not uncommon for workers and entrepreneurs (both formal and informal) on the Costa del Sol and Canary Islands to describe Swedes as 'ideal', especially in comparison to customers from Spain or the UK. Simultaneously, there are Swedish retirement migrants in Spain who lack the capability to be profitable customers in either formal or informal labour market segments of the tourist regions of the country. There are even those who need to provide services to other retirees in order to survive, intertwined with social and volunteer networks providing unpaid peer support. What strategies are available for different groups of Swedish retirement migrants in Spain? In this chapter the conditions for differently positioned providers who serve retirement migrants in Spain – such as Swedish entrepreneurs, Spanish workers and those as Paula, the Third Country Nationals- will be discussed.

This chapter analyses Swedish international retirement migrants (IRMs) in Spain and their consumption of domestic services (cleaning, care and domestic work) as part of the privatisation of elderly care consumed on an international arena. In particular, paid and unpaid, as well as formal and informal (regulated and unregulated), arrangements for domestic services formed around IRMs in Spain will be explored.

Through their dreams, frustrations and practices in Spain, IRMs are grappling with the changing welfare state in the Sweden they left behind and eventually tend to return to. Caught between collectivism and individualism, IRMs are reimagining and imagining Sweden, while facing a patchwork of options for survival. In this context, IRMs' moral economies mitigate the changing conditions of family and transnational gaps between welfare states. Solidarity and care among IRMs, as well as relations with informal workers and intermediaries, form a moral economy in IRM zones whereby increasing international gaps and inequalities appear more manageable, while enmeshed in the wider market of globalised labour.

This chapter argues that Swedish retirement migrants create a moral economy of care, between themselves and in relation to entrepreneurs and workers. Moral economy is here defined, following Andrew Sayer (2007: 262) as: 'the moral norms and sentiments that structure and influence economic practices, both formal and informal, and the way in which these are reinforced, compromised or overridden by economic pressures'. It is argued that the moral economy reflects the collective and individual consequences of the privatised migration context in Spain, as well as the shrinking Swedish welfare state. Proponents of the moral economy framework emphasise how this concept highlights possibilities for people to defend social commitments and obligations from the erosive tendencies of economic processes (Bolton and Laaser 2013: 510). As an analytical framework, moral economy 'connects the analysis of radical political economy, the (a)morality of markets under liberal capitalism and the lived reality of the everyday work situation for a range of people' (Bolton and Laaser 2013: 511). By addressing the moral economy concept to the study of the service economy around IRMs (and particularly domestic services), how the market is a social and political construction being shaped and reshaped by social, political and moral struggles, as well as mediated by institutions, individuals and communities are to be investigated. In other words, the dimensions of actors' reflections, norms, practices and social connections, within national and international markets, will be illuminated.

For instance, within the literature on domestic services and global care chains, one can see how emotional aspects of work, in addition to gift giving may play into the labour process itself (Näre 2012; Aguirre 2013; Anderson 2000; Lutz 2011). In this context, a moral economy approach can illuminate research on insecure and precarious employment, connecting the logics of family, community and workplace, and the dilemmas of people trying to balance these (Bolton and Laaser 2013: 518).

All actors involved in IRM strategies for survival in Spain (IRMs, workers and entrepreneurs) blur together as part of a moral economy of service and care. According to a moral economic logic, the relations between service providers and customers are based on notions of solidarity, gratitude, duty and 'familial' responsibility, entailing highly personalised labour relationships rather than merely economic profit maximisation. The term moral here refers to exchanges that have other goals than merely economic profit, such as the accumulation of symbolic and social capital, as well as social cohesion (Näre 2012: 400). As will be demonstrated, when related to paid labour (for instance migrant or Spanish domestic workers and carers, employed formally or informally), the moral economic aspect is reflected in workers' and entrepreneurs' preference for clients and employers who are considered good, just and treat them with respect, rather than necessarily paying much more than other potential clients/employers (Näre 2012: 407). Additionally, how all this is connected to neoliberal labour market relations and globalisation will be explored.

This chapter is based on interviews with both parties involved in the economy of care around Swedish IRMs: eighty IRMs, one-hundred and twenty workers/entrepreneurs (who perform IRM related services), as well as twenty experts (public and organisational officials, and specialised media) in twenty-four villages and towns located in two of the three main destination regions for Swedish

IRMs: the Southern coast of mainland Spain (the "Costa del Sol" in Andalucía) and the Canary Islands[3]. The large number of interviewees encompasses a great variation in the conditions, arrangements and motivations of IRMs, as well as the entrepreneurs and workers who provide their services.

Privatisation, Swedish Tax Deductions and Domestic Services in Spain

Swedish retirees are part of a growing number of Northern European International Retirement Migrants (IRMs) who reside seasonally or permanently in Southern European destinations – especially in the coastal areas of Spain. The transnational lives of Swedish IRMs are situated within and between the Swedish and Spanish welfare states, involving different ways of distributing the responsibility for elderly care between state, market and family. Sweden represents one of the highest, and Spain one of the lowest, levels of state funded provision in Europe (Lister et al. 2007; Williams and Gavanas 2008).

Eldercare is increasingly a private affair for Northern Europeans given the marketization, privatisation and welfare state reductions there since the 1990s, including Sweden (Meagher and Szebehely 2013a). Thus, the conditions for ageing in Europe are changing. In the words of gerontologists John A. Vincent, Chris Phillipson and Murna Downs (2006: 217):

> [...] it appears most likely that a person's 'welfare' and 'quality of life' in old age will increasingly reflect their individual life course and their achieved material, knowledge, social and entitlement resources. The complement is that an older person's welfare situation will be less and less a function of the welfare regime in their country or countries of residence.

However, as argued in this chapter, this only applies to a very few who are in an economic position to pick and choose on the international market. The other elderly are still tied to welfare state provision, even though it is shrinking; not the least from the point when they become dependent on extensive eldercare. In other words, there are significant socio-economic asymmetries between wealthy, middle income and low income IRMs, as well as between service providers with backgrounds in Spain, (Northern) Europe and third country nationals such as Paula.

---

3 Fieldwork was realised by Gavanas and Calzada in two different Spanish regions (and a range of IRM destinations within these) in order to maximise variation among the interviewees, as well as control for the regional welfare and labour contexts to shape the options and strategies of IRMs concerning the provision of services.

When care must be bought onto the market (due to insufficient public provision), access is unequally distributed (Ibañez and Léon 2014). This too applies to Swedish IRMs, whether they belong to the minority of IRMs registered as residents in Spain, or the majority of IRMs registered as residents in Sweden. The international retirement migration of the relatively wealthy baby boom generation born in the 1940s highlights privatisation developments on the transnational scale. These occur alongside the decline of inter-generational family support obligations, decreasing local ties, cheaper international travel and communication, as well as the enhanced international portability of pensions in the EU, encouraging more Northern European retirees to move or live transnationally (King, Warnes and Williams 2000: 13). In other words, the transnational residential patterns of IRMs 'manifest not only increased affluence and the revolution in transport technology, but also rising inequalities on the regional, national, continental and global scales' (Vincent, Phillipson and Downs 2006). Throughout their migration trajectory, IRMs re-evaluate their situations and reformulate their strategies, switching strategically. IRMs tend to reconsider their plans when reaching a point of dependency and facing slim public, and unaffordable private, alternatives in Spain. Until that point, some IRMs are making themselves consumers of services and care on an international market, without access to the Swedish public provision of eldercare.

Swedish retirees, especially those born in the 1940s, are considered a growing cohort of relatively wealthy consumers, with more cosmopolitan preferences and habits compared to previous generations (Gavanas 2013; Meagher and Szebehely 2010; Thelin 2013). This generation spent their working years under a system characterised by job stability that allowed uninterrupted social contributions and strong social protection. Today's retirement migration among Swedish elderly can be understood as a (partial) product of the 'golden years' of the Swedish welfare state (Meagher and Szebehely 2010, 2013a, 2013b). Thanks to their relatively beneficial retirement conditions, there is a group of middle- to upper-class Swedish elderly that can afford to maintain dual residence (in Spain and Sweden), enabling them to maximise their social/family resources, quality of life, wealth and welfare benefits (Åkerlund 2013). However, there is a large variety of socio-economic conditions, as well as residential arrangements among IRMs; including those with scarce economic means, and IRMs from working/lower middle class backgrounds (Blaakilde and Nilsson 2013).

While the warmer winter climate is a major motivation for Northern European retirees to move to Spain (combined with health reasons), the relatively lower prices of living, as compared to Sweden, is another important factor that motivates international retirement migration. In Spain, rental and property costs are much lower than in Northern Europe, the food, drinks, heating and services are much cheaper and thus, regardless of income level, Northern European IRMs get more for their pensions in Spain (King, Warnes and Williams 2000: 32–33). In other words, the different groups among Swedish IRMs there may thus have different reasons, financial conditions and motivations to migrate. These could be health, lifestyle and/or economic related. The majority of IRMs return to Sweden when they or their partner are in need of extensive elderly care, which would be too costly for anyone to pay for privately in Spain, except for the very wealthiest. Despite this, there are IRMs who stay on deliberately in Spain, and a minority of these may get 'stranded'; unable to manage everyday life independently, with a lack of funds and social contacts. Hence, on the one hand, Swedish IRMs get more for their money in Spain, but on the other hand it becomes too expensive to remain in Spain when in need of costly eldercare services.

During the 1990s, the private provision of eldercare increased from three percent to thirteen percent of the Swedish workforce. From then, it has continued to grow in Sweden, and in 2012, twenty-one percent of residential care, and twenty-three percent of home based care, were provided by private companies, driven by for-profit providers (Erlandsson et al. 2013: 23). Together with new public management reforms and shrinking public provision in elderly care, tax deductions for domestic services, introduced in 2007, have become part of a dual privatisation process in Sweden (Gavanas 2013). Over the last two decades there has been a marked increase in privately provided elderly care in Sweden, whilst tax deductions for private domestic services have encouraged these as a substitute for public home care among the elderly. Nevertheless, even though public care is eroding in Sweden, it is still one of the world's most generous countries when it comes to eldercare spending according to Organisation for Economic Cooperation and Development (OECD); care recipients only pay five to six percent of the cost, and those with low incomes are exempt from care fees and may also receive a housing allowance (Erlandsson et al. 2013: 25). However, the coverage of needs assessed eldercare services has not kept pace with the ageing population in Sweden, which has been compensated for by either privately purchased care or unpaid family members; the latter especially in low income families (Erlandsson et al. 2013: 49; Ulmanen 2015). Petra Ulmanen (2015) describes how the shrinking resources for eldercare since the 1990s have been paralleled with increasing unpaid care by family members. Between 1988 and 2010, the share of elderly with unpaid family care increased from forty to sixty-five percent (2015: 21–22). Ulmanen (2015: 22) also shows how unpaid family care is clearly gendered as between 1994 and 2000, the share of elderly with help from adult daughters increased from twenty-two to thirty-three percent, while the share of those with help from sons stayed at twelve to thirteen percent.

Along with the increased privatisation of eldercare in Sweden there have been recurring 'care scandals' over the quality and staffing of private elderly care providers (Jönson 2015), and several public opinion polls have shown that Swedes are very sceptical about the increasing impact of profit driven actors in welfare services (Erlandsson et al. 2013: 74). Simultaneously, during the years since the introduction of the tax deductions in 2007, domestic services have become increasingly normalised in Swedish middle-class homes (Gavanas and Calleman 2013). This partly stems from the prevalence of neoliberal values driving forward the transformation of formerly unpaid or state funded services into market based paid work (Lutz 2011: 8). In other words, the care services that were formerly realised by partners and family members have become increasingly outsourced to a market for paid services. Notwithstanding, despite the tax deductions' aim to formalise domestic services and thereby provide regulated labour market opportunities, informal domestic services still proliferate in Sweden, even though the tax authority estimates a shrinking informal sector, as well as decreasing cultural acceptance to purchase informal services (Skatteverket 2011). Even though elderly over the age of sixty-five are the largest consumer group for tax deduced domestic services in Sweden (after families with dependent children), services purchased informally are still considered more flexible and affordable by some consumers (Gavanas 2013: 98). The larger the tax wedge (i.e. the price increase due to taxes and social security fees), the bigger incentive for informal arrangements (Nyberg 2013: 116). Furthermore, income differences between customers and providers of domestic services are conducive to demand for such services (Nyberg 2013: 117).

The Spanish Destination Context

Similar to Sweden, the Spanish state has sought to formalise domestic services, but despite recent reforms (i.e. the 2006 Dependency Law and the 2011 reform on The Social Security Regime of Household Employees), elderly care and domestic services are still largely channelled through the informal labour market (Ibañez and Léon 2014). The informal economy covers one third of the domestic service market in Spain (Simonazzi 2009: 226). It is estimated that it corresponds to almost twenty-five percent (24.6) of Spanish gross domestic product (GDP) according to a report released by *Gestha* (the union of the technical staff of the Spanish Finance Ministry) entitled: "The Underground Economy Takes Its Toll. The Increase in Fraud during the Crisis" (Sardà 2014). The informal economy has increased particularly in the regions most affected by unemployment and the property market crash, and here IRM destinations such as Andalucía and the Canary Islands are mentioned among those affected[4]. Zyab Ibañez and Margarita Léon (2014) argue that the existence of a strong informal market in Spain reflects an institutional and social inertia towards the informal sector, and policy attempts at formalising domestic services have had limited effect.

Since the late 1990s, the Spanish labour market has been characterised by segmentation, temporary contracts (over 30 percent), weak unions, an extensive informal economy and low wages; the national minimum wage was approximately six-hundred and fifty (645.30) Euros per month in 2013, and fifty percent of formal employees in Spain earn less than one thousand Euros per month (Ibañez and Léon 2014). High unemployment, above twenty percent, has been a steady feature during the last three decades. According to Spanish National Statistics (INE), twenty-three percent of all contracts in Spain are temporary, and this number is higher than thirty percent in touristic and agricultural regions such as Andalucía and the Canary Islands (2012).

Because public Spanish welfare state provision has thus far been very weak in terms of social protection, unpaid family support (mostly realised by women) has functioned as a buffer to fill in the gaps of the Spanish welfare regime (Lister et al. 2007). This further disadvantages migrants, as compared to Spanish nationals who have access to wider and stronger social and family networks. More than seventy-five percent of IRMs (from all countries, including Sweden) do not have any eldercare assistance or home service. Among those who do, the most common option is domestic service (93 percent), while a minority receives public home-based care. Service provided by Spanish public social workers to IRMs is practically non-existent (Rodríguez, Ángeles Casado and Huber 2005).

The privately hired cleaners, carers and handymen (men will be used herein throughout for handy-work as odd-jobs are primarily conducted by men) who

4 Despite the economic crisis of 2008, migrant women, predominately from Latin America, representing thirty-six percent of the Spanish domestic service sector, have not been as affected by unemployment as their male counterparts (Ibañez and Léon 2014). There are some unskilled jobs in specific sectors, particularly services related to domestic help and care achieved mostly by migrant women, which have not so far declined despite the economic crisis (Godenau 2012). Migrant women represent thirty-six percent of domestic workers in Spain, the largest percentage in Europe, and only twenty percent of them are in labour market positions corresponding to those of non-migrant formal workers in the country (González 2013). This situation translates into more precarious jobs for women, mostly for migrants according to SEDOAC, a migrant domestic workers' association based in Spain (Álvarez 2014).

provide domestic services to IRMs are Spanish and Nordic citizens, as well as Third Country Nationals, mostly from South America. IRMs' consumption is surrounded by a long-standing tourist infrastructure (Woube 2014) and a Nordic labour market where companies related to tourism, property or health are managed by hiring Scandinavian speaking staff (Breivik 2015: 37). Low-skilled work, such as cleaning and certain subcontracted odd-job services were usually conducted by Spanish or South American workers according to the interviewees herein. Scandinavian migrant workers managed and performed services in cases where IRMs (who tend not to speak fluent Spanish) require Swedish speaking intermediaries or providers. Different types of domestic services for IRMs in Spain are clearly segmented by language, nationality and gender. For cleaning services, IRMs usually require no specific trained skills: low prices are important to customers and positions are filled by low waged Spanish or South American women who speak Spanish only. IRMs did not tend to apply specific language requirements when selecting whom to conduct cleaning services: they turn to Spanish or South American women recommended through social networks. Very rarely did interviewees or their social networks use Eastern European or North African women or men offering domestic services in these areas. In contrast, IRMs may require that domestic services involving eldercare are performed by Swedish speaking workers, who tend to charge higher rates per hour than informal cleaners.

As consumers of domestic services on a privatised, segmented and international market, Swedish IRMs may use tax deductions in Spain, which are part of Swedish privatisation and formalisation policies. However, because the rates for both formal and informal domestic services are much lower in Spain compared to Sweden, IRM interviewees do not find it worthwhile to use the Swedish tax deductions – called RUT – for cleaning and care, even though they have a right to use these if they are registered as residents and taxpayers in Sweden. In contrast, the ROT deductions for domestic handyman services, which can be more costly than cleaning and care services, were more frequent among IRM interviewees. Differing from the feminised and female dominated domestic services, masculinised handyman services, where workers are generally men and considered higher skilled, charge relatively higher rates (Kilkey, Perrons and Plomien 2013). However, ROT services are another matter as therein the workers' skill level is a factor, and major repair and renovation projects can be costly. For example, regarding the ROT deduction, one Swedish handyman interviewee with a company formally registered in Spain, said that a Swedish couple can save fifty-thousand SEK for each person, thus saving one-hundred thousand SEK per year using ROT.

Handymen who know how to get the Swedish ROT deductions for their clients may have a competitive advantage. These businesses do not need to be run by Swedish citizens in order for their customers to be approved for tax deductions by the Swedish tax authority. There are companies headed by Spanish citizens that offer ROT deduced services. Additionally, on the Costa del Sol and the Canary Islands two companies that used the RUT deductions for domestic services such as cleaning and care were found. Albeit, they seemed to have difficulties finding enough clients. A Swedish entrepreneur who runs a domestic service company on the Canary Islands said that formal cleaning services in Spain are much cheaper than in Sweden, so using RUT does not make sense.

Some of the domestic service providers with companies registered in Spain, offering the equivalent of Swedish *hemtjänst* (home based eldercare services), say they have IRM customers who cannot actually afford these services. There are IRMs who do not have a high enough income from which to deduce any taxes. In Sweden, those who consume ROT and RUT services are generally middle- to upper-class (Gavanas and Calleman 2013). In a privatised Spanish context, informal domestic services become one of the most accessible and affordable options for IRMs. This brings us to the issue of domestic service and its connection to cultural preferences.

Location of Formal and Informal Domestic Services within 'Cultural' Preferences

Similar to British IRMs in Spain, Swedish IRM interviewees maintain an ethos of helping each other and being 'like a family' (King, Warnes and Williams 2000: 148–152; Oliver 2008: 113). Those who have lived there longer, and those who have mastered the Spanish language, mediate for recently arrived IRMs. One interviewee described this in term of military service; an obligation that is compulsory for the sake of the migrant community during a certain phase or generational period. IRMs may volunteer in order to keep themselves busy, to meet people, to feel useful, or because they (also) need some extra income (O'Reilly 2000). This widespread work by IRMs within the IRM community is part of the unregulated and informal economy which is blurred with the formal economy in the sense that those who are working formally (IRMs as well as not-yet-retired workers) at real estate agencies, restaurants, etc. are often involved informally in the form of labour or goods exchange (O'Reilly 2000: 122–123).

There are IRMs who work informally for other IRMs, providing care and intermediary services (O'Reilly 2000: 122–123; Woube 2013). Some IRMs use unpaid volunteer services, which are another type of informal service, although not paid for on a market, which sometimes blends with the informal segment. At these organisations, those volunteering are often IRMs who help other IRMs with 'everything' out of solidarity; especially IRMs who have lived in Spain for many years and speak Spanish fluently. For instance, a Spanish speaking IRM on Isla del Sol provides unpaid services to the IRM community by translating Spanish news ('a hobby that costs money'), accompanying IRMs to doctors, dealing with IRMs who die and their mourning relatives, and helping IRMs with computers (he initially tried to charge 20 Euros per hour but this transpired not to be popular). In addition to official organisations, there were also some somewhat organised volunteer care networks among IRMs. For instance, an IRM interviewee on Isla del Sol spoke at length of the many benefits of the IRM care network that he was starting where IRMs would help each other out by providing unpaid elderly care. This could both enable IRMs to stay active and independent, as well as replace the need for family help among those IRMs who are widows, widowers or single. There are also intermediaries, i.e. workers and entrepreneurs at companies catering for IRMs, such as hair salons, real estate agencies, cafés, etc., who help with 'everything' for no extra charge.

When IRMs require cleaning services, interviewees tend to turn to the cheapest and most convenient option: informal services for five to ten Euros per hour obtained through word of mouth in social networks. IRM interviewees may legitimise these practices with the moral benefit of 'helping out' someone unemployed or poor by consuming their services. IRMs may combine cleaners (who tend to speak Spanish only, and possibly some English) with a Swedish speaking carer who they hire formally or informally at an hourly rate of fifteen to twenty Euros per hour.

There are also formally registered cleaning, care, and handyman service companies run by Scandinavians or Spaniards in IRM areas, advertising their services through Scandinavian contact zones (churches, organisations, hair dressers, cafés, etc.) and magazines. For instance, a Swedish woman in Guadamecer on the Costa del Sol is working formally as a home nurse at a Swedish domestic service company. She describes her services as offering 'the whole package', including general help at home, as opposed to specific nursing tasks. She believes IRMs prefer a Swedish nurse as her language skills give her an advantage on the labour market. Formal domestic service companies in Spain may subcontract some of the work to self-employed workers and charge much lower prices than their equivalents in Sweden. A Swedish man on Isla Bonita described how things work according to his experiences when hiring domestic workers:

> After half a year we started to get to know some people here and they had hired handymen through others. We are talking about Brits, and through Brits we got in touch with

> local Spanish workers. The rules here say that if I am a construction worker, working in a company here, a local Spaniard, everything top notch, everything okay by the book, then I have the right to carry out certain tasks outside of my company. Those (subcontracted) workers are so loyal and relatively cheap. If you want to know about prices I think we're paying, last time around, eight Euros per hour or something like that. And we get invoices. If they need help carrying out tasks they don't do by themselves, they can handle that. They take on full responsibility. [...] As for cleaning, some Brits – mostly Brits – and some Spaniards, locals, at the same price level. I would say those are more black [informal] than white [formal].

Thus, according to the Spanish regulatory system for formal domestic service companies, it may be unclear to the customer whether the subcontractors are hired informally or not. Additionally, whether subcontracting self-employed workers pay taxes and social security fees may too be vague.

Domestic services provided by Scandinavians and requiring Scandinavian language skills tend to be more expensive than services provided and managed by Spanish locals, Eastern Europeans or Third Country Nationals. An established Swedish handyman/cleaner/carer couple on Isla del Sol, with decades of experience working on the island, noted that their only competition is from Eastern Europeans, who are cheap but considered a disaster by customers (as they do really terrible and unreliable work). As such, the couple have not needed to lower their prices: the customers know what they get and prefer this security, although some have complained about the high prices. Another advantage they have is their established relation (over a long time) with the customers making it very difficult for newcomers to compete. However, Swedish handymen (and other Swedish migrant workers in Spain) may have to adjust to Spanish payment levels (and working hours) and thereby experience downward mobility as compared to handymen in Sweden (Lundström 2014). Moreover, Swedish handymen who have recently arrived may have difficulties in competing with more established ones who are familiar with the ways things work in Spain. As a Spanish handyman in Valleviejo on Costa del Sol noted:

> The problem is that in order to help out Swedes one needs to have lived in Spain and worked in Spain. A Swede who comes here and doesn't know Spanish can't do it either. It has to be a Swede who has lived here for seven or ten years and worked in Spain. It's not just the language, the system is so different, Spaniards are so different. Here there are a thousand rules as in Sweden, but the difference is that here there are rules to follow and rules you don't need to follow. You can disregard it. In Sweden a rule is a rule and that's it. But that's not how it works in Spain.

When it comes to selecting providers for handyman work (repairs and maintenance), IRM interviewees often compared Spanish and Swedish or other migrant workers in terms of 'cultural traits'. Among IRM interviewees, discussions on whether Spanish handymen have a '*mañana* attitude' were frequent, referring to timeliness. For instance, a female IRM in Valleviejo on the Costa del Sol explained that many Spanish handymen adopt the '*mañana*' attitude, but instead she wants order and timeliness (*punktlighet*). In contrast to such ideas, Swedish handymen could advertise their formal or informal services through IRM social networks and platforms, and offer 'Swedish' quality and timeliness. However, as IRM interviewees highlighted: they also charge 'Swedish' prices, and some questioned the perceived '*mañana*' stereotypes around Spanish handymen among fellow IRMs. A group of IRMs in Torremoros on the Costa del Sol discussed the '*mañana*' phenomenon as follows:

> Those who say that Spaniards are lazy, they haven't seen them work; they work hard as hell I think. I just hear what [my friend] Felipe says, that 'they can't make it in time, goddamn Spaniards', he says. [...] That mentality is there, *mañana* lives on a lot, especially for those who hire handymen, they can sit around and wait for them in vain for a whole day: nobody shows up. [...] But if you are stricter with them I think it actually works quite well.

An IRM couple in Fuenterredonda on the Costa del Sol hired a Spanish handyman recommended by Swedish friends as they said that he does everything, and works extra informally in addition to his regular job. The couple noted that when they (Spanish handymen) say '*mañana*' (tomorrow), you do not know which tomorrow they mean (i.e. which day the handyman will arrive).

Social norms around family, care and community are influential when it comes to the organisation of domestic services. These draw upon IRMs' background contexts in Sweden, as well as their social networks in Spain. Cheaper informal alternatives for domestic services and elderly care are easily available and normalised among customers as an acceptable option. Moreover, the importance of trust, personal recommendations and social networks in selecting domestic service providers increase tendencies towards informal alternatives. In Spain among IRM customers, informal providers are able to compete against formal providers by offering significantly cheaper prices, especially when it comes to services considered unskilled and with no language requirements, such as cleaning. Worker and entrepreneur interviewees with formal domestic service companies do experience competition from informal providers in Spain. One Swedish interviewee, the head of a company that provides domestic services to Swedish IRMs on the Costa del Sol, said: 'I dare not send one of my workers to any household for cleaning services, because I know shortly an informal worker would offer to do the same job for five Euros an hour'. She is annoyed with informal competitors who offer cleaning services for half the normal salary: 'You know how much effort it will take to raise these salaries? We live in a banana republic'. Competition with the informal market for cleaning jobs led her to abandon this area of services and concentrate on care where the demand for Swedish speaking staff is higher among IRM customers.

As apparent above, when it relates to cleaning services, informal workers may compete by offering lower prices, but not with services where language skills in Swedish are required, such as for care. For instance, a Swedish entrepreneur in Guadamecer on the Costa del Sol claimed that IRMs can hire a domestic cleaner informally, but they will never hire someone informally for important matters such as going to the doctor. For such matters, they prefer not to take the risk and instead hire a formally registered company such as hers. Likewise, a Swedish speaking formal care worker stated that IRMs require a worker they can communicate with, and therefore there are not many Spaniards among carers. IRMs legitimise their use of informal options in a number of ways. For example, they propose hiring informal staff is how things work in Spain. Additionally, it is cheaper (i.e. salary levels are lower in Spain), there is such high unemployment, the worker is a friend of a friend and it is helping them, or that Spaniards are more interested in informal arrangements. Beyond economic arguments, Swedes expose a contrasting perspective to their homeland when compared to Spain, and in this they illustrate how structural aspects of the changing welfare state in Sweden interplay with personal needs and desires, as well as with comparatively positive cultural perspectives on Spain.

Swedishness and Spanishness; the Intersection of the Personal, Structural and Cultural

To some interviewees, Sweden, 'Swedishness' and the Swedish welfare state represent safety and familiarity in the face of the Spanish context when they are no longer physically active and independent (Spanish provision of elderly care being practically non-existent to them). Some IRM interviewees feel that they are paying too much tax in Sweden without receiving enough returns (whilst residing in Spain). In addition, IRM interviewees expressed critique towards Swedish elderly care as being too impersonal, of low quality and scarce: resonating with common critique in Sweden towards Swedish '*hemtjänst*' (home based elderly care). Swedish retirement migrants, from all income categories, generally perceive Spanish health care as superior to the Swedish equivalent – especially interviewees on Costa del Sol. However, views on the Swedish alternative seem to shift when IRMs face alternatives for eldercare. Thus, while Spanish health care is a pull factor to migrate to Spain, Spanish eldercare later becomes a push factor to leave and eventually return to Sweden. Regardless, IRMs seek to extend their days under the Spanish sun, opting out of Swedish public provision while making themselves into consumers on an international market. Janne, an IRM in Valleviejo on the Costa del Sol, comments on the wealthy retirees born in the 1940s and that they have higher demands than Sweden offers:

> It is an enormous buying power that Swedish society will lose. [...] We demand a new society on our conditions.

Unless Sweden improves, Janne says that him and his wife will move to Spain and bring their resources along with them. Likewise, Donna in Carejas on the Costa del Sol is in a similar economic position, with a similar outlook:

> In my opinion, if there is anything one should use one's money for, it is to buy oneself wellbeing, when one finds oneself in my life stage. I can't afford to be unwell, Anna, it's about quality time, it's carpe diem!

Swedish IRMs are often very critical towards Sweden and Swedes. Especially critiqued is the perceived Swedish conformity, anti-sociality, jealousy, boredom and boastfulness. In contrast, life in Spain is considered more socially active, less narrow minded, livelier, less stressful and Spaniards are considered to have more respect for the elderly. For instance, Roland on the Costa del Sol states:

> I think that despite the economic situation, many people in Europe live a richer life, have a richer life than the Swede. They have more well-being, they socialise. They don't have our standard, but I mean, the Swede is actually very, very poor. Spaniards get more out of their time and feel much better [...] I don't think there is any society in the world as fabulously boring as Swedish society. There you go out and just do shopping; here you go out and it down at a bar and drink coffee and someone always comes around and talks to you. In Sweden, if you sit at the bar and rattle a bit too much with your glass or cup, they turn around and stare. Here one talks loud and yell at the waiter or waitress in any way one likes.

Lasse, another IRM on the Costa del Sol, speaks of similar advantages in Spain as compared to Sweden, especially when it comes to the segregation between generations in Sweden:

> If one disregards the economy I think Spaniards have a much better life, a cooler life, more chilled in relation to material means and the like. They take care of each other, they are there for each other in a different way than us Scandinavians. While there (in Sweden) one can almost expect that if something happens to you, then I think my son will more or less stay away. I might exaggerate, but I think there are a lot of ways in which I think he wouldn't help me out.

In Spain, beyond the warmer winter climate and lower prices, IRM interviewees seek the social life they are lacking in Sweden: an active life outdoors with social interaction among peers. Interviewees especially value the solidarity between IRMs: that Swedes in Spain help and take care of one another in ways which are considered non-existent among Swedish retirees in Sweden. The worst case scenario for many IRMs is to be forced to move back to Sweden and be isolated, fading away alone in an apartment. Within their social networks, IRMs are forming systems for checking on each other and helping in emergencies, for instance by phone chains. However, none of the initiatives discovered during the fieldwork of this research, in neither the Canary Islands nor the Costa del Sol, have become substantial enough to persist over time. This lack of collective capability can also become a source of disappointment, especially for IRMs who are single or widowed, whose friends have passed away or returned to Sweden.

Sigrid on Costa del Sol is one of the widowed IRMs who were planning to return to Sweden; most of her friends had already returned. When she considered the option to stay on in Spain she noted:

> There is nothing here – there is no *hemtjänst* [home based eldercare]. So you need to get private [services]. That's the thing: everyone starts looking around when the clock ticks: 'now it's time, we are moving back home!' It's like you enter safety when you come home to Sweden, that's the thing. You don't get that safety here, you don't. Especially when it comes to those of us [widows and singles] who live alone, that's the thing.

For retired migrants, as well as migrant workers, the heavy reliance on unpaid family care in Spain becomes problematic (Hardill et al. 2005). When economic, physical and social resources diminish, as IRMs gradually reach dependency on eldercare and their partners and friends pass away, life in Spain changes abruptly. Lack of fluency in the Spanish language may cause desperate situations for IRMs who do not return to Sweden: 'When a migrant needs health care or personal support, especially 24 hour care, limited Spanish-language skills pose major problems' (Hardill et al. 2005: 777). This is particularly important for IRMs with dementia or Alzheimer's. Unless they have the resources to pay privately or have access to unpaid family support, low to medium income Swedish IRMs who remain in Spain rely on charities and volunteer organisations that provide home or hospital visits and interpretation (Hardill et al. 2005), as well as the peer support and moral economy of their social network.

There is a tension between critiquing Sweden and fellow Swedes on the one hand (for being un-social, boring, mainstream, 'too Swedish' and lacking cosmopolitanism), and seeking solidarity between Swedes in Spain; between IRMs' individualist pursuits as consumers on an international arena, and forming collectivist moral economies in Spain. The bottom line is that there are fewer options when one is no longer physically capable to choose, and at this point the moral economy becomes the last stronghold before returning to the Swedish welfare state.

Moral Economy Within and Beyond Markets

The moral economy among IRMs occurs beyond and within market orientated exchanges and relations. It consists of solidarity, family-like obligations and gratitude between IRMs, but also between IRMs and workers, entrepreneurs and intermediaries who serve them. Thus, as Philip Whitehead and Paul Crawshaw argue (2014), the moral economy constitutes a challenge to the capitalist political economy that constantly stirs a competitive individualist spirit driven by the stimulation of consumer desires. Moral economy asserts human over economic interests and the value of collective before self-interest, prioritising duty to neighbour and rejecting the notion that an elite should profit from the necessities of others as woven into the natural order of things. However, neoliberal capitalist relations, as well as welfare states encompass moral economies constraining the options of actors.

In IRM destination zones the moral economy operates. This is apparent for all involved parties as everyday survival strategies and negotiations which are encompassed by exploitative neoliberal markets, the shrinking Swedish (or practically non-existent Spanish) welfare states and the physically absent family. However, different actors in IRM fields have different in-roads to this economy:

- **IRMs** are in the same situation and help each other out of solidarity and obligation as in turn, they might be the ones in need of help; widow(er)s are particularly looked after by the community. Some are simultaneously seeking a social life in Spain which they are missing in Sweden.
- From the perspectives of **workers** (Spanish and others), Swedish IRMs have a good reputation compared to other customers because they are generally considered 'grateful' and respectful. In other words, these workers select Swedish IRMs as customers out of other reasons than necessarily paying higher rates for their services.
- Among **intermediaries/entrepreneurs/migrant workers** with backgrounds in, or relations to, Sweden are those who express a wish to help Swedish IRMs out of obligation or compassion: to symbolically 'return' help one has received oneself in a similar situation (for instance as a migrant in Sweden).

One aspect to the moral economy is the family-like obligations and interactions between some providers and customers of domestic services, such as the notion that Swedish IRMs are particularly 'grateful' in the views of many domestic worker interviewees. Swedish IRMs are described as preferable as customers by workers and entrepreneurs, and are also considered popular as migrants contributing to the local economy through their consumption (see also Lundström 2014; Woube 2014). Worker interviewees demonstrate that Swedish IRMs clearly have a good reputation among domestic workers, within those who work both formally and informally. Swedes are thought to be respectful (particularly in comparison to the employers/customers from other countries) and reliable with payments and agreements. The preference for Swedish customers/employers appears among workers of all national backgrounds (Swedish, Spanish and South American). For instance, one Spanish cleaner at a Swedish apartment complex in Guadamecer says that working for Spaniards and Swedes is completely different. She feels that Swedish people value her work and that makes her feel good.

In sum, filling the gaps between family, state and the market provision of services, IRMs and the workers and entrepreneurs that cater for them, form a moral economy where provider–customer relations are characterised by obligations and solidarity. These non-monetary aspects of market connections may provide social cohesion and personalised labour relationships. The moral economy and its tendencies for unpaid work may eventually further workers' and entrepreneurs' interests in economic and social capital, but may also become a burden for providers with weak positions in the labour market. IRMs' continued existence in Spain is, however, conditioned by the unemployment, segmentation and precarity of the Spanish labour market in tourist regions: workers with low wages and 'flexible,' unpredictable, insecure and partly informal working conditions (Gavanas and Calzada 2016a, 2016b).

Concluding Discussion

IRM interviewees cast their community in Spain as the socially active and solidaristic alternative to a Sweden considered cold and boring with low quality public provision. Caught between individualist consumerism and collectivist survival strategies, some IRM interviewees seek to mobilise unpaid volunteer networks where IRMs provide help to each other but are often frustrated in the process. As discussed, moral economies are filling the void in the absence of the (imagined) Swedish welfare state and the physically present family: care by the community. However, health, family situation, nationality and socio-economic conditions impact the constraints and options for different actors to navigate. In addition, there are power relations between different groups among IRMs, as well as between different groups of service providers.

Despite the past Swedish social democratic welfare state tradition, aspiring to provide equal access to elderly care across socio-economic class, and the solidaristic efforts in IRM social networks, demand for domestic services is partly conditioned by socio-economic polarisation (Milkman et al. 1998) and this is equally true on a cross-national scale. When the market (as opposed to the state or the family) provides domestic services, its costs rises as wages do, and this means that workers' wages are always being forced down by strategies such as employing those with least bargaining power (Williams and Gavanas 2008). This is clearly demonstrated by the strategies among IRMs when related to unskilled, low wage and informal services on the segmented labour markets for domestic services in Spain. As Zoran Slavnic (2010) argues, informalisation occurs from above (by corporations, governments and subcontractors) and below (by marginalised actors such as low-income workers and self-employed/small business owners) in this field, but also from the middle, through IRM strategies. However, the moral economy formed in IRM zones makes these cleavages appear more legitimate to all involved parties while simultaneously 'levelling the playing field', at least cosmetically.

Asymmetric working conditions, and possibilities for future mobility and independent retirement, persist within a polarising context where privatisation and shrinking public provision across an ageing Europe intersects with economic crises and austerity measures in Southern Europe. Those who have the most disadvantaged conditions in IRM destinations are workers in unskilled jobs – such as Paula – struggling with unemployment or temporary contracts, and migrant workers because their salaries and social rights are the lowest, and their risks of poverty are higher. They are also part of a moral economy where personal relations of respect and family-like exchanges matter. These dimensions intersect with the gendered dimensions of the labour market conditions, as female domestic workers tend to have lower salaries than males. Notwithstanding, IRMs with low pensions, alone and in need of care, that cannot afford to pay professional services are forced to rely on informal carers with uncertain qualifications and with whom, for the most part, they cannot adequately communicate.

Intergenerational, socio-economic, gendered and racialised inequalities in domestic services relations, which are considered problematic in Swedish public discourse (Gavanas 2006), are outsourced to Spain where they become normalised among social networks of IRMs in the "foreign" context (Lundström 2013). Despite possibilities for free movement within Europe, and despite the migration- and work strategies of providers to improve the lives for themselves and their families, substantial inequalities, within and between the background and destination countries of migrants across a North-South EU axis, as well as between Third Country and EU nationals, persist unchallenged (Kilkey, Perrons and Plomien 2013: 66). Moral economies both mitigate such inequalities and make them more bearable. They provide survival strategies and respect while being enmeshed in neoliberal market logics and shrinking welfare provision.

References

Aguirre, G. 2013. 'Om känslor på jobbet. Intimitet, känslor och hushållstjänster i Barcelona.' In Gavanas, Anna and Catharina Calleman (eds.) *Rena hem på smutsiga villkor? Hushållstjänster, migration och globalisering*. Göteborg and Stockholm: Makadam, 143–160.

Álvarez, C. 2014. 'La importancia de la igualdad de derechos laborales para las trabajadoras del servicio doméstico.' *SEDOAC*, October 24. Accessed August 5, 2016. <http://serviciodomesticoactivo.blogspot.com.es/2014/10/la-importancia-de-la-igualdad-de.html>

Anderson, B. 2000. *Doing the Dirty Work? The Global Politics of Domestic Labor*. London and New York: Zed Books.

Åkerlund, U. 2013. 'The best of both worlds. Aspirations, Drivers and Practices of Swedish Lifestyle Movers in Malta.' PhD diss., Umeå University.

Blaakilde, A. L. and Nilsson, G. 2013. *Nordic Seniors on the Move: Mobility and Migration in Later Life*. Lund Studies in Arts and Cultural Sciences, Lunds Universitet.

Bolton, S. and Laaser, K. 2013. 'Work, employment and society through the lens of moral economy.' *Work, employment and society* 27/3, 508–525.

Breivik, J.K. 2015. '"Lille Norge": Emigranters Felleskapsutfordringer i Spania.' *Tidsskrift for Velferdsforskning* 18/1, 34–47.

Erlandsson, S., Storm, P., Stranz, A., Szebehely, M. and Trydegård, G.-B. 2013. 'Marketising trends in Swedish eldercare: competition, choice and calls for stricter regulation.' In Meagher, Gabrielle and Marta Szebehely (eds) *Marketisation in Nordic eldercare: a research report on legislation, oversight, extent and consequences*. Stockholm University: Stockholm Studies in Social Work 30, 23–85.

Gavanas, A. 2006. 'De Onämnbara: jämlikhet, "svenskhet" och privata hushållstjänster i pigdebattens Sverige.' In de los Reyes, Paulina (ed.) *Arbetslivets (o)synliga murar*, SOU 2006:59. Stockholm: Kulturdepartementet, 305–348.

Gavanas, A. 2013. 'Elderly Care Puzzles in Stockholm. Strategies, on formal and informal markets.' *Nordic Journal of Migration Research* 3/2, 63–71.

Gavanas, A. and Calleman, C. 2013. *Rena hem på smutsiga villkor? Hushållstjänster, migration och globalisering*. Göteborg and Stockholm: Makadam.

Gavanas, A. and Calzada, I. 2016a. 'Multiplex migration and axes of precarization: Swedish retirement migrants to Spain and their service providers.' *Journal of Critical Sociology*, Special issue on precarity edited by Carl-Ulrik Schierup and Martin Bak Jørgensen.

Gavanas, A. and Calzada, I. 2016b. 'Swedish retirement migrants in Spain: mobility and elderly care in Ageing Europe.' In Kilkey, Majella and Ewa Palenga-Möllenbeck (eds) *Family Life in an Age of Migration and Mobility: Global Perspectives through the Life Course.* New York: Palgrave.

Godenau, D. 2012. *El papel de la inmigración en la economía española.* Observatorio de Dovulgación Financiera, N°7.

González, J.S. 2014. 'Gestha dice que la economía sumergida creció al 24,6% del PIB por la crisis.' *El País,* January 29. Accessed August 5, 2016. <http://economia.elpais.com/economia/2014/01/29/actualidad/1390995231_745540.html>

Hardill, I., Spradberry, J., Arnold-Boakes, J. and Marrugat, L. M. 2005. 'Severe health and social care issues among British migrants who retire to Spain.' *Ageing and Society* 25, 769–783.

Ibañez, Z. and Leon, M. 2014. 'Resisting crisis at what cost? Migrant care workers in private households.' In Anderson, Bridget and Isabel Shutes (eds) *Migration and Care Labor: Theory, Policy and Politics.* New York: Palgrave, 110–130.

INE (Instituto Nacional de Estadística) 2012. *Encuesta de Población Activa* [Survey on Active Population]. Madrid: INE.

Jönson, H. 2015. 'Framing scandalous nursing home care: what is the problem?' *Ageing and Society* 36/2, 400–419.

Kilkey, M., Perrons, D. and Plomien, A. 2013. *Gender, Migration and Domestic Work. Masculinities, Male Labour and Fathering in the UK and USA.* Hampshire and New Yrk: Palgrave Macmillan.

King, R., Warnes, T. and Williams, A. 2000. *Sunset lives: British retirement migration to the Mediterranean,* Oxford and New York: Berg.

Lister, R., Williams, F., Anttonen, A., Bussemaker, J., Gerhard, U., Heinen, J., Johansson, S. and Leira, A. 2007. *Gendering citizenship in Western Europe: New challenges for citizenship research in a cross-national context.* Bristol: Policy Press.

Lundström, C. 2013. '"Maid" Sökes: 'Live In Maids' och skillnadsskapande praktiker i svenska migranthem i Singapore.' In Gavanas, Anna and Catharina Calleman (eds.) *Rena hem på smutsiga villkor? Hushållstjänster, migration och globalisering.* Göteborg and Stockholm: Makadam.

Lundström, C. 2014. *White Migrations. Gender, whiteness and Privilege in Transnational Migration.* Hampshire and New York: Palgrave.

Lutz, H. 2011. *The New Maids. Transnational Women and the Care Economy.* London och New York: Zed books.

Meagher, G. and Szebehely, M. 2010. *Private financing of eldercare in Sweden: Arguments for and against.* Working Paper 1/2010. Stockholm: Institute for Futures Studies.

Meagher, G. and Szebehely, M. 2013a. *Marketisation in Nordic eldercare: a research report on legislation, oversight, extent and consequences*. Stockholm: Stockholm Studies in Social Work 30.

Meagher, G. and Szebehely, M. 2013b. 'Long-term care in Sweden: Trends, actors, and consequences.' In Ranci, Costanzo and Emmanuele Pavolini (eds.) *Reforms in Long-Term Care Policies in Europe. Investigating institutional change and social impacts*. New York: Springer Science+Business Media, 55–78.

Milkman, R. et al. 1998. 'The Macrosociology of Paid Domestic Labor.' *Work and Occupations* 25/4, 483–510.

Näre., L. 2012. 'Moral Economies of Reproductive Labour. An ethnography of Migrant Domestic and Care Labour in Naples, Italy.' PhD diss., University of Helsinki. SSKG Skrifter 33.

Nyberg, A. 2013. 'RUT-avdraget.' *Fronesis* 42–43, 114–130.

Oliver, C. 2008. *Retirement Migration. Paradoxes of ageing*. London: Routledge.

O'Reilly, K. 2000. *The British on the Costa del Sol. Transnational identities and local communities*. London and New York: Routledge.

Rodríguez, V., Ángeles Casado, M. and Huber, A. 2005. *La migración de retirados europeos en España*. Consejo Superior de Investigaciones Científicas (CSIC), Unidad de Políticas Comparadas (UPC), Madrid.

Sardà. J. 2014. *La economía sumergida pasa factura: El avance del fraude en España durante la crisis*. Gestha (Union of the Technical Staff of the Spanish Finance Ministry).

Sayer, A. 2007. 'Moral economy as critique.' *New Political Economy* 12/2, 261–270.

Simonazzi, A. 2009. 'Care regimes and national employment models.' *Cambridge Journal of Economics* 33/2, 211–232.

Skatteverket 2011. *Om RUT och ROT och VITT och SVART*. Rapport 2011: 1.

Slavnic, Z. 2010. 'Political economy of informalization.' *European Societies* 12/1, 3–24.

Thelin, A. 2013. 'Äldrefattigdom, Ekonomisk utsatthet i yngre älderspensionärers vardag.' PhD diss., Linnaeus University. Dissertation No 154/2013, Växjö.

Ulmanen, P. 2015. *Omsorgens pris i åtstramningstid. Anhörigomsorg för äldre ur ett könsperspektiv*. Report in Socialt Arbete no. 150. Stockholms Universitet: Doktorsavhandling i Socialt Arbete.

Vincent, J. A., Phillipson, C. and Downs, M. 2006. *The Futures of Old Age*. London, Thousand Oaks and New Delhi: Sage.

Whitehead, P. and Crawshaw, P. 2014. 'A tale of two economies: the political and the moral in neoliberalism.' *International Journal of Sociology and Social Policy* 34/1–2, 19–34.

Williams, F. and Gavanas, A. 2008. 'The Intersection of Child Care Regimes and Migration Regimes: a Three-country Study.' In Lutz, Helma (ed.) *Migration and Domestic Work: a European Perspective on a Global Theme*. London: Routledge.

Woube, A. 2013. 'Transnational Voluntarism among Senior Swedish Migrants on Costa del Sol in Spain.' In Blaakilde, Anne Leonora and Gabriella Nilsson (eds.) *Nordic Seniors on the Move. Mobility and Migration in Later Life*. Lund Studies in Arts and Cultural Sciences 4. Lund: Lunds Universitet, 153–175.

Woube, A. 2014. 'Finding One's Place. An Ethnological Study of Belonging among Swedish Migrants on the Costa del Sol in Spain.' PhD diss., Uppsala University.

Magnus Dahlstedt & Anders Trumberg

7. Towards a New Education Regime: The Neoliberal Turn in Swedish Education Policy*

Abstract: The chapter focuses on the neo-liberal changes of Swedish education policy since the early 1990s and its consequences for the democratic and egalitarian visions of the education system. Policy changes, it is argued, have carried with them a reproduction and increase of inequalities between different students, along ethno-cultural/racial, gender, and class lines, in terms of educational options and outcomes.

Introduction

The education system in Sweden was for a long time segregated. The minority of mostly privileged, mostly male students could study at the upper levels of the education system while the majority – following the lines of the underprivileged population in terms of gender and social class – were bound to the lower levels. The idea of a more equal school system was first presented as a governmental report in the 1940s. But it was only in the 1960s that the system changed and became oriented towards social equality and equal distribution of educational opportunities (Trumberg 2011). Under the development and implementation of the post-war school system one aim of the government was to secure a democratic distribution of education. This new democratic orientation included the goal of fostering responsible and active democratic citizens.

The institution of the school was regulated by the state with the aim of being as equal as possible, independent of which school students attended. Between the 1960s and the 1980s the education system was characterized by a low proportion of private and independent schools, limited freedom of choice, and centralized regulation (Richardson 2004; Wahlström 2002). The organization of schools rested on the main pillars of non-segregation, social levelling, equality, general citizen-competence, and public responsibility for education (Rothstein 1998).

---

* This chapter is based on previously published work: Dahlstedt and Olson (2013), Dahlstedt and Neergaard (2015), Schierup and Dahlstedt (2015), Trumberg (2011).

One overarching objective of educational policy in the classical Swedish model was to gradually level social and economic gaps, and in this way to counteract the most polarizing effects of the market (Lindblad and Popkewitz 2001). The educational policy discourse was dominated by a view of education as a 'public good' (Englund 1993). Every individual growing up should be guaranteed the right, under such an educational policy, to equal education, understood and institutionally underpinned as a fundamental social right, in which the structure and content of education is deeply ingrained as a basic dimension of a welfare society's democratic order.

However, the school system in Sweden was highly debated in the 1970s. The main objections were that the central regulation of the schools did not take any consideration of local levels, that it did not involve the citizens in the decision-making process, and that there was a lack of effectiveness in terms of learning, financing and organisation, caused by the centralization (Wahlström 2002). It was, as in many parts in the Swedish welfare sector, the beginning of a process of decentralization that started at the end of the 1980s and the beginning of the 1990s, which has resulted in an offset of responsibility from the state to local municipalities, the market, civil society, and the individual. This development, following the lines of a neoliberal economic re-orientation in Sweden, and its consequences for the democratic visions and realities of the education system, will be discussed further in the following chapter. Focusing on the relationships between the goals of equality and equivalence, and the neoliberal turn in Swedish education, we argue that the changes in the Swedish education system in the last two decades illustrate the effects of the priorities of the market principles that, when normalized in education, have created the foundation of the present divisions of school, educational options and outcomes for different students, along ethno-cultural/racial, gender, and class lines.

This chapter is structured according to the following: Firstly, it focuses on some of the main neoliberal reforms initiated in Sweden since the early 1990s, most importantly the freedom of choice reform. With these reforms, there has been an increasing focus on the responsibilities and active participation of the individual, where education is conceptualized as a 'private good' rather than as a 'common good'. Secondly, these reforms relate to issues of diversity and the inclusion of migrants. Thirdly, some of the consequences of the reforms initiated in the last two decades are discussed, with a particular focus on issues of segregation and increasing polarization. Fourthly, the main conclusions of the chapter are summarized and discussed.

Market-Oriented Reforms and Freedom of Choice

Generally, several of the comprehensive changes that have occurred in the Swedish welfare model since the 1980s (See the chapter of Schierup and Scarpa in this volume; Schierup and Dahlstedt 2015) have left clear impressions on the educational policy (Dahlstedt and Olson 2013). Swedish educational policy has gradually shifted from having been regarded as a 'public good', schools are now seen more as a 'private good', with a focus on individual choice, parental responsibility for education, efficiency and competition, and the development of individual competence as guiding principles of how schools should be run (Englund 1993). Influential voices stressed that schools should not only provide certain common basic knowledge, but they should also offer more opportunities for individuals to develop their potential and their interests. By the end of the 1980s the responsibility for schools shifted from central government to local municipality authorities.

The 1991 change of government, when Sweden elected a centre-right coalition, was a key change in direction for Swedish educational policy. Freedom of choice was introduced, the regulations regarding independent schools were changed, and several municipalities brought in school voucher systems. Both compulsory and upper-secondary schools were also given greater scope for creating a profile of their own. The schools gradually adapted to the new rules, and it was at the end of the 1990s that a major change in the school market became visible in the form of an increase of new, independent schools with specialized profiles (for example sport, culture, health).

One of the consequences of the political shift in the 1990s, primarily in the big cities, was a rapid rise in the number of students attending an increasing number of independent schools, which had profit, not uncommonly, as an important driving force (Arnman, Järnek and Lindskog 2004). In 1992, 1.1 percent, or 5000 students, attended independent schools. In 2015, the figure was 14.1 percent, or 134 000 students. Today there are 800 independent schools at the compulsory level (from first to ninth grade), and most of these independent schools are run by large companies specializing in the school sector. There are also various municipal, organizational hybrids, for example schools that are municipality schools but are called *'Intraprenad'* schools which function as independent schools regarding the economy. They can keep any profit they make, while at the same time receiving public funds based on the number of their students. This means that the profits from these independent schools do not go into the municipal budget to be redistributed among local schools.

Sweden thereby made a dramatic switch to '…in international terms, extremely generous legislation when it comes to the right of privately organized schools to receive public funding', and independent schools keeping their profits (Rothstein and Blomqvist 2000: 164). With the overall changes in the education system, Sweden went from having one of the world's most government-dominated and unified education systems, to one with the highest level of freedom of choice; a change that even the OECD (2012) classified as 'radical'. So, what effects have these changes had on the levels of equality and equivalence in the school system?

Though present for a long time in the Swedish debate, the concept of equality (*jämlikhet*), and later the concept of equivalence (*likvärdighet*), came in during the 1980s at the centre of the political debate regarding the organizational development of schools and the related changes to the education system (Englund and Quennerstedt 2008). At the beginning of the 1960s the concept of equality (*jämlikhet*) meant that schools should be equal. It should not matter which school a person studied in or which social class they belonged to, the education system would give equal opportunities to all. The content of the education was the same in all schools; the books and other material were the same, and so on. This development of the school system after the Second World War was in many ways a reaction to the previous school system, that to a large extent was highly segregated (Wahlström 2006).

The concept of equivalence (*likvärdighet*) was first used in the 1970s and had in the beginning the same meaning as equality. It was in the late 1980s that the meaning of equivalence was challenged by the centre-right-wing parties. When using the concept, they gave it a more individualistic meaning. The traditional meaning of equity and equivalence, as creating good and responsible citizens within the societal collective, was re-interpreted as the individual right for students to develop their comparative advantages. In that way, 'equivalence' created inequalities within the school organization, such as freedom of choice, independent schools, and different school profiles. Thus, the centre-right-wing parties associated the concept of equivalence with students' rights to choose their school, and the uniform system was seen as a restriction of individual freedom and therefore also a restriction regarding equivalence (Englund and Quennerstedt 2008). In this new interpretation, equivalence should be guaranteed by directly formulated goals in the curriculum, admission requirements for the teachers, and different forms of evaluation within the school system.

At the beginning of the 2000s, this shift in the concept of equivalence was furthermore linked to the results of students. It was argued that if students did not reach their educational goals the system could not guarantee equivalence. This meant that equivalence was associated with the quality of education, evaluation, and reviews. For example, a Government Official Report suggests radical changes to the aim of improving the quality of schools (SOU 2007:28). Among others, the changes aimed at reducing the number of national goals and introducing more national tests. Those tests should then be used to measure the knowledge base (*kunskapsnivå*) of the students, as well as the efficiency of the schools (Bergh 2008).

The discussion about equity and equivalence is by no means over, and it will continue. However, the change of the concept of equivalence at the end of the 1980s was a precursor to the reforms that were initiated at the beginning of the 1990s. These neoliberal reforms have, in a very short time, resulted in a fundamental change of the Swedish education system (Trumberg 2011).

Neoliberal Partnerships for Lifelong Learning

The changes of the education system were in accordance with the premise of the market economy, including a greater element of competition, which was assumed to lead not only to a higher degree of *cost-effectiveness*, but also to higher *quality* and extended *offerings*. The heightened competition was also assumed to 'unleash' creativity among staff, parents, and students.

At the same time, individual students were given more latitude to shape their own 'knowledge profile'. Students' extended possibilities for choosing courses and subjects and for participating in the planning and assessment of teaching was now put forward as being central to the 'fostering of democracy' in the schools (Department of Education 1994). Even before the new national curriculum took force in 1994 the centre-right government had decided that students/parents should have the right to choose their school, and that at least 85 percent of the cost per student was to be defrayed by the home municipality.

These changes illustrate a move towards a policy of 'partnership' as a vehicle for developing the characteristics of a new form of embedded neoliberal policy. Education policy is one of the areas of public policy in Sweden where discourses on partnership has had an especially strong impact. Ever since the late 1980s, it has been strongly emphasized in Swedish education policy that schools should be organized and run by teachers, parents, students, in cooperation with other players in the local community, rather than by the state and the central bureaucracy (Lindblad and Popkewitz 2001; Dahlstedt and Hertzberg 2011). Taking effect in the 1990s, this policy change embodied a wish to counter the negative effects of the deregulated market through cooperation between players *across* sector and purview demarcations, and between state/municipality and business, and elected representatives/civil servants and civic associations.

One issue that has recently attracted both public and political attention is the partnership of schools with the business community. This is an issue that encompasses several dimensions. There are a number of examples of how organizations representing business interests participate in the system of education, for example by offering schools free instructional materials that are geared in various ways to influence students in a more business-friendly direction (Confederation of Swedish Enterprise 2006). A form of cooperation between schools and business that has become increasingly common is for privately run schools to offer instruction in the workplace and in companies with the aim of establishing contact points between students and the labour market.

Apace with the shift of focus in politics from central regulation to goal-oriented control, collective to individual, public to private, and external to internal demands, schools have successfully moved from being regulated by 'decree' to being about freedom of choice and responsibility. Demands for conformity have been turned into demands for variety, direct control has turned into accountability, and sanctioning into self-discipline. The operational forms of schools have been adapted to the changing needs of the labour market. The growing amount of student-led instruction is only one example of how students are introduced to a working life characterized by uncertain terms of employment and flexible organizations (Österlind 1998).

This trend, however, is not unique to Sweden. Corresponding adjustments to the demands and expectations of the labour market have taken place in several OECD countries. The OECD itself has long played an influential role as both a source of inspiration and a foundation for legitimizing various reforms of economic and educational policy in its member countries (Dovemark 2004).

Within the European Union there is at the turn of the millennium a lively discussion on how it can strengthen its competitiveness in the global knowledge economy. Here, 'lifelong learning' is promoted as an important part of the economic growth potential of education: 'the move towards lifelong learning must accompany a successful transition to a knowledge-based economy and society'. Lifelong learning is seen here as essential for the individual as well as for society.

> All those living in Europe, without exception, should have equal opportunities to adjust to the demands of social and economic change and to participate actively in the shaping of Europe's future (Commission the European Communities 2000: 3).

Here, the focus is on the individual as a learning subject. Responsibility for learning should be transferred from the state to the individual, while the responsibility of the state is to 'create opportunities and incentives for individuals, businesses, and governmental actors in order to invest in education and learning' (Skolverket 2001: 12). The keyword is 'invest'. Education and learning should be understood as investments for 'individuals, businesses, and governmental actors'. The reform of secondary education – senior high school – is a telling example of the special kind of adjustment to a working life taking place in the early years of the new millennium (Dahlstedt and Hertzberg 2011; Lundahl and Olson 2013; Öhrn, Lundahl and Beach 2011). If the goal of education policy in the early post-war years was, step-by-step, to create a school for all students, the reform of secondary education in the new millennium, to an extent, means a return to a more divided secondary education in which vocational and academic programs are more distinctly separated. Academic programs are meant to lead to continued studies, while vocational programs are meant to lead to 'acknowledged competence and employability' (SOU 2008: 24). This is one of several signs of the far-reaching reformation of education during the early part of this millennium.

Another sign of this reformation is a gradually increasing emphasis on entrepreneurship in educational contexts. Between the years 2005 and 2008, a nationwide program for education in entrepreneurship was carried out across the country: the so-called 'national entrepreneurship program'. This program is aimed at the whole educational system since the intention is to create a 'leitmotif' in the Swedish educational landscape.

> When entrepreneurship runs like a recurring theme through all the educational system it will have an impact. An individual who is formed by entrepreneurial learning in school becomes a workforce asset for the existing organizations. Entrepreneurship also brings with it the courage to take off—to start one's own business and realize lifetime dreams (Nutek 2008: 11).

A result of this ambition is that entrepreneurship was written into the new curriculum for secondary education, launched with the new curriculum of 2011 (Öhrn, Lundahl and Beach 2011). As stated by the Swedish National Agency for Education:

> An important function for school is to provide a general view and coherence. School should stimulate the students' creativity, curiosity, and self-confidence as well as their will to try out their own ideas and solve problems. The students should have the opportunity to take an initiative and take responsibility as well as develop their ability in working independently and together with others. School should through this contribute to the students developing an approach that promotes entrepreneurship (Skolverket 2011: 9. Author's translation).

The inclusion of entrepreneurship in the curriculum points to how the principles of the market have been normalized in education. What previously stood out as a contradiction between the ambition of education to educate citizens for democracy on the one hand, and to educate the workforce requested by the market on the other hand (Englund 2005 [1986]), now seems to have dissolved. Education for democracy and education for entrepreneurship at this time became integrated parts of the same educational project. The ends and means of politics are, as in the 1990s, responsible citizens – individuals who can and want to take responsibility for forming their own lives. The role of education is to make these young people *want to* take responsibility for their own lives in the future (Fejes and Dahlstedt 2013). However, less attention has been paid to collective, public, and civic factors, such as the social and economic circumstances which characterize the conditions for the will and responsibility of the individual.

Education between Homogeneity and Diversity

In education policy there has for a long time been an ideal of ethno-cultural homogeneity – this applies to Sweden as well as to many other countries. In the process of nation-building, a large-scale educational project was initiated – i.e. shaping the population into an imagined national community. In Sweden, the elementary school system, established in 1842, became a central arena for such an educational project (Ehn, Frykman and Löfgren 1993). However, in a world increasingly formed by migration, the vision of a national community (as well as the role of education within the national project) has gradually changed. With migration, some notions that were previously considered as self-evident have been seriously challenged. In education policy, the main focus has shifted from seeing migration as a problem (in terms of, for instance, adaptation and language difficulties, cultural clashes, crises of identity, and rootlessness) to an emphasis on migration primarily as a resource, where the focus is on ethno-cultural diversity and the recognition of differences (Olson 2008; Dahlstedt and Hertzberg 2011).

However, in the Swedish education system of the new millennium, the relationship between the notions of ethno-cultural homogeneity and ethno-cultural diversity is somewhat contradictory. There is a tension between a transgressing approach on the one hand – challenging borders and boundaries – and a preserving approach on the other, based on a strong insistence on education for a Swedish ethno-cultural community defined in terms of particular 'core values' (*värdegrund*) (Dahlstedt and Olson 2013). During the early 1990s, there was something of a return to an older way of imagining 'Swedish core values' taking place. In the curriculum of 1994 'Swedish core values' were defined as a reified cultural community tied to religion, or rather Christianity, and a set of particular, deeply rooted traditions. At the same time, there has been sharp criticism directed towards an explicit emphasis on single-direction assimilation of certain categories of migrants to a predefined Swedish ethno-cultural community. In the public discussion about 'core values' in Swedish schools, the 'values' referred to appear as both universal and inclusive, but, at the same time, some 'values' – as well as their adherents – appear in themselves to be problematic and in need of 're-education'.

These negotiations and contradictions are not only visible at the level where policies are *formulated,* but also at the level where policies are actually *realized* (cf. Lindensjö and Lundgren 2000). There is a range of studies indicating the differing treatment of students in Swedish schools, where some are portrayed and treated as problematic, and 'the Others' as being in need of assimilation into a Swedish, imagined community (Lundquist 2010; Mulinari and Neergaard 2010). The same goes for parents (Dahlstedt 2009). Migrants are, in a variety of settings, defined in terms of their supposed deficits or shortcomings, focusing on either ethno-cultural features (such as 'loss of identity', 'cultural clashes', and language problems), or socio-economic features (such as lack of 'social capital', unemployment, 'social exclusion', and 'welfare dependency') (Runfors 2003; Dahlstedt 2009). Some students, particularly those categorized as 'non-Western', 'non-European', and 'non-Christian', are portrayed and treated as migrants, although they might have been born in Sweden and are Swedish citizens. Their actions, for example in classroom situations, tend to be interpreted in terms of their attributed belonging to a certain collective; that is, their 'ethno-cultural belonging', and not in terms of their individuality (Runfors 2003; Hällgren 2005; Mulinari 2015).

Segregation, Differentiation and Unequal Opportunities

In parallel with the reforms that since the 1990s have gradually transformed the Swedish educational landscape, there has also been an intensive debate on their possible negative consequences (Lindensjö and Lundgren 2000; Arnman, Järnek and Lindskog 2004). A recurring theme has been the risk of increased segregation and differentiation; a theme that has been addressed in a number of official reports. These reports have pointed to a connection between decentralization and the freedom of choice reforms of the 1980s and 1990s, and increased differentiation. Despite increased opportunities to make individual decisions, 'differentiation of students largely follows earlier patterns' (Arnman, Järnek and Lindskog 2004: 161). Study choices, school achievement, and higher education continue to be segregated along socio-economic lines. Moreover, the reforms implemented since the 1980s and 1990s have tended to *reinforce* prevailing patterns of differentiation and segregation – particularly in urban areas, where the establishment of an increasing number of independent schools has led to keener competition for both students and staff. Since the 1990s, Swedish schools have increasingly become more homogeneous in terms of class as well as ethno-cultural background, and thus function less as places where students from different ethno-cultural and class backgrounds can meet (Trumberg 2011).

The fact that schools have become more socially and ethno-culturally homogenous has often been said to be the effect of an increasingly residential segregation – following the argument that if the neighbourhood around a school becomes more homogenous, the school also tends to become more homogenous (Lindbom 2010). But recent research has shown that the freedom of choice has reinforced segregation between schools (Östh, Andersson and Malmberg 2013; Böhlmark, Holmlund and Lindahl 2015; OECD 2015). Anders Böhlmark, Helena Holmlund and Mikael Lindahl (2015) show that regions with a higher degree of school choices have a higher level of school segregation than regions with fewer choice opportunities. From quantitative analysis they conclude that the increase in school segregation cannot be fully explained by the current residential segregation, and that school segregation was less if the students had attended their assigned schools. Students' choices of independent schools have an impact on school segregation (Böhlmark, Holmlund and Lindahl 2015). John Östh, Eva Andersson and Bo Malmberg, studying the increased differentiation in terms of performance between schools, conclude that:

> The most likely driving force behind the increasing differentiation is not residential segregation, but rather the rapid structural transformation of the Swedish school system. A rapid growth in the number of students attending voucher-financed, independent schools has been an important element in this process (Östh, Andersson and Malmberg 2013: 422).

The practical teaching itself could make it more difficult for some students to attend some schools. The more project-based teaching, with less teacher-led time – which is most common in independent schools – and less support from home, make it difficult for students to manage the courses. Therefore, schools can use the way of organizing the teaching as a means to select students with a certain socio-economic background. In addition, independent schools have lower teacher-pupil ratios than schools managed by the municipality (Skolverket 2016). The teacher-pupil ratio is one way for independent schools to cut costs and yield a profit, but reducing levels of teaching staff also reduces the amount of teacher-led time.

A pattern well-known in the sociology of education is that student achievement is strongly influenced by the learning environment at the school. It has been shown that students whose parents have low levels of education perform better in classes dominated by students with highly educated parents than they do in classes where the parents have low levels of education (Arnman and Jönsson

1983). The freedom of choice reform has led not only to increased segregation in schools – in the form of a greater concentration of students on the basis of the educational background of their parents – but also to greater differences in student achievement, both across schools and among students (Skolverket 2006, 2012). Students of foreign background show lower levels of achievement than their native Swedish counterparts. This is a pattern that pervades all subjects. On the other hand, girls of foreign background achieve better results in school, on average, than do boys of native Swedish background (Arnman, Järnek and Lindskog 2004).

Independent schools are for example overrepresented in the 100 schools in Sweden, with the lowest teacher-pupil ratio. While the students in these schools have very high grades compared with students from other schools, this could be explained by the students' socio-economic background and their highly educated parents (Svensson and Wingborg 2015).

The key explanation for differences in achievement therefore seems to be the social, rather than the ethno-cultural, background of the students. The importance of students' social backgrounds seems to have increased in this case as well. At the same time, owing to a complex interaction of class divisions and ethno-cultural and geographic segregation, the effects of attending a school dominated by students of foreign background have increased since the late 1990s:

> The higher the proportion of foreign-born students in a school, the lower the achievement expected from a student at that school, regardless of whether a student is foreign-born or not (Skolverket 2006: 38).

These effects of segregation have become even more visible in the new millennium (Skolverket 2012). This is probably due to an increase in movement from one school to another, where it is, above all, students with foreign backgrounds who have lived in Sweden for a longer period who 'move away from immigrant-dense schools, while relatively recently arrived foreign born students start or remain in schools with a high proportion of foreign-born students' (Skolverket 2006: 38–39).

But you could also argue that more than student achievement is affected. Segregation also affects school goals regarding the formation of 'democratic citizens'. This can be seen mainly in two ways. When school is no longer a meeting place for students of different social and cultural backgrounds, students tend to grow up in different social worlds. This has an impact on their attitudes, behaviour, and ideas of reality, and also forms their ideas of the people they do not meet in everyday life: 'the Others' (Trumberg 2014; Nielsen-Schjellerup 2006; Strömblad 2003; Karsten 1998). But you could also see that the students' civic competence (*medborgarkompetens*) would be affected. By 'civic competence' we mean democratic values, trust in politicians, trust in political institutions, and trust in their own ability to communicate and shape values and ideas. Such competence is high in schools with a high proportion of students with well-educated parents, although students from different socio-economic backgrounds can also benefit from being part of this milieu. In other words, students from low-educated, low-income households can achieve better civic competence if they attend schools with students from high-educated and high-income households (Ekman and Zetterberg 2010). In this way, the homogenization of schools also has an impact on the democratic goals of the Swedish education system.

School Choice and Labour

As discussed above, during the economic crisis of the 1990s, a number of dramatic changes in the Swedish welfare model took place that also created severe problems in the schools (Broady 2000). The crisis brought with it an increased polarization, by gender, ethnicity, and age, where single mothers, individuals of non-European background, and young people were among the worst affected (SOU 2000:39). The labour market for young people largely evaporated in the economic crisis. Cuts in municipal budgets hit schools and child care harder than other spheres. Funding per student for teaching declined drastically. The number of students per class grew. Many schools made major cuts in special education. Those students who had the greatest difficulty in completing compulsory schooling were no longer welcome in working life, which meant that within a landscape that was segregated geographically along class and ethno-cultural lines, they were forced to pursue upper-secondary programs characterized by circumscribed opportunities for development and careers. This placed young people of foreign background in a particularly precarious situation. Vocational education of a traditional type hardly existed anymore. Even though an ever-growing component of theoretical studies may be seen as justified by the heightened demands from employers in more sectors of the labour market, the result was an increase in drop-out rates (Broady 2000).

At the same time as the competition for attractive educational opportunities has grown stiffer, upper-secondary schools are offering an ever more varied choice of educational alternatives. The educational field has gradually turned into a market (Lundahl et al. 2014) that is more and more difficult to define for those participating in it (Broady 2000). Besides the fact that the choices that have been circumscribed for both students and parents, it is becoming increasingly difficult to get an overview of the concrete possibilities that any choice offers (Dovemark 2004). The crucial decisions about students' schooling are made earlier and earlier in their lives, whereas the consequences of those decisions appear later and later. Poorly considered decisions entail a risk of having only limited choices in the future and can lead to multiplying the exclusionary effects. For individual students to be able to take advantage of the opportunities offered by freedom of choice, they must possess a great awareness of what possible future benefits – or limitations – the choices entail (Skawonius 2005; Lundahl et al. 2014). For students to have the support and help of their parents and other family members may be an indispensable asset – not only in terms of getting help with homework but also when it comes to navigating the tortuous terrain that freedom of choice presents (Dovemark 2004). Parents with access to economic resources, educational capital, robust and influential networks, and cultural assets acquire a good knowledge of the educational field and the labour market, and on this basis they can tailor special educational niches to fit their own children perfectly (Broady 2000), thus making effective decisions that further their children's educational and labour market careers.

Ethnic Polarization and 'White Flight'

At the turn of the millennium, Bo Rothstein and Paula Blomqvist (2000: 185) proposed three serious warning signs regarding the impact of the freedom of choice reform on ethnic segregation: (1) it is primarily children of native Swedish parents who choose to leave municipal schools in favour of independent schools, (2) native-born Swedish parents tend to move away from schools in areas with a high concentration of people of foreign background; a pattern of movement that is usually termed *white flight* in the Anglo-American literature, and (3) an increasing number of free schools with specific language, ethnic, or religious orientation, which they maintain 'by definition, increases ethnic segregation'. Fifteen years later, these three warning signs are still highly relevant. Anderson, Östh and Malmberg (2010) have studied 'white flight' and shown that the student population that is defined as a majority population (all students except students with fathers born in Africa, the Middle East, or South America) moves out when the population of students from the visible minority (students with fathers born in Africa, the Middle East, or South America) increases in the schools. The study also shows that the socio-economic characteristics of students in schools are more important for student achievement than the socio-economic characteristics of the surrounding neighbourhood (Anderson, Östh and Malmberg 2010; Bergsten 2010).

If too many students of foreign background attend a school, that school tends to get a bad reputation, which in turn diminishes its attractiveness to native-born students of middle class background (Bunar 2001, 2009; Skawonius 2005; Kallstenius 2010). Such schools soon run the risk of starting a downward spiral of continued student flight, dwindling resources, bad reputation, budget cuts, staff flight, etc.

The rumours about bad reputation that follow certain schools often develop from the characteristics of the surrounding neighbourhood, when people living outside the area see the neighbourhood and the school as a segregated, 'no-go area'. Bad reputations are often based on the socio-economic and cultural characteristics of the neighbourhood (basically the social and ethno-cultural backgrounds of its inhabitants), and are often formed through the media. The inhabitants are seen as violent, different, and poor. The schools are often stigmatized by rumours of an unsettled and violent milieu, and their achievements, measured by student grades, are relatively low. But schools can have a rather good student milieu and reputation regarding student achievement if, for example, progress of student achievement is measured by following a cohort between seventh and ninth grade instead of aggregating students' grades year by year (Trumberg 2011). The causes that most parents specify when they choose schools are often driven by emotions and based on feelings instead of the more rational considerations described in neoliberal economic theories. Many parents also have limited knowledge about the different alternatives and the choices that could be made (Skawonius 2005; Skolverket 2003).

A bad reputation eventually influences the economic budget, and schools that are not capable of reversing such trends may ultimately face the threat of closure. But in reality relatively few 'low performing' municipality-managed schools are closing. Neoliberal theory postulates free entry to and exit from schools that compete in the school market, which means that schools that cannot compete are going to be closed. But the political reality is different as it is quite hard to close schools down. Thus, if a politician makes a decision to close a school down, he or she is at risk of not being re-elected. From the local political perspective, the closing of a school also has to be balanced against other factors, such as the overall municipality service grade in the area. So in reality, it is not so easy for municipality-managed schools to exit the market, though it might be easier, taking parental resistance into account, to close a school with a bad reputation in a low status area than one with a bad reputation in a high status area (Trumberg 2011).

Among families whose children attend schools in areas with high concentrations of people of foreign background, there is often a concern – regardless of the families' own background – that the children will not learn Swedish properly, precisely because of the low proportion of native Swedish students. Concern about the language development of children is often an important reason that parents give when choosing to move their children to other higher status and 'Swedish-dense' schools (Kallstenius 2010).

Within the category of parents of foreign background, it has been shown that there are major differences regarding their choice of schools. Some parents are strongly inclined to make an active school choice, while others do not make an active school choice. These differences are greater within the category of native Swedish parents. In this respect it is possible that Sweden will gradually establish school patterns similar to those in a number of other countries, namely, that some parents of foreign background actively use, or have the opportunity to use, their right to choose schools to get away from 'immigrant-dense schools' (Trumberg 2011; Skolverket 2006). Since parents who make use of their school choice are normally relatively well-educated, the effects are a small but noticeable and parallel decrease of *ethno-cultural* segregation, and an increase of *social* segregation (Rothstein and Blomqvist 2000). For the individual, education can open up new opportunities. However, as long as successful individuals opt to move out of 'vulnerable' suburban areas, while less successful individuals move in, these environments will continue to be segregated (Arnman, Järnek and Lindskog 2004; Kallstenius 2010; Trumberg 2011). There seems to be little evidence that the existing school hierarchy is breaking up. Rather, as shown by international research, the free choice reforms tend to set the hierarchy in stone (Bellei and Vanni 2015; Musset 2012; Ladd 2003).

> Even though theoretically, choice can be introduced into schooling systems to improve the opportunities disadvantaged children can receive, at the same time, the same policy arrangements have other effects that hinder equity, as the possibility of exercising choice is not the same for all parents (Musset 2012: 33).

And today, the education system is, to all intents and purposes, subordinated to this driving force of free choice.

Concluding Reflections

Summarising this chapter, we have outlined the various education reforms initiated in Sweden since the 1990s, with the main goal – in line with a broader neoliberal agenda – of reducing state power and reinforcing individual choice. The result of these reforms has been that the Swedish education system of today functions more as a springboard for the individual than as a policy instrument for the equal redistribution of educational options. As in other policy areas, the principle of equality, in the sense of equal *outcomes*, has gradually been replaced by the principle of equity, in the sense of *opportunities* (Lindensjö and Lundgren 2000). The conditions of education are dictated more and more by the demands and expectations of the (labour) market. The increasingly influential doctrine of 'lifelong learning' challenges individuals to secure their 'enterprise' and 'employability' on their own, continuously, through various kinds of continuing education and (re)training. An active, self-aware, and responsible subject, modelled on the *entrepreneur*, is the prototype for such education. This subject is no longer an equal citizen but an individual, constantly updating his/her qualifications, learning to make well-considered, independent choices, and continually searching for new possibilities to invest in (Rose 1998). This perpetual process of becoming successful is understood as being of considerable value, not only according to the logic of the market (that is, to start and run a business), but also beyond the domains of the market.

> Entrepreneurial competences increase the opportunities of the individual to start and run a business. Competences such as to see opportunities, to take an initiative, and to turn ideas into action are of considerable value to the individual and to society in a wider sense (The Government Office 2009: 12).

The concept of lifelong learning rests on an understanding of society that carefully *avoids* further analysis of politico-economic power relationships, which legitimates and reproduces a segmented society along ethno-cultural/racial, gender, and class lines. The dominant ideal that the educational system should 'focus on the individual' and provide individuals with the scope to realize themselves to the best of their ability, obscures symbolic and material inequalities. The philosophical figure of 'the free individual' is cut off from conditions that are decidedly real. Inequalities are parenthesized as if they did not exist (cf. Fraser 1992). Furthermore, such a 'focus on the individual' tends to provide greater scope for the unequal preconditions that students and parents bring with them when they make their individual school choices.

The connection between work, the labour market, and education is strong. Those who do not manage in school are almost automatically disqualified in the labour market. Together, schooling and education in the new millennium are more than ever seen as a national comparative advantage, and therefore linked to efficiency, growth and profit. Students are the people who would carry and realize this value. Successful students are those who can navigate the education system and make all the right choices. The changing meaning of equivalence has contributed to relativizing the notion of equality, adjusting it to the leading principles of competitiveness in a market-driven knowledge society.

Acknowledgement of Funding

This work was supported by the Swedish Research Council (grant number 721-2013-2009).

References

Andersson, E., Östh, J. and Malmberg, B. 2010. 'Ethnic Segregation and Performance Inequality in the Swedish School System.' *Environment and Planning A* 42/11, 2674–2686.

Arnman, G., Järnek, M. and Lindskog, E. 2004. *Valfrihet – fiktion och verklighet.* Department of Pedagogy, Uppsala University.

Arnman, G. and Jönsson, I. 1983. *Segregation och svensk skola.* Lund: Arkiv.

Bellei, C. and Vanni, X. 2015. 'Chile: The Evolution of Educational Policy 1980–2014.' In Schwartzman, Simon (ed.) *Education in South America.* New York: Bloomsbury, 179–201.

Bergh, A. 2008. 'Från likvärdighet till kvalitet.' In Englund, Tomas and Ann Quennerstedt (eds.) *Vadå likvärdighet?* Daidalos. Göteborg, 165–182.

Bergsten, Z. 2010. 'Bättre framtidsutsikter?' PhD diss., Department of Cultural Geography, Uppsala University.

Böhlmark, A., Holmlund, H. and Lindahl, M. 2015. *School choice and segregation.* Uppsala: Institute for Evaluation of Labour Market and Education Policy.

Broady, D. (ed.) 2000. 'Skolan under 1990-talet.' In SOU 2000. *Välfärd och skola,* SOU 2000: 39. The Committee of Welfare Closing. Stockholm: Fritzes.

Bunar, N. 2001. *Skolan mitt i förorten.* Stehag: Symposion.

Bunar, N. 2009. *När marknaden kom till förorten.* Lund: Studentlitteratur.

Commission of the European Communities 2000. *A Memorandum on Lifelong Learning.* Commission Staff Working Paper. SEC(2000) 1832. Brussels: Commission of the European Communities.

Confederation of Swedish Enterprise 2006. *I praktiken.* Stockholm: Confederation of Swedish Enterprise.

Dahlstedt, M. 2009. 'Parental Governmentality.' *British Journal of Sociology of Education* 30/2, 193–205.

Dahlstedt, M. and Hertzberg, F. 2011. *Skola i samverkan.* Malmö: Gleerups.

Dahlstedt, M. and Neergaard, A. 2015. 'Conclusion: Swedish exceptionalism and beyond.' In Dahlstedt, Magnus and Anders Neergaard (eds.) *International Migration and Ethnic Relations.* London: Routledge, 249–271.

Dahlstedt, M. and Olson, M. 2013. *Utbildning, demokrati, medborgarskap.* Malmö: Gleerups.

Department of Education 1994. *Lpo 1994. Läroplan för det obligatoriska skolväsendet, förskoleklassen och fritidshemmet.* Stockholm: Department of Education.

Dovemark, M. 2004. 'Ansvar – flexibilitet – valfrihet.' PhD diss., Department of Pedagogy and Didactics, Gothenburg University.

Ehn, B., Frykman, J. and Löfgren, O. 1993. *Försvenskningen av Sverige*. Stockholm: Natur & Kultur.

Ekman, J. and Zetterberg, P. 2010. 'Vad förklarar skillnaden mellan 14-åringars medborgarkompetens?' In Skolverket (ed.) *Skolor som politiska arenor*. Stockholm: The Swedish National Agency for Education, 80–103.

Englund, T. 1993. 'Utbildning som "public good" eller "private good".' Department of Pedagogy, Uppsala University.

Englund, T. 2005 [1986]. *Läroplanens och skolkunskapens politiska dimension*. Lund: Studentlitteratur.

Englund, T. and Quennerstedt, A. (eds.) 2008. *Vadå likvärdighet?* Göteborg: Daidalos.

Fejes, A. and Dahlstedt, M. 2013. *The Confessing Society*. London: Routledge.

Fraser, N. 1992. 'Rethinking the Public Sphere: A Contribution to the Critique of Actually Existing Democracy.' In Calhoun, Craig (ed.) *Habermas and the Public Sphere*. Cambridge: MIT Press, 109–143.

The Government Office 2009. *Strategi för entreprenörskap inom utbildningsområdet*. Stockholm: The Government Offices.

Hällgren, C. 2005. '"Working Harder to Be the Same".' *Race, Ethnicity and Education* 8/3, 319–342.

Kallstenius, J. 2010. 'De mångkulturella innerstadsskolorna.' PhD diss., Department of Sociology, Stockholm University.

Karsten, L. 1998. 'Growing up in Amsterdam.' *Urban Studies* 35/3, 565–581.

Ladd, H. 2003. 'Introduction.' In: Plank, David. N. and Gary Sykes (eds.) *Choosing Choice: School Choice in International Perspective*. New York: Teachers College Press, 1–24.

Lindblad, S. and Popkewitz, T. S. (eds.) 2001. *Education Governance and Social Integration and Exclusion: National Cases of Educational Systems and Recent Reforms*. Uppsala Reports on Education 34. Department of Pedagogy, Uppsala University.

Lindbom, A. 2010. 'School Choice in Sweden.' *Scandinavian Journal of Education Research* 54/6, 615–630.

Lindensjö, B. and Lundgren, U. P. 2000. *Utbildningsreformer och politisk styrning*. Stockholm: HSL.

Lundahl, L., Erixon Arreman, I. Holm, A.-S. and Lundström, U. 2014. *Gymnasiet som marknad*. Umeå: Boréa.

Lundahl, L. and Olson, M. 2013. 'Democracy Lessons in Market-Oriented Schools.' *Education, Citizenship and Social Justice* 8/2, 201–213.

Lundquist, C. 2010. 'Möjligheternas horisont.' PhD diss., Department of Social and Welfare Studies, Linköping University.

Mulinari, D. 2015. 'Kalla mig vad fan du vill, men inte invandrarförälder!' In: Dahlstedt, Magnus, Fredrik Hertzberg, Susanne Urban and Aleksandra Ålund (eds.) *Utbildning, arbete, medborgarskap*. Umeå: Boréa, 189–213.

Mulinari, D. and Neergaard, A. 2010. 'The "Others" in Sweden.' *The Journal for Critical Education Policy Studies* 8/2, 130–164.

Musset, P. 2012. *School Choice and Equity: Current Policies in OECD Countries and a Literature Review*. OECD Education Working Papers, No. 66. OECD Publishing.

Nielsen-Schjellerup, H. 2006. *Gemenskap och utanförskap*. Stockholm: Liber.

Nutek (The Swedish National Board for Technical and Industrial Development) 2008. *Entreprenörskap i stort och smått*. Stockholm: Nutek.

OECD 2015. *Improving Schools in Sweden: An OECD Perspective*. OECD.

Olson, M. 2008. 'Från nationsbyggare till global marknadsnomad.' PhD diss., Department of Behavioural Sciences and Learning, Linköping University.

Öhrn, E., Lundahl, L. and Beach, D. 2011. *Young People's Influence and Democratic Education*. London: Tufnell Press.

Österlind, E. 1998. 'Disciplinering via frihet.' PhD diss., Department of Pedagogy, Uppsala University.

Östh, J., Andersson, E. and Malmberg, B. 2013. 'School Choice and Increasing Performance Difference.' *Urban Studies* 50/2, 407–425.

Richardson, G. 2004. *Svensk utbildningshistoria*. Lund: Studentlitteratur.

Rose, N. 1998. *Inventing Ourselves*. Cambridge: Polity Press.

Rothstein, B. 1998. *Just Institutions Matter*. Cambridge: Cambridge University Press.

Rothstein, B. and Blomquist, P. 2000. *Välfärdsstatens nya ansikte*. Stockholm: Atlas.

Runfors, A. 2003. Mångfald, motsägelser och marginaliseringar. Stockholm: Prisma.

Schierup, C.-U. and Dahlstedt, M. 2015. 'Bortom den svenska modellen?' In Dahlstedt, Magnus, Fredrik Hertzberg, Susanne Urban and Aleksandra Ålund (eds.) *Utbildning, arbete, medborgarskap*. Umeå: Boréa, 27–56.

Skawonius, C. 2005. 'Välja eller hamna.' PhD diss., Department of Pedagogy, Stockholm University.

Skolverket 2001. *Det livslånga och livsvida lärandet*. Stockholm: The Swedish National Agency for Education.

Skolverket 2003. *Valfrihet och dess effekter inom skolområdet*. Stockholm: The Swedish National Agency for Education.

Skolverket 2006. *Vad händer med likvärdigheten i svensk skola?* Stockholm: The Swedish National Agency for Education.

Skolverket 2011. *Lgr 11. Läroplan, examensmål och gymnasiegemensamma ämnen för gymnasieskola 2011*. Stockholm: The Swedish National Agency for Education.

Skolverket 2012. *Likvärdig utbildning i svensk grundskola?* Stockholm: The Swedish National Agency for Education.

Skolverket 2016. 'SIRIS Database.' Accessed February 10, 2016. <http://siris.skolverket.se/siris/f?p=Siris:1:0>

SOU 2000. *Välfärd och skola*. SOU 2000:39. Socialdepartementet. Stockholm: Fritzes.

SOU 2007. *Tydliga mål och kunskapskrav i grundskolan*. SOU 2007:28. The Commission on Goals and Evaluation in Primary Education. Stockholm: Fritzes.

SOU 2008. *Framtidsvägen*. SOU 2008:27. The High School Commission. Stockholm: Fritzes.

Strömblad, P. 2003. 'Politik på stadens skuggsida.' PhD diss., Department of Political Science, Uppsala University.

Svensson, S. and Wingborg, M. 2015. *Färre lärare ger vinsten*. Stockholm: Katalys.

Trumberg, A. 2011. 'Den delade skolan.' PhD diss., Örebro studies in human geography 6, Örebro University.

Trumberg, A. 2014. 'You and the Other: the school as a meeting place.' In Eimermann, Marco and Anders Trumberg (eds.) *Place and Identity*. Stockholm: Santérus Academic Press.

Wahlström, N. 2002. 'Om det förändrade ansvaret för skolan.' PhD diss., Department of Pedagogy, Örebro University.

Wahlström, N. 2006. 'Likvärdighet – ett begrepp med skilda demokratiska dimensioner.' In Ekström Mats (ed.) *Om demokratins villkor II*. Örebro: Örebro University, 59–75.

Magnus Dahlstedt & Vanja Lozic

8.
Problematizing Parents: Representations of Multi-Ethnic Areas, Youth and Urban Unrest

Abstract: The causes of and solutions to juvenile delinquency and social unrest among youth in so-called Swedish multi-ethnic urban areas are frequently represented in public-institutional discourse as related to migrant parents. These are, the authors argue, consequently exposed to policies for 'activation', 'responsibilisation' and 'normalisation'.

> Is it possible to make new citizens? Yes. [...] they are made all the time. But if their social constitution is erected upon what they are said to lack, then citizens will always fall short of democratic expectations.
>
> Barbara Cruikshank (1999: 123)

Introduction

One of the central debates on social policy and social cohesion in Sweden revolves around the country's disadvantaged, so-called Urban Development Areas. The centre of attention has been, time and again, the suburban areas built as part of the large-scale housing projects of the 1970s, the so-called Million Programme (Abiala 2014; Hallin et al. 2010; Magnusson 2014). From the start these areas were represented as a problem in public debate, defined in terms of social and/or ethno-cultural Otherness (Ristilammi 1993; Molina 1997; Brune 2004). In the new millennium, these areas were once more constructed as a problem in the public discourse. At this time, multi-ethnic suburbs were referred to as 'areas of exclusion' (*utanförskapsområden*) (Dahlstedt 2015). These changes in ways of representing the suburbs as a problem, in turn, are part of wider transformations in welfare policy and the governing of citizens, where there has been a shift of focus from centralism and social inclusion to autonomy and responsibility of the individual (See the chapter by Schierup and Scarpa in this volume). The focus on multi-ethnic suburbs was further emphasized by a series of violent uprisings, setting cars and schools on fire, and local confrontations with the police, throughout Sweden – for instance in 2005 in Ronna, Södertälje, 2008 in Rosengård, Malmö, and 2013 in Husby, Stockholm (see the chapters by León Rosales and Ålund, Schierup and Ålund in this volume; de los Reyes et al. 2014).

The focus of this chapter is on examples of juvenile delinquency and social unrest among youth in so-called Swedish multi-ethnic areas during this decade.[1] Using interviews with police informants, schools, voluntary organizations, and social services, and as researchers involved in working on social inclusion among youth in one of the Million Programme areas in Sweden, we analyzed various discursive conceptualizations of the causes of urban unrest and the means to solve these problems. With an analytical framework inspired by Michel Foucault (1991) and his theorization of governing as a point of departure, the analysis of interviews indicates a strong focus on the family in general, and migrant parents in particular, as problems in need of normalization to Swedish core values. Briefly, we argue that these conceptualizations of problems and solutions may be seen in the light of on-going changes in welfare policy, where the main responsibility for the welfare of citizens is put on the individuals themselves rather than on the collective and the state.

Analytical Framework

The theoretical point of departure for this chapter is the concept of *governmentality* (following Foucault 1991; Cruikshank 1999; Dean 1999; Rose 1999; Hindess 2002). The focus is on 'different mentalities of government' (Dean 1999: 16), drawing attention to the complex ways in which thought is linked to a wide range of procedures and techniques. According to Foucault (1991), governing does not originate from, or belong to, the state apparatus. Rather, governing is made up of a broad repertoire of government technologies operating throughout the *entire* social field. Governing is not only restrictive but is also productive, argues Mitchell Dean (1999). According to Carol Bacchi (2010: 4) individuals 'are governed through problematization' and the problem representations they contain.

In line with such an approach, we analyze the representation of a problem, or rather how different organizations create a problem, and what they propose to do about it (Bacchi 2010). Thus, governing may be understood as problematizing activities, in the sense that certain phenomena, domains, or subjects in society are represented as problematic and thus in need of intervention. This means that 'problems are not pregiven, lying there waiting to be revealed. They have to be constructed and made visible...' (Miller and Rose 2008: 14). Through such problematizing activities, certain phenomena, domains, or subjects are made *governable*, i.e. the target of governing practices which operate throughout society. Thus, every problematization or construction of *problems* is intimately related to the

1 This work was supported by the Swedish Research Council (Grant number 721-2013-885).

construction of *solutions*: 'every postulated "solution" has built into it a particular representation of what the problem is…' (Bacchi 1999: 21).

The classic formula for governing the welfare state is, according to Nikolas Rose (1996), state-centric. The formula consists of making the state the primary agent that forms, guides, and controls events and people, based on uniform policies. However, according to Rose, today we are living in a society formed by neoliberal governmental rationalities, where governing 'does not seek to govern through "society", but through the regulated choices of individual citizens, now constructed as subjects of choices and aspirations to self-actualization and self-fulfilment' (Rose 1996: 41). Here, governing is about constant *responsibilization*, i.e. the creation of active and responsible citizens who take charge of the entire course of their own lives (from education and work, to politics and housing, to family and leisure activities etc.) on the basis of their *own* ideals, circumstances, ambitions and, of course, *efforts*. Hence, the objective of these interventions is 'implanting in citizens the aspiration to pursue their own civility, well-being and advancement' (Rose 1996: 40), i.e. the creation of individuals who are *motivated, willing,* and *able* to be active and take initiative. The creation of such active and responsible citizens consists of a broad repertoire of technologies which operate in different fields and which form subjectivities in ways that make individuals, on their own, *want* to take initiatives (Popkewitz, Olsson and Petersson 2007).

The *family* is one of the most crucial domains where such governing is taking place (cf. Donzelot 1977; Popkewitz 2008). The family, according to Rose (1999: 74), 'has a key role in strategies for the government of freedom', as it 'links public objectives for good health and good order of the social body with the desire of individuals for personal health and well-being'. The formation of citizens is not only about fostering children to become certain kinds of subjects, it is also about enabling parents to raise their children in a 'desired' direction, i.e. they also need to be fostered as parents (Vincent 2000; Dahlstedt 2009a). Interventions in one direction or the other therefore cannot easily be distinguished from one another; they are intimately woven together in a complex 'government through the family' (Donzelot 1977: 92). Through a wide range of problematizations, the family is targeted as being in need of certain interventions, and thus made governable. Such problematizations make families, as well as society at large, governable. An important research question is thus: How are families of different kinds problematized in relation to certain norms – for instance the 'black', 'migrant', or 'socially excluded' family (cf. Lawrence 1982; Grillo 2008; Vanderbreck, Rose and De Bie 2011; Eliassi 2014; Franklin and James 2015)? As we will see in this chapter, in Sweden of today there is a strong problematization of parents' migrant backgrounds.

Based on these analytical points of departure, interviews were conducted with twenty representatives of municipal, state, and non-governmental organizations, working for and with young people in the Area.[2] Even though the interviews cover a variety of themes, they mainly revolve around the interviewees' work with young people, and the way they describe and rationalize this work. In our analysis, we focus on the interviewees' understanding of juvenile delinquency as a *problem*, and on the *solutions* they advocate. Drawing on a discourse analysis influenced by the work of Foucault (1991), discourses are seen not simply as reflections of 'reality', but rather as structuring what is thinkable and sayable about certain issues, and as defining problems as well as proper solutions to these problems. In the interviews, a variety of representations of, and solutions to, the problems are included. These representations are often intertwined with each other and thus difficult to separate. Nevertheless, an analysis of the interviews highlights several prevailing representations of problems and solutions, and these will receive prominence in the analysis.

However, before we begin the analysis, we would like to contextualize this study by referring to the political transformation of Sweden's welfare model.

Governing Welfare, Governing the Multi-Ethnic Suburb

The governmental rationality of the Swedish welfare model, developed in the post-war period, was – referring to Rose (1996) – state-centric. Inspired by Keynesian ideas, it emphasized full employment, including government intervention, to secure demand and active labour market policies. This welfare model was based on the pillars of centralism and universalism, social intervention, and consensus (Rothstein 1998). According to this governmental rationality, the state had the legitimacy as well as the authority to intervene in the social body. This principle was further closely interrelated to another important notion in the Swedish welfare model, *social engineering*, according to which governing society was seen as being based on social planning, expertise, and scientific knowledge.

2 The Area, situated in a large Swedish city (the City), has for decades been at the forefront of public debate on the so called Million Programme. In recent years, the focus of these debates has been on the repeated incidents and confrontations between young people living in the Area and the forces of order. The interviewees, employed as social workers, principals, police officers, risk and safety workers, psychologists, youth coaches and youth leaders, project managers, borough coordinators, and drama teachers, are working on improving the situation in the Area in general, and supporting children, adolescents, and young adults in particular.

However, starting in the late 1980s, the 'Swedish model' and the governmental rationality on which it was based, were challenged and criticized, among other things, for their alleged inefficiency and centralized micro-management (Boréus 1994; Hugemark 1992; see also the chapter by Schierup and Scarpa in this volume). Since the late 1980s, the Swedish model has experienced a gradual shift towards a welfare model shaped by more neoliberal governmental rationalities (Larsson, Letell and Thörn 2012), emphasizing individual autonomy, initiative, and freedom of choice vis-à-vis the principle of state intervention as a means of achieving equality and the redistribution of societal resources (Ryner 2002; Lindvall 2004).

With this shift, the notion of *active citizenship* has become part of the mainstream policy discourse in a number of different arenas – for instance in the areas of the labour market, education, and social policy – where there is a strong focus on 'activating' citizens and making citizens take responsibility and including themselves in society (cf. Dahlstedt 2009b, 2015; Carlbaum 2012; Vesterberg 2013; Larsson 2015). In several policy domains, political reforms have been implemented which have gradually turned welfare from being a collective social right into being a commodity, i.e. an individual enterprise – for instance education (Lundahl et al. 2014; Fejes and Nordvall 2014; see also the chapter by Dahlstedt and Trumberg in this volume) and eldercare (Andersson and Kvist 2014). In this respect, being a citizen-subject has increasingly come to mean acting as a consumer in a welfare market. Thus, the contours of a *new Swedish model* are emerging, with this new model emphasizing the obligations, duties, and moral fibre of active citizens over their rights (Johansson 2001; Junestav 2004; Schierup, Krifors and Slavnic 2015).

In the 1990s, the public sector came to be seen by Swedish policy-makers as a service producer first and foremost, whose main task it was to satisfy citizens' demands. Moreover, public sector performance has increasingly been evaluated on the basis of its ability to deliver its services at the lowest possible cost. This is a far cry from the traditional, social democratic view of the public sector as an instrument of social transformation, providing citizens with a refuge from the stratifying effects of a capitalist society (Blomqvist 2004: 151).

These transformations have implied significant changes in the way the welfare sector is organised and run, not least for those working with the issues that we analyze in this chapter, namely young people and youth problems. The on-going transformations in governing the welfare state are visible not least in the areas of the Million Programme. Since the 1990s, these areas have been transformed from being 'mixed neighbourhoods' into areas with a vast majority of inhabitants with migrant backgrounds. During the same period, the general rise of inequality in the

Swedish welfare model at large has become more visible – in the broader Swedish urban landscape as well – with increasing polarization in the cities (Bustos Castro and Lindblad 2004; Scarpa 2015). It has been evidenced that in-movers to areas of the Million Programme are 'less educated, more often unemployed, have lower disposable income, and… [are] less often natives or have a Western background compared to those who move elsewhere…' (Andersson 2013: 184). In other words, there are parallels between developments in Swedish cities and the patterns of segregation and urban polarization found in other Western countries, for instance in the US (cf. Wilson 1987; Wacquant 2008).

The number of people receiving income support in areas of the Million Programme is many times higher than for Swedish society as a whole (Socialstyrelsen 2010). In these areas the interplay between spatial segregation, marginalization in the labour market, and stigmatization generate social and economic as well as educational inequalities (Bunar 2001). Poverty is heavily concentrated in the peripheral suburbs of the large cities throughout Sweden (Scarpa 2015). Schools in these areas tend to be highly stigmatized, which has led to a 'flight' of pupils to more 'reputable' schools. As the pupils who are left in the suburban schools usually come from families with low levels of social, economic, and cultural capital, school results tend to deteriorate and the schools get even lower status and quality ranking in the educational field (Kallstenius 2010).

In Swedish urban policy in the new millennium, multi-ethnic 'areas of exclusion' have appeared in contrast to the norm of active citizenship (Dahlstedt 2015). These areas, together with their inhabitants, have increasingly become identified as a serious political problem that needs to be dealt with (Bustos Castro and Lindblad 2004; Tedros 2008). The issue that has repeatedly been raised in public discourse is how to get the suburban population to transform its morals of dependency and passivity into the diligence, confidence, employability, and enterprise of the surrounding Swedish society. In urban policy discourse, exclusion is first and foremost to be resolved from inside the 'areas of exclusion'. On the basis of such rationality, a range of 'activating' initiatives have targeted the multi-ethnic suburbs, providing opportunities, removing obstacles, and motivating and stimulating self-sufficiency among the inhabitants (Davidson 2010).

This representation of the problems of 'areas of exclusion' and the proposed solutions to these problems has several parallels to the 'moral underclass' discourse that has been quite influential in the political debate in other countries, for example Britain and the US (Levitas 1998). As in the 'moral underclass' discourse, the primary focus is on the various shortcomings and responsibilities of 'the excluded', rather than on the hierarchies and inequalities of the economy or society in general (cf. Schierup, Krifors and Slavnic 2015).

How, then, do the interviewees understand the issue of juvenile delinquency in the Area - as a *problem* and what *solutions* do they advocate in order to deal with this problem? The analysis begins with the interviewees' representations of the problems, followed by the solutions that they emphasize.

Dominant Problematizations

When it comes to representations of problems there are four main and interrelated problematizations in the interviews: the locality as a problem; parent's lack of involvement; family issues, and not least, migrants' backgrounds.

The Locality as a Problem

In the interviews, the problematization of the young is first of all related to *the urban environment* of the Million Programme. In the interviews, the urban environment appears as a frame in which the lives of young people are made comprehensible (cf. Bustos Castro and Lindblad 2004). It is on the basis of the urban environment in which young people reside that their behaviour is being construed. In the interviews, the Area is generally described as a locality situated on the outskirts of, or outside, the City, and outside the rest of Swedish society. Different conditions, rules, and norms seem to apply to the Area than to the rest of the City and society. In the interviews, the urban environment is represented as a breeding ground for young people who end up with different kinds of problems, which the interviewees are then forced to respond to and manage. A recurring representation is that there is a lack of positive role models in the Area who can serve as good examples for children and adolescents of how a good life can be lived.

In the interviews, two aspects appear to make the Area problematic. Firstly, the Area has (too) high a concentration of inhabitants born abroad, and they have established (too) strong a group of ethnic enclaves. As a result of this, it is argued, a form of parallel society has evolved. For instance, youth aid worker Maria describes how a large percentage of the residents of the Area are 'left out of the rest of the country', and how they are contained in 'small communities' where 'they live in their own reality'. In this environment, even young people who were born and raised in Sweden, and are thus in a sense 'Swedish', consider themselves first and foremost 'migrants' or 'non-Swedish' on the basis of their parents' country of birth. In these communities developing over time, a distrust grows of society, of its institutions and its representatives. Many parents 'have not learned the language', Maria notes, adding that they are more or less exclusively engaged in ethno-cultural associations, and obtain information primarily by watching foreign satellite and TV channels.

The second problem that is evident in the interviewees' talk about the Area is the high unemployment rate, which according to social welfare worker Olivia is so palpable that there is virtually 'no one they know who goes to work'. This condition implies that the unemployed parents 'become role models for children, and unemployment becomes the norm'. Following this line of argument she asserts that, to the question 'What will you be when you grow up?', the answer from young people is 'Well, I do not know, I will be nothing'.

On the whole, the Area is represented as an insecure and disorderly neighbourhood – a locality 'excluded' from society. It is said that criminals here act as role models, particularly for young men for whom they offer economic gains, security, and a sense of belonging, in exchange for a hiding place, selling drugs, and stealing. Police officer Andreas contrasts the situation in the Area with the living conditions that exist in other localities, 'where school activities work; where you have motivated friends who invest in the sports and education'. In these, more 'normal functioning' localities, the young are not attracted to crime and the drug trade as potentially the only possible way to achieve success.

Unconcerned Parents as a Problem

In this particular urban context, as depicted by the interviewees, even parents emerge in a distinctive way insofar as they are frequently described in terms of problems, not least because they appear to be unconcerned. School principal Henrik's standpoint is an example of such problematization. Based on his experiences in a compulsory school in the Area, he argues that 'parents care very little about the school', despite the fact that the school premises and the learning environment have for a long time been very unsatisfactory. Another school principal, Carina, is also concerned about the lack of parent engagement in school issues, and she argues:

> We rarely succeed in getting many parents at parent-teacher conferences. The biggest turnout is amongst the parents who have a job and are part of society; and it's not all parents who have managed this. [...] Among the more economically powerful groups, [in the areas] where there are more highly educated parents, there the schools come into question. It is not the best thing for the school to be challenged by the parents, but the parents in [the Area] are passive.

Carina distinguishes between parents from the Area and the residents from the City's more affluent areas, where parental involvement in children's schooling and in society at large is greater. Even if she makes a distinction between different neighbourhoods in terms of parental involvement, she is careful not to present a too generalized picture of parents from the Area. School principal Carina distinguishes, for example, between parents who have paid work, and thus are implicitly equated to being integrated in society, and those who do not work, and who are more passive and uninvolved with regards to school issues. Similarly, school principal Henrik emphasizes that the Area is characterized by a high turnover of residents, and that many parents drive their children to other neighbourhoods, with the aim of providing them with better prospects. It could be argued that these parents are in fact *highly* involved in their own and their children's living conditions, and that they take active decisions about the future.[3]

A characteristic example of parents' lack of involvement in their children's lives is, according to the interviewees, the parents' inability to encourage their children. An important part of the work that youth aid worker Maria conducts is to learn more about young people's lives, understand their living conditions, promote equality, and adapt her work to their schedules, interests, and needs. She notes that many parents she encounters 'do not encourage their children, not in any way, or rather they do not have the ability to encourage children and give them positive attention that strengthens them'. Based on this observation, she draws the conclusion that 'parents do not know in all situations how to encourage children'.

How is it then that parents are not sufficiently involved in their children's lives? The interviewees put forward two main reasons: first, generally problematic family situations, and second, parents' migrant backgrounds.

The Family as a Problem

In the interviewees' accounts, the family is identified as a major cause for the emergence of diverse problems among young people. However, not all families are portrayed as problematic. Rather, a problematic family is essentially characterized as being permeated by destructive relationships between partners, divorce, mental health problems, substance abuse, and domestic violence. In the problematic family, support and care, both of which are required as necessary for children to

3 Support for this argument is also found in current statistics, showing that the parents from the Area are those who make the greatest use of the possibility to freely choose a school. While a large proportion of the students from the Area commute to other districts, there are almost no students from other districts who come to any of the schools in the Area (cf. Dahlstedt and Lozic 2017).

grow up to be well-functioning and law-abiding citizens, are missing for various reasons.

When youth aid worker Boris discusses his experience of working with young people, who for different reasons have had difficulties adjusting to current social norms, he especially emphasizes children and adolescents who are exposed to physical and/or psychological abuse. According to him, these children and adolescents gradually lose confidence in the adult world, and in their despair they may become belligerent. Based on his work experience, Boris gives the following example of how these processes may materialize:

> [The guy] was quite often beaten by his father. […] And then there was a divorce, but it was not an ordinary divorce, but rather harsh one. This made this guy react aggressively, but this is a normal reaction. […] Many people around me are victims, so you feel like the whole world falls apart.

According to Boris, children and adolescents 'do not get support at home', because the parents 'are not able to cope', so young people run the risk of resorting to the street 'gangs and subcultures'.

Child psychologist Esther suggests that in the Area there is a large percentage of 'ruptured families', where parents have their own problems, not least the abuse which leads children and adolescents to feelings of 'loneliness, fear, and abandonment'.

> The parents of these young people have considerable needs, so they have not been able to see [their] children's needs, and this has consequences later in life. […] These parents feel that they are not enough and relieve the anxiety with other means. Children become psychologically abandoned. Instead of rejection, a child who is sad needs closeness and nearness. But if this happens over and over and over again, it will lose trust and confidence in the adult world.

She believes that the development of a positive identity among children requires a stable childhood and a safe home environment, both of which are lacking in these 'ruptured families'. Parents' own problems may have a significantly negative impact on young people's prospects, and instead of creating trust and confidence, their relationships with their parents create distrust and suspicion.

Similarly, youth aid worker Thalia exemplifies that 'many [parents] have come from difficult circumstances and can't bother to get involved'. While she expresses that these parents are indeed uninvolved, she underlines that they 'are not bad parents'. Their attitude is more about 'the situation they are in that makes it difficult for them to act in accordance to their desire', as well as the knowledge that 'they cannot support their child in the way they would like'. The family is once again described as being in a social context where relationships do not really work, and where conditions are such that parents can hardly live up to the accepted norms for good parenting. Responsibility and commitment are the key elements of these norms.

Migrant Background as a Problem

The problematization of the parents' lack of involvement is directly connected with another form of problematization that recurs in the interviews: the parents' *migrant background* as a problem in itself, which supposedly shapes the parents' views on parenting (cf. Ålund 1991; Mattsson 2005; Grillo 2008; Eliassi 2014). However, the parents' migrant background is not problematized in one, but in various ways.

One way to problematize migrant background is to present it as a breeding ground for miscellaneous broken relationships and social problems. As Secure Safe worker, Patrik, puts it: parents have 'seen terrible things, which they have not been able to deal with, so they cannot move on with their lives'. One can recognize the outline of this kind of problematization, for instance from Ylva Brune's (2004) analysis of media representations of the problematic family.

The parents' problems are frequently derived from their insufficient knowledge of Swedish and a lack of understanding of Swedish society. Youth aid worker Maria speaks of many 'parents, who cannot find their bearings in society' and who thus 'lead a life of their own, which is quite different from the norm'. She believes that this greatly hampers the future prospects of children and adolescents. School principle Carina is one of those who see a clear link between language problems and passivity, and accordingly she concludes, 'if about half of parents don't understand what you're saying then there is no purpose in that kind of [parent-teacher conference]'. Respectively, police officer Ingmar emphasizes language as a serious barrier, but he accentuates an additional language issue as particularly alarming, namely the inverse dependency relationship emerging between parents and children.

> I have employees who hold inquiries at home, in an apartment, talk to parents who don't speak Swedish. Children speak better Swedish, so the kids deceive the parents by lying or not telling the whole truth to their parents, because they don't speak the language.

From his point of view, parents' language deficiency results in an inversion of parent-child relationships. Not only do children act as interpreters, but parents also become dependent on their children as well as becoming isolated in their homes, finding it increasingly difficult to set limits on their relationship with their children. A municipality manager, Nicklas, makes a similar argument, explaining how the inverted family relationships may imply that 'the son dominates very much; he starts to call the shots and pull the strings', which in turn 'will result in growth of criminality and drugs'.

This problem is not only about parents lacking knowledge on the whole, but more about them having wrong and/or inappropriate knowledge. A recurring problem description is that some parents have experience of living in political systems and cultures that are very different from 'Swedish', which in itself is said to have a number of problematic consequences (cf. Gruber 2007; Dahlstedt and Hertzberg 2011). Social worker Lars demonstrates that 'parents come from countries where the school system is completely different', implying that they have completely different views on upbringing and the expectations of schools:

> Teachers cannot handle this. They set no boundaries, they are wimpy. Parents are more familiar with an authoritarian school system, where school steers, so then they say: 'In school, the kids are those who decide'.

Comparably, the police officer Andreas speaks of 'migrant parents' who have a 'completely different mindset about sentence than they have in the so-called West', and they think that society 'indulges' and 'pets with people'. According to police officer Ingvar, there are significant differences between Swedish authority and these parents' views on both society and upbringing: 'if you are talking to a father here, he could hit a child', which, according to police officer Ingmar, would not be possible in other parts of the City.

In the interviews, the parents' authoritarian approach is frequently associated with gender issues and their different ways of bringing up girls and boys (cf. Eriksson 2003; Mattsson 2005; Eliassi 2014). When, for instance, police officer Andreas discusses his work with disorderly adolescents, he points out that girls seldom pose any real problem, because they are 'usually controlled hard'. Boys, however, 'are let loose'. In other words, families make a sharp distinction between how girls and boys are supposed to be brought up. This is also noted by female aid worker Daniella who talks about parents who 'do not think that girls should engage in recreational activities', and instead insist that girls should engage in tasks that belong to the private sphere. Nevertheless, it is not only parents who exercise control over family; in these situations children in general, and sons in particular, play an important part. According to Daniella, brothers play an exceptionally important role in maintaining the authoritarian upbringing and patriarchal relationships that exist in some 'migrant families':

> Girls should take care of their older brothers. [...] They cannot even imagine that their older brother could take care of her, cook and wash or similar. She must do this on his older brother's behalf. However, if older brother comes here and says, 'Now you have to

> go home!' then she must go home. There is no way of saying 'no!' So the control doesn't only come from parents.

All things considered, there is quite a contradictory problematization of the parents' migrant background in the interviews. On the one hand, parents are described as being unable to draw boundaries, as well as being excessively indulgent and irresponsible, and on the other hand they are regarded as overly controlling, and advocating an authoritarian and patriarchal upbringing, which is not consistent with the norms that prevail in Sweden. In this regard, the differentiation between the upbringing of males and females is referred to as a clear example of the disproportionate control said to characterize upbringing in 'migrant families'. In both cases, the 'migrant family' is represented as problematic.

Proposed Solutions

Accordingly, in the interviews there are a number of different problematizations of young people's troublesome behaviour, for instance the urban environment, parents' lack of involvement, problematic families, and migrant status. The causes are related to unemployment and spatial segregation in the Area, but the main focus is put on the parents, the family, and the relationships within the family. On the subject of the solutions to the defined problems, in terms of civil unrest and crime among young people, we can observe that the emphasis on parents and the family is even more evident, as most of the measures suggested are directed towards the transformation of the family in general, and parents in particular.

Fostering Parents

When the interviewees talk about counter-measures for youth unrest and criminality, they generally argue for the necessity of activating and involving the parents, so that they can take responsibility not only for their children's learning and future, but also for their own learning and the Area's future. Thus, one could argue that parents need to be fostered/educated in order to become more active and responsible.

According to youth aid worker Karl, solutions include 'strengthening parents, which is not just about them learning classical things, such as information about our society'. Such strengthening involves parents being made to participate in the change process, and becoming experienced, knowledgeable, and active agents. Along similar lines, municipality coordinator Nicklas argues that 'you need to work with parents, teach them how to deal with kids'. In other words, managing parents involves not only providing them with information, but also shaping their thoughts and values, and defining the horizon of their understanding. If parents are to educate and bring children up in the right way, they first need to be taught the rules of parenting.

The guiding principle of fostering is *involvement.* For instance, leisure activities chief Raul and police Andreas put emphasis on the importance of 'achieving parental involvement', denoting 'build vigilance among parents in their children's schooling'. Similarly, acting teacher Gabriella argues that it is challenging to 'find parents' involvement in children but also to get parents to feel engaged as well as *acquire* their engagement'. Police officer Ingvar describes this fostering mission it terms of enlightening parents about 'what child upbringing is about'. In his mind it is particularly important that parents understand that 'if you are here in Sweden then you raise children in one way, and if you are in African countries then you raise them in a different way'. In a sense, fostering 'involved parents' implies assimilation of an implicit Swedish normality, not least when it comes to upbringing and gender norms. In Sweden certain norms apply; in Africa other norms apply.

For such fostering to be created, communication is indispensable, as are the platforms enabling such communication. An important factor in this context is *trust,* and in order to evoke trust it is crucial to establish relationships with parents. Youth aid worker Karl self-critically argues for long-term efforts to involve the residents in the Area and to understand their needs and experiences.

> People need to feel that they belong somewhere, that they contribute, that they have a meaning and they do not feel that in the systems available today. […] You are nowhere viewed as an individual; no one sees your ambitions and potentials.

Against this background, a range of initiatives for approaching the residents and the parents of the Area are suggested, with the aim of understanding their needs and expectations. Here, a better understanding is regarded as a prerequisite for creating trust and confidence, while without trust and confidence, the desirable fostering of parents is not possible. However, according to municipal coordinator Nicklas, this is a big challenge, as the residents are 'tired of projects and other people coming here, while nothing significant is being done'. In order to tackle this challenge it is seen as necessary to motivate the residents and make them more receptive to communication.

The repertoire of initiatives suggested as a means of encouraging communication between organizations and citizens includes workshops and parenting classes, cultural events, information meetings with representatives of the authorities, organizations, and associations, door-to-door campaigns, and civic centres where residents can obtain free counselling on security, housing, education, job-seeking, parenting, and consumer rights.

One of the guiding principles for such initiatives is *partnership*, emphasizing the necessity of developing communication and contacts between organizations and citizens. Among the interviewees, partnership is seen as being able to catalyze new ideas, provide a better overall picture of the challenges in need of certain responses, enable more effective authority, and perhaps above all embody local support and reliance. Partnerships between schools, social services, the police, voluntary organizations, and other institutions, are expected, in particular, to improve school performance; reduce conflicts both inside and outside schools; increase parental involvement; provide trainee jobs for young people, and enable the use of schools as communication and information platforms, to name a few of the possibilities (cf. Dahlstedt and Hertzberg 2011).

One specific initiative, highlighted as particularly successful in several interviews, is a kind of 'home-party', arranged by a number of organizational representatives visiting the homes of female residents in the Area (Lozic 2016). According to security worker Stefan, an important goal of these meetings is to bring about 'mutual learning' between the representatives and female residents. Instead of the residents visiting the organisations during office hours, as is customary, home meetings bring the representatives, dressed in civilian clothes, to the homes of local women after office hours. Thus, a seemingly neutral arena for fostering and education is initiated, where participants from both sides can meet on ostensibly equal terms, as equal partners. On the one hand, these events provide the representatives of the authorities with an opportunity to reach out and communicate information to a category of people that is otherwise represented as particularly difficult to reach through the usual communication channels. On the other hand, through these learning occasions, the female residents can be 'strengthened' in their role as citizens, as they are given an opportunity to articulate their own opinions, expectations, and experiences, while also setting the agenda for the meetings. At the same time, the meetings can bring about a kind of active, committed, and responsible group, engaged in its own development as well as in the development of the local community. Furthermore, organizational representatives can gain insight into, and a greater knowledge of, the lives of the female participants. All things considered, the 'home-party' is one of the initiatives developed in order to enhance communication with, and fostering of, residents in the Area.

Preventive Measures

Another recurring theme in the interviews is *prevention*, a notion that has become widespread in the last decade's policy debates about crime in Sweden as well as in several other countries (cf. Hörnqvist 2010; Wahlgren 2014; O'Malley 2012).

The reasoning is that crime should be prevented from occurring, and in order to hinder the occurrence of juvenile crime it is necessary to implement immediate and preventive measures. Child psychologist Esther is one of the interviewees emphasizing the importance of preventive interventions: 'society should act beforehand, and not when they are already stuck in addiction and crime, because then there is no turn back'. In other words, the earlier the intervention, the easier it is to tackle crime. Similarly, municipality manager Nicklas argues:

> When one is little, then one has minor problems and if you wait until [children] grow up [then you have greater problems]. One can immediately see that some children have [...] a certain personality type. It feels appalling to say that about small children, but it is a fact, and with these kids one needs to be more vigilant. You have to catch them much, much earlier, and work more with parents.

This quote exemplifies the ways in which the reasoning about prevention is closely linked to efforts to foster not only youth but also parents. In order to hinder the rise of crime among youth it is necessary to foster them in an effective way; they have to be caught early in their lives, and the support services need to 'work more with parents'. By all accounts, prevention needs to be based on knowledge about the children's lives and experiences, as well as how they might develop in the future. This implies that the interviewees see a need to identify various risks which will enable them to implement necessary preventive measures (cf. O'Malley 2012). The question is how and where will they gather the necessary knowledge?

From the interviews, two central areas of care emerge which are regarded as suitable for collecting pieces of knowledge that would enable the implementation of preventive measures. Prenatal care is one such arena.

> You can see [potential problems] early, already at prenatal period, that is to say [...] when you are going on to have a child; so you should [help] at an early stage, and especially in the areas where there are special needs. You should be sturdier and be there. [...] If you want to affect a person's life, [...] then in my mind you must be there from the start, already in infancy. During infancy, you have the opportunity to [...] influence a child and [...] have a pretty big impact even with quite limited and simple means (Police officer Jesper).

Prenatal and childcare appear as particularly apt for detecting problems, intervening early in family life, shaping parents, and providing them with the right tools so that they can in turn bring up their children in a desirable way. Because all potential parents pass through these care centres, they can help with information gathering, and thus facilitate detailed analysis, differentiation and prognosis of each case. Under the aegis of care centres special effort can be deployed to specific localities where such actions are required.

School is another institution that is well-suited for preventive work, the interviewees conclude. Not only does school foster law-abiding citizens, and examine and differentiate them, it is also superior when it comes to crime prevention because 'one can quite early see that certain students: "Shit, this one is going to be a problem!"', police officer Andreas says. Therefore, he believes that schools need 'huge resources' and need to be given 'support' and 'backing'. Police officer Jesper also emphasizes this aspect of the role of schools in crime prevention.

> School is a foundation for intervention in [children and parents]. [...] In fact, it is only when you get to school, that you are seen and heard as an individual, and it is here where society for the first time can really map the individual and family, and see how they have it. [...] It is in school that one has an opportunity to make an assessment for the first time.

In schools, as in care centres, it is possible to reach everybody, because elementary education is compulsory. Indeed, school is engaged in the mapping and comprehensive examination of students, in terms of what is occurring both inside and outside the classroom walls. School makes children and their families visible and accessible, and is therefore an important arena for acquiring knowledge about them, as well as being a point of contact between children, parents, and the agents engaged in preventive work, such as the police and social services (see Wahlgren 2014).

Concluding Reflections

This chapter has focused on the organizational representatives' way of understanding and dealing with youth and unrest in multi-ethnic areas in Sweden. More specifically, we have analyzed interviews with people working within the police, schools, voluntary organizations, and social services in the Area, a location in a large Swedish city characterized in political debates and by the media as an 'area of exclusion', a 'multi-ethnic suburb', or the 'Million Programme'. Following Bacchi (2010: 4), we have focused on 'the ways in which particular representations of "problems" play a central role in how [individuals] are governed, in how [they] are ruled'. How do organizational representatives conceptualize the causes of juvenile delinquency and urban unrest among youth, and what measures do they propose as a means to address these problems? From the interviews, we analyzed a range of descriptions of both the causes of, and the solutions to, youth problems in an urban setting.

Regarding the problems represented in the interviews, a *segregated urban environment* emerges as an important explanation for the problems. In these problematizations, primarily two circumstances are emphasised as particularly urgent: firstly socio-economic exclusion, and secondly the concentration of residents with migrant backgrounds. It is argued that both of these circumstances create an environment with no truly positive role models that young people can use as learning examples of how they can/should act in order to succeed in life and in society.

In this highly segregated urban environment, as it is described, parents are portrayed primarily as a problem. It is argued that parents in these particular areas are too seldom engaged in the upbringing of their children, for example by participating in parent-teacher conferences or information sessions. One recurrent problematization is that parents are not able to encourage their children, i.e. there is a problem of *parenting*. In the interviews, two main reasons that contribute to the parents' lack of involvement were presented: firstly, a troublesome situation in the family in general, and secondly, the migrant background of the parents. It is argued that in this so-called problematic family, there is a lack of the support and protection needed for fostering well-functioning and law-abiding citizens. According to the interviewees, this is due to – among other things – destructive relationships between partners, divorce, mental health issues, drug abuse, and domestic violence. Additionally, the migrant background of the parents is highlighted as another major factor causing difficulties of the youth in these urban settings to adapt to current norms, and thus contributing to the development of urban unrest. In these problematizations, the migrant parents' lack of knowledge about how to foster children in accordance with desirable norms, and about the inequality between boys and girls, are two issues represented as particularly serious problems. Put simply, it is concluded that migrants' approach to parenting runs counter to the principles applicable in Sweden.

All in all, in the various representations of problems and their causes, both structural and individual problems are identified. This problematization identifies certain subjects and areas as particularly problematic, thus justifying certain measures for transforming these subjects/objects (Bacchi 2010). In other words, the analysis of problematization directs attention to the reasons that the family and the Area are made *governable,* and are the targets for a range of interventions.

In fact, when it comes to solutions to the problems, there is a strong focus on the family and the parents, leading to the situation in which the main solutions are more or less decoupled from the structural circumstances. In general, it is the family and the parents who are made responsible, and are thus constructed as the objects of transformation, i.e. *fostering* and *prevention*. In order to deal with the problem of 'disorderly suburban youth' there is, first and foremost, an urgency for parents to change. In other words, it is not only the young who are in need of being fostered, the parents also need to be fostered in the role of being a parent. They need to be fostered in how to take responsibility and become more involved according to current conventions – i.e. *responsibilized* (Rose 1999). Here, it is the individual who has the responsibility for making change happen; not the organizational representatives or anyone else. As several of the interviewees described it, this fostering is about 'strengthening parents', establishing channels and arenas, thus making it possible for suburban residents, parents, and others to get involved and to take responsibility (cf. Rose 1999; Popkewitz, Olsson and Petersson 2007). This may involve, for example, urging residents to come to parent-teacher conferences and information meetings; to participate in various social activities (such as summer festivals and safe walks); to visit local civil society organizations or to open their homes to representatives of different organizations, and informing parents about various issues. Through such initiatives there is hope that parents can become the *role models* they need to be in order to raise their children as good citizens. Here, parents not only need knowledge about how to think as good parents, and be good parents, they also need to develop the *will* to participate and to change (cf. Vincent 2000).

Alongside fostering the parents, early interventions are seen as the most crucial action when it comes to dealing with unrest among the youth in multi-ethnic areas. Early interventions require the development of a certain *prognostic vision*, i.e. knowledge about *risks*, and 'early signals' of things that are likely to go wrong (Hörnqvist 2010; O'Malley 2012). Here, school as well as maternal health are highlighted as two particularly important domains, as all children – and with them their parents – pass through them. Among these two domains, school is described as particularly important, not only because of its mission to foster the citizens of tomorrow, but also because of its great potential as a source of knowledge about children and the family, as well as being a domain where both children, parents, and other actors can meet (cf. Dahlstedt 2009a; Wahlgren 2014).

The particular understanding of problems and solutions emerging from the interviews should be seen in the light of the *makeover* of Swedish welfare policy, briefly described at the beginning of this chapter. With this *makeover*, greater responsibility for the welfare of individual citizens has been put on the individuals themselves (Larsson, Letell and Thörn 2012). In contrast to the conception of welfare within the framework of the traditional Swedish welfare model, the welfare of the individual is no longer seen as a fundamental citizenship right. Rather, welfare has increasingly been conceptualised as the responsibilities, priorities, and choices of the individual citizen. In accordance with a neoliberal governmental rationality, there are good citizens of a certain kind emerging – active, committed, responsible, and making choices (Hindess 2002; Dahlstedt and Olson 2013).

It is also, essentially, the profile of such citizens that is emerging in the stories of the interviewees. The good citizen, according to this conception, is never a finished subject – she is in constant becoming, and constantly in need of learning. In order to achieve success – as parent, child, and future citizen – one needs to constantly 'reinvent oneself', to be 'in step with the times', to be prepared to adapt to the demands of the situation. Constant *makeover* is the ideal, not only for the welfare model, but also for the new citizen. 'The new citizen is required to engage in a ceaseless work of training and retraining, skilling and reskilling, enhancement of credentials and preparation for a life of incessant job-seeking: life is to become a continuous economic capitalization of the self' (Rose 1999: 161). Thus, life itself appears as a lifelong process of learning, and self-becoming (Popkewitz, Olsson and Petersson 2007). Similarly, Bacchi (2010: 12) argues that citizens today are constructed as, and 'encouraged to think of themselves as, (personally) responsible for all the ills ("problems") in their lives; subjects who must continually reinvent themselves through lifelong learning'.

Furthermore, it is the 'excluded' parents and other residents living in 'areas of exclusion', who appear as the antithesis from which the ideal of the good citizen is carved out. It is towards the figure of the desirable good citizen that the problems – the parents and the residents of the Million Programme areas – are to be fostered, with the help of the various interventions (Dahlstedt 2015). Suburban residents may live in a situation of profound exclusion, but the *solution* to the problems associated with this exclusion are nonetheless to be found within those who are identified as constituting the *problem* (Vanderbreck, Rose and De Bie 2011). Even the excluded can 'take control over their own lives', if only they are given the opportunity and are 'activated'. Referring to Cruikshank (1999), these technologies of activation, targeting suburban inhabitants, parents, and youths, could be understood as quite a paradoxical form of governing – a *will to empower*. On the one hand *empowering*, in the sense of striving to motivate and release the inner creativity of the individual, on the other hand *disciplinary*, in the sense of emphasizing active participation and adaptation as obligations to the norms of Swedishness (cf. Hörnqvist 2010; Lozic 2016). In line with this rationality, those who choose *not* to become activated, those *not* making the right active choices, and those who are *not* capable of realizing and taking the long-term consequences of their choices into consideration, only have themselves to blame (Vanderbreck, Rose and De Bie 2011). Although migrant parents have also been problematized previously, and targeted by various fostering interventions (Ålund 1991), in the context of the on-going transformation of welfare policy, such problematization could be seen as part of a shift of responsibility for welfare from the public/collective to the private/individual. However, it is not only parents of migrant backgrounds who appear as problematic in accordance with a neoliberal governmental rationality, but also categories such as single mothers and the unemployed. These categories of citizens also seem to fall outside the current norm of the good, responsible citizen.

However, as argued previously, the targets of governing practices are not passive objects. They are rather, in various ways, made into active subjects who govern themselves according to certain norms and conventions. This means that there are always possibilities for citizen-subjects-in-the-making to become active citizens in other ways. As also shown by recent developments in peripheral suburban areas throughout Europe, the on-going transformation of welfare policies can also make multi-ethnic suburbs into sites of confrontation, where it is possible for the inhabitants to articulate alternative ways of becoming citizens, and to organize themselves towards a citizenship beyond the prescribed models, and beyond hierarchies and unequivocal distinctions. As shown in suburban Sweden, these confrontations may involve suburban youths, struggling for equal social rights, claiming their right to the city, and challenging current notions of citizenship in contemporary multi-ethnic Sweden (de los Reyes et al. 2014; Schierup, Ålund and Kings 2014). Violent or not, the future outcome of these struggles is anything but a given.

References

Abiala, K. (ed.) 2014. *Brinner 'förorten'? Om sociala konflikter i Botkyrka och Huddinge.* Samtidshistoriska Frågor 30. Huddinge: Södertörn University.

Andersson, R. 2013. 'Reproducing and Reshaping Ethnic Residential Segregation in Stockholm: The Role of Selective Migration Moves.' *Geografiska Annaler: Series B, Human Geography* 95/2, 163–187.

Andersson, K. and Kvist, E. 2014. 'The Neoliberal Turn and the Marketization of Care: The Transformation of Eldercare in Sweden.' *European Journal of Women's Studies* 22/3, 274–287.

Ålund, A. 1991. *Lilla Juga: Etnicitet, familj och kvinnligt nätverk.* Stockholm: Carlssons.

Bacchi, C. 1999. *Women, Policy and Politics*. London: Sage.

Bacchi, C. 2010. *Foucault, Policy and Rule: Challenging the Problem-Solving Paradigm*. FREIA's text series No. 74, Aalborg University.

Blomqvist, P. 2004. 'The Choice Revolution: Privatization on Swedish Social Services in the 1990s.' *Social Policy & Administration* 38/2, 171–193.

Boréus, K. 1994. *Högervåg: Nyliberalismen och kampen om språket i svensk debatt 1969–1989*. Stockholm: Tiden.

Brune, Y. 2004. 'Nyheter från gränsen: Tre studier i journalistik om "invandrare", flyktingar och rasistiskt våld.' PhD diss., Göteborgs Universitet.

Bunar, N. 2001. *Skolan mitt i förorten. Fyra studier om skola, segregation, integration och multikulturalism.* Eslöv: Symposion.

Bustos Castro, P. and Lindblad, E. 2004. 'Place, Discourse and Vulnerability: A Qualitative Study of Young Adults Living in a Swedish Urban Poverty Zone.' *Health & Place* 10/3, 259–272.

Carlbaum, S. 2012. 'Blir du anställningsbar lille/a vän?' PhD diss., Department of Political Science, Umeå University.

Cruikshank, B. 1999. *The Will to Empower: Democratic Citizens and Other Subjects.* Ithaca: Cornell University Press.

Dahlstedt, M. 2009a. 'Parental Governmentality: Involving "Immigrant Parents" in Swedish Schools.' *British Journal of Sociology of Education* 30/2, 193–205.

Dahlstedt, M. 2009b. *Aktiveringens politik: Demokrati och medborgarskap för ett nytt milennium.* Malmö: Liber.

Dahlstedt, M. 2015. 'Discourses of Employment and Inclusion in Sweden.' In Righard, Erica, Magnus Johansson and Tapio Salonen (eds.) *Social Transformation in Scandinavian Cities.* Lund: Nordic Academic Press, 61–82.

Dahlstedt, M. and Hertzberg, F. 2011. *Skola i samverkan.* Malmö: Gleerups.

Dahlstedt, M. and Lozic, V. 2017 [Forthcoming]. 'Färgblind rasism.' In Hübinette, Tobias (ed.) *Kritiska ras- och vithetsstudier.* Lund: Studentlitteratur.

Dahlstedt, M. and Olson, M. 2013. *Utbildning, demokrati, medborgarskap.* Malmö: Gleerups.

Davidson, T. 2010. 'Utanförskapelsen. En diskursanalys av hur begreppet utanförskap artikulerades i den svenska riksdagsdebatten 2003–2006.' *Socialvetenskaplig Tidskrift* 17, 149–169.

de los Reyes, P., Hörnqvist, M., Boréus, K., Estrada, F., Flyghed, J., González Arriagada, A., Lundgren, M and Lundström, M. 2014. *Bilen brinner, men problemen är kvar: Berättelser om Husbyhändelserna i maj 2013.* Department of Criminology, Stockholm University.

Dean, M. 1999. *Governmentality.* London: Sage.

Donzelot, J. 1977. *The Policing of Families.* London: John Hopkins.

Eliassi, B. 2014. 'Constructing Cultural Otherness within the Swedish Welfare State: The Cases of Social Workers in Sweden.' *Qualitative Social Work* 14, 554–571.

Eriksson, M. 2003. *I skuggan av pappa.* Stehag: Gondolin.

Fejes, A. and Nordvall, H. 2014. 'Folkbildning och vuxenutbildning i sjuggan av skolkrisen.' In Stenberg, Lina (ed.) *Skolan ut ur krisen: En forskarantologi om framtidens utbildningspolitik.* Stockholm: Tiden, 93–105.

Foucault, M. 1991. 'Governmentality.' In Burchell, Gordon, Colin Gordon and Peter Miller (eds.) *The Foucault Effect*. Chicago: The University of Chicago Press, 87–105.

Franklin, D.L. and James, A.D. 2015. *Ensuring Inequality*. Oxford: Oxford University Press.

Grillo, R.D. (ed.) 2008. *The Family in Question. Immigrant and Ethnic Minorities in Multicultural Europe*. Amsterdam: Amsterdam University Press.

Gruber, S. 2007. 'Skolan gör skillnad: Etnicitet och institutionell praktik.' PhD diss., Department of Social and Welfare Studies, Linköping University.

Hallin, P.O., Jashari, A., Listerborn, C. and Popoola, M. 2010. *Det är inte stenarna som gör ont*. Malmö: Malmö University Publications in Urban Studies (MAPIUS).

Hindess, B. 2002. 'Neo-liberal Citizenship.' *Citizenship Studies* 6/2, 127–143.

Hugemark, A. 1992. *Den fängslande marknaden*. Lund: Arkiv.

Hörnqvist, M. 2010. *Risk, Power and the State: After Foucault*. London: Routledge.

Johansson, H. 2001. 'Activation Policies in the Nordic Countries: Social Democratic Universalism under Pressure.' *Journal of European Area Studies* 9/1, 63–77.

Junestav, M. 2004. 'Arbetslinjer i svensk socialpolitisk debatt och lagstiftning 1930–2001.' PhD diss., Department of Economic History, Uppsala University.

Kallstenius, J. 2010. 'De mångkulturella innerstadsskolorna: Om skolval, segregation och utbildningsstrategier i Stockholm.' PhD diss., Faculty of Social Sciences, Stockholm University.

Larsson, J.K. 2015. *Integrationen och arbetets marknad*. Stockholm: Atlas.

Larsson, B., Letell, M. and Thörn, H. (eds.) 2012. *Transformations of the Swedish Welfare State*. Basingstoke: Palgrave Macmillan.

Lawrence, E. 1982. 'Just Plain Common Sense: The "Roots" of Racism.' In Centre for Contemporary Cultural Studies (ed.) *The Empire Strikes Back – Race and racism in 70s Britain*. London: Routledge, 47–94.

Levitas, R. 1998. *The Inclusive Society? Social Exclusion and New Labour*. Basingstoke: Palgrave.

Lindvall, J. 2004. 'The Politics of Purpose: Macroeconomic Policy in Sweden After the Global Age.' PhD diss., Department of Political Science, Gothenburg University.

Lozic, V. 2016. 'Normalisering av ungdomar i problem genom styrning av föräldrar: Från strukturella orsaksförklaringar till familjecentrerade lösningar.' *Sociologisk Forskning* 53/2, 151–174.

Lundahl, L., Erixon Arreman, I., Holm, A.-S. and Lundström, U. 2014. *Gymnasiet som marknad*. Umeå: Boréa.

Magnusson, S. 2014. 'Att säkerställa att vi är välkomna.' PhD diss., Department of Strategic Communication, Lund University.

Mattsson, T. 2005. 'I viljan att göra det normala: En kritisk studie av genusperspektivet i missbrukarvården.' PhD diss., Lund University.

Miller, P. and Rose, N. 2008. *Governing the Present: Administering Economic, Social and Personal Life*. Cambridge: Polity.

Molina, I. 1997. 'Stadens rasifiering.' PhD diss., Department of Social and Economic Geography, Uppsala University.

O'Malley, P. 2012. *Risk, Uncertainty and Government*. Hoboken: Taylor and Francis.

Popkewitz, T. 2008. *Cosmopolitanism and the Age of School Reform*. New York: Routledge.

Popkewitz, T.S., Olsson, U. and Petersson, K. 2007. 'The Learning Society, the Unfinished Cosmopolitan, and Governing Education, Public Health and Crime Prevention at the Beginning of the Twenty-First Century.' *Educational Philosophy and Theory* 38/4, 431–449.

Ristilammi, P.-M. 1993. *Rosengård och den svarta poesin*. Stehag: Symposion.

Rose, N. 1996. 'Governing "Advanced" Liberal Democracies.' In Barry, Andrew, Thomas Osborne and Nikolas Rose (eds.) *Foucault and Political Reason*. London: Routledge, 37–65.

Rose, N. 1999. *Powers of Freedom: Reframing Political Thought*. Cambridge: Cambridge University Press.

Rothstein, B. 1998. *Just Institutions Matter*. Cambridge: Cambridge University Press.

Ryner, M.J. 2002. *Capitalist Restructuring, Globalization and the Third Way: Lessons from the Swedishh Model*. London: Routledge.

Scarpa, S. 2015. 'The Spatial Manifestation of Inequality: Residential Segregation in Sweden and its causes.' PhD diss., Department of Social Work, Linnaeus University.

Schierup, C.-U., Ålund, A. and Kings, L. 2014. 'Reading the Stockholm Riots – A Moment for Social Justice?.' *Race & Class* 55/3, 1–21.

Schierup, C.-U., Krifors, K. and Slavnic, Z. 2015 'Social Exclusion: Migration and Social Vulnerability.' In Dahlstedt, Magnus and Anders Neergaard (eds.) *International Migration and Ethnic Relations*. London: Routledge, 200–227.

Socialstyrelsen 2010. *Social rapport 2010*. Stockholm: Socialstyrelsen.

Tedros, A. 2008. 'Utanför storstaden: Konkurrerande framställningar av förorten i svensk storstadspolitik.' PhD diss., School of Public Administration, Gothenburg University.

Vanderbreck, M., Roose, R. and De Bie, M. 2011. 'Governing Families in the Social Investment State.' *International Critical Childhood Studies* 4/1, 69–85.

Vesterberg, V. 2013. 'Ethnicised Un/employability: Problematized Others and the Shaping of Advanced Liberal Subjects.' *Ephemera* 13/4, 737–757.

Vincent, C. 2000. *Including Parents?* Buckingham: Open University Press.

Wacquant, L. 2008. *Urban Outcasts*. Cambridge: Polity.

Wahlgren, P. 2014. 'De laglydiga: Om skolans brottsförebyggande fostran.' PhD diss., Department of Criminology, Stockholm University.

Wilson, W.J. 1987. *The Truly Disadvantaged*. Chicago: The University of Chicago Press.

Randi Gressgård

9. Welfare Policing and the Safety-Security Nexus in Urban Governance: The Expanded Cohesion Agenda in Malmö[1]

Abstract: Based on a critical policy study of crime prevention in Malmö, this chapter discusses how partnership agreements between the police and local authorities intensify and widen the scope of policing in immigrant-dense areas, conflating welfare with crime prevention.

Introduction

Critical urban theorists have emphasised the vanishing of spaces for collectivisation, or urban commons, resulting from privatisation of public goods and services, the dismantling of municipal infrastructures and other neoliberal features of contemporary urban governance (Mayer 2012: 78). At the same time, discourses on social cohesion and civic integration have taken a stronghold in urban governance, particularly in Europe. Rather than seeing this as a contradiction, I attempt to demonstrate how cohesion discourse underpins neoliberal trends of moralisation of citizenship and responsibilisation of subjects in urban governance. I do not see this as a dismantling of municipal infrastructures, however. I shall argue instead that established welfare state structures and institutions form the basis for variegated modes of security: more police enforcement in conjunction with more police involvement in 'social' policy interventions.

In the first part of the chapter, I will probe the safety–security nexus from a theoretical point of view, arguing that crime prevention has less to do with preventing people from violating the law and more to do with securing order and regulating spaces in urban areas designated as problematic (McGhee 2003: 390). I will demonstrate, in accord with Mustafa Dikeç (2007), how practices of articulation (policy documents, polls, media reports, spatial designations, etc.) constitute specific urban spaces as objects of policy interventions. Precisely because the

1 This chapter is re-published with permission from *Nordic Journal of Migration Research* (NJMR). The text was originally published in *NJMR* 6/1, 2016 – a special issue on 'Planning for Pluralism in Nordic Cities' (guest-edited by Randi Gressgård and Tina G. Jensen).

safety–security nexus relates to the environment of which it is a part, I intend to analyse demands for safety and security in their broader political and economic context, demonstrating how policing serves the purposes of social cohesion and economic growth at once. Based on a study of policy frames in urban governance in Sweden, with a special focus on Malmö,[2] I proceed to discuss, in Part II, how various techniques of control are entwined with 'social' crime prevention, amounting to what I term welfare policing. I am particularly concerned with how partnership agreements between the police and local authorities intensify and widen the scope of policing in deprived, immigrant-dense areas, conflating welfare with crime prevention. My principal argument is that the expanded cohesion agenda, which opens up for far-reaching security politics in specific districts, renders entire sub-populations legible as dangerous 'others' against which society, or the city, must be defended.

Part I: Construing the City as an Entity to be Defended

Images of the city as an entity to be defended are often established in discourses on competition, 'rhetorically bolstered through recourse to the establishment of external enemies' (Massey 2005: 158). The external enemies could be other cities and regions that compete in the same market, or it could be the national government pursuing a policy that privileges other national cities and regions at the cost of one's own city, thus making the city less successful than it otherwise would be. In Malmö, this kind of message is conveyed in the political rhetoric of former social democrat mayor (between 1994 and 2013), Ilmar Reepalu, who takes issue with the national government's unwillingness to change the country's asylum legislation that enables refugees to choose freely where to live while waiting for their asylum applications to be processed. In Reepalu's view, the asylum legislation can be blamed for the city's problem of segregation and, in effect, for raising the level of (organised) crime that threatens the inhabitants' security and feeling of safety (Fjellman Jaderup 2012a, 2012b; Kommunstyrelsen 2012). In this line of reasoning, the cumulative effects of the national immigration control are segregated and criminalised ethnic minority communities that do not contribute to Malmö's overall positive development.

2 The empirical part of the chapter is mainly based on local media reports and policy documents published between 2011 and 2015. The empirical material of the entire PLANPLUR study includes participatory observation in public meetings, seminars etc. on social sustainability between 2011 and 2013 (see Gressgård 2015a, 2015b).

To increase the city's economic productivity and attractiveness, while decreasing street crime and unsocial behaviour, it is imperative that problematic and threatening difference gives way to prosperous diversity (Mukhtar-Landgren 2012). In accordance with this view, Malmö City's visionary comprehensive plan depicts ethnic and cultural diversity as a potential asset that fuels the city's economy (Malmö City Planning Office 2013). The corresponding view is that economic development for the city eventually benefits all inhabitants, including the least privileged subpopulations (Massey 2005). In either case, the city's positive development hinges on security measures that come to grips with differences impacting negatively on the city as a whole (Gressgård 2015b). Based on idealised and idealising notions of the city, urban governance aims to recreate the urban characteristics that are needed for the city to be whole (once again) (Tunström and Bradley 2015: 77). Those who pose a threat to the city are hence not only – and not primarily – external enemies, but include also undesirable migrants and minority groups in its midst.

Security and the Expanded Cohesion Agenda

The connection Reepalu makes between urban segregation (disintegration), immigration politics and crime is indicative of an expanded social cohesion agenda that has evolved in Europe over the past decades.[3] Based on a comparative study of the turn to cohesion politics in France, Germany and the UK, Jan Dobbernack (2014: 128, 175) observes that the agenda-setting around cohesion has extended the domain of problematic behaviour, accompanied by (discursively asserted and constructed) anxieties of declining levels of trust, decaying norms of collective conduct and loosening communal ties. In a British context, Anne-Marie Fortier (2010) sees the chain-linking of criminal justice, immigration and civic integration as an expansion of the remit of cohesion from the management of diversity to involving the fight against crime and security threats. Willem Schinkel and Friso van Houdt (2010: 707) point to a similar nexus of immigrant integration and crime control in Dutch politics, manifested in a 'safety chain' of collaborative partners (the justice department, police, local municipality, housing corporations, etc.) that work together at the local level of the neighbourhood, especially where large number of so-called non-Western migrants are 'concentrated'. Because crime is regarded as a 'social' problem resulting from lack of responsibility and lack of

3 According to Katarina Nylund (2014: 52), the concept of social cohesion was introduced for the first time in Malmö's current comprehensive plan (Malmö City Planning Office 2013). The politics associated with the cohesion agenda is far from new, however; it has evolved since the 1980s in Scandinavian countries (Borch 2005).

cultural adjustment and community, Dutch policy-makers have stressed the need for normative attachment to society alongside more surveillance (Schinkel and van Houdt 2010: 708, 709; Schinkel and van den Berg 2011). According to Carl-Ulrik Schierup and Aleksandra Ålund (2011: 56), Swedish policy documents echo contemporaneous cohesion discourses in the UK, the Netherlands and elsewhere in Europe when advocating cultural unity rather than cultural plurality backed by equity or equality. To secure social cohesion, they critically remark, 'a shared vision and sense of belonging must be extended to those who live "outside society"' (Schierup and Ålund 2011: 56; see also Dikeç 2007).

In Sweden, there has been a welfare state critique following an era of social-democratic dominance, accompanied by a gradual political shift away from a 'strong' welfare state towards a politics that places much stress on civil society as a moral collectivity (see e.g. Dahlstedt 2008; Kings 2011; Lozic 2010; Tunström and Bradley 2015). Whereas the traditional welfare state redistributed public goods and services to citizens on the basis of their given membership in 'the social' (identified with nation-state citizenship), more recent neoliberal governance is preoccupied with the building of responsible communities (O'Malley 2004: 74). People are made personally responsible for their belonging to 'the social', notably in the context of debate and policy on immigrant integration (Kofman 2005; O'Malley 2004; Schinkel and van Houdt 2010). Schinkel and van Houdt (2010: 697) maintain that the moralisation of citizenship pertaining to cultural assimilationism is intertwined with the responsibilisation of subjects that is characteristic of neoliberal forms of governing. Moralisation and responsibilisation come together in moralised notions of the 'good' and 'active' citizen. Another way of putting this – paraphrasing Pat O'Malley (2004: 74) – would be that moralisation and responsibilisation come together in cohesion discourse's emphasis on the responsibility people own to society and their communities.

When civil society is transposed into the concept of community, community is no longer merely the territory of government, but has become a means of government (McGhee 2003: 380, 390; see also Cruikshank 1999: 93; Rose 1999). We shall see below how community is promoted as a way of both preventing and combating crime, and how the supposed restoration of community is, in turn, regarded as necessary for a smoothly functioning economy. In Part II, we shall see how collaborative authorities in Sweden have initiated crime-preventive empowerment programmes aimed at enabling the formation of local community bonds and capabilities, in conjunction with intensified pre-emptive order enforcement by the police. First, however, I shall elaborate on how the security-safety nexus, through cohesion discourse, works to extrapolate from peoples' fear of being attacked by criminals of immigrant or ethnic minority background to society being under attack as a whole.

Fear of Disintegration, Moralisation of Citizenship and Order Maintenance

Fortier (2010) demonstrates how cohesion politics is centred on the subjects' desires to belong on the one hand, and their emotive responses to perceived threats to cohesion and safe living on the other. The expanded cohesion agenda evolves into a form of 'governing through affect', where emotive responses are the subject of polls, etc. (Fortier 2010: 20, 22). As of 2006, the Swedish government has commissioned the National Council for Crime Prevention (*Brottsförebyggande rådet* [BRÅ]), with the assistance of Statistics Sweden, to conduct an annual national survey on people's felt security and vulnerability to crime. Among the questions are: 'Were you threatened last year in such a way that you were frightened?'; 'Are you anxious about crime in society?' and 'What is the extent of your confidence in the way the police carry out their work?' (BRÅ n.d.). Malmö City and the police also conduct their own annual survey on issues of safety in different urban districts. The results of these polls are disseminated to the public through local media and commented upon by the police and local authorities.

In line with Fortier (2010), it could be argued that the questionnaires are designed to address an anxious and affective subject. It is also possible to argue that the measurement of inhabitants' felt safety or fear of crime instigates and aggravates a particular kind of xenophobia pertaining to fear of disintegration. Bryan Turner (2007: 300) sees this escalating form of xenophobia as part of a modern culture of fear, maintaining that '[t]he essential political condition xenophobia is a situation in which the majority feels that it is under attack'. In a similar vein, Les Back and Shamser Sinha (2012: 140) argue that it is fear and insecurity that give the racism of today its affective energy and force, connecting the personal state with the battle to secure and defend society itself. Migrants and ethnic minorities might be portrayed as refusing injunctions to care for the neighbourhood as well as the nation due to a lack of solidarity and loyalty (Erel 2011; Fitzgerald and Smoczynski 2015; Schierup and Ålund 2011; Skey 2011). Such apocryphal storytelling (moral panics) characteristically play on the interrelated registers of safety and security. In a Dutch context, van Houdt and Schinkel (2014: 52) remark that feelings of insecurity (i.e. unsafety) have become leading targets of intervention, while also giving rise to legitimate policy targets.

In many cases, (un)safety (i.e. the level of anxiety) figures as an index of (dis) order, and security politics is carried out as a means to restore order and continuity

(Hills 2009: 14, 216, 222). Didier Fassin (2013: xv) is among the critical scholars who have identified a shift in recent years from law enforcement to enforcing order in urban security politics. Order enforcement policy draws attention to 'populations at risk' in so-called problematic areas, disharmonious neighbourhoods, districts out of control, defect places, security hot spots, combat zones, etc.[4] From a critical point of view, order enforcement is seen as a *projection* of order more than as an imposition of order on the given (Castel 1991: 295). The point to be made here is that the safety-security nexus plays a formative role in this process: the designation of populations at risk in so-called problematic areas propels fear of disintegration and works to construe specific spaces as objects of policy interventions (see e.g. Dikeç 2007; Van Houdt and Schinkel 2014).

Part II: Combining Pre-Emptive and Preventive Crime Fighting

The police are vested with statutory powers, over and above those of ordinary citizens, which allow them to use force in their exercise of crime-fighting tasks. These powers may be extended under special circumstances and in specific areas. I shall refer to such force-based crime fighting as *pre-emptive*, characterised by a 'will to power'.[5] On the other hand, the police are involved in a number of crime-preventive practices that do not involve force and restraining control but contain a strong social element, characterised by a 'will to empower' vulnerable groups and individuals (Cruikshank 1999).[6] In the remaining part of the chapter, I shall focus attention on collaborations between the police and local authorities, and how collaborative efforts combine pre-emptive and preventive crime fighting through plural forms of policing (Jones and Newburn 2006a). Using Malmö as

---

4 See e.g. Amin 2012; Dikeç 2007; Dobbernack 2014; Fassin 2013; Garland 2001; Schierup, Ålund and Kings 2014; Schierup and Ålund 2011; Schinkel and van den Berg, 2011; Van Steden and Huberts 2006; Wacquant 2008a.

5 My definition is different from Nietzsche's conceptualisation of 'will to power' in terms of a primordial force (*Kraft*). Informed by Michel Foucault's (2007, 2008) conceptual vocabulary, I take 'will to power' to mean the exercise of authority over others through constraining techniques of power, centred on prohibitions and disciplinary rules, as distinct from powers of (self)regulation by way of empowerment.

6 The distinction between pre-emptive and preventive crime fighting converges with the conventional distinction between reactive and pro-active policing inasmuch as pre-emptive policing includes techniques characteristic of reactive policing. However, both pre-emptive and preventive crime fighting are pro-active in that they are aimed at preventing crime from taking place.

a case in point, I shall elaborate on how the coercive 'will to power' is entwined with the care-oriented 'will to empower' in partnerships against crime, and how these new assemblages entail a transformation of welfare provision towards crime prevention within an expanded cohesion agenda. I am particularly concerned with how a long-established welfare state tradition has become enmeshed in preventive programmes that combine coercion and care in specific territorial areas (De Koning 2015).

Partnerships against Crime

There has been a gradual change in the policing landscape, in and beyond the heartlands of social democracy. A number of hybrid forms of crime-fighting strategies are emerging, especially in big cities, and the importance of partnerships in the provision of policing services and community safety is growing steadily (Jones and Newburn 2006b). Partnership in policing signals that the authorities wish to spread responsibility for public safety and security across society. Responsibility for crime prevention is devolved to a variety of governmental and non-governmental actors to engender the spirit of community responsibility and active citizenship.

Although the responsibility for safety and security is less dispersed in Sweden than it is in many other countries (Amin 2013), Sweden has witnessed a rapid increase in partnership in policing in recent years. The idea of collaboration in crime prevention was initially introduced in a national programme initiated by the Swedish government in 1996, and further propelled by a plan of action from the National Police Board (Rikspolisstyrelsen 2008) that vindicates formal collaboration agreements. In 2010, a handbook was published to support and stimulate a long-term collaboration between the police, municipalities and other parties (Berg, Gustafsson and Johansson Meinke 2010: 8). While the plan of action applied exclusively to the police authorities, the handbook caters for the needs of both the police and the local authorities (Patel 2013: 23).

The inspection report, *Police and Municipality Collaboration* (*Samverkan polis och kommun*), states that crime prevention is generally understood as 'activities that the police carry out in collaboration with other actors or independently in order to prevent or hamper commitment of crime, criminal actions or breach of the peace' (Rikspolisstyrelsen 2012: 7, my translation). The report concedes that this broad definition of crime prevention, aimed at increasing safety and preventing crime, is problematic because the relationship between safety and security is not clarified; it is just assumed (Rikspolisstyrelsen 2012: 35). Nevertheless, the safety–security nexus is described as a robust basis for local security politics, and the report underscores the importance of local crime prevention initiatives in this respect.

The importance of a shared understanding of the local safety–security situation is furthered stressed in a follow-up evaluation report by the National Council for Crime Prevention (Patel 2013), and is central to a major reform of the Swedish Police Service that involves a new national Police Authority as of 2015 (Polissamordningen 2015). Through so-called citizen commitments (*medborgarlöften*) the police commit themselves more to the citizens they serve: 'focus on things that people who live and work in an area take to be most important in order to feel safe and secure' (Implementing Committee for New Swedish Police Service 2015: 4, my translation; see also Polisen 2015: 30). In the National Police Commissioner's report for 2015–2016, it is stated that '[p]eople should feel that the police care and take their problems seriously. That makes more people willing to collaborate and assist the police' (Polisen 2015: 5, my translation). The overall focus is on how to improve police responses to (risks of) crime through community involvement, rather than questioning the broader effects of policing and the idea that policing is about safety and security for all (see Lamble 2013: 239–240).

Swedish crime-fighting programmes are tailored to the same pattern as British programmes, which combine pre-emptive enforcement activities, for example crackdowns and surveillance, with long-term interventions to prevent youngsters from being recruited to criminal networks (Bullock and Tilley 2008: 40). In the so-called Manchester model, police enforcement activities are meant for non-cooperative individuals who have been offered help and support to remain clear from offending and gang membership but who in spite of all that continue to offend. The enforcement activities function as a coercive, authoritarian threat behind the care-oriented preventive measures undertaken by other agencies. This is by some involved actors described as a 'carrot and stick' dynamics (Bullock and Tilley 2008: 40), resembling the power of surveillance described by Frantz Fanon (1986: 117): 'As long as everything went well, he was praised to the skies, but look out, no nonsense, under any condition!'

As distinct from their British counterparts and most other European partnerships in policing, there is a persistent focus in Swedish policy reports on social problems and a robust faith in the social sciences and their professions. When social problems are put on the policy agenda, however, the framing tends to shift from welfare issues to security and safety, drawing attention to 'populations at risk' and emphasizing self-governing subjects aided by an empowering, enabling state (O'Malley 2004: 57, 59, 62.). In a recent report that discusses how to improve local crime prevention, the Council for Crime Prevention looks for greater willingness to contribute with new ideas and innovation (BRÅ 2015). Within the frame of collaboration agreements and citizen commitments, this probably means eclipsing socio-structural perspectives more still by moralisation and responsibilisation. As already mentioned, attached to the preventive practices of responsibilisation of subjects (who have been offered choices) is the blaming and sanctioning – the threat of penalisation and incapacitating – of those who are 'unwilling' to comply with the norms of the inclusive state (Miller and Rose 2008: 105; Schierup, Ålund and Kings 2014; Schierup and Ålund 2011). This is not to say that empowerment programmes are repressive policing in disguise. Rather, it is to suggest that the social inclusion of 'good', responsible citizens is conditioned on a normative and often spatial exclusion of 'bad' citizens or non-citizens who allegedly do not belong to the city and thus have no 'right to the city' (Lefebvre 1996). Collaborative efforts in Malmö involve, as will become evident in the following, an affective mobilisation of responsible people who belong to the city or community against internal and external enemies. This, in turn, serves to construe the city as an entity to be defended.

Crime-Fighting Collaborations in Malmö

Like other Swedish municipalities, the city administration of Malmö and the local police have initiated a joint security–safety agreement, Malmö – A Safe and Secure City (*Malmö – en trygg och säker stad*), running from 2012 to 2016.[7] In keeping with the cohesion agenda and the emphasis on community involvement, the document underscores that the preventive practices are aimed at activating citizens and increasing their feelings of trust, confidence, belonging, etc. For the collaboration to work, it is argued, the collaborating parties have to trust one another, develop a common view of their work and deploy a common vocabulary (Malmö City 2012). Irrespective of its actual effects on crime, I would argue that the partnership agreement testifies to what Fortier (2010: 21, 24), in British cohesion politics, identifies as a political will to unity, in combination with a post-political framework of a 'shared future vision'.

One example of collaborative efforts in Malmö is the campaign 'Heja Malmö!' from 2012. The campaign blog urged the city's inhabitants to ask for a receipt when buying alcohol, taking a taxi, etc. to undermine the informal economy associated with criminal gangs. The slogan 'Heja Malmö!' is an encouragement to join in the cheers: 'Come on, Malmö!' The campaign attempts to create enthusiasm and love for the city by promising 'a good strong dose of Malmö love' (Heja Malmö! Website 2012; Vårt Malmö 2012a). One of the campaign blog headings was 'We

7 It succeeded the agreement on Five Focal Points for Increased Safety in Malmö (*Fem Fokus for ökad trygghet i Malmö*) from 2011.

love our city' – a common statement from the then-mayor and social democrat, Reepalu, and the leader of the conservative, oppositional party at the time, Anja Sonesson. On behalf of the municipality, the politicians promised to do whatever they can, in collaboration with the police, to prevent youngsters from being recruited by the criminal networks, but they need help from the local community:

> Together with the police, we will support persons who want to change their life style and leave their criminal life behind [...] But even here we need help from Malmö's inhabitants, associations and businesses that want to back up the youth [...] We love our city. And to the criminal gangs we say in unison: You are not welcome in our lovely Malmö! (Heja Malmö! Website 2012, my translation).

The campaign blog and leaflet also announced that civilians are the best detectives – in popular discourse called 'the detective civil society' (*Detektiven Allmänheten*) – when it comes to reporting and combating crime. An interviewed police officer, cited in the local broadsheet under the heading 'The best detective is oneself' (*Själv är bästa detektiv*), commented that the police are increasingly tipped by people who suspect crime or observe criminal activities. On the other hand, he explained, there are groups of people who do not feel that they belong to society and therefore do not feel solidarity. 'It's about loyalty and what people identify with', he concluded (Vårt Malmö 2012a, my translation).[8]

There have also been other collaborative efforts that address the informal economy in Malmö, such as a crime-fighting programme that targeted illegal businesses, which are considered to form a major part of the city's crime scene (Höök 2011). The programme included collaboration with the tax authorities, but was chiefly concerned with pre-emptive crime fighting in urban micro-places, so-called hot spots, where the risk of crime is considered to be particularly high. In the summer of 2011, the police set off in pursuit of the criminal gangs in Norra Grängesbergsgatan, a street in the southern inner city dominated by small migrant-run businesses (various shops, hairdressers, food stalls, workshops, etc.) and minority associations and clubs, some of them illegal (in popular discourse referred to as 'black clubs'). The city authorities gave the police permission to close the street for traffic between 9 p.m. and 5 a.m., and those who did not comply with the restrictions risked having

8 During 2015, there were a series of detonations (mainly by hand grenades) in Malmö. When commenting on the frequent attacks in the local newspaper, a local Social Democrat politician, responsible for issues relating to safety and security in Malmö municipality, used a similar rhetoric of cohesion, responsibilisation and attachment to the one used in the 'Heja Malmö!' campaign: 'Everyone who loves Malmö has a shared responsibility for sticking together and doing whatever they can to stop the wave of violence' (Schönström 2015, my translation).

their cars searched by the police (Polisen 2011). In an interview with the local newspaper, *Sydsvenskan*, the commander-in-chief of the programme declared that the police will be more visible in this particular area of the city, and the undercover police will actively target Malmö's criminal underworld. According to the newspaper article, this is an established method; other streets have previously been closed for traffic during night time to prevent street prostitution. The article also listed a number of other criminal activities that are associated with 'the underworld', including shootings, trafficking, rapes and attacks and assassinations by explosives. The crime-fighting strategy has had a smoothing effect on the whole area, the police representative assured (Mikkelsen 2011), thereby suggesting that ordinary citizens can feel more safe in the previously dangerous area.

The first case serves to illustrate how preventive policing involves the use of information, in combination with measures aimed at increasing feelings of safety and cohesion (these constitute two separate crime prevention categories within the frame of collaboration agreements) (BRÅ 2013: 52, 54). Most importantly for purposes of our argument, the example demonstrates how incivility is associated with criminal networks – consisting mainly of so-called alienated young men of immigrant or ethnic minority background – that pose a threat to 'our city' and jeopardize the inhabitants' safety. The appeal to the city's inhabitants – used as a generic term in the 'Heja Malmö!' campaign – reflects a view of civil society as basically homogenous and, as a whole, worthy of protection from destructive forces (Mayer 2012: 74). Through interpellation, the campaign seeks to engage civil society, using a narrative of belonging to mobilize people *for* the city, *against* criminal gangs and networks. The campaign affectively plays upon and exacerbate distinctions between loyal inhabitants and failed citizens or non-citizens who are either figured as disloyal (feel no solidarity), or the cause of insecurity (Lamble 2013: 231). The latter category should either be voluntarily enrolled in empowering programmes, or – alternatively – forcefully excluded, in accordance with the politicians' proclamation that criminal gangs are not welcome in 'our city'.[9] As for the safety–security nexus, we could infer that when civilians are made into detectives, suspicion of crime is inevitably directed towards particular groups of people, marked by difference, in specific areas or streets. It also seems pertinent to note that the marginalisation of areas designated as problematic is more or less

9 People who want to 'leave their criminal life behind' are eligible for support from Malmö's Consultation Team (*Malmös Konsultationsteam*), which is a collaboration between Malmö City, the police, local crime prevention authorities (*Kriminalvården*), and a national institution for crime prevention amongst youths (*Statens Institutionsstyrelse*) (Vårt Malmö 2012b: 3; see also Malmö City 2014).

disconnected from wider structures and processes in society (Schierup and Ålund 2011: 55, 57; Tunström and Bradley 2015: 78), attesting to the conjoined power mechanisms of moralisation and responsibilisation described above.

The second case demonstrates how the police use pre-emptive measures to make it more difficult for targeted populations to commit crime and increase both the feeling and the actual risk of being caught. The police categorise these measures as crime-preventive in a 'strict' sense, and they use a separate category for measures that target populations at risk (BRÅ 2013: 52, 54). According to Mats Franzén (2001: 206), the general decline of the welfare state is being compensated for by the police's extended authority to use situational crime-fighting techniques 'directly aimed at inhibiting criminal and other threatening acts in particular spaces'. However, it could be argued that the policing activities not only work to inhibit criminal acts; they also serve to produce spaces of intervention by identifying ethnic minority populations in designated areas with criminal activities such as illegal businesses, drug offences, violence, among others (Turner 2007: 289) – in short, the criminal 'underworld' that threatens 'our city'. The designation 'underworld' signals that those who belong to this world exist outside of society; they do not belong to the city. Taken together, the cases exemplify how issues of migration and integration are tied in with criminal justice.

As indicated above, the combination of more force-based policing and more 'social' policing makes it virtually impossible to discern between welfare provision and crime prevention in specific urban districts. The conflation of welfare provision and crime prevention effectively blurs the boundaries between police interventions based on concrete suspicion of crime on the one hand, and 'social' interventions that target whole subpopulations of emplaced and unprivileged people of minority background on the other. As Robert Castel (1991: 288) notes, it is no longer necessary to manifest symptoms of dangerousness to be suspected; 'it is enough to display whatever characteristics the specialists responsible for the definition of preventive policy have constituted as risk factors'. In line with Castel, Carl-Ulrik Schierup, Aleksandra Ålund and Lisa Kings (2014: 7, 12) maintain that 'socially marginalised places have become stigmatised and criminalised and it is enough to live in or to be present in a certain area to be subject to control'. This, in turn, entails a potentially infinite multiplication of the possibilities for intervention (Castel 1991: 289). Obviously, people's fear of crime can never be completely eliminated and safety never guaranteed entirely. The preoccupation with feelings of safety in contemporary policy thus paves the way for endless public critique of defective interventions, alongside demands for new and more effective security measures (Borch 2005: 159).

Collaboration for the City's Prosperity and Attractiveness

At this juncture, it is important to note that policing in terms of punitive paternalism (at the bottom) is tied in with practices of economic (neo)liberalism (at the top) (Wacquant 2008b: 203). For instance, the national inspection report assumes that the municipalities want their inhabitants to be safe because it makes the municipalities more attractive to businesses, investments and people looking for jobs. This is crucial, the report states, because it makes the municipalities more willing to co-fund the safety surveys (NPB 2012: 33; see also BRÅ 2013: 44; Berg, Gustafsson and Johansson Meinke 2010: 12). Malmö is not included in the inspection report, but Sweden's second largest city, Gothenburg, is among the evaluated municipalities. The Gothenburg partnership agreement is particularly instructive in so far as it is influenced by the Manchester model and because it explicitly links security politics to the city's overall economic development, which is indicative of the transmuted welfare state. The document establishes that the collaboration between the police and other actors will contribute to a positive development of vulnerable urban districts through a combined focus on safety, employment, education and economic growth from a 'holistic' point of view. A positive development in all the involved areas (officially designated as 'improvement areas') is, according to the document, conditioned upon their inclusion in the development of the city as a whole, as well as that of the region (Gothenburg City 2010; NPB 2012: 20).

With regard to the 'holistic' approach to prosperous urban development, it should be noted that partnership agreements are without a clear point of fixation. Niels Å. Andersen (2008: 115, 122) remarks that in contrast to the pre-determined purposes of traditional welfare politics, quasi-contractual partnership agreements flexibly seek out possibilities for new couplings, and their open character creates particular ideas and visions of the problems to be solved within the post-political, visionary framework of the cohesion agenda (Fortier 2010: 28). This is evident in the above-mentioned policy documents that stress the importance of developing a common view, deploying a common vocabulary and creating a sense of belonging and feeling of safety through citizen commitment (see also Gressgård 2015a, 2015b). According to O'Malley (2004: 64), critics of (state) bureaucracy imagine a different way of governing the future that embraces the intuitive, daring and imaginative. So, rather than representing dead (contract) texts that can gradually become fixed through *interpretation* (Andersen 2008: 123), partnership agreements seem to be about *imagination*; the future is waiting to be formed by the power of will and imagination, as it were (O'Malley 2004: 71). It could be argued that visionary planning, aimed at moulding and strengthening shared identities, leaves little room for political struggles or ideological battles, and it weakens the democratic transparency and accountability of the planning process (see e.g. Baeten 2012; Dannestam 2008; Gressgård 2015a, 2015b; Nylund 2014). In largely uncontested, managerial terms, specific spaces and populations are constituted as a form of exteriority that menaces the integrity and development of the city (or society) (Dikeç 2007: 172).

Concluding Remarks

We have seen that the police and local authorities in Malmö seek to develop a common view of their work – a shared problem focus – based on quasi-contractual trust and a view of the city as an entity. Urban governance seeks to facilitate couplings between various actors, ultimately aimed at recreating the urban characteristics that are needed for the city to be a cohesive whole (again). The discussion has suggested that this holistic ambition (Lithman 2010) emerges from an expanded cohesion agenda and a concomitant safety–security nexus in urban governance. I have argued that in spite of the fact that the scope of policing is widened and the efforts are intensified, policing is hardly a contested issue within this policy framework. Instead of debating (politically) whether policing is a reasonable way of dealing with problems related to segregation and marginalisation, the problems are framed in such a way that more comprehensive (holistic) policing appears like an obvious solution.

Given the strong emphasis on the reformist 'will to empower' in welfare policing, the integral 'will to power' is somewhat obscured. This haziness is further compounded by the open, quasi-contractual character of partnership agreements, not to mention the proliferation in actors involved in crime prevention and their diffuse mandate. Within the limits of the law, albeit in a legal grey zone, welfare policing allows of expansive policy interventions in specific neighbourhoods and domestic domains, which makes it virtually impossible to discern between welfare and security politics. I have argued that people of immigrant or ethnic minority background who happen to live in deprived neighbourhoods are targeted for crime-preventive interventions, not on the basis of concrete imputations of dangerousness, but because their marginalised status in society is coded as a security threat. Emplaced minority groups are cast as potentially dangerous populations based on a combination of factors liable to produce risk (Castel 1991: 288; Schinkel and van den Berg 2011: 1924).

The conflation of welfare provision and crime prevention is not an entirely new phenomenon in Scandinavia; crime prevention has been part of social-democratic welfare politics for decades (Borch 2005). However, the importance of collaborative efforts has become ever more articulated, notably through partnerships in policing and subsequent citizen commitments, which means that new possibilities of interventions are opened up. As for the safety–security nexus, I have argued that cohesion discourse extrapolates from people's fear of being personally attacked by criminals of immigrant or ethnic minority background to society (or the city) being under attack as a whole. We have seen that mediated stories about the criminal underworld versus ordinary citizens (who are loyal and love their city) affectively play upon distinctions between inhabitants worthy of protection and enemies of the city who are spotted as the cause of unsafety. Moreover, safety polls that measure feelings of (un)safety give legitimacy to more expansive security politics. The examples from Malmö demonstrate that the safety–security nexus constitutes a vital part of the expanded cohesion agenda that links security, criminal justice and issues of immigration and integration as a chain.

Within the expanded cohesion agenda, I have argued, crime prevention has less to do with preventing people from violating the law and more to do with securing order (Fassin 2013). This is not to say, however, that concerns over public order have given priority to security over welfare, as Turner (2007: 295) suggests in a British context. There is no contradiction between enforcing order and providing welfare (in a transmuted form) (see Baeten 2012: 26; Dannestam 2008).[10] In the Swedish case, the inherited institutions and infrastructures of the social-democratic welfare state seem to offer favourable conditions for expanded policing in urban space.

Acknowledgement

I am grateful to Lisa Kings, Aleksandra Ålund, Kari Anne Drangsland, Ana Ivasiuc, and Anouk de Koning for having commented on earlier versions of this text. I would also like to thank the *Nordic Journal of Migration Research*'s two anonymous referees and the journal editors for their valuable comments.

10 Much like the security apparatus of the *Ancien Régime* in the context of European urbanisation, the neoliberal (transmuted) welfare state utilises police forces both to control and to manage populations, dealing with law and order enforcement as well as the well-being of citizens and economic circulation (see Foucault 2007: 65, 343; 2008: 253).

Funding Acknowledgement

The work was conducted within the research project 'Planning for pluralism in Malmö' (PLANPLUR), supported by a research grant from the Meltzer fund, University of Bergen.

References

Amin, A. 2012. *Land of Strangers*. Cambridge: Polity.

Amin, A. 2013. 'Surviving the turbulent future.' *Environment and Planning* 31/1, 140–156.

Andersen, N.Å. 2008. *Partnerships: Machines of Possibility*. Bristol: The Policy Press.

Back, L. and Sinha, S. 2012. 'New hierarchies of belonging.' *European Journal of Cultural Studies* 15/2, 139–154.

Baeten, G. 2012. 'Normalising neoliberal planning: The case of Malmö, Sweden.' In Tasan-Kok, Tuna and Guy Baeten (eds.) *Contradictions in Neoliberal Planning, Cities, Policies and Politics*. London: Springer, 21–42.

Berg, G., Gustafsson, C., and Johansson Meinke, M. 2010. *Samverkan i lokalt bråttsförebyggande arbete*. Stockholm: Brottsförebyggande rådet.

Borch, C. 2005. *Kriminalitet og magt*. Copenhagen: Politisk Revy.

BRÅ (National Council for Crime Prevention) n.d. 'The Swedish Crime Survey.' Accessed March 6, 2016. <http://www.bra.se/bra/bra-in-english/home/crime-and-statistics/swedish-crime-survey.html>

BRÅ 2015. *Förstärkt stöd till – och samordning av – det lokala brottsförebyggande arbete*. Stockholm: Brottsförebyggande rådet.

Bullock, K and Tilley, N. 2008. 'Understanding and tackling gang violence.' *Crime Prevention and Community Safety* 10/1, 36–47.

Castel, R. 1991. 'From dangerousness to risk.' In Burchell, Graham., Colin Gordon and Peter Miller (eds.) *The Foucault Effect: Studies in Governmentality*. Chicago: University of Chicago Press, 281–298.

Cruikshank, B. 1999. *The will to Empower: Democratic Citizens and Other Subjects*. Ithaca: Cornell University Press.

Dahlstedt, M. 2008. 'The politics of activation: Technologies of mobilizing "multiethnic suburbs" in Sweden.' *Alternatives* 33/4, 481–504.

Dannestam, T. 2008. 'Rethinking local politics: Towards a cultural political economy of entrepreneurial cities.' *Space and Polity* 12/3, 353–372.

De Koning, A. 2015. 'This neighbourhood deserves an espresso bar too: Neoliberalism, racialization, and urban policy.' *Antipode* 47/5, 1203–1223.

Dikeç, M. 2007. *Badlands of the Republic: Space, Politics and Urban Policy*. Oxford: Blackwell.

Dobbernack, J. 2014. *The Politics of Social Cohesion in Germany, France and the United Kingdom*. New York, NY: Palgrave Macmillan.

Erel, U. 2011. 'Complex belongings: Racialization and migration in a small English city.' *Ethnic and Racial Studies* 34/12, 2048–2068.

Fanon, F. 1986 [1968]. *Black Skin, White Masks*. London: Pluto.

Fassin, D. 2013. *Enforcing Order: An Ethnography of Urban Politics*. Cambridge: Polity.

Fitzgerald, I. and Smoczynski, R. 2015. 'Anti-Polish migrant moral panic in the UK: Rethinking employment insecurities and moral regulation.' *Czech Sociological Review* 5/3, 339–386.

Fjellman Jaderup, E. 2012a. 'S vill styra asylboende hårdare.' *Sydsvenskan*, April 1. Accessed March 6, 2016. <http://www.sydsvenskan.se/malmo/s-vill-styra-asylboende-hardare/>

Fjellman Jaderup, E. 2012b. 'Intern debatt om Reepalu.' *Sydsvenskan*, March 28. Accessed March 6, 2016. <http://www.sydsvenskan.se/malmo/intern-debatt-om-reepalu/#Scen_1>

Fortier, A.-M. 2010. 'Proximity by design? Affective citizenship and the management of unease.' *Citizenship Studies* 14/1, 17–30.

Foucault, M. 2007. *Security, Territory, Population: Lectures at the Collège de France 1977–1978*. New York, NY: Palgrave Macmillan.

Foucault, M. 2008. *The Birth of Biopolitics: Lectures at the Collège de France 1978–1979*. Translated by G. Burchell. New York, NY: Palgrave Macmillan.

Franzén, M. 2001. 'Urban order and the preventive restructuring of space: The operation of border controls in micro space.' *Sociological Review* 49/2, 202–218.

Garland, D. 2001. *Culture of Control: Crime and Social Order in Contemporary Society*. Chicago, IL: University of Chicago Press.

Gothenburg City 2010. *Överenskommelse om samverkan mellan Göteborgs Stad och Polisområde Storgöteborg*. Gothenburg.

Gressgård, R. 2015a. 'The power of (re)attachment in urban strategy: Interrogating the framing of social sustainability in Malmö.' *Environment and Planning A* 47/1, 108–120.

Gressgård, R. 2015b. 'The whole city or the city as a whole? Questioning the conceptual assumptions of social sustainability in urban governance.' In Righard, Erica, Magnus Johansson and Tapio Salonen (eds.) *Social Transformations of Scandinavian Cities: Nordic Perspectives on Urban Marginalisation and Social Sustainability*. Lund: Scandinavian Academic Press, 199–216.

Heja Malmö! website (2012). Accessed March 6, 2016. <http://hejamalmo.se/vad-ar-heja-malmo/>; <http://hejamalmo.se/category/malmokarlek/>; <https://sv-se.facebook.com/hejamalmo>

Hills, A. 2009. *Policing Post-Conflict Cities*. London: Zed Books.

Höök, L. 2011. 'Polisen ska återta "laglös" gata.' *Sydsvenskan,* September 11. Accessed March 6, 2016. <http://www.sydsvenskan.se/malmo/polisen-ska-aterta-laglos-gata/>

Implementing Committee for New Swedish Police Service 2015. *Pilotprojekt lokala medborgarlöften – slutrapport*. Statens Offentliga Utredningar. Ju 2012:16. Polisen.

Jones, T. and Newburn, T. (eds.) 2006a. *Plural Policing: A Comparative Perspective*. London: Routledge.

Jones, T. and Newburn, T. 2006b. 'The United Kingdom.' In Jones, Trevor and Tim Newburn (eds.) *Plural Policing: A Comparative Perspective*. London: Routledge, 34–54.

Kings, L. 2011. *Till det lokalas försvar: Civilsamhället i den urbana periferin*. Lund: Arkiv förlag.

Kofman, E. 2005. 'Citizenship, Migration and the Reassertion of National Identity.' *Citizenship Studies* 9/5, 453–467.

Kommunstyrelsen 2012. 'Brev från kommunstyrelsen Malmö: Goda krafer räcker inte.' *Dagens Arena,* March 16. Accessed March 6, 2016. <http://www.dagensarena.se/wp-content/blogs.dir/8/files/2012/03/Brev-fra%CC%8An-kommunstyrelsen-Malmo%CC%88.pdf>

Lamble, S. 2013. 'Queer necropolitics and the expanding carceral state: Interrogating sexual investments in punishment.' *Law Critique* 24/3, 229–253.

Lefebvre, H. 1996 [1969]. *Writing on Cities*. Oxford: Blackwell.

Lithman, Y. 2010. 'The holistic ambition: Social cohesion and the culturalization of citizenship. *Ethnicities* 10/4, 488–502.

Lozic, V. 2010. 'I historiekanons skugga: Historieämne och identifikationsformering i 2000-talets mångkulturella samhälle.' PhD diss., Lund University.

Malmö City 2012. *Malmö – en trygg och säker stad. Samverkansöverenskommelse mellan Malmö stad och Polisområde Malmö 2012–2016*. Malmö.

Malmö City 2014. 'Stöd för avhoppare – Konsultationsteamet.' Accessed March 6, 2016. <http://malmo.se/Kommun--politik/Trygghetsfragor-i-Malmo/Sarskilda-utmaningar/Stod-for-avhoppare.html>

Malmö City Planning Office 2013. *Översiktsplan för Malmö ÖP 2012. Planstrategi. Utställningsförslag*. Adopted by the City Council May 22, 2014.

Massey, D. 2005. *For Space*. London: Sage.

Mayer, M. 2012. 'The "Right to the City" in urban social movements.' In Brenner, Neil, Peter Marcuse and Margit Mayer (eds.) *Cities for People, Not for Profit: Critical Urban Theory and the Right to the City*. New York, NY: Routledge, 63–85.

McGhee, D. 2003. 'Moving to "our" common ground: A critical examination of community cohesion discourse in twenty-first century Britain.' *The Sociological Review* 51, 376–404.

Mikkelsen, J. 2011. 'Grängesbergsgatan stängs.' *Sydsvenskan,* June 27. Accessed March 6, 2016. <http://www.sydsvenskan.se/malmo/grangesbergsgatan-stangs/>

Miller, P. and Rose, R. 2008. *Governing the Present: Administering Economic, Social and Personal Life*. Cambridge: Polity.

Mukhtar-Landgren, D. 2012. 'Planering för framsteg och gemenskap: Om den kommunala utvecklingsplaneringens idémässiga förutsättningar.' PhD diss., Lund University.

Nylund, K. 2014. 'Conceptions of justice in the planning of the new urban landscape: Recent changes in the comprehensive planning discourse in Malmö, Sweden.' *Planning Theory and Practice* 15/1, 41–61.

O'Malley, P. 2004. *Risk, Uncertainty and Government*. London: Routledge.

Patel, E. 2013. *Samverkan mellan polis och kommun*. Report 2013:5. Brottsförebyggande rådet (BRÅ). Vällingby: Elanders Sverige AB.

Polisen 2011. 'Fokus på unga och riskhelger – i samverkan med Malmö stad.' Last modified April 10, 2014. Accessed March 6, 2016. <https://polisen.se/Arkiv/Nyhetsarkiv/Skane/Fokus-pa-unga-och-riskhelger---i-samverkan-med-Malmo-stad/>

Polisen 2015. *Polismyndighetens verksamhetsplan för 2015–2016*. Stockholm: Polismyndigheten.

Polissamordningen 2015. 'Reforming the Swedish Police.' Last modified March 31, 2015. Accessed March 6, 2016. <http://polissamordningen.se/english>

Rikspolisstyrelsen 2008. *Samverkan polis och kommun – för en lokalt förankrad polisverksamhet i hela landet*. Stockholm: Rikspolisstyrelsen.

Rikspolisstyrelsen 2012. *Samverkan polis och kommun. Inspektionsrapport 2012:2.* Stockholm: Rikspolisstyrelsen.

Rose, N. 1999. *Powers of Freedom: Reframing Political Thought*. Cambridge: Cambridge University Press.

Schierup, C.-U. and Ålund, A. 2011. 'The end of Swedish exceptionalism? Citizenship, neoliberalism and the politics of exclusion.' *Race and Class* 53/1, 45–64.

Schierup, C.-U., Ålund, A. and Kings, L. 2014. 'Reading the Stockholm riots – A moment for social justice?' *Race and Class* 55/1, 1–21.

Schinkel, W. and van den Berg, M. 2011. 'City of exception: The Dutch revanchist city and the urban *Homo Sacer*.' *Antipode* 43/5, 1911–1938.

Schinkel, W. and van Houdt, F. 2010. 'The double helix of cultural assimilationism and neo-liberalism: Citizenship in contemporary governmentality.' *The British Journal of Sociology* 61/4, 696–715.

Schönström, A. 2015. 'Detta är inte ett tillfälle för partipolitiskt käbbel. Samling behövs mot våldsdåden.' *Sydsvenskan,* July 26. Accessed March 6, 2016. <http://www.sydsvenskan.se/opinion/aktuella-fragor/detta-ar-inte-ett-tillfalle-for-partipolitiskt-kabbel-samling-behovs-mot-valds/>

Skey, M. 2011. *National Belonging and Everyday Life: The Significance of Nationhood in an Uncertain World*. Basingstoke: Palgrave.

Tunström, M. and Bradley, K. 2015. 'Opposing the postpolitical Swedish urban discourse.' In Metzger, Jonathan, Philip Allmendinger and Stijn Oosterlynck (eds.) *Planning against the Political: Democratic Deficits in European Territorial Governance*. New York: Routledge, 69–84.

Turner, B. 2007. 'The enclave society: Towards a sociology of immobility.' *European Journal of Social Theory* 10/2, 287–303.

Van Houdt, F. and Schinkel, W. 2014. 'Crime, citizenship and community: Neoliberal communitarian images of governmentality.' *The Sociological Review* 62/1, 47–67.

Van Steden, R. and Huberts, L. 2006. 'The Netherlands in plural policing.' In Jones, T. and Tim Newburn (eds.) *Plural Policing: A Comparative Perspective*. London: Routledge, 12–33.

Vårt Malmö 2012a. 'Heja Malmö.' *Vårt Malmö* 45/2.

Vårt Malmö 2012b. 'Nu vill fler lämna det kriminella livet.' *Vårt Malmö* 45/3, 3.

Wacquant, L. 2008a. *Urban Outcasts: A Comparative Sociology of Advanced Marginality*. Cambridge: Polity.

Wacquant, L. 2008b. 'Relocating gentrification: The working class, science and the state in recent urban research.' *International Journal of Regional Research* 32/1, 198–205.

PART III: REIMAGINING COMMUNITY

Diana Mulinari & Anders Neergaard

10. From Racial to Racist State? The Sweden Democrats Reimagining the Nation[1]

Abstract: Controversies over citizenship and belonging have lately become pivotal to Swedish politics. The growing strength of the extreme right party, the Sweden Democrats' reimagination of Sweden, indicates, the authors argue, Sweden's shift from being a 'racial' to a 'racist' state. Analysing women and migrants within the party, the chapter highlights the paradoxical politics of a political programme that is anti-feminist and racist, but seek support from (some) women and (some) migrants.

Introduction

Controversies over citizenship, national identities and belonging have been central to Swedish public discourse since the 1990s, and have lately become the very bases of Swedish politics. In the early 1990s, New Democracy, a short-lived parliamentary party, attempted to combine populism and racism at a time when Neo-Nazi-inspired social movements were burgeoning in the streets. These movements were followed by the successful establishment of the Sweden Democrats (*Sverigedemokraterna*), a racist party that has played a major role in Swedish national parliamentary politics since 2010. The growing role of the Sweden Democrats and the social movement that they may be seen as a representative of was manifested by increasing racist violence against those perceived as non-Swedish, as well as systematic claims that migrants constitute a threat to Sweden; claims that up to a certain extent have been included in most mainstream political parties[2]. However, the establishment of these parties encountered extensive forms of resistance from diverse civil society organisations and labour unions to extra-parliamentary

1 This chapter is a result of our research project, 'An impossible equation? The activity of women and immigrants in radical far-right populist parties: a case study of the Sweden Democrats', financed by the Swedish Research Council.
2 Two political parties with parliamentary representation challenged these racist representations: *Vänsterpartiet* (Left party) with 6% of electoral support at the national Parliament and *Feministisk Initiativ* (Feminist Initiative) with 2% of electoral support only represented at the municipality level.

groups, in the struggle against racism and the support of refugee and migrant rights (see Chapters Eleven to Fourteen in the volume).

'Not my Sweden' is a slogan often posted on social media by an increasing number of citizens who no longer recognise their society, where racist violence erupts regularly, ranging from insults and physical attacks on migrants, especially Roma EU migrants trying to make a living through begging, to the torching of accommodation hosting refugees[3]. These and other instances of violence have however, also been accompanied by a racist discourse that is gradually becoming more pronounced thanks to the important role played by social media[4]. Examples of this include comments by local representatives of the Sweden Democrats such as 'hope they starve themselves to death', made in response to a protest by unaccompanied refugee children and adolescents, or 'couldn't anyone stand on Oresund Bridge with a machine gun?' made in reference to stopping refugees from coming to Sweden through the Copenhagen-Malmö Bridge (Baas and Holmén 2013). This symbolic, as well as corporeal and politically articulated racist violence, is occurring in a country with a social democratic leadership that seemingly lacks moral authority, as well as the political vision to offer an alternative that it is capable of acting upon. A manifestation of this apparent political paralysis was the government's agreement to a broad political compromise with established right-wing parties in October, aimed at halting the inflow of refugees to Sweden. In the process of arriving at the agreement, basic principles governing Swedish asylum and refugee policy for decades (although with exceptions) were rapidly forsaken, along with central principles at the heart of social democracy and the labour movement concerning labour market issues. This was met by reactions from thousands of human rights activists, who criticised Prime Minister Stefan Löfven for hypocrisy due to the betrayal of the promises, he had made as late as August 2015 (Nilsson 2015b), solemnly championing open borders for refugees and a generous and inclusive asylum policy.

Departing from these controversies of the present, this chapter will identify and develop several topics evolving from the research on Sweden Democrats starting seven years ago[5]. The political projects of the Sweden Democrats will be

---

3 Roma Camp sites attacked in Sweden (Sveriges Radio 2014).

4 For an antiracist use of social media, see next chapter (Eleven) in this volume.

5 The collection of the empirical material occurred between 2008 and 2014. Close to 20 interviews were conducted with female municipal representatives of the Sweden Democrats, including some with migrant backgrounds. The official documents from the electoral board and the municipalities were used to create the population, employing a saturation approach (Guest, Bunce and Johnson 2006).The interviews were

discussed, which have been framed as wider projects aimed at reimagining Sweden. The term 'reimagining' is used to indicate a party that is discursively stronger but, despite growing parliamentary strength, is still[6] quite weak in institutionally shaping Swedish politics. A short history of the Sweden Democrats will initiate the discussion, alongside the party's contextualisation within the changing political landscape. This is followed by the introduction of postcolonial, neo-Marxist, and feminist perspectives on racism. The emergence and development of extreme right-wing parties (ERP) will then be explored, a phenomenon understood as being connected with both the continuity and transformation of racism as an ideology and stratagem in Swedish politics. Together with exacerbated exclusionary as well as exploitative representations of migrants, this development is seen as indicating Sweden's shift from being a 'racial' state to a 'racist' one. These points are used to scrutinise two particular topics that has been marginalised in much ERP research. By focussing on women and migrants within the party we aim at analysing tensions and conflicts between a party that is anti-feminist and racist, but at the same time seek support from (some) women and (some) migrants. First, we look at the centrality of gender in the political discourse and support of the Sweden Democrats, analysing the ambivalence of being anti-feminist and at the same claiming a Swedishness in which gender equality is an important trait. Second, the party's articulation of ethnicisation and racialisation will be analysed through its programme and public discourse, exploring the position of migrants within. We explore migrant positionality in relation to political discourse and support of the Sweden Democrats. The chapter concludes by emphasising the interplay between the Sweden Democrats' increasingly successful political position and their reimagination of a new Sweden.

The Rise of the Sweden Democrats

The Sweden Democrats have grown quite rapidly since their first electoral participation in 1988. Until 1998, they received less than 0.4% of the votes, but in 2002, they broke past the 1% mark and started gaining double percentage figures in almost every election, before finally achieving parliamentary representation in

semi-structured and realised individually by a research assistant. In addition, the official documents of the party available on the web were considered, as well as on their website, their party newspaper *SD-kuriren*, mainstream media and secondary literature.

6 As the speed of change has been extremely fast, it is important to note that this was written in the winter of 2015–16.

2010. In the 2014 national election, the party received 13% of the votes (and subsequent opinion polls have signalled about 20% voter support for the part). Thus, the Sweden Democrats have become the third-largest party in the parliament and, in the opinion polls, very close to the size of the Swedish Social Democratic Party and *Moderata samlingspartiet* (the Moderate Party, neoliberal and conservative).

Before the Sweden Democrats achieved their breakthrough in the national elections, there was a short-lived right-wing populist party called New Democracy (1991–1994) that increasingly developed a racist interpellation. Whereas established politicians and mainstream scholarship have generally framed the ideology, politics and actions of both parties in terms such as 'populist', 'xenophobic', 'immigrant-hostile' or 'immigration negative', they have rarely explicitly used the term 'racist'. This, in combination with the Sweden Democrat's systematic strategy of repeating the slogan 'we are not racist; we only want to discuss the problem of migration' have most likely helped the party's electoral success[7]. It is, however, quite difficult to deny that racism, especially when phrased in terms of an anti-Muslim racist discourse, has been an intrinsic component in the political interpellation that has made the Sweden Democrats into Sweden's third-largest party.

Contrary to mainstream scholarship on these parties, which will be returned to, the Sweden Democrats as a product of the Swedish 'racial formation' is analysed, that is, the wider social processes related to the use and meaning of race and racial categorisation within the political discourses. The notion of racial formation is used, referring to what Michael Omi and Howard Winant define as:

> The process by which social, economic and political forces determine the content and importance of racial categories, and by which they are in turn shaped by racial meanings. Crucial to this formulation is the treatment of race as a central axis of social relations which cannot be subsumed under or reduced to some broader category or conception (2014: 4).

In focusing on the Sweden Democrats, a number of questions emerge, such as: 'Why has the party achieved electoral success now?' Moreover, 'Why is the party growing that rapidly?' An important conceivable explanation is that the controlled rhetoric of the Sweden Democrats no longer includes the vulgar and coarse racism seen when the party first emerged as an outgrowth of the racist and neo-Nazi social movement of the 1990s (Larsson and Ekman 2001). Today, the party's politics are broader in scope and reflect a nuanced, tactical and strategically designed ideology,

---

7 While cultural racism is intrinsic to the Sweden Democrats, they have launched a policy of zero tolerance on (biological) racism, under which they expelled a number of Sweden Democrats as (too) racist.

which nevertheless fail to distance itself from fundamental ideas of race[8]. While an explicit language of 'race' is rarely used by the party, except through the mediums of social media and blogs, a racist discourse is nevertheless present, as, for example, in this statement from the party's document on democratic development:

> It is necessary to state that by 'special populations' we refer to those ethnic groups that have no natural residence in our country. It has now been made into an almost accepted view that democracy is equated with the right for anyone to settle in Sweden and to enjoy the Swedish welfare system. This is obviously an incorrect interpretation. Sweden is the country of the Swedes, and from this it follows that Swedish norms and values will have a special status in Sweden (Sverigedemokraterna 2004).

There is no direct mention of 'Islam' or 'Muslims' in this quote. However, the party's perception of Muslims is made explicit in other contexts such as in a 2009 article (published for the first time in one of Sweden's major newspapers) written by the party chairman Åkesson, in which Muslims are described as the largest 'foreign' threat since WWII (implying that they are in the same league as the Nazis) (Åkesson 2009). Another example is a campaign video by the Sweden Democrats for the 2010 election, where the image of 'a horde of oriental women' dressed in *niqab*, wearing diamond rings and joined by many of their children in baby strollers, are juxtaposed with an old, grey-haired, light-skinned, obviously 'Swedish' woman (Mulinari and Neergaard 2012). She is shown to be on the losing side in an unequal race towards an office desk with two emergency brake handles, supposedly representing a crisis-ridden Swedish welfare state caught between a rock and a hard place. One brake is the 'pension brake' (implied to be the target of the *niqab*-wearing women and their children), while the other is the 'immigration brake', which the old 'Swedish' woman is supposedly reaching for. The video exposed the seemingly successful strategy of the Sweden Democrats pitting one group against another – in this case, the bereaved benefactors of the decaying system of Swedish elderly care against the 'luxury Muslim refugees', and the supposedly extravagant costs of integrating the latter into the country. The video invokes the metaphor of cuckoo eggs to depict the destruction of Sweden from within. A same type of propaganda, but in a considerably more fine-tuned form, was repeated in the party's campaign in advance of the 2014 election.

Despite this evidence, the rise of the Sweden Democrats is only partly seen as the result of a successful strategy of distancing the party from a crude and overt

8 The concept of race referred to in the context of the Sweden Democrats is mediated through concepts such as religion (especially Islam and Muslims) ethnic groups, natural residence, nationality, ethnicity and culture.

racism, by progressively replacing it with more subtle metaphors. This attempt at distancing continues to come into question by the overt and crude racism of some members and supporters of the Sweden Democrats[9]. Despite the party leadership's strategy of avoiding coarse rhetoric, it passively and sometimes even actively supports the activities of its members and supporters on social media. An example of these connections was the speech given on the 18th of October 2015 at Trelleborg by Kent Ekeroth, a Sweden Democratic Member of Parliament. He was inspiring supporters by saying that

> 'Swedish people have a long fuse. But when it burns clear … then there will be a bang! We'll show them that now is the time, now the bang will come', and continued addressing the listeners: 'You who are here today, you are the spearhead that we need to take our country back' (Quoted and translated from Olsson 2015)[10].

In this sense, the Sweden Democrats may be seen as the principal parliamentary manifestation of a contemporary 'Polanyian' countermovement (see the introduction to this book). The party is still at the centre of a social movement that keeps switching emphasis between protest, racism and extreme-right interpellations. In line with Barbara Perry (2001), the Sweden Democrats may be understood as a political node for the clustering of a range of minor organisations, networks and individuals for voicing their thoughts on racism and neo-fascism, bridging parliamentary organised members and Neo-Nazi activists realising violent actions.

The Sweden Democrats in a Changing Political Context

The 2014 electoral success of the Sweden Democrats created a serious institutional crisis in national parliamentary politics, which has historically been dominated by two competing blocs: centre-left and centre-right. The seven other Swedish parliamentary parties, besides the Sweden Democrats, declared in advance of both the 2010 and 2014 parliamentary elections that they would not collaborate with what is often called a 'xenophobic' or 'immigrant critical' party. However,

---

9 There are a number of websites documenting these numerous outbursts, some leading to expelling or warning members, but many passively accepted by the Sweden Democrats. To take just one example to understand the language used in some of the cases during the autumn of 2015, when thousands of refugees were coming to Sweden, a Sweden Democrats municipal council member and juror asked in a Facebook comment: 'Couldn't anyone stand on the Oresund Bridge with a machine gun?' (See Nilsson 2015a).

10 The full speech is accessible at https://www.youtube.com/watch?v=pb1wltJMabs (Accessed March 24, 2016).

the strength of the Sweden Democrats as a strategic balancer in parliament has obstructed effective governing. One short-lived attempt to circumvent the parliamentary power of the Sweden Democrats, the so-called December Agreement of 2014, was crafted in order to allow the largest bloc at the time to pass its budget in Parliament[11]. Although supposed to last until 2022, the agreement collapsed less than one year later as a consequence of opposition from conservative members of the small Christian Democratic Party. This opposition was given strength by another looming opposition within the largest right-wing party *Moderaterna* in the Swedish Parliament.

Prior to this, there had been a certain political rapprochement offered by three of the right-wing parties to the Sweden Democrats on migration and refugee issues. At the same time, the Confederation of Swedish Enterprise (*Svensk Näringsliv*) and its affiliated employers' associations approached the Sweden Democrats with the aim of guiding their politics into a more business-friendly direction. Despite the Sweden Democrats' insistence on staunchly defining themselves as a neither politically left nor right, but a social conservative party, and despite the strong electoral support shown to the party by mostly white working class men, the party is slowly positioning itself in a conservative and neoliberal corner, by offering to form a government coalition with the Moderate Party and Christian Democratic Party (Larsson 2015). During the 2010–2014 parliamentary period, the Sweden Democrats voted substantially more with the right-wing alliance than with the red-green opposition, despite their rhetoric of being welfare friendly. This rapprochement with the political right is increasingly resulting in a shift in the party's rhetoric. From once being against the privatisation of the publicly financed welfare service, and defending the collective agreements according to which trade unions are fairly free to go on strike to advance their positions, the Sweden Democrats have now effectively switched to the conservative and neoliberal camp.

Until recently, there was general agreement among all parties, except the Sweden Democrats, on a comparatively generous refugee policy at the European level. Following the success of the Sweden Democrats in the 2014 election, the Social Democratic Party, and especially the right-wing parties, have been bleeding potential voters to the Sweden Democrats. Additionally, three right-wing parties have embarked on shifting their positions on refugee and integration policies. On the background of a substantial increase in the number of asylum seekers,

11 The objective was to avoid the repetition of the fate of the first budget following the 2014 election, in which the right-wing opposition's budget was passed with the active support of the Sweden Democrats.

Sweden – according to OECD (n.d.) the country in Europe accepting most refugees per capita – recently dramatically transformed its policies. In October of 2015, the government came to an agreement with the four right-wing parties in Parliament on the matters of refugee and integration policy. The agreement focused on making Sweden less open by introducing temporary residence permits, combined with employer-friendly policies directing refugees towards low-wage (especially service-orientated) sectors of the labour market (Regeringen 2015). While the policy's central focus is on migration, one of the its main consequences will be a labour market that will provide employers with easy access to cheap and weak organised labour (Dadgostar and Esbati 2015).

In the early 1990s, Sweden, together with Germany, was already becoming infamous for racist and neo-fascist violence. Several scholars have emphasised the similarities of the situation back then with the situation today. There were around 15 cases of attacks on refugee housing in 2015. Roma European Union migrants, working as beggars, are constantly harassed. A fatal terrorist attack on a school in Trollhättan in October of 2015 was clearly an exceptional racially motivated event, but it is illuminating to examine how the media and the mainstream society in general handled it. Trollhättan is a midsized Swedish industrial town with a high degree of racialised segregation. In the 1990s, the town witnessed neo-Nazi movements; these movements have resurfaced in the last few years. There in October of 2015, a young white Swedish man dressed up as a character from the Star Wars film franchise and armed with a sword, entered a schoolyard located in an ethnically segregated area, explicitly selected and attacked non-white children and teachers, and killed a fifteen-year-old boy and a young teacher.

There was a reluctance in Sweden to see this massacre as being racially motivated or as a case of terrorism. Even the public service media reproduced the division between 'true Swedes' and 'Others' when reporting on the massacre. In the aftermath of the attack, a Swedish television journalist asked the police if the killer avoided 'Swedish children completely'. The following day, a reporter questioned the municipal communications director: 'It's an extremely segregated school with very few Swedish children. What do you have to say about this?' (Fossbo 2015). This shows that the word 'Swedish' was coded in this context as 'white', and that the term refers to city areas in which more than half of the population are foreign-born or children of migrants. Taken together, this is a social context for racialisation of Swedish citizens, further referred to as racialised Swedes.

A Post-Colonial Reading of European Extreme Right-Wing Parties

While there are large variations among European extreme-right parties that are represented by rapidly shifting interpellations (e.g. protest, racist and extreme-right) over time (Fennema 1997), there seem to be some commonalities which make most researchers view them as an ideological family (Mair and Mudde 1998). In summarising a broad range of attempts within mainstream political science and sociology to capture the essence of ERP, Cas Mudde argues that they end up claiming 'that populist radical right values are alien to western democratic values, but [...] a small potential exists for them in all western societies' (2010: 1170).[12]

Mudde contends that this line of reasoning is not substantiated by ideology of these parties or by data on attitudes among electorates. Instead he argues that the available data support an understanding of establishment and support of ERPs as linked what we call 'racist normalcy'. ERPs reflect and mobilise a radicalisation of mainstream views and 'that key aspects of the populist radical right ideology are shared by the mainstream, both at the elite and mass level, albeit often in a more moderate form' (2010: 1178). This he substantiates by arguing that surveys have demonstrated significant racism among respondents, a fact that should place racism at the core of understanding ERP's ideologies. However, there is a solid refusal among these influential researchers to see racism as integral to 'western' ideology and political thought (Bonilla-Silva and Baiocchi 2001).

This is again apparent in literature on European history, in which colonialism, imperialism and other forms of western geopolitical domination appear to be completely silenced or forgotten. As a number of scholars have demonstrated, there is a normalisation of colonial and imperialism expression, for instance: 'The white man's burden', 'Manifest Destiny', 'Dia de la Raza'[13], 'the Commonwealth' and 'the Orient (see for instance Dussel 1995; Said 1978; West 1999; Bonilla-Silva and Baiocchi 2001). In transcending these self-imposed limits by ERP scholars, strong reasons are found for the argument that the racist normalcy, that ERP represent, is a radical version of the racism of today.

Inspired by postcolonial research and transcending Mudde's that do not recognise the intrinsic problem of racism, we argue with reference to Karl Polanyi

12 He exemplifies with established researchers such as Betz (1994), Ignazi (1992) and Kitschelt and McGann (1995).

13 Over the last decade, progressive governments in Latin America have denounced the racist legacy of Columbus Day, renaming it instead 'Indigenous Resistance Day'. This content was originally published by teleSUR (2015).

(2001) that the neoliberal creed is a reinforced version of an exploitative racist normalcy that has dominated the political discourse of western elites since the early 1980s. The rise of ERP, of which the Sweden Democrats is an example, represents an exclusionary racism that is partially posited against the neoliberal onslaught. Thus, the neoliberal creed of 'the market' harbours a contemporary project of commodification based on an exploitative racism, pointing back to the legacy of the racism geopolitics represented by colonialism, imperialism and neo-colonialism (Miles 1993; Ross 2012; Goldberg 2006). Although more covert forms of western imperialism continue to be a driver of exploitative racism in spite of the formal decolonisation of the global South, they have been increasingly accompanied by another manifestation of the racialised exploitation embodied in migration from the global South to North.

By viewing ERP through an antiracist/postcolonial perspective, it becomes possible to capture what seems to be a general shift from biological to cultural racism as central to the creation and establishment of a historically specific European 'racial formation' (Omi and Winant 2014), what political philosopher David Goldberg conceptualises as the establishment of 'racial states' (2002). This reflects an understanding that the emergence of ERP requires a historical frame that explains both the continuity and change in the role of racism as an ideology essential for the construction of Europe and its states.

Exploring Swedish Racial Formation: Exploitative and Exclusive Racism

As earlier argued, racialised politics and discourses in Sweden may be understood through the distinctions and varying balances between 'exploitative' and 'exclusionary' racism (Mulinari and Neergaard 2014; for a different categorisation, see Essed 1996). Exploitative racism operates by producing a usable (exploitable) labour force through discursive and institutional practices. Additionally, exploitative racism is linked to people with the power and the possibility *to exploit* and thus, principally, to the 'elite', that is, the political parties formulating policies that place workers vulnerable to exploitation on the one side, and employers using the precarious labour market positions of workers on the other. Meanwhile, exclusionary racism emphasises the threat of the 'Other'.

Of the two forms of racism, the institutionally dominant form in Sweden continues to be exploitative racism, intersecting with capitalist exploitation, especially expressed through a neoliberal agenda that does not replace, but often subsumes neoconservative policies. Exploitative racism may be seen as a practice that is ideologically framed in the win-win policies of managed migration (Fekete 2001;

Lentin and Titley 2011). It is shaped by an idea of producing cheap (including educated) labour through processes of racialisation and curtailed rights.

Exclusionary racism is linked to the construction of 'Others' as a threat that is always present, but it only crystallises at certain moments, which leads to the spurious causal argument in mainstream research that crisis produces racism. Here, understanding of exclusionary racism is inspired by how the concept of ethnopluralism is conceptualised by Michael Minkenberg (1997). It rejects the notion that biological racism is in principle (but rarely in practice) non-hierarchical; a horizontal dimension emphasising incommensurability. An ERP '... disguises [...] its racism and anti-semitism in the concepts of ethnopluralism' (Minkenberg 1997: 74). In this sense, exclusionary racism may be conceptualised as defensive at its core, although in general, it is practiced through offensive border maintenance. Thus, in its extreme form, exclusionary racism may take the form of racist terrorism, as in the case of Lasermannen, Peter Mangs and the Trollhättan school murders[14]. However, the dominant form of exclusionary racism focuses on separation and exclusion, as in the culturally racist discourse of the Sweden Democrats. Here, ethnopluralism is converted into politics and practices of separation and policies for stemming immigration, and into strategies for expulsion/repatriation.

Exploitative and exclusionary racism should be seen as two different modes that, in many ways, coexist in different constellations of hierarchy and balance. While it would be too simplistic to trace a definitive link between class position and forms of racism, it is contended that people championing exploitative racism generally do so from a more privileged class position, whereas people advancing exclusionary racism do so from a more subordinated or peripheral class position.

Further, the more visible exclusionary racism of the Sweden Democrats is still, on a policy impact level, peripheral, compared to Denmark and Norway (Widfeldt 2014; Berggren and Neergaard 2015), to exploitative racism. Thus, it is contended that exploitative racism has dominated the racial formation of Sweden for some time, and it is only fairly recently that expanding policies of exclusionary racism have been seen.

14 Lasermannen ('the Laser Man') and Peter Mangs are two Swedish serial killers that targeted migrants (Tamas 2002; Gardell 2015), and the racist Trollhättan school murders was the worst terror act in Sweden since 1940 (Cantwell 2015).

From Subordinated Inclusion to a Racist State

In historicising the intersections of the exclusionary and exploitative, four periods are differentiated[15]. The first period, where exclusionary racism dominated Swedish racial formation for long periods occurred in the 19th and early 20th centuries. The secondary exploitative racism to be discussed was mainly shaped by imperialism towards the global South, and the internal colonialism towards the Sami as First Nation people as explored (Öhman 2016). The internal colonial legacy was based on certain forms of exploitative racism that are in place today in the continuity of the Swedish state's appropriation of land and water (or the third world). This was a period in which Sweden was among the leading countries in scientific racism (Broberg 1995). It was a time when racialised eugenics, related to forms of internal colonialism, became a frame for racist practices targeting Sweden's Sami and Roma population (Lundmark 2002). These practices, such as the sterilisations of the Sami and Roma, also targeted non-racialised people, particularly people with mental disabilities and marginalised groups of women who were seen to lack the qualities needed for reproducing a 'healthy' nation (Broberg and Tydén 2005).

Following World War II, during a second period, biological racism was discredited, although eugenics survived. In the context of refugee and labour migration and a booming economy, there was a slow but substantial shift in Swedish racial formation. In earlier studies on the Swedish Trade Union Confederation, LO, it was argued (Mulinari and Neergaard 2004) that this was a time of inclusionary subordination, which – seen from a wider societal perspective – was marked by a decrease in exclusionary racism. However, this was also a time when an exploitative racism, based on racialisation of migrant populations, was institutionalised, particularly through ethno-racial discrimination and labour market segregation.

The 1968 radicalisation created a space for identification with antiracism. Support for anti-colonial movements and US civil rights can be considered central to what Hübinette and Lundström (2014) call 'white solidarity', a term that, however, risks essentialising the linkage between social location and political identity. The decline of the social democratic project, which began with the 1991 financial crisis, gave rise to a third period, a period of Sweden's reimagination, in which neoliberal exploitative racism has increasingly merged with a new exclusionary racism, related to the successful establishment of racist parties.

15 For an inspiring approach of historicising through whiteness, see Hübinette and Lundström 2014.

The interpellation of aggressive white nostalgia[16] has become a trademark feature of the Sweden Democrats in their project for reimagining the nation. In this interpellation, exclusionary racism is central, and it is becoming more hegemonic, shaping what could transform into a fourth period. This period would represent a fusion between migration and refugee policies, focused on the securitisation of borders, both externally and internally, often discursively constructed in relation to the 'Other'. To the extent that migration and refugee policies are fused with the more crude exclusionary racism of the Sweden Democrats, it may imply a shift from a Swedish racial formation, regulated through subordinated inclusion, towards a racist Swedish state.

A central shift has already occurred from forms of exclusion towards systems of expulsion in refugee policies, and this is clearly indicated in the Sweden Democrats' reimagination of the nation. Such hegemonic discourses, while underlining the centrality of 'open societies', create and recreate boundaries of expulsion through the category of race; normalising the state of emergency that legitimates state intervention towards specific categories of people.

While a *racial state* regulates the presence of migrants through forms of subordinated inclusion, a *racist state* operates through a classification system that creates boundaries between accepted and undesirable migrants, a system that is contained within the bodies of migrants themselves. A racist state embodies what Giorgio Agamben (1998) describes as the systematic state of emergency that enables the state to turn the lives of those under its rule into what he calls 'homo sacer', or 'bare life'.

Finally, if a shift from a racial to a racist state is occurring, this shift is also gendered. Discourses of security and migration control, aimed at protecting the nation, reconstitute gender relations through forms of militarised masculinity. They also transform the defensive caring racism of the Sweden Democrats into a regime of caring racism classification that defines who within the nation is worth caring for.

Gender Politics in a Racist Party

The relationships between women and nationalism, as well as between gender, nationalism and racism, have been central to feminist scholarship in recent decades. Scholars have argued that women play a leading role in the symbolic construction of the nation and its boundaries, and that they are key actors in the construction of the narratives of belonging (Bulbeck 1997; Mulinari and Neergaard 2015; Kaplan

16 The concept of white nostalgia is used where people mourn the passing of what they themselves have transformed, inspired by Renato Rosaldo (1993; see also hooks 1992; Gilroy 2004).

and Weinberg 1999; Yuval Davis 2011). However, according to Kathleen Blee (2011), to argue that the politics and practices of ERP are gendered is not enough. Four relevant questions should be asked: What does it mean (theoretically and analytically) that gender matters in the analysis of the right-wing? When is gender more salient? Why does gender matter? To whom does gender matter?

Following the Swedish election in 2010, partially because of the Sweden Democrats entry into parliament, the percentage of overall female MPs decreased, which led a Swedish TV journalist to ask the Sweden Democrats' chairman how it feels to have less than half the share of female parliamentary representation than in Muslim countries such as Afghanistan, Pakistan and the United Arab Emirates[17]. In so doing, the journalist played on the racism of the Sweden Democrats against Muslims by emphasising that even reactionary Muslim parliaments have a better representation of women than the Sweden Democrats.

While the Sweden Democrats have over 9,000 members, only slightly more than a fifth of these are women, and their increase is very slow. Furthermore, women are strongly underrepresented in national, regional and local parliamentary bodies (see Table 1).

Table 1: Percentage of women elected to the Sweden Democrats and to all other parties (2002–2014)

	2002	2006	2010	2014
Sweden Democrats, municipal elections	12.2	16.9	18.7	23.4
All other parties, municipal elections*	47.3	42.8	44.2	46.1
Sweden Democrats, county elections	-	12.5	17.1	29.8
All other parties, county elections**	47.3	48.0	48.8	50.1
Sweden Democrats, national elections	-	-	15	22.4
All other parties, national elections***	45.3	47.3	46.8	47.0

*Lowest share among other parties in 2014 municipal elections, 44.2% (*Moderata samlingspartiet*)
**Lowest share among other parties in 2014 county elections, 34.5% (*Centerpartiet*)
**Lowest share among other parties in 2014 national elections, 26.3% (*Liberalerna*)

Source: Authors' compilation based on SCB (2016a)

With regard to opinion polls and gendered differences in the support for the Sweden Democrats, table 2 below shows a similar picture, with much higher support (generally more than double) for men than for women:

17 See <http://www.youtube.com/watch?feature=player_detailpage&v=H--Q-atkZqg#t=346s> (Accessed November 11, 2013, no longer publicly accessible).

Table 2: Party sympathy survey

Percentage (by sex) that consider the Sweden Democrats to be the best party

	Nov 2010	May 2011	Nov 2011	May 2012	Nov 2012	May 2013	Nov 2013	May 2014	Nov 2014	May 2015	Nov 2015
Men	4.3	4.4	5.3	5.5	8.1	7.9	9.5	8.7	10.5	14.4	20.0
Women	2.1	2.1	1.5	2.3	3.1	3.6	3.8	3.4	4.9	6.5	8.8

Source: Authors' compilation based on SCB (2016b)

When the Sweden Democrats doubled their electorate in the 2014 national election, they did so in many ways by repeating their 2010 campaign. The central target remained the Muslim threat, and the welfare costs of immigration. However, in relation to gender, there were some novelties compared to 2010. These included a more pronounced and developed political programme on gender issues, advocated by the new gender equality representative of the party, who, in response to criticism of the party's antifeminism, defined herself as an 'uniqueness feminist' (in Swedish, *särartsfeminist*). With the explicit aim of securing stronger electorate support from women, the party advanced some new policies. A specific proposal centred on the right of auxiliary nurses and others (mainly women) employed in welfare services to full-time employment (as women are often directly or indirectly forced to take part-time jobs). This was a paradoxical proposal, as it included a large share of racialised nurse's aides, who are often disproportionally overrepresented among part-time and temporary employees. There was also an increase in the number of women on the Sweden Democrats' parliamentary lists, although the number was still substantially lower than in other parties. These changes did not result in any substantial shift in the gender ratio. However, by doubling the votes, the Sweden Democrats attracted more women voters.

In their critical review of the explanations provided for understanding gender as one of the clearest barriers to support for racist parties (Betz 1994: 142), Elisabeth Gidengil et al. (2005) asserted that one of the most serious shortcomings of these explanations is the focus on women's lack of identification with racist parties. The authors argued that if the focus was shifted towards men, the gender gap would be explained as a male response to second-wave feminism, a point also stressed by other research (Norocel 2013; Keskinen 2014). Furthermore, women's lack of identification with these parties is according to Gidengil et al. (2005) to a certain extent based on the centrality of gender equality for most women across the political spectrum. Another explanation is that women with conservative values in gender relations prefer voting for mainstream right-wing parties, to voting for ERP (Mudde 2007). However, not all racist parties are uniformly conservative on moral issues. Tjitske Akkerman and Anniken Hagelund (2007) argued that in Norway there has been a shift in the Progress Party's politics towards what could be considered 'feminist' values regarding family and sexuality, a shift that has boosted support from women in the form of votes.

The Sweden Democrats are strongly anti-feminist. They frequently criticise various aspects of gender equality policy, arguing that it violates 'human nature' and weakens 'normal' family cohesion (Towns, Karlsson and Eyre 2014: 237). Notwithstanding, in the construction of 'Swedishness', and against immigrants, especially Muslim 'Others', the Sweden Democrats identify certain positive aspects of gender equality on the grounds that formal gender equality, which acknowledges the innate differences between women and men, is culturally Swedish and can thus be contrasted with the position of (Muslim) immigrants. In other words, gender equality is highlighted the most when the Sweden Democrats talk about 'the Other'.

On the 8th of March 2012, the Sweden Democrats women's network presented a campaign film that aimed to put the topic of 'honour killing' on the public agenda. The first scene of the film showed a female body brutally beaten, in the second a young blonde woman cleaned the blood, accompanied by a speaker's voice saying: 'Do you know that culture can kill?' (Vergara 2012). The Sweden Democrats women active in Almedalen before the 2014 Swedish elections systematically linked rape to migration, asserting that the courses offered to refugees seemed unable to teach them Swedish cultural values regarding women: 'The Alliance has introduced community education classes for asylum seekers, but apparently without success… Look at the increasing number of honour crimes and the exploding figures regarding rape' (Borg 2010).

The Sweden Democrats paradox regarding gender is that, as an ethno-nationalist party, they argue that gender equality is a Swedish cultural trait, yet as an anti-feminist party, they assert that feminism has destroyed the Swedish family. The Sweden Democrats paradox regarding ethnicity (or culture) is that, as a nationalist party, they want to celebrate Swedish culture, while as a neo-conservative party, they want to introduce the cultural values they believe other cultures embody, as one informant asserted:

> […] I believe that they do not feel well because everything is so fuzzy here. Everybody does what they want. Women leave their children, and children can scream to their parents. And I have spoken with many migrants, and they think I am right. They would like more authority and more order. It is in their culture (Informant C).

Whereas it is argued that the patriarchal culture of many migrants is a problem vis-à-vis what is constructed as Swedish gender equality, what is seen as these migrants' respect for authority (or their desire for discipline and punishment) is celebrated.

Women who represent the Sweden Democrats have expressed feelings of inadequacy and insufficiency regarding the demands that the gender regime in Sweden poses on women, both as workers and as mothers. They have reacted against the social-democratic-inspired gender regime (the double-income household model), a type of gender equality promoted to a certain extent by second-wave feminism (Bergqvist, Olsson Blandy and Sainsbury 2007). It is a model that has decreased (but not wiped out) some forms of male power within the family and workplace. It has implied a process of decreasing patriarchal power, but at the same time, has placed conflicting and difficult demands on women as citizens, workers and mothers. In studying women activists in the Sweden Democrats, the informants also reacted to the introduction of neoliberal policies that, following an appropriation of feminist ideas (cf. Fraser 1998), have transformed gender equality into an individual issue of personal success, and linked the potential for equality to higher income (Mulinari and Neergaard 2014). A salient characteristic of the female Sweden Democrats politicians in this study, is that they rarely spoke about male dominance and when they did, they never described it as something negative; in contrast to Swedish female politicians of other parties. These Sweden Democrat women tended to enter parliamentary politics both through an exclusionary racist project, and as a reaction against the Swedish women's movement and its demands for gender equality. Thus, they saw themselves as challenging the parliamentary dominance of gender equality policies, a dominance that, according to them, has gone too far. In the words of an informant:

> Children abandoned in the day care centres and mothers dying, really dying of stress. For what? For gender equality? What is wrong if women want to be mothers…? I mean if they want to stay at home with their children. It is only natural. All these work demands. People get sick. I got sick (Informant A).

Their insistence that they were not racist, despite sometimes being called racist, was a statement important to the informants, and was used repeatedly, not only in relation to party policies but in their understanding of self-identity. The informants often returned to their (strong) feelings of self-esteem regarding their understanding of the personality traits needed to be a member of the Sweden Democrats, and of the pride carried in the 'us' created; in contrast to all the (Swedish) others who have failed to organise themselves (even though they actually think as 'us').

For these women, 'coming out' as one of the Sweden Democrats was related to discovering that they were 'normal' and 'nice' people. This 'coming out' was also shaped by how they linked their self-image as open, generous and caring people to the Sweden Democrats' project, as illustrated in the following quote:

> I've always been a person who thinks, we live here, but all people are equal and also live here. People who are Muslims or this and that or Chinese, it made no difference to me, because we're all just people. I've always thought that before. So I've tried to raise my kids, but it's been impossible, because they have lived in a completely different world where there's been a lot of gangs, where there's been a lot of assaults, where there's been a lot … and it's been [because of the] the migrants. And it was probably then when I started to react and think that, but come on [name], your … your ideology, it doesn't work that way, it's a nice thought, but it doesn't work that way in real life. It does not work for those that you care the most for. I would be a bad mother if I did not acknowledge this. At the same time I started talking to the people coming from the former Yugoslavia, where they really hate each other now, and then I thought, they lived in the same country, and they hate each other now, [and] they're crude and racists. And then I feel like that there are a lot of people coming here, bringing this hate, [and] they don't really want to live in harmony with us. It is neither good for them nor for us. And that's where I feel strongly about doing something (Informant S).

This informant provided two basic explanations for why she changed her view of people from other backgrounds. On the one hand, her experience as a mother with what she perceives as her humanism, collided with her children's experiences of (gangs of) migrants. On the other hand, she explained her own racism using her impression of others' racism. It is 'they' who come here bringing hate and prejudice and forcing the informant to change her ideology, which according to the informant herself, is not sustainable 'in real life'. In her account, racism is a cultural product brought to Sweden by immigrants, and it forces Swedes who have previously followed an equality ideology to think differently. In other words, it is the immigrants' own fault that the Sweden Democrats are forced to think the way they do. However, it is also because she wants to be a good mother, or actually, because the migrants and migration hinder her from being a good mother, that she has changed her outlook on people from other backgrounds.

In a short sentence ending this quote, the informant added an interesting comment when she expanded on who she cares for, stating: 'It is neither good for them nor for us'. At the crossroads of the cultural racist politics of the Sweden Democrats and gender maternalism, a form of 'caring racism' (Mulinari and Neergaard 2014) has evolved. Here, care is most often expressed as 'We' against an 'Other'; a natural love (Ahmed 2003) for 'our people', constituted through racial fantasies of those 'Others' threatening their wellbeing. At times, this caring racism is shaped through an ethnopluralist frame, in which caring for the 'Other' becomes an argument for the 'Other' to leave, to return home, where they will ostensibly be better off.

Patricia Hill Collins (1998) argued that the idealised traditional family combines a seemingly natural hierarchy with a feeling of unity among its members. Another characteristic of the traditional family, which the author suggested, is its location in discourses of belonging through genetic links, that is, blood ties. If the nation is understood in terms of family bonds, the control of women's sexuality for the 'purity of the race' becomes central, and blood ties enter into the conceptualisation of the nation. Demands for restricted immigration, closed borders and assimilation are logical consequences of this line of thought. The model is moved from the family towards the public legitimisation of hierarchies among societal groups. It is, in this sense, a re-politicisation of the private as a model for the public.

For the Sweden Democrats, reimagining Sweden is not only an issue of cleansing Sweden of 'foreign' elements, it is also an issue of family and gender, in which two contradictory positions are balanced. On the one hand, the Sweden Democrats use gender equality as a value of Swedishness against (Muslim) migrants who can never become 'us'. On the other hand, the party is building on a supposedly patriarchal migrant 'Other', defending what they see as traditional family roles and values against the onslaught of what they see as an aggressive Swedish feminism.

Migrants in a Project of Racist Nationalism?

The success of the Sweden Democrats in the national elections of 2010 and 2014 raised the question of who votes for that party. The available statistics, especially the Statistics Sweden (SCB) party sympathy (see table 3 below) and exit polls, should be read at best as indications. Typically, they have been poor at predicting election outcomes concerning the Sweden Democrats.

Table 3: Party sympathy survey

Percentage (by sex and foreign/native-born) of people who consider the Sweden Democrats to be the best party

	Nov 2010	May 2011	Nov 2011	May 2012	Nov 2012	May 2013	Nov 2013	May 2014	Nov 2014	May 2015
Men, Swedish born	4.6	4.7	5.7	5.9	8.5	8.3	9.8	9.3	11.2	14.9
Men, foreign born	1.6	1.5	1.4	1.9	5.4	4.6	7.3	2.5	5.2	9.8
Women, Swedish born	2.2	2.2	1.5	2.2	3.0	3.6	4.2	3.7	5.3	6.4
Women, foreign born	1.4	1.4	1.5	3.5	3.9	3.3	1.4	1.3	2.2	7.3
All, foreign born	1.5	1.5	1.5	2.7	4.7	3.9	3.9	1.8	3.5	8.5

Source: Authors' compilation based SCB (2016b)

With the exception of the category 'Men, foreign born' in the November 2013 and May 2015 polls (in which the error margin was almost 4 per cent), sympathy for the Sweden Democrats among people with foreign backgrounds, or people who are foreign born, is very much below the percentage for white Swedish men. It is interesting to note that the difference between Swedish-born and foreign-born men is generally substantially larger than the difference for the same groups of women; a result caused by the low percentage of Swedish-born women voting for the Sweden Democrats.

Despite substantially fewer foreign-born (especially women) voting for the Sweden Democrats, this figure is rising over time. Thus, an interesting question is 'why would foreign-born Swedes want to vote for the Sweden Democrats, a racist party?' One factor to take into account is that the category 'foreign born' is very heterogeneous. Based on regimes and conjunctures of racialisation, and how the Sweden Democrats profile their racism, together with other political questions and the policies the party has had, and continues to have, a different impact on various groups suffering racialisation is an issue that now turned to (Poohl 2010).

According to Pontus Mattson (2009), there are two categories of migrants that have been interpellated by the Sweden Democrats, one being the first wave of labour migrants and the other being the groups that have experienced a minority religious position in states dominated by repressive Islamic governments. These categories of migrants identify themselves through references to whites, Christian, Europeans, civilised people, etc. Some came to Sweden during the time of labour migration and refugee migration from Eastern European countries, all before the early 1970s, when labour migration basically stopped. A third category of migrants, are those that identify with the Sweden Democrat's conservative values, which are exceptional in Swedish policy[18].

Nima Gholam Ali Pour had a strong position as Chairman of one neighbourhood associations of the Social Democratic Party in Malmö. He left the Party for the Sweden Democrats when a member with a Muslim background, who was already a board member of the Islamic Association, was elected to the Social Democratic Party board. He argued that he did not understand why he (as a migrant) was not allowed to be a member of a party that aimed to limit migration. He asserts that as a migrant (maybe more than other Swedes), he is able to witness how unfair the system is, for those that work versus those that cheat (criminals, welfare dependants etc.)(Ljungberg and Hashemi 2013).

The credibility of the Sweden Democrats, and particularly in its difficulties in distancing from Nazism, puts the topic of migrants (or rather the Party's relations with both with migrants as a social category and the people embodying the

18 While the Christian Democratic Party has competed on conservative values concerning gender and sexuality, it has slowly adapted to its liberal alliance parties on these issues, and has also generally been a staunch defender of a comparatively generous refugee policy.

category) in a sensitive position. 'If the Sweden Democrats are not racist, how come there are so few migrants in their ranks?' This was a question posed by the antiracist movement before the elections. Thus, still struggling with trying to distance itself from its history, the Sweden Democrats 2014 election video presented two racialised representatives arguing that one could be proud of Sweden and still be concerned about migration policies.

In the following quote, one of our informants, a Sweden Democratic woman representative, with a migrant background that in Sweden risks racist discrimination, illustrates this position:

> I think it's great that the Sweden Democrats dare to stand for it, and that they dare to speak loudly what the Swedish people only talk about at the kitchen table and around the cottage. And I know that because when I meet Swedes who do not know me, they are so very careful. But then when I bring up the subject of the problem of migration myself, then they begin to talk. Otherwise, they dare not, for they get the stamp of being racist directly. And what they say – elderly, plain people, Swedish workers that have retired – they say that nobody asked them if they wanted foreigners in their buildings. I have worked all my life to live here. So I must say, they, the Muslims, destroy much, I do not know how, they can get hold of our houses, how they can afford to buy the condominium. And then it happens that they are forced to sale; for they cannot pay for it. I sit on the board here too, so I have some insight on that, it's a disaster. We always had such a fine order in the laundry room and in the garden and the basement. They are more and more moving in, [and] they are destroying the area. I asked them why move here if you cannot follow the rules? Because it is so nice here, they answered. But why do you think it is so nice here? Because of us, we keep everything clean and in order. I am a migrant and follow the rules. That's it, that's what people see. Now I'm not saying that all of them are like that, but the ones I have met (Informant K).

This narrative can be inscribed within the rhetoric of the Sweden Democrats. The argument that 'everybody thinks like us, but nobody has the courage to speak' is very common and it is conveyed here in an account of what people actually feel but dare not say. The rhetoric of 'out in the cottages' follows Sweden Democrats' nostalgic reading of the Swedish as rural people. The narrative of the Swedish seniors also follows the Sweden Democrats, in terms of the groups with which the party has been successful. Finally, a racism that is always defensive ('I am not saying that all of them are like this or do this but …') follows a common rhetoric in the other interviews.

There is, however, a specificity in this narrative that has qualities in common with Sweden Democrats members with migrant backgrounds. At a certain level, their investment in what could be conceptualised as respectability is perceived as being threatened by two groups: on the one side, the younger generation of Swedes with a migrant background, Swedes who are quite outspoken about racism, and on the other side, the new migrants, the refugees. The narratives of these two groups of migrants are often presented in juxtaposition with the speakers' own careers in Sweden, and their lifestyles are characterised as accepting of the rules and as those of good and respectable immigrants. They took the jobs that Swedes did not want, they found work from day one, they moved around looking for jobs, they had to struggle but they learned Swedish, they paid taxes and contributed to the welfare of Sweden. All the Sweden Democrats' activists of migrant backgrounds that were spoken to, also repeated this narrative, or parts of it. Anna Hagwall from Hungary, at times one of the most prominent women members of the Sweden Democrats, in the same interview highlights a different argument, based on economic capital. She explains that the support for the party by people with Eastern European backgrounds (respectable middle-class citizens in the present day) is grounded in their successful adaptation in Sweden (Poohl 2010).

Jasbir K. Puar (2007) used the concept of homo-nationalism to describe how the category of 'queer' shifted from being a construction of figures of death during the AIDS epidemic, to becoming a construction of productive (neoliberal) subjects tied through happy gay marriage to ideas of success. The author argued that this fragile inclusion was accompanied and accomplished by the production of populations of Orientalised terrorist bodies. A similar argument could be developed regarding the category of migrants in Sweden. Violence against refugee camps, attacks on mosques and narratives of Islamisation go hand in hand with the creation of forms of migrant respectability, regulated by a binary opposition between 'good' (working hard, 'integrated', read: white, Christian) migrants and 'bad' (living on welfare, exclusionary ethnicity) migrants (Davies and Harré 1990). These new forms of respectability that regulate the inclusion of subordinated racialised supporters are at the core of the reimagination of the Swedish racist state.

Conclusion

Borrowing the title for this chapter from a text by Ronit Lentin (2006), it has been asked if Sweden is in a state of transition from a racial state to a racist state. Inspired by the literature on racial formation that bridges productively the category of race with societal structures, the need to discuss these topics in the context of Sweden has been argued for. As such, the concepts of exploitative and exclusionary racism was introduced and discussed in the preceding discussion.

Few would disagree that Sweden is in transition, and many would also use the term crisis. However, there is little agreement on *what kind of crisis*, or transition towards *what*? The growth of the Sweden Democrats, a racist ERP, has played an increasingly important role in reimagining Sweden; in a context where migrants' loyalty to the nation is always at stake, and in which gender conservative agendas are introduced and established. This reimagination, as demonstrated above, is located in an exclusionary racism that is powerfully and, at times, violently coded. It is increasingly successfully through the normalisation of the racism that the Sweden Democrats embody in the discourse and policies of the established political parties. It is this normalisation of racism that provides the shift from a racial to a racist state.

Finally, such racist reimagination of the nation is systematically challenged by diverse social movements from sections of the Swedish Church to grass-roots movements of social protest against neoliberalism and racism. In other words: Sweden Democrats' reimagination of the nation is resisted, among other things, through emerging notions of solidarity and inclusion.

In concluding this chapter, noting the distinction between 'reimagination' and 'reimagineering' is crucial. The growth of the Sweden Democrats in electoral strength has created the basis for formulating an exclusionary and anti-democratic racist project. Some of its central tenets have been discussed, highlighting how racism and anti-feminism guide the party's vision for a new Sweden. However, despite pursuing a political project that seemingly produces, or at least facilitates, both racist and sexist symbolic and physical violence, it is contended that societal processes of transformation are still at a level of reimagination. Parallel to the reimagination by the Sweden Democrats, there is a project of political reimagineering that is fusing increasingly exploitative and exclusionary racist ideas into a conglomerate of political concrete reforms. This is partially being done under the radar of racism, and is at most used in connection to the Sweden Democrats. A major issue in the future will be how the balance between the reimagination of the Sweden Democrats and the reimagineering of the government and parliamentary parties which will shape a possible transition of Sweden from a racial to a racist state.

References

Agamben, G. 1998. *Homo Sacer: Sovereign Power and Bare Life*. Stanford, Calif.: Stanford University Press.

Ahmed, S. 2003. 'In the Name of Love.' *Borderlands* 2/3, 1–41.

Akkerman, T. and Hagelund, A. 2007. '"Women and children first!" Anti-immigration parties and gender in Norway and the Netherlands.' *Patterns of Prejudice* 41/2, 197–214.

Åkesson, J. 2009. 'Muslimerna är vårt största utländska hot.' *Aftonbladet*, October 19. Accessed August 5, 2016. <http://www.aftonbladet.se/debatt/debattamnen/politik/article12049791.ab>

Baas, D. and Holmén, C. 2013. 'Flera politiker skriver anonymt på hatsajter.' *Expressen*, December 10. Accessed August 5, 2016. <http://www.expressen.se/nyheter/expressen-avslojar/flera-politiker-skriver-anonymt-pa-hatsajter/>

Berggren, E. and Neergaard, A. 2015. 'Populism – Protest, democratic challenge and right-wing extremism.' In Dahlstedt, Magnus and Anders Neergaard (eds.) *International Migration and Ethnic Relations: Critical Perspectives*. London: Routledge, 169–199.

Bergqvist, C., Olsson Blandy, T. and Sainsbury, D. 2007. 'Swedish State Feminism: Continuity and Change.' In Outshoorn, Joyce and Johanna Kantola (eds.) *Changing state feminism*. Basingstoke: Palgrave Macmillan, 224–245.

Betz, H.-G. 1994. *Radical Right-Wing Populism in Western Europe*. New York: St. Martins Press.

Blee, K. M. 2011. 'Does Gender Matter in the United States Far-Right?' Paper presented at the conference *Reasoning with Cases in the Social Sciences*, Pittsburgh, PA, USA, November 11–12.

Bonilla-Silva, E., and Baiocchi, G. 2001. 'Anything but racism: How sociologists limit the significance of racism.' *Race and Society* 4/2, 117–131.

Borg, T. 2010. 'Problem måste belysas för att kunna lösas.' *Therese Borgs Blogg*, August 30. Accessed August 5, 2016. <https://thereseborg.wordpress.com/2010/08/30/problem-maste-belysas-for-att-kunna-losas-2/>

Broberg, G. 1995. *Statlig rasforskning : en historik över Rasbiologiska institutet*. Lund: MediaTryck.

Broberg, G. and Tydén, M. 2005. 'Eugenics in Sweden: Efficient Care.' In Broberg, Gunnar and Nils Roll-Hansen (eds.) *Eugenics and the Welfare State: Norway, Sweden, Denmark, and Finland*. East Lansing: Michigan State University Press, 77–149.

Bulbeck, C. 1997. *Reorienting Western Feminisms: Women's Diversity in a Postcolonial World*. Cambridge: Cambridge University Press.

Cantwell, O. 2015. 'Värsta terrorattentatet i Sverige sedan 1940.' *Aftonbladet*, October 23. Accessed August 5, 2016. <http://www.aftonbladet.se/nyheter/kolumnister/oisincantwell/article21634251.ab>

Collins, P.H. 1998. 'It's All in the Family: Intersections of Gender, Race and Nation.' *Hypatia* 13/3, 62–82.

Dadgostar, N. and Esbati, A. 2015. 'M ville sänka löner – och lyckades bra.' *Aftonbladet*, October 28. Accessed August 5, 2016. <http://www.aftonbladet.se/debatt/article21654875.ab>

Davies, B. and Harré, R. 1990. 'Positioning: The Discursive Production of Selves.' *Journal of the Theory of Social Behaviour* 20/1, 43–63.

Dussel, E. D. 1995. *The Invention of the Americas: Eclipse of 'the Other' and the Myth of Modernity*. New York: Continuum.

Essed, P. 1996. *Diversity: Gender, Color, and Culture*. Amherst: University of Massachusetts Press.

Fekete, L. 2001. 'The Emergence of Xeno-Racism.' *Race & Class* 43/2, 23–40.

Fennema, M. 1997. 'Some Conceptual Issues and Problems in the Comparison of Anti-Immigrant Parties in Western Europe.' *Party Politics* 3/4, 473–492.

Fossbo, H. 2015. 'SVT anklagas för att bidra till rasistisk upptrappning.' *SVT*, October 26 (Updated October 27). Accessed August 5, 2016. <http://www.svt.se/kultur/medier/en-uppdelning-byggd-pa-en-framlingsfientlig-logik>

Fraser, N. 1998. *Social Justice in the Age of Identity Politics: Redistribution, Recognition, Participation*. Wissenschaftszentrum Berlin für Sozialforschung.

Gardell, M. 2015. *Raskrigaren: seriemördaren Peter Mangs*. Stockholm: Leopard Förlag.

Gidengil, E., Hennigar, M., Blais, A. and Nevitte, N. 2005. 'Explaining The Gender Gap in Support for the New Right: The Case of Canada.' *Comparative Political Studies* 38/10, 1171–1195.

Gilroy, P. 2004. *Postcolonial Melancholy*. Columbia University Press.

Goldberg, D. T. 2002. *The Racial State*. Oxford: Blackwell.

Goldberg, D. T. 2006. 'Racial Europeanization.' *Ethnic and Racial Studies* 29/2, 331–364.

Guest, G., Bunce, A. and Johnson, L. 2006. 'How Many Interviews Are Enough? An Experiment with Data Saturation and Variability.' *Field Methods* 18/1, 59–82.

hooks, b. 1992. *Black looks: race and representation*. Boston, Mass.: South End Press.

Hübinette, T. and Lundström, C. 2014. 'Three phases of hegemonic whiteness: understanding racial temporalities in Sweden.' *Social Identities* 20/6, 423–437.

Ignazi, P. 1992. 'The Silent Counter-Revolution: Hypotheses on the Emergence of Extreme Right-Wing Parties in Europe.' *European Journal of Political Research* 22/1, 3–34.

Kaplan, J. and Weinberg, L. 1999. *The Emergence of a Euro-American Radical Right*. New Brunswick: Rutgers University Press.

Keskinen, S. 2014. 'Re-constructing the peaceful nation: negotiating meanings of whiteness, immigration and Islam after a shopping mall shooting.' *Social Identities* 20/6, 471–485.

Kitschelt, H. and McGann, A. J. 1995. *The Radical Right in Western Europe: A Comparative Analysis*. Ann Arbor: University of Michigan Press.

Larsson, M.J. 2015. 'Åkesson vill bilda regering med M och KD.' *Dagens Nyheter*, November 28. Accessed August 5, 2016. <http://www.dn.se/nyheter/politik/akesson-vill-bilda-regering-med-m-och-kd/>

Larsson, S. and Ekman, M. 2001. *Sverigedemokraterna: Den nationella rörelsen*. Stockholm: Ordfront.

Lentin, A. and Titley, G. 2011. *The Crises of Multiculturalism: Racism in a Neoliberal Age*. London: Zed Books.

Lentin, R. 2006. 'From racial state to racist state? Racism and immigration in 21st century Ireland.' In Lentin, Alana and Ronit Lentin (eds.) *Race and State* (1st unabridged edition). Newcastle: Cambridge Scholars Publishing, 255–273.

Ljungberg, A. and Hashemi, Z. 2013. 'Allt fler män med utländsk bakgrund stöder SD.' *Sveriges Radio,* December 12. Accessed August 5, 2016. <http://sverigesradio.se/sida/gruppsida.aspx?programid=3993&grupp=20769&artikel=5730771>

Lundmark, L. 2002. 'Vetenskap i rasimens tjänst: så fick skallmätning av samer vetenskaplig legitimitet.' *Tvärsnitt* 2, 4–15.

Mair, P. and Mudde, C. 1998. 'The Party Family and its Study.' *Annual Review of Political Science* 1, 211–229.

Mattsson, P. 2009. *Sverigedemokraterna in på bara skinnet*. Stockholm: Natur & Kultur.

Miles, R. 1993. *Racism after 'race relations'*. London: Routledge.

Minkenberg, M. 1997. 'The New Right in France and Germany: Nouvelle Droite, Neue Rechte, and the New Right radical parties.' In Merkl, Peter H. and Leonard Weinberg (eds.) *The Revival of Right-Wing Extremism in the Nineties*. Frank Cass & Co. Ltd.

Mudde, C. 2007. *Populist Radical Right Parties in Europe*. Cambridge: Cambridge University Press.

Mudde, C. 2010. 'The populist radical right: A pathological normalcy.' *West European Politics* 33/6, 1167–1186.

Mulinari, D. and Neergaard, A. 2004. *Den nya svenska arbetarklassen: rasifierade arbetares kamp inom facket*. Umeå: Boréa.

Mulinari, D. and Neergaard, A. 2012. 'The Sweden Democrats, racisms and the construction of the Muslim threat.' In Morgan, George and Scott Poynting (eds.) *Global Islamophobia: Muslims and Moral Panic in the West*. London: Ashgate, 67–83.

Mulinari, D. and Neergaard, A. 2014. 'We are Sweden Democrats because we care for others: Exploring racisms in the Swedish extreme right.' *European Journal of Women's Studies* 21/1, 43–56.

Mulinari, D. and Neergaard, A. 2015. 'Racist dreams and municipal budgets: Women representing a culturally racist party in local politics.' *Social Identities* 21/5, 506–523.

Nilsson, M. 2015a. 'SD-politiker: Kan ingen ställa sig på bron med en kulspruta.' *Kvällsposten*, September 9. Accessed August 5, 2016. <http://www.expressen.se/kvallsposten/sd-politiker-kan-ingen-stalla-sig-pa-bron-med-en-kulspruta/>

Nilsson, M. 2015b. 'Kritiserad Löfven håller tal om kris.' *Expressen*, September 5. Accessed August 5, 2016. < http://www.expressen.se/nyheter/kritiserad-lofven-haller-tal-om-kris/>

Norocel, O. C. 2013. '"Give Us Back Sweden!" A Feminist Reading of the (Re)Interpretations of the Folkhem Conceptual Metaphor in Swedish Radical Right Populist Discourse.' *NORA. Nordic Journal of Feminist and Gender Studies* 21/1, 4–20.

OECD. n.d. 'Migration Insights.' *OECD*. Accessed August 5, 2016. <http://www.oecd.org/migration-insights/>

Olsson, E. 2015. 'Hård retorik kan trigga våld, anser polis och forskare. Vad SD anser får vi inte veta.' *KIT*, October 26. Accessed August 5, 2016. <https://kit.se/2015/10/26/17799/hard-retorik-kan-trigga-vald-anser-polis-och-forskare-vad-sd-anser-far-vi-inte-veta/>

Omi, M. and Winant, H. 2014. *Racial Formation in the United States*. New York: Routledge.

Öhman M.-B. 2016. 'Embodied Vulnerability in Large-Scale Technical Systems: Vulnerable Dam Bodies, Water Bodies, and Human Bodies.' In Folkmarson Käll, Lisa (ed) *Bodies, Boundaries and Vulnerabilities*. Switzerland: Springer International Publishing, 47–79.

Perry, B. 2001. *In the Name of Hate: Understanding Hate Crimes*. London: Routledge.

Polanyi, K. 2001. *The Great Transformation: the Political and Economic Origins of Our Time*. Boston, MA: Beacon Press.

Poohl, D. 2010. 'Malmös nya ansikte.' *EXPO*, July 23. Accessed August 5, 2016. <http://expo.se/2010/malmos-nya-ansikte_3189.html>

Puar, J. 2007. *Terrorist Assemblages: Homonationalism in Queer Times*. Duke University Press.

Regeringen 2015. *Insatser med anledning av flyktingkrisen*. Stockholm: Regeringskansliet.

Rosaldo, R. 1993. *Culture and Truth. The Remaking of Social Analysis*. London: Routledge.

Ross, R. J. (ed.) 2012. *Racism and Colonialism: Essays on Ideology and Social Structure*. Leiden: Springer Science & Business Media.

Said, E. W. 1978. *Orientalism*. London: Routledge & Kegan Paul.

SCB (Statistics Sweden) 2016a. *Allmänna val, nominerade och valda. 2002–2014.* <http://www.scb.se/sv_/Hitta-statistik/Statistik-efter-amne/Demokrati/Allmanna-val/Allmanna-val-nominerade-och-valda/#documentation> SCB: Örebro.

SCB (Statistics Sweden) 2016b. *Partisympati efter kön och utrikes/inrikes född (urvalsundersökning). 2 ggr/år 2006M05–2016M05.* SCB: Örebro.

Sverigedemokraterna 2004. *Idédokument – Demokratisk utveckling*. Antaget vid extra Riksårsmötet den 27 november 2004. Accessed Feb 13, 2009 on <http://sverigedemokraterna.se>

Sveriges Radio 2014. 'Roma camp sites attacked in Sweden.' *Sveriges Radio,* July 19. Accessed August 5, 2016. <http://sverigesradio.se/sida/artikel.aspx?programid=2054&artikel=5917888>

Tamas, G. 2002. *Lasermannen : en berättelse om Sverige*. Stockholm: Ordfront.

teleSUR 2015. 'Honoring Indigenous Resistance Day, Exposing Colonial Crimes.' *teleSUR*, October 11. Accessed August 5, 2016. <http://www.telesurtv.net/english/telesuragenda/Indigenous-Resistance-Day-20151011-0016.html>

Towns, A., Karlsson, E. and Eyre, J. 2014. 'The equality conundrum: Gender and nation in the ideology of the Sweden Democrats.' *Party Politics* 20/2, 237–247.

Vergara, D. 2012. 'SD vill debattera hedersvåld – saknar åtgärder.' *EXPO*, March 7. Accessed August 5, 2016. <http://expo.se/2012/visionslost-nar-sd-kvinnor-vill-lyfta-debatt_4829.html>

West, C. 1999. *The Cornel West Reader*. New York: Basic Books.

Widfeldt, A. 2014. *Extreme Right Parties in Scandinavia* (1 edition). London; New York, NY: Routledge.

Yuval-Davis, N. 2011. *The Politics of Belonging: Intersectional Contestations*. SAGE.

Paula Mulinari

11. Workplaces on the Move: Professional Mobilisation against the Extreme Right

Abstract: The chapter explores organised resistance by employed in the Emergency Room in Malmö, Sweden. It was provoked by a planned visit of the leader of the Sweden Democrats, a right-wing xenophobic party. The case is explored along three interlacing themes: the politicisation of public care, the subversive potential of following codes of the profession and the meaning of racism. Based on professional core values workers created a new political space that made it possible to mobilize against the extreme-right.

Introduction

In the spring of 2014, Jimmie Åkesson, leader of the Sweden Democrats (SD), went on a national tour to visit workplaces. On April 9, he and his team planned to visit three workplaces in Sweden's third-largest city, Malmö: the Emergency Room (ER) at a local hospital, a fire station and a police station. At both the fire station and the ER, workers mobilised to stop the visits.

This article explores the events that occurred at the ER, as told by some of the workers who initiated and organised the resistance against Åkesson's visit. It aims to highlight how resistance was explained, carried out and affected the relations between workers.

Interviews and dialogues with the informants form the empirical focus of the text.[1] This approach aims to highlight the centrality of 'our story', as one informant put it, which frames, as its point of departure how the events are explored and analytically organised through three topics: the politicisation of public care, the subversive potential of following the rules and, finally what is defined as the meaning of racism and who can embodied it.

I argue the workers have created a new political space through their actions, making it possible to mobilise against the extreme-right through mobilising arguments

1 The findings discussed in this article are based on a larger study on forms of workplace resistance. The empirical material is based on ten interviews with health-care professionals who, in different forms, participated in the events in Malmö. The informants include 5 nurses, 3 doctors and 2 assistant nurses, covering different positions within the workplace.

of professionalism and care. The article shows that the actions against the Sweden Democrats were not organised around arguments against racism but around arguments that conceptualised racism as the antithesis of their professional training; further, it explores how workers were able to challenge the silence that normalises racism in the workplace by using documents on core values, referring to the work ethics of welfare professionals. Finally, it analyses how a resistance within the resistance was shaped that challenged the boundaries and meaning of racism. Theoretically, the article uses the concept of moral and affective economies in order to locate patterns of negotiation and struggles over what is just, fair and right and to elucidate how these struggle interconnect the ethical with the political and the emotional.

Background

In 2014, with two upcoming elections in Sweden (European Parliament elections in May and national elections in September), there was extensive activity by political parties, visiting schools and workplaces, organising debates and holding public rallies. The ER in Malmö was the first public health-care workplace that Åkesson would visit in the city of Malmö.

> It was during a morning meeting that our supervisor informed us that Jimmie Åkesson would visit our ER. She sounded a little like she was apologising but still emphasising that Åkesson visit was something that was going to happen. No questions about it. I was not the only one who felt really uncomfortable with the whole thing. We did not want to be used for his political purpose, so we began to talk to each other. We felt that something needed to be done (Maria, emergency-room nurse)

As Maria recounts, the workers in the ER learned about Åkesson's visit at a regular morning meeting six weeks before his visit. According to Maria, the weeks that followed the morning meeting would change the atmosphere of the ER. The coffee-break conversations, which usually were concerned with issues such as last night's TV drama, holiday plans and working conditions were transformed into an arena for exploring the meaning of antiracism.

What began as a small group of colleagues who wrote a letter stating that they did not want Åkesson to visit their ER would develop, through the active engagement of some workers in the ER, into a massive workplace manifestation. Six weeks after the morning meeting, 750 employees had signed the letter, and support on social media was enormous for both the ER workers and the fire fighters who also took a stand against Åkesson's visit.

It could be argued that the employees' resistance strategies, which are the focus of this article, are not particularly original or innovative. To use sociologist Charles Tilly's (2006) concept, the use of petitions, opinion articles, badges and Facebook activities belong to a common repertoire in the Swedish political landscape. When the actions analysed in this article took place, the SD was the third-largest party in Sweden. The party has always met with public protests when holding public meetings, and when it entered the National Parliament in 2010, several newspapers took a public stand against the party (Lundström and Hübinette 2011). Hence, there was nothing new in protesting against the SD; however, what was innovative were the location of and argument used in the mobilisation. What makes this act of resistance different from others is the intersection of *location* (workplace), *topic* (antiracism) and *arguments* (professional values). This intersection created (if only for a short span) a new political space, with workplaces entering into public debates and challenging a right-wing and xenophobic, but democratically legitimated, leader's right to enter workplaces using their professional identity as an argument. As workplaces in Sweden had never been mobilised against right-wing, xenophobic parties or organisations, this action was path-breaking.

Antiracist Mobilisation of the Workplace

Movements against racism are growing and encompass a variety of expression. In their analyses of European antiracism, Stefano Fella and Carlo Ruzza (2013) argue that social movements that identify themselves as antiracist differ in terms of what they define as racism and antiracism as well as in terms of their political agenda and forms of activism (Fella and Ruzza 2013). However, as stressed by a number of researchers, one central aspect of otherwise diverse antiracist movements is the idea of antiracism as a question of human dignity (Jämte 2013). Workplace mobilisation is seldom included in these topographies of antiracist mobilisation; the social movements explored often find themselves outside of the workplace. One the other hand, in the field of labour studies, antiracist resistance is often understood as a conflict between management and the labour force, hence, often marginalising antiracist mobilisation.

The action that occurred in Malmö challenges this divide. While this action was workplace-centred, its major aim was to make a public stand from the workplace position, In this article, I will approach the health care workers action against racism through the concept of moral economy as it illuminates how professional values and norms – conceptualising racism as the antithesis of professional training – were central to the protest actions at the ER in Malmö.

According to Knut Laaser and Sharon Bolton, the concept of moral economy is underutilised in the study of work (2013: 510). The authors argue that the concept provides 'endless analytical opportunities through which the contemporary lived experience of work can be analytically examined' (2013: 509). Central to the concept is the assumption that economies are socially, historically and politically embedded systems that are regulated by norms that may be compromised, overridden or reinforced by economic pressures (Sayer 2004: 2). The concept has been used in a range of research fields: in analyses of resistance and its absence (Thompson 1971; Scott 1977, 2008), in studies of science and epistemic values (Daston 1995) as well as in analyses of the phases of capitalism (Burawoy 2013). Historian E. P. Thompson and sociologist James C. Scott made a significant contribution to the understanding of moral economy and resistance. Through the concept of moral economy, they examined why organised collective resistance occurs at specific times and why it is absent at others (even though exploitation and oppression are permanent). E. P. Thompson's now legendary analyses of the British Crowd argued that 'riots' were a consequence of market transformations that challenged common ideas about obligations and the economic function of different groups and rights. According to Thompson, these common ideas constituted the moral economy of the poor. Collective resistance movements were not rebellions of the belly (1971: 77), but were organised to defend the moral economy that was being destroyed by the liberation of the market. In his words, 'An outrage to these moral assumptions, quite as much as actual deprivation, was the usual occasion for direct action' (1971: 79). Scott presents a similar argument in his analyses of acts of rebellion by peasants in Southeast Asia. He explores what he defines as the moral economy of the peasants and the consequences when this moral economy is confronted and transformed. Scott defines moral economy as follows:

> Their notion of economic justice and their working definition of exploitation— their view of which claims on their product were tolerable and which intolerable. (Scott 1977:3)

Scott's notion of everyday resistance and its hidden aspects, along with postmodernism and feminism research on resistance, has broadened the concept by making visible the more informal, invisible and individual forms of resistance in workplaces (Prasad and Prasad 2000, 1998). Thompson and Scott share an interest in exploring resistance as socially embedded acts influenced by the moral economy of their time and not as a 'natural' act against oppression. These writers' contributions to the analysis of resistance have expanded the notion of what resistance can be and how it can be articulated.

I agree with Laaser and Bolton that the concept of moral economy can be used to study working life, in general, and workplace resistance, in particular, as it aids exploration of the hegemonic discourses concerning what is defined as entitlement, unequal, fair and rights in workplaces and the processes that can change and challenge these notions.

Another author who has used the concept of moral economy more recently is the sociologist Andrew Sayer. According to Sayer, one is not able to see the norms and values that surround institutions – concerning, for instance, rights, responsibilities and appropriate forms of behaviour – as they become invisible when they are socially established. It is only when they are contested that we are able to identify and grasp the norms and values which have constituted them (2011: 249). Taking this as a point of departure, and inspired by Laaser's and Bolton's argument regarding the centrality of the concept for the field of labour, I use it to highlight the negotiations of the meanings of being professional.

One shortcoming of the concept is its lack of theorisation regarding the role that particular (gendered) bodies play in economic interactions. Even if authors such as Sayer examine organisation and gender in the moral economy (2011: 13–14), the concept tends to understand gender in terms of effects rather than as a social process that shape the economy itself (Acker 2006). Therefore, in this article, I draw theoretically also on feminist analyses of the gendering of professions and resistance (Briskin 2013).

The Moral Economy of Public Care Work

I start by presenting the issues of antiracist mobilisation and moral economy among professional staff at the ER where the mobilization begun. Some of the workers had themselves experienced racism and played a central role in naming the tension between the articulation of the fight against racism to the outside and the silencing of racism to the inside.[2] This can be illustrated through Anel's experience, who felt that the supervisor knew that the SD visit could create problems but did not want to talk about it.

> They said it quickly, at the end of the meeting (staff meeting), as if it was something not particularly relevant or important, like 'by the way', they informed us. It was not something they wanted to discuss. It was information. We were informed. I think that their silence, to some extent, also provoked me, us. At least, they could admit that it was a problem, that it could be offensive to many of us: a racist party in our workplace. The visit was a fact. If you were against, it was like you were a drama queen or an angry teenager.

According to Anel, the manager's strategy of silencing the visit of a racist party leader was one of the reasons that inspired the creation of a shared point of departure for resistance. Note that Anel underlines the manager's strategy of what she

2 The article is based on 12 interviews. In order to reduce the possibility of identification neither age, profession nor gender is presented. All workers that have been interviewed have been given Swedish gender-neutral names.

calls 'informing' instead of opening a dialogue; moreover, note that Anel considered the supervisors' silence as a provocation, particularly what hir experiences as a marginalisation of *hirs* own feelings ('an angry teenager'). Listening carefully to Anel, it seems as if the managers broke the moral economy through which relations between managers and employees was regulated in the ER. It is the tension between the ideology of collaboration central to democratic aspects of staff meetings in Sweden and the practice of authority that opens the way for the conflict.

Charlie begins his narrative by asking, 'The question was what we could do?' The first suggestion, as Charlie recalls, was that they call in the sick.

> Many felt bad, really bad, and there were discussions about taking sick leave that day. But then we felt that it is their ideas that are sick, not us. We felt that we needed to do something here because it was here that we did not want the racists to be. It was our ER, and they should not use it for their hate propaganda.

Charlie and hir colleges moved from an act of individual des-identification towards an act of collective resistance. They moved from a defensive strategy aimed at protecting those who felt bad towards a collective strategy of making these feelings a public issue. The decision turned the workplace into a site where the struggle over the meaning of what it means to 'care' would become central.

Anel and Charlie knew each another from before they worked at the ER. They had not only worked together but also been active in the mobilisation against funding cuts to public health. Charlie says they had a 'political confidence in one another'. They began to write a letter with another colleague that would be posted in different spaces within the workplace.

> We wanted to gather as many colleagues as possible, so we narrowed down the argument to the question of our profession. And we argued that the values of the SD are inconsistent with the idea of providing equal care. Actually, both the laws and rules that regulate our job state that even people without legal permits, people that are hidden, clandestine, have the right to emergency care. Actually, as we argued in the letter, it should not be a big thing for the managers to say 'no' to the visit. Just follow the rules, as they often say [laughs].

The ER workers organised the resistance against the Sweden Democrats not through arguments against racism but through arguments that conceptualised racism as the antithesis of their professional training. While many began to collect signatures, a doctor in another city in northern Sweden, Umeå, tried to block Åkesson's entrance to his ward, arguing that Åkesson's visit would create a disturbance among co-workers and patients and thereby jeopardise the patients' safety (Turborn 2014). When Åkesson visited a fire station in Södertörns, near Sweden's capital, Stockholm, workers hung a banner with the words 'Fight racism'. Indeed, work-place mobilisations were occurring at other places.

The argument that the values of the SD were not consistent with the work ethics of welfare professionals was also raised by fire fighters in Malmö in an open letter published in Sweden's largest morning newspaper, three days after the health-care professional published theirs.

> All people's equal and inviolable value is an important foundation for our profession in the emergency services – a basis that is incompatible with racist policies (Dagens Nyheter 2014).

Similarly, Remy stressed the security aspect of the visit to a doctor in Umeå:

> To let Åkesson in would jeopardise patient security. It is essential that the patient in the ER feels secure. The ER needs to be a safe place. To let Åkesson stroll along the corridors would endanger this. Personally, I think it was a really irresponsible and unprofessional decision to allow his visit.

This comment highlights both the connection between professional ethics and antiracism and the ways in which it can be conceptualised and used in professional practice.

Linda Briskin (2013) places nurses' activism in Canada in the context of the neoliberal restructuring of public health care, as well as in the context of gendered care work (see Chapter Four in this volume for a discussion on the Swedish case). She uses the concept of the 'politicising of caring' to understand nurses' and health professionals' mobilisations. The politicising of caring 'emphasizes patient care, and calls for the re-valuing of both the expertise and caring involved in nurses' work' (Briskin 2013: 106).

Briskin argues that the politicising of caring resulted in widespread public support for nurses' strikes and offers a paradigm which supports the expansion, rather than the narrowing, of the collective bargaining agenda at the same time that public support for other forms of collective-based workplace actions is diminishing. In Sweden, both Rebecca Selberg (2012) and Magnus Granberg (2014) have studied nurses' resistance and have shown how this gendered politicisation of care is central to workplace mobilisation.

In my study, the politicising of care is central to the mobilisation against the presence of a racist party in the public workplace. Resistance was legitimated through references to the need for caring and through arguments that the SD and its leader, as well as racism inhibiting SD politics, is threatening care work in different ways. The politics of caring appears in my data from the perspective of professional knowledge and skill as many informants used it in their statements – for example, 'It is our obligation' and 'We are forced' – to take a stand against the SD. The actions were grounded in a moral argument of the inherit contradiction between Åkesson's politics and the professions values, which made the claim for action and resistance legitimate.

This repertoire was not new. Health-care professionals have been active in social movements against financial cuts that they have argued carry risk for the lives of patients. They have also been active in expanding the institutional framework by, for instance, giving care to patients without legal papers before it was mandatory. What was special about this form of resistance was that the politicisation of care was used to take a stand not for workers' interests or rights but for a public issue: a stand against racism.

However, the politics of caring went beyond the patients themselves to include the city of Malmö as a whole. A central argument in the letters of both the fire fighters and the health care professionals was that it was their job to protect members of the 178 nationalities in the city and that for doing so, and in order to do a good job, it was essential to treat all people equally.

In Briskin's (2013) analysis, in which the gendered dimensions of the politicisation of care are central, health care is coded as women's work. In the events described in this study, perhaps because of the presence of the fire fighters and of men and women among the ER activists, the gendered dimension was regulated by encompassing all forms of femininity and masculinity that performed care in public work, with a focus on protection and service rather than caring.

The workplace actions were not related to an unequal distribution of economic resources or exploitation, they were motivated by the workers' idea of what is just and fair care to give and by their experience of their professional identity being questioned by managers. In this way, the action questions ability of managers to determine what it means to provide 'care' and 'safety'. The culturally accepted idea that care workers can mobilise due to their concern for the public was re-interpreted to allow mobilisation to take a stand against racism – which the workers, connecting to the ethics of welfare work stressed – as the 'natural' thing to do from where they stand. And it is in positioning themselves as just professionals that the locus of moral economy within workplace resistance illuminates connections between antiracist struggles within the workplace and beyond. In the next section this is discussed in relation to the workers use of different forms of organisational documents.

The Subversive Potential of Following the Rules

Resistance was also organised by reframing managerial speech documents and rules arguing that not only was the action morally right as a defence of their profession but also was sanctioned by the documents and rules that guide their work. One participant, Mio, argues the following:

> He wants to divide people, to say that some are better than others, but to us, all people are equal, and all people have the right to the same care. That's fundamental in our profession. You do not need to be extremely courageous to say 'no' to their visit. Managers can depart from our professional code.

The letter that was placed in the ER coffee rooms, and which soon circulated among all hospital employees through mails and social media, begins with a reference to the core health-care document that states that care should be given with respect. The letter takes as a point of departure the motto '*allas lika värde*' ('the equal value of all people') and continues by quoting the hospital's equal treatment policy, which states, 'all co-workers have the obligation and responsibility of working against discrimination in their everyday jobs'.

At an early stage, the organisers decided to make badges stating, 'Care workers against racism'. Jona explains the idea:

> We had the idea of the badges early. We thought that people could put them on as a form of silent protest so at least, he [Åkesson] would know that we took a stand against racism.

The badge has the same shape as the badge first used by the French organisation SOS-racism (Benhabib 2002) in the early 1980s that read, 'Do not touch my friend'. The symbol is widely known in Sweden as one of the first antiracist symbols responding to the neo-Nazi violence of the 1990s. The new badge follows a similar design and states, '#health professionals against racism'.

Photo: Paula Mulinari

However, the badges were not allowed in the ER, as Tiger explains:

> They [the managers] literally ran down from their rooms and told people to take it off, one by one. I think they were really scared. It was like in a Hollywood movie. You had the badge on, and then they appeared from nowhere. And it was the higher supervisors, and they had that crazy look. I think they were afraid of what the managers would say, that they would be punished for it. I liked the badge. It felt right to have it on. And I like looking at others who had it. It created a sort of silent understanding.

The supervisors experienced the silent protest that Tiger describes as a serious threat to the social order of the ER. Tiger and Jona felt that their supervisors were more afraid of what their own managers would do than they were angry at the statement itself. I read this form of resistance as an illustration of the originality of the actions – because it succeeded in disabling the order in the ER and creating a zone of discomfort – as there were no regulations concerning the wearing of badges in the workplace.

The managers first attempted to identify the badges as political. If the resistance was conceptualised as irrational before, now it was named as political. Tiger puts it as follows:

> It [the badge] only said that we are professionals against racism. We defend our values that all people should be treated equally, and they said that it was political. But they are the ones that made it a political issue. They should be proud and support that we fought for our values that should be theirs.

Hospital managers asserted that workers' uniforms had to be free from political 'manifestations of any kind' and added that the workplace should free from political statements. The hospital chief also identified the badge as something to which patients holding racist views could take offence:

> Even the ones with racist opinions need to feel that she or he will get the same care as all other people (Åberg 2014; My translation).

This statement made many of the people I interviewed angry because they understood the statement as expressing a lack of confidence in their ability to provide equal care to all patients. For example, Anel argued the following:

> The badge said 'against racism', not against patients who hold racist views. The badge took a stand against racism that wants to put people against people here in the city. And the strange thing is that, in all the documents, it states that we need to work against all forms of discrimination and for equal treatment, so for me, the badge was a sign of doing what the documents regulating our work, what the employers, wanted me to do [laughs]. But I guess they never thought that we took their documents seriously. Maybe because they themselves seldom do it.

The badge with the phase '#healthcare professional against racism' was prohibited in the ER and other wards where people were wearing it. At this point, Tiger had an idea.

> When we were writing the letter, I remember that one of the core values of the hospital was respect for humans, so I thought, 'Let's do a new badge', and so we did.

Photo: Paula Mulinari

The new badge states, 'respect for humans' and has the hospital logo, as Kalle explains:

> At first, they came down and said we could not wear that badge either. But then we calmly explained that the phrase was taken from one of the documents that identify the core values of the hospital. Then they could not say much. The words on the badge were the words they had written.

At that point, the managers did not argue that the badges were political but that they were unhygienic, instead. Jan Eriksson, chief of the University Hospital of Skåne (SUS) argued that the rules were clear when it comes to 'manifestation of different kinds'. To the TV station SVT, he stated the following:

> The uniform is designed to wear when giving care, and it should be free from manifestations of any kind. In part it is also about infection control and that you should not wear anything that may accumulate microbes and other things that can spread infection. But it is also that we do not want to end up in the discussion concerning that or that message, neither in a discussion about how many buttons you can have (Åberg 2014).

According to Ahmed, institutions themselves engage in 'speech acts' that make claims 'about' or 'on behalf' of an institution' (2006). A central part of these speech acts is the documents about gender equality, diversity and anti-discrimination laws that regulate public-welfare organisations. Sara Ahmed argues that these texts (documents) are never 'finished' as forms of action as what they 'do' depends on how they are 'taken up' (2006: 105). During the conflict, workers put these documents on their working bodies, giving them a new place and meaning. Following the rules and putting the public transcript in a new context forced managers to make visible the limits that the public transcript had, beyond the formal terms in the document.

The End or a New Beginning

The public letter written by the health-care workers was published on April 4, 2014 in *Sydsvenskan*, the largest newspaper in the South of Sweden (#vårdpersonalmotrasism 2014). More than 750 hospital workers wanted to sign the letter, but only ten were allowed to do so by the newspaper. On April 7, the fire fighters' letter was published in *Dagens Nyheter* (DN 2014). Both events were covered in all national newspapers and television channels and were prevalent on social media, with the hashtags #firemen against racism and #care workers against racism.

Only two days after the publication of the letter, four of the workers who had signed it received death threats. Three had migrant backgrounds, and the fourth was a nurse who the newspaper had classified as belonging to the Left. The health-care workers' Facebook group was closed due to security reasons.

Until then, the leadership of unions that collectively organise more than 2 million workers (the Swedish Municipal Workers' Union, the Swedish Association of Health Professionals and the Swedish Medical Association) had been rather silent, but at this point, they took a stand supporting the action. The event was historic in the Swedish context. Even though the unions had criticised the SD's values, it was the first time that three unions together had stressed that they not only understood but also supported the protest.

> It is natural that, for instance, midwives, doctors, nurses and nursing assistants protest when a party that does not believe that all humans are equal wants to visit their workplace. As the basis of the care system rests on the health, and the care system's ethical platform emphasises all humans' dignity (Nordström, Ribeiro and Flodin 2014; Author's translation).

The union letter also acknowledges the existence of racism in Swedish workplaces.

> Racism is a structural problem in Sweden, and it occurs at all levels and in all sectors of society. Workplaces are no exception to this. It is our job as trade unions to counteract the forces trying to tear apart our society (Nordström, Ribeiro and Flodin 2014).

When Åkesson finally arrived in Malmö on Wednesday, April 9, the unions had taken an extraordinary stand legitimising workplace mobilisation against right-wing, xenophobic parties. According to many of my informants, Åkesson never talked to the workers in the ER but walked through the hall and left through the backdoor. Some of the fire fighters had decided to spend their workday outside the workplace, so Åkesson visited an empty workplace. The police officers never took a public stand against his visit.

The actions created a new space in the political landscape. It was now possible, even morally and professionally right, to act against the presence of a racist party in the workplace. By combining the rules of the game, the centrality of professional care and positioning racism outside the workplace, the health-care workers were able to challenge the silence that normalises racism in the workplace. However, the focus on professional and institutional core values had shortcomings, primarily the neglect of racism in the workplace. Additionally, the campaign created a binary opposition between good, antiracist workplaces and bad, racist SD which obscured the experience of discrimination within the workplace.

Racism in the Margin

While the focus of the resistance was the visit of the SD, the agenda of employees, particularly those who had experienced racism in their everyday lives, expanded the meaning of the action and raised the question of racism in the workplace. This is especially relevant when exploring what it meant to take a stand against racism. The problem of not talking about racism (while resisting the visit of a racist party) was present throughout the event. Alex, who also was involved in the beginning of the actions, speaks about this topic:

> In the beginning, we wanted to highlight racism within our own organisation, and that there; of course, it is also so that we treat people differently, for instance, depending on their skin colour. However, we wanted to write a letter that as many as possible could feel comfortable with, so the focus was placed on the idea of being a health care worker.

It became clear during the conversations that a central issue was the tension between naming racism (outside) and making it invisible (inside the workplace), a tension created by the idea that the workplace was free from racism. Paradoxically, the resistance against racism became an illegitimate topic of discussion. Mio illuminates this aspect, illustrating, further on, how racism becomes a political issue and hence a non-professional issue. Further on hir marks the importance on migrant background (as dividing line) in this connection.

> You are not allowed to be political in our profession, but it annoys me that racism has been so normalised to the point where being antiracist is defined as a political stance. We have come to the point where not taking stand against racism is seen as being neutral. For us who experience racism, that is a privileged position we cannot take. But, of course, it silences us. I think it was easier for the Swedes to wear it in some sense because they are not identified as talking for themselves; it is nicer in some way, more noble.

The badge was a disturbance as it took a stand and gave the words written in a policy a place and time, demands for action here and now. Mio raises other questions: Who may embody and represent the professional/caring subject? Who may embody the non-political professional 'caring for all'? Hir seems to fear that hir (as an employee with a migrant background) will be experienced as more aggressive, or as somebody with personal interests.

However, it was not only the managers who were against the badges. Some colleagues defined it as too political, as Charlie describes:

> What I experienced as the worst thing when I had the badge on me was all the other colleagues who sighed or said, 'Ahh, do you really have to do politics in everything?' Most of our people supported the action, perhaps over 90%, but still there were people that—it is as if they do not understand that to not take action is also a position.

According to Anel, the badge that states, 'Professional health-care workers against racism' was important in a different way.

> It would not only show the patients where you stand but also your colleagues that you will not take their crap. That would be nice, instead of being angry all the time, as I am now. I do not like to argue. I do not like to confront people, and I do not think it is funny. It is difficult and hard, and I feel weak, and it makes me feel vulnerable. I know that the pin would not change racism, but perhaps, it would make some things easier. It would show that you're against racism and place the problem on those who are, rather than on me. Do you know what the funny thing or, really, the sad thing is? That the pin was seen as a problem but not the racism we suffer.

For Tatum, who works in another section but who brought several badges to hir wards so people could wear them the visibility of the badge created a feeling, for a short time, that hur was not fighting racism alone.

> It felt that we were more than two. Actually, when things got rough I saw that we where more than I had guessed. For me that is important in my daily work, to know that, to know that I am not alone.

In analysing the enormous protests against the entrance of the SD into Parliament in 2010, Catrin Lundström and Tobias Hübinette (2011) argue that, despite the massive resistance, the mobilisation was coded with a white nostalgia frame that mourned the loss of old Sweden coded through banal forms of nationalism that located racism outside the nation.

To some extent, the events in the ER in Malmö, created the idea of good workplaces beyond racism. In that sense, the events can be re-read as an illustration of Lundström and Hübinette's arguments. However, the actions also seem to have given those workers who suffer from racism a sense that during a short span of time, racism was a public concern, and not defined as only their problem. While most of them expressed ambivalence and discomfort that the SD was the only organisation defined as racist (and, for instance, not theirs workplace), they also identified with the solidarity they enjoyed from colleges and the support of people outside of the workplace, as Tara states, 'At least, you knew who is ready to support you, and who is not, and from there I can work'. The action made visible both the limits and possibilities of antiracist solidarity within workplaces and among co-workers.

Concluding Remarks

The forms of resistance developed by the health workers and fire fighters in Malmö seem to have inspired other public institutions and civil-society organisations. Even different municipalities took a public stand against racism. The police was not one of them. I did not have the opportunity to interview police workers and discuss their decision not to take a public stand against Åkesson. For further analysis of this or similar future actions, it would be interesting to explore the difference between different professions and how they understand their moral economy.

The ER workers challenged the dominant discourse aiming at normalising the presence of the Sweden Democrats and, thus, the presence of racism. While the action was not a direct resistance against exploitation, it was a struggle for control and autonomy of their workplace. It questioned managers' ability to decide, determine and control employees' work. It was also a struggle that challenged managers and their stance on what was normal, natural and right. A new moral and affective economy was put in place, providing room for a discussion of racism that was previously a suppressed topic. The action neither changed the rules of the game nor transformed unequal workplace relations; however, it did create new forms of solidarity within the workplace that followed the moral economy of the workers – not that of the managers.

The resistance was motivated by the health-care workers' conviction and understanding of what is good care and, particularly, of the obligations implied by caring for others. The resistance was also motivated by their disappointment and anger when what they considered to be core values of their professional identities was put into question by the managers. According to the workers, to take a stand against racism was the 'natural' thing to do, from the standpoint of moral and affective economy that has defined the meaning they, themselves, gave to their work.

The managers reaction to that the action, especially when the workers placed antiracist badges on themselves also grasp the pressure that is placed on workers by managers when they engage in actions that are defined as 'political'. As the material shows, the managers defined antiracism as a political issue and tried to delink issues of tolerance and respect from the political domain. In a context in which the extreme right-wing party the SD is growing, this will become a key challenge for workers.

Although the relationship between political mobilisation and race has gained increased attention, much of this work consists of studies outside the workplace. This lack could be linked to political and theoretical arguments that identify workplaces and paid work as less central to both political mobilisation and personal identity (Weeks 2011). However, the action analysed in this article challenges this assumption. Rather than trying to reinforce the dichotomy between the workplace and public spaces or between labour struggles and struggles for human rights, we need to examine how workplace mobilisations are shaped at the cross-roads. The concept of moral economy can be useful in this analysis as it can grasp the often invisible racial norms embedded in organisations and the obstacles that workers encounter when challenging them, as well as the organisational limits (such as, in this case, the idea of the organisation itself as racist). Further, the concept of moral economy helps us explore the struggles in workplaces that are not always expressed in economical terms or in terms time recourses but instead are entrenched into the idea of what professions are and the role they should play.

I hope that this article will contribute to the expansion and redefinition of the workplace as a space of resistance and interconnect research on workplace antiracism to research on other forms of resistance against racism.

Acknowledgement of Funding

This work was supported by the Swedish research Councils, FORTE [2011-0826].

References

Acker, J. 2006. 'Inequality Regimes: Gender, Class and Race in Organizations.' *Gender and Society* 20/4, 441–464.

Ahmed, S. 2006. 'The Nonperformativity of Antiracism.' *Meridians: feminism, race, transnationalism* 7/1, 104–126.

Åberg, J. 2014. 'Därför får vårdpersonal inte bära knapp mot rasism.' *Svt,* April 9. Accessed August 6, 2016. <http://www.svt.se/nyheter/lokalt/skane/brickan-personalen-inte-far-bara>

Benhabib, S. 2002. *The Claims of Culture: Equality and Diversity in the Global Era.* Princeton, N.J.: Princeton University Press.

Briskin, L. 2013. 'Nurse militancy and strike action.' *Workers of the World: International Journal on Strikes and Social Conflicts* 1/2, 105–135.

Burawoy, M. 2013. 'Ethnographic fallacies: Reflections on labour studies in the era of market fundamentalism.' *Work, Employment & Society* 27/3, 526–536.

Dagens Nyheter 2014. 'Protestbrev mot Jimmie Åkesson från brandmän i Malmö.' *DN.se,* July 4. Accessed August 6, 2016. <http://www.dn.se/valet-2014/protest-brev-mot-jimmie-akesson-fran-brandman-i-malmo/>

Daston, L. 1995. 'The Moral Economy of Science.' *Osiris* 10/1, 2–24.

Fella, S. and Ruzza, C. 2013. *Antiracist Movements in the EU: Between Europeanisation and National Trajectories.* Basingstoke: Palgrave Macmillan.

Granberg, M. 2014. 'Manufacturing dissent: Labor conflict, care work, and the politicization of caring.' *Nordic Journal of Working Life Studies* 4/1, 139–152.

Jämte, J. 2013. *Antirasismens många ansikten.* PhD diss., Department of Political Science, Umeå University.

Laaser, K. and Bolton, S.C. 2013. 'Work, employment and society through the lens of moral economy.' *Work, Employment & Society* 27/3, 508–525.

Lundström, C. and Hübinette, T. 2011. 'Sweden after the Recent Election: The Double-Binding Power of Swedish Whiteness through the Mourning of the Loss of "Old Sweden" and the Passing of "Good Sweden".' *NORA – Nordic Journal of Feminist and Gender Research* 19/1, 42–52.

Mirsch, H. 2014. 'Vårdpersonal får inte bära knapp mot rasism.' *Vård Fokus,* April 9. Accessed August 6, 2016. <https://www.vardfokus.se/Webbnyheter/2014/April/Vardpersonal-far-inte-bara-knapp-mot-rasism>

Mårtensson, F. 2014. 'Läkaren som försökte stoppa Åkesson kritiseras av landstinget.' *Läkartidningen,* March 13. Accessed May 3, 2016. <http://www.lakartidningen.se/Aktuellt/Nyheter/2014/03/Reprimand-vantar-lakaren-som-forsokte-stoppa-Jimmie-Akesson/>

Nordström, A., Ribeiro, S. and Flodin, T. 2014. 'Vi är stolta över att våra medlemmar protesterar.' *Aftonbladet,* April 8. Accessed August 6, 2016. <http://www.aftonbladet.se/debatt/article18685955.ab>

Prasad, P. and Prasad, A. 2000. 'Stretching the Iron Cage: The Constitution and Implications of Routine Workplace Resistance.' *Organization Science* 11/4, 387–403.

Sayer, A. 2004. 'Moral Economy.' Published by the Department of Sociology, Lancaster University, Lancaster. Accessed July 29, 2016. <http://www.comp.lancs.ac.uk/sociology/papers/sayer-moral-economy.pdf>

Sayer, A. 2011. *Why Things Matter to People: Social Science, Values and Ethical Life.* Cambridge: Cambridge University Press.

Scott, J.C. 1977. *The Moral Economy of the Peasant: Rebellion and Subsistence in Southeast Asia.* New Haven: Yale University Press.

Scott, J.C. 2008. *Weapons of the Weak: Everyday Forms of Peasant Resistance.* New Haven: Yale University Press.

Selberg, R. 2012. *Femininity at Work: Gender, Labour, and Changing Relations of Power in a Swedish Hospital.* Lund: Arkiv.

Thompson, E. P. 1971. 'The Moral Economy of the English Crowd in the Eighteenth Century.' *Past and Present* 50, 76–136.

Tilly, C. 2006. *Regimes and Repertoires.* Chicago: University of Chicago Press.

Turborn, E. 2014. 'Läkare stoppade Sverigedemokraterna.' *Västerbottens-Kuriren,* March 13. Accessed August 6, 2016. <http://www.vk.se/1147972/lakare-stoppade-sverigedemokraterna>

Weeks, K. 2011. *The Problem with Work: Feminism, Marxism, Antiwork Politics, and Postwork Imaginaries.* Durham: Duke University Press.

#vårdpersonalmotrasism 2014. '"Jimmie Åkessons värderingar är inte välkomna på vår akutmottagning".' *Sydsvenskan,* April 3. Accessed August 6, 2016. <http://www.sydsvenskan.se/2014-04-03/jimmie-akessons-varderingar-ar-inte-valkomna-pa-var-akutmottagning>

Nedžad Mešić

12. Framing Solidarity in the Unionisation of Undocumented Migrant Workers

Abstract: This chapter explores the capacity of two Swedish trade union initiatives, SAC Syndicalists and LO-TCO centre, to extend solidarity to undocumented migrant workers. The author asks what solidarity linkages have been established since the shift of millennia and what obstacles encountered in forging solidarity between workers with strong versus weak legal status. He illuminates the emergence of a transformative form of solidarity, which may open for protection of new groups of disadvantaged workers.

Introduction

Trade unions have, as their primary purpose, the organisation and defence of employee interests in the labour market in order to secure the best terms and conditions, available through exercising their collective bargaining strength. Traditionally, addressing the balance of power between labour and capital has been based on the calibration of conflicting interests by domestic labour market actors. The 'age of migration' has brought new complexities to this equation marked by the emergence of a new 'worker' category, among which, the undocumented migrant has been increasingly prominent. The status of undocumented migrants in the labour market is problematic and, at first glance, trade unions may have little to offer. Likewise, as collective labour representation agencies, trade unions seemingly have little to gain from the presence of undocumented migrant workers in their ranks. This raises issues for trade unions of the appropriate forms of organisational response, and not least, the reach of solidaristic inclusion of a more complex and diversified workforce. Forging solidarity between workers with strong versus weak legal status, dependent on citizenship, impacts collective bargaining and attempts to fight 'social dumping'. For more than a decade, particularly since European enlargement in 2004, this challenge has embroiled trade unions and social movement actors.

The chapter investigates two Swedish trade union initiatives in providing protection for undocumented migrant workers. It asks what solidarity linkages have been forged, and what lessons can be learned from attempts to mobilise workers whose legal status may be unclear.

In the following sections, a short background on current Swedish unions will be presented, followed by the theoretical and methodological framing of the study.

Subsequently, two cases of union intervention will be discussed, illustrated by interviews with both union representatives and migrant activists. The major argument is that conflicts between the 'self-interest' of the union (members) and protection of the undocumented workers' interests, add further weight to the duality of inclusion (right to association), and exclusion (irregularity of work). These create obstacles for rhetoric realisation in the practice of solidarity, and it is therefore proposed that forging collaborations with support organisations for undocumented migrants can deliver alternative approaches.

The Recent Agenda of an Old Movement

During recent decades, internationally trade unions have been losing members and have seen a weakening of influence (see MacDonald 2014; Balasubramanian 2015; Farber 2015). The Swedish self-regulation model, based on collective bargaining agreements between labour market parties covering ninety percent of employees, has however remained relatively strong in comparison to other countries. Yet, Swedish unions have also been affected by a decline in union density from eighty-five percent in the early 1990s to sixty-nine percent in 2015 (Kjellberg 2013, 2016).

Union decline through membership loss has prompted the search for union revitalisation initiatives. A recurring argument is that extending solidarity through coalition building with other social movements may create pathways to strengthening union influence in the labour market and society at large (Frege and Kelly 2003; see Turner 2005). Revitalisation strategies propose that the labour movement, which traditionally has taken a protectionist stance towards migrants (see Penninx and Roosblad 2000), 'should recognise that migrant workers are an integral part of the working class, and that they have often played a pivotal role in the making of labour movements' (Munck 2015: 105).

In the context of the United States of America (USA), Ruth Milkman (2015) pinpoints the potential of alliances with progressive movements to address the discrepancies between out-dated protective structures and the increasing challenge of a precarious labour market. Milkman illustrates synergies in cooperation between labour unions and community-based workers-centres' movements. Together, they have shared challenges of strengthening low-wage immigrant workers' bargaining capacity. In so doing, this has helped overcome a lingering myth of the 'unorganisability' of undocumented workers. Although mobilising and forging long-term relationships with such workers has proved difficult, not least due to the risk of employer complaints to the authorities resulting in deportation, the number of workers' centres providing direct assistance and advocating for the rights of precarious migrant workers have increased (see Fine 2011; see also Milkman, Bloom and Narro 2010). However, with the deportation of close to four-hundred thousand migrants in 2011, and the continued difficulties in organising workers, Lee H. Adler and Daniel B. Cornfield (2014: 51) contend that unions and immigrant worker advocates, hoping for (still elusive) labour and immigration legislation reforms, might 'need to consider different approaches or strategies in order to succeed'.

In a comparative analysis on the Global North's (The USA, France, Germany and the United Kingdom) union activities to mobilise precarious migrants, Gabriella Alberti, Jane Holgate and Lowell Turner (2014) identify a slow, but increasing, drift from restrictive to inclusive approaches. In relation to the most concealed workers, including those undocumented, they underline that there are great challenges and considerable varieties in methods across countries. Notwithstanding, the authors propose that 'best practice' is found in social movement inspired tactics of grassroots activism and coalition-building. Such may include: industrial approaches targeting employers in subcontracting chains; the recognition of ethic identities, e.g. through separate structures, yet with close links to mainstream union channels; and, the development of coalitions with social justice groups, pursuing community support built on a harmonised division of labour.

In Sweden, there has been a growing research on irregular migrants (Khosravi 2010; Holgersson 2011; Sager 2011; Sigvardsdotter 2012), however few studies have more extensively centred on undocumented migrants and trade unions. In this context, Anders Neergaard (2015a: 232) argues that three parallel solidarity approaches to labour migration can be identified among the unions. Firstly, in the shape of 'subordinated inclusion', a term directing attention to members' perceptions of labour migration as a threat to '"our" situation,' further strengthened through union scepticism regarding the feasibility of organising new worker groups. Secondly, a vertical form of solidarity that invokes human rights through 'idealist rhetoric of support and help'. Thirdly, a stance on workers' community interests as considered threatened by capitalist-antagonists' dividing politics and schemes. In regards to undocumented migrants, these differences are ascribed to the different realms of the labour market, and the economies that the respective unions are active within. Yet, also the differential relationships between capital and labour, as well as particular forms of regulation therein. Neergaard contends that therefore it is understandable that, for example, the Building Maintenance Workers' Union that mobilises in a sector with low degree unionisation[1] and is

1 From 2008 to 2014, union density fell from sixty to fifty percent in the private sector (Kjellberg 2016: 12, 41).

composed of high numbers of precarious workers, has most passionately undertaken the development of an inclusive strategy (Neergaard 2015a).

Although undocumented migrants are prohibited to stay and work in Sweden, they could be entitled to protection through the right of association stipulated in the labour law. The latter guides such unions' practical and strategic agenda. The strategy of unions that have shifted perspective from 'illegal' to 'workers', representing undocumented workers, has also been discussed as a form of 'semi-organising', mainly because such unions have not fully succeeded in employing traditional bargaining power in this sphere. Furthermore, the implementation of the EU Sanctions Directive[2] carries the potential to moderately improve undocumented workers' legal situation through the right to back pay[3]. Notwithstanding, this is only feasible if becoming appropriately recognised by the judicial system and labour market actors (Selberg 2014). In the case of unions, where exclusionary membership practices have applied to effectively organising these workers, it 'obviously has turned out to be a hard nut to crack' (Inghammar 2010: 211). Undocumented migrants are thus, to some extent, protected as workers by the law, yet the conduct of such work is sanctioned, forcing them to admit their 'crimes' in order to secure rights. Through this contradiction, the state adds to workers' subordination from the employers by equating both parties' crimes and shared self-interest in concealing such labour. Compared to the conventional workings of criminal law, this construct is further considered an anomaly, by which the criminalisation of labour is also coincided with the criminalisation human beings. Decriminalising the work carried out by undocumented migrant workers, but not the employers' part in the arrangement, is therefore held as the only feasible measure to suppress employers of means of eroding working conditions, hence securing all workers' positions by dampening the demand for this labour force. This consequently corrects the 'unjust' punishment of people whose lives depend on such work and is seen to be 'of great importance for all workers that the legal sanctions on regulated labour migration are not, under any circumstances, directed to (irregular) migrant workers' (Selberg 2015: 394).

Some Swedish trade unions have begun to develop positioning towards undocumented workers in line with such line of reasoning, notably the Building

---

2 Directive 2009/52/EC of the European Parliament and of The Council of the 18th of June 2009, providing for minimum standards on sanctions and measures against employers of illegally staying third-country nationals. In 2013, implemented into Swedish legislation (Svensk författningssamling [SFS] 2013:644).

3 Undocumented migrants are entitled back payments for the work they have done, equivalent to the wages of a 'legally' employed worker.

Maintenance Workers' Union (BMWU). Other unions have previously adopted directly exclusionary practices, including as in some cases, joint passport inspection raids with the police, aimed at apprehending and removing irregular migrants from their workplaces (see Frank 2012). However, as previously noted, there has been a general shift towards involving the undocumented as fellow workers and building new inclusionary organisational forms. The manner in which this collective action approaches solidarity is the theme of the following section.

Elucidating Solidarity through Frame Analysis

Even if they are prohibited of staying and working in Sweden, undocumented migrant workers have the right of association. These contradicting conditions contribute to ambivalent union responses, as well as from salient undocumented migrant organisations. With this background, a frame analysis in order to elucidate the engagement of undocumented migrant activists and core union organisers in collective action will be employed. The focus is on organisational challenges within unions seeking to articulate constructive and inclusionary responses to undocumented migrants. Discussing the issues of solidarity, the chapter asks how the geography of solidarity is formed and subsequently reformed, as well as how it is conditioned, and what kind of political agency can be identified in trade union strategies.

Solidarity emerges over spatial and ideological boundaries that, following David Featherstone (2012), may go far beyond binary notions of similarity and dissimilarity that prescribe identities as pre-formed, fixed or given. Instead, he argues that solidarity is a transformative process through which alliances are constructed, reconfigured and contested. Solidarity is thus understood as provisional, unpredictable and dynamic, evolving with the reconfiguration of political identities. This highlights the transformative potential of political solidarity, i.e. the openness of political identities to negotiation in relation to political alternatives made through political struggles. Political agency is thus seen as a creative practice within particular geographies of solidarity.

The breadth of solidarity in the organisation of labour, as Ingemar Lindberg (2013) claims, is best understood as a chain-linked construct of mutual self-interest, perceived fellowship and communal conduct. Tracking the occurrence of this tri-linked chain construct, and aligning it with a transformative approach to solidarity, will be the points of departure for solidarity scrutiny. As such, how it is formed and reformed, and what forms of political agency can be identified, and related, to solidarity in trade union strategies will be addressed.

Frame analysis literature is useful in examining different unionisation initiatives that attempt to articulate a collective agenda of inclusion towards the undocumented (see Gahan and Pekarek 2013). David Snow et al. (1986: 464) hold that successful mobilisation depends on *frame alignment* – that is, 'the linkage of individual and SMO (social movement organisation) interpretive orientations, such that some set of individual interests, values, and beliefs and SMO activities, goals, and ideology are congruent and complementary'[4]. By focusing trade unions' public communications and the accounts of core activists and union representatives, the correspondence and divergence between prevailing frames can be examined. This enables an analysis of consensus framing vis-à-vis *diagnostic frames*, which identify injustices and attribute blame, and *prognostic frames*, which propose solutions, strategies and tactics in response to the diagnosis (Snow and Benford 1988). It is important to underline that frames are never static and that the 'development, generation, and elaboration of collective action frames are contested processes' (Benford and Snow 2000: 625). Willeam A. Gamson and David S. Meyer (1996: 286–287) further stress that the framing of political opportunities may in itself generate new possibilities:

> It is not merely about seeing the glass half-full rather than half-empty but seeing it as half-full when it is often 90 percent empty. [...] There are numerous examples of past movements that demonstrated the possibilities of change that few had thought possible in advance. If movement activists interpret political space in ways that emphasise opportunity rather than constraint, they may stimulate actions that change opportunity, making their opportunity frame a self-fulfilling prophecy.

Furthermore, by way of theoretical approach, the concept of *frame disputes* will be employed when referring to disagreements over present and projected reality within and between actors (Benford 1993). In part, frames can be conceptualised in terms of their degree of *resonance* – exploring why some frames are more persuasive, salient or effective in mobilisation campaigns than others. In this study, this will be actualised through the concept of *experimental commensurability*, which prescribes that resonance is conditioned by the degree to which frames correspond to the everyday lives of the mobilisation targets. In addition to this, *frame amplification* will be used when referring to processes in which existing values or beliefs become invigorated and clarified, *frame extension* when discussing specific concerns to draw connections to more general interests and values, and

4 In the present study, the term *social movement organisation* comprises trade union confederations, trade unions and their local offices or sections, and organisations of undocumented migrants.

boundary framing when exploring the introduction of attributional demarcations in regards to the diagnosis (Benford and Snow 2000).

Contextualising the Research Field

The global city literature pinpoints nodes of major cities in the global economy that have produced both informalisation of migrant labour and strong forms of contention among their citizens (Sassen 2006; Stahre 2007). The Stockholm area, as research field for the study of organisation forms of undocumented migrants, provides pertinent examples. They are, first, the Undocumented Migrants' Group (UMG), which was a local Stockholm-based group that organised the undocumented within the Syndicalist union from 2004–2010[5]. Second, the Undocumented Migrants Stockholm (UMS) group that was founded by undocumented migrants in conjunction with a partial regularisation in the period 2005–2006. Third, the Trade Union Centre for Undocumented Migrants (TUCUM) that was established in 2008 through collaboration between the major trade union confederations LO and TCO, as well as a number of affiliates and other trade unions, as well as the aforementioned organisation UMS.

The present study is based on the analysis of documents and interviews with union representatives, movement leaders and undocumented migrant activists directly engaged in claiming rights. In the following, they are referred to as *core organisers* or *union representatives,* and *core activists*[6]. For many, their engagements have not been confined within these specific venues, but included relations with actors in neighbouring interest areas, such as: agencies founded on ethnic grounds, underground health-clinics, soup-kitchens, anti-deportation campaigns, social media campaigning etc. In the following sections, focus on UMG will be initially

5 Parallel to this initiative, another Stockholm-based SAC-Syndicalist 'co-organisation', Västerorts LS, has offered undocumented migrants membership in the sub-group 'Register'. One Västerorts LS representative maintained in 2010 that the majority of this union's members were undocumented migrants (Lag och Avtal 2010). In 2013, this local union organisation was excluded from SAC by its central committee, who claimed that the 'co-organisation' had acted against union statues and principles (SAC 2016).

6 A *key informant* and *oral history interviewing* approach to in-depth qualitative interviews was adopted. The informants were encouraged to share their experiences in order to understand the predicaments and outcomes of the collective actions they had participated in. The time-period that data was collected stretched from 2008 to 2015, and has thus provided some longitudinal insights into the characteristics of mobilisation as different collective actions having evolved over time (see Blee and Taylor 2002).

explored, thereafter followed by TUCUM and UMS initiatives. The chapter ends with a discussion on the variations of these mobilisation efforts and their outcomes.

Syndicalists of a Distinctive Sort – the Undocumented Migrants' Group (UMG)

The Swedish Workers' Central-Organisation, or SAC Syndicalists in popular parlance, is a union confederation that comprises fifty-two local 'co-organisations', which organise some five-thousand six-hundred members (Karlsson and Warlenius 2012). The union was established in the aftermath of the 1909 'Grand Strike'[7] that not only proved politically and economically ineffective, but also marked a major setback in the history of the blue-collar trade union confederation known as *Landsorganisationen (LO)*, halving its membership-base between 1908 and 1910. In response to this, many workers would seek alternatives to the reformist labour movement (Schiller 1967). Hence, in 1910 a 'youth socialist' initiative, comprising unions from southern Sweden, organised a congress marking the founding of a trade union guided with syndicalist principles. It condemned bureaucratisation and centralisation in the established labour movement and envisioned a revolutionary union striving for socialist societal transformation (Gunnarson 1965: 202). Throughout its history, the SAC Syndicalist's union has carried a radical identity, not least by being the first union to organise undocumented workers. According to the SAC secretariat (Correspondence, the 24th of August 2015) the union had already in 2002 at its twenty-seventh Congress, adopted a formal decision to organise all workers independently of legal status. While this entailed the acceptance of undocumented migrants as union members in all local organisations, the district offices have remained autonomous in regards to matters of practical inclusion. Some local organisations had already, prior to the congress, enrolled undocumented migrants as members who, while awaiting asylum decisions, had found jobs, joined the union and remained members even after negative asylum rulings.

The Undocumented Migrants' Group (UMG) was, according to its representatives, formed irrespectively of any general union policy. Instead, they maintained that this formal SAC union decision on unionisation of undocumented migrants was unknown to them, and that inspiration rather was found in unionisation initiatives in the USA and southern Europe.

In 2004, the group's core organisers invited a representative of the *Spanish Confederación General del Trabajo (CGT)* to a conference for members and an

7 I.e. general strike.

additional public meeting. A local Spanish-language radio station acknowledged the event and invited the representatives to a live broadcasted programme. The immediate positive response came as a surprise to the organisers, especially when thirty people in the live-session called the studio to declare interest. One activist recalls this event and subsequent meetings:

> The listeners called in and the radio personnel wanted to let us know before we had left, and we were rather worried [...], what if the secret police arrive, what if the Iranian embassy... One gets all sorts of ideas, or if the regular police arrive and people do not have residence permits. Then, lots of people came to the meeting [...] there were maybe 100 people there.

The group established subsections specialising in union rights, but also some non-traditional union matters, such as ways to find work, access to healthcare and Swedish language studies. This initial phase was however, according to the organisers, also characterised by internal debates, both at local and regional levels, over whether the unions should be organising any workers in informal employment:

> They were ombudsmen, employed within SAC, who were older men from northern Sweden where the SAC had a strong anchoring in the forest industry, but also those from Stockholm were rather critical. [...] Several people from the local organisation in Gothenburg were critical; they [too] were of the opinion that this [activity] was organising undeclared work.

Despite these internal framing disputes, the UMG developed strategies, accumulated external support from refugee rights groups, and succeeded in settling a series of conflicts with employers. However, they would also encounter various organisational difficulties, a weakening of internal support, and eventually organisational decline and dissolution. In the following development, the core organisers' experiences of this trajectory are described.

Conflicts with employers, in almost all cases, predominantly focused on retroactive compensations after workers were dismissed. Fear often prevented workers from improving conditions as it was 'difficult, because one is afraid as an undocumented migrant [...], because one is so exploited'. Thus, the majority of those who joined the UMG as regular paying members would do so in relation to an ongoing conflict. This meant that labour conflicts would serve as pathways to union membership. Despite being supported by the 2002 SAC congress decision to elaborate new organisational strategies, the local organisation would diverge from customary SAC prognostic frames by offering representation to people who prior to a conflict had not been members. One of the organisers expands on the matter:

> Officially, we do not negotiate for people's conflicts unless they are members. We have not dealt with this formally. But rather, taken on what we believed we could do something

about. […] Then the rest of the local organisations demanded more or less that we change this policy. […] We would not have (represented) done so with someone who was employed in a rule-abiding way. We signed them up and started to negotiate over old things anyway. […] We quite simply accepted the employee's version, we believed them (laughingly), and then we put forward their demands. […] What they have agreed on as pay, that's what we have pursued.

The disputes were commonly resolved by invoking the legally sanctioned bargaining rights, which ordinarily would result in conciliation over compensation and thus would not require further industrial action. The organisers explained however that, if needed, they used industrial action such as blockades of various premises linked to the employer's business:

In no case that I was involved in have they [the employers] tried to deny that this or that someone has carried out some job. Rather, it is only a lot of fuss around the scope and what already has been paid. […] And then this, that they are forced to negotiate, it does not mean that they are obliged to get along with us. […] So those [laughingly] who do not comprehend that they shall come to the proceedings, they probably think that they are obliged to get along with us too. […] The [LO] tradition is more that one is to get along by not spoiling the good atmosphere and so on. And we [Syndicalists] could not care less about the good atmosphere. It may become as mean as it wants, particularly in those situations when our member has decided to no longer work there – in principle then we can be as mean as it gets.

While the 'winning' or settling of 'some thirty to forty' negotiations with employers were described as events that re-energised collective action mobilisation, not all disputes would however lead to settlements, and would thus impact on the organisers' motivation:

If you negotiate and do not reach a result for the member it will drain one's powers. It is not always as fun [as in those successful cases] […], rather it may be that one chases a small construction company composed of one person who you never get hold of.

This was however not the only negative implication that emerged prior to the ensuing termination of the group's collective mobilisation actions in 2010. The core organisers pointed to a set of interlinked factors concerning the incorporation of undocumented workers into the trade union's organisational form. The traditional SAC prognostic frames for defending their members' position on the labour market – through local club mobilisation in workplaces, and active member participation in all union activities – resonated poorly with the undocumented workers avoiding deportation. One organiser explained further:

We became as our own group within the local organisation, and then we maybe did not make more of the regular members become conscious about these questions, […] [we became] a bit isolated and separatist [...] [At local organisation meetings] there were a lot of formalities and arid matters that did not deal with undocumented workers' every-day lives. [...] Now we are in the same trade union...but... we never discussed my work conditions in these meetings because it was something totally different or far distant.

According to the organisers of undocumented workers, the establishment of a discrete group was initially anchored in the idea that it would provide a 'secure venue' for examining the working and living conditions, and developing appropriate strategies. In addition to this, language barriers could be more easily overcome in a narrower setting. Altogether, the special features of undocumented workers' legal status, the activist character of the union and the language barriers would amount to obstacles for conducting joint meetings and articulating collective action frames resonating with both the documented and undocumented members alike, thus fostering solidarity (cf. Lindberg 2013). The differences in members' working conditions were described as pivotal, negatively impacting factors on mobilisation efforts. The frames of collective action would thus lack congruence across memberships in relation to the 'personal, everyday experiences of the targets of mobilisation' (Benford and Snow 2000: 621). Although the matters of the UMG would be raised at local union office meetings, the organisers explained that interest was weak. One of them stated that the group was:

[...] tolerated in the meetings, but not much more than that. [...] Those [Syndicalists] that are established at the workplace, who enjoy their jobs, they do not want the reputation of being troublemakers, they do not want to stand in a blockade and yell 'damn work-buyer'. [...] I remember that I was rather disappointed that so few 'normal' members, if one could say so, arrived at our blockades. [...] Those who hold a steady job, enjoy their job, have a boss they can talk to, they [...] may think that we cause more harm than good.

The impediments to pursuing collective action through consensus attitudes of members of the union and the norms of 'communal conduct' (cf. Lindberg 2013) clashed with the pursuing claims on behalf of the new (undocumented) members. The union organisers found themselves in a situation of becoming proxies for undocumented workers in conflicts with employers – a task that would prove overwhelming without the active backing from the rest of the SAC membership. One of them described:

The Syndicalist idea is that one works together and is active as a member. One does not walk up to an ombudsman, put forth demands and walk home, and let the bureaucracy deal with the misery. [...] But, when it comes to the undocumented migrants, it was often so, that they were too afraid to show themselves, they are afraid even of riding on the subway, and then we in a way end up in this situation that we functioned as ombudsmen and that was not fun. [...] That way of working, it is not 'Syndicalistic'. Rather, one should engage the members, including those one negotiates for. [...] 'There are twenty

> thousand undocumented migrants in Sweden', so we used to say sometimes, and all of them are mistreated in one or another way. How were we to clear this up with four people?

This dependency on a few volunteers was, according to another organiser, further underpinned by the declining degree of engagement by those formerly undocumented union members who had received residence permits:

> Some of them I was in contact with in UMG who had received amnesty [...] did not continue to be active afterwards. Maybe it is so, that one has lived in really tough conditions here, worked informally, not dared to ride on the subway, and in addition to this have children, then when one gets the residence permit there are other things in life than attending [union] meetings. Also, maybe one does not want to remember this [period in life]. [...] When one is in an exposed situation, then this is priority number one [gaining a residence and work permit], of course. Just because one is a refugee, it is not necessarily so [...] that one is all that interested in other refugees or refugee-law, and maybe one wants that to be a [closed] chapter.

Such divergences of interests, norms and contingent circumstances call attention to varieties of framing disputes and efforts to achieve resonance for solidarity during the collective action mobilisation. The unionists' experiences and assessments of undocumented unionisation disclose a context where justice only partially can be served. Such accomplishments seem both to be contingent on substantial individual sacrifices outside ordinary unionist commitments, and on outcomes from clashes with contemporary union customs. Accordingly, whilst those workers who are immediately concerned, in the best of scenarios, only may afford offering limited fellowship and conduct (cf. Lindberg 2013).

The Trade Union Centre for Undocumented Migrants (TUCUM)

In this section the Trade Union Centre for Undocumented Workers (TUCUM), which is supported by unions in the LO, TCO[8] and Saco[9] confederations, is examined. The establishment of the TUCUM in 2008 is bound with previous union initiatives, and at least three cornerstone events. In 2007, the TCO adopted a policy on undocumented migrant workers in which they were recognised as covered by the labour law. Second, the RITA-project, initiated by the BMWU, had the goal of countering the exploitation of such workers within the cleaning sector (Holmgren 2007). The project report estimated that at least ten percent of the workers in this

8 The Swedish Confederation of Professional Employees.
9 The Swedish Confederation of Professional Associations.

sector were undocumented and provoked one union representative to refer to 'our criminal cleaning sector'. In this initiative, the BMWU developed an inclusive strategy, and through its advocacy of undocumented migrants' rights at the 2008 and 2012 LO congresses, it has slowly succeeded in developing the LO's position on those (Neergaard 2015b).

The third development was the entrance of the association Undocumented Migrants Stockholm (UMS) into public debate following the 2005/2006 partial regularisation programme. Through subsequent political collective actions, the UMS attracted wide media interest and political support in its struggle for union rights. As a result, it became recognised as a legitimate representative body for undocumented migrants, not least through invitations to parliamentary hearings (Sigvardsdotter 2012; Hellgren 2014). The trade unions followed by inviting UMS to participate in the preparatory work that would become the TUCUM, and in which four UMS representatives were offered board positions, including that of vice chairman.

Union representatives have praised the centre for its uniqueness and capacity to bring together the three larger trade union confederations in joint collaboration to resolve practical matters regarding the exploitation of undocumented migrants. Today (2016), eight years after its ceremonial inauguration by the LO and TCO chairs, the centre is endorsed by some thirty union member organisations that support it through a 500€ yearly membership fee, as well as staff it during its one-day-a-week opening hours, and twelve hours-a-day, seven-days-a-week telephone service. Each Monday, TUCUM is open to migrants received by union representatives who listen to their employer-related problems, and if considered feasible, forward the case to the corresponding union. In its public communications, TUCUM has stated that working or employing someone without a work permit is illegal, but if it occurs, the workers' rights nonetheless, are protected by law. Accordingly, the centre provides advice and support to workers in conflicts (TUCUM 2016). TUCUM representatives claim that cases have been forwarded to eight trade unions, of which today four – Hotel and Restaurant Workers' Union, Food Workers' Union, Municipal Workers' Union and the aforementioned BMWU – also offer union membership to the undocumented (see Selberg 2014). Thus, through its intermediate position between the workers and specific trade unions, TUCUM provides the liaison for Swedish trade union engagement[10] in defending the labour rights of undocumented migrants.

10 SAC organisation of the undocumented has proceeded in parallel to this venue.

Compared with the various estimates on the number of undocumented migrants in Sweden, it can be assumed that the centre has not dealt with an overwhelming number of cases. 'At most two, sometimes just one, arrive, and some Mondays, none', according to one representative. During the first couple of years, the majority of visits to the centre have had not been forwarded to the unions, either because workers have been cautious about direct union interference in their workplace conflict, or because other matters have predominated, such as healthcare, financial or legal support. This trend has, according to representatives, changed over the years through targeted information campaigns in collaboration with support organisations for undocumented migrants. In 2015, twenty-five cases had reached the unions, half of the total number of visits to the centre that year. However, where trade unions have intervened, the employment outcome for the individual worker has not been good, even if an immediate redress in terms of wage issues was achieved. One representative stated: 'We have not had anyone who has remained employed after we make the claim'.

The collaboration with the UMS was initially greatly valued for the organisation's direct channels to the undocumented, or as one union representative noted: 'when we started up, our driving forces were the contacts with the UMS'. However, within one year these ties would be strained to the breaking point, and result in the UMS resignation from the TUCUM board. One former core UMS activist pinpointed the discrepancies in perspectives and expectations between the UMS and TUCUM:

> [...] enormous expectations that this huge trade union, gigantic trade union [LO] would help with the right to stay and right to work. [...] The problem with unions and TUCUM, and the problem with the whole civil society working with this unionisation matter, is that it doesn't understand that it also must work with the right to stay. [...] They [undocumented workers] don't give a damn about the working conditions sometimes. They are afraid of death if sent back. [...] [Unions] have their own purposes. [...] Primarily, they don't want salaries being dumped and that the workers' general rights diminish. [...] They do not want to help undocumented migrants, they want to frame the employers. But, they have to think further. [...] They have a rather poor understanding of asylum politics [...], which creates undocumentedness, and it is there the core [problem] lies, [and] solutions as well. [...] There is a will [in unions], people are goodhearted, [...] but it is not enough.

According to one TUCUM representative, unrealistic expectations were being placed upon them by the UMS (2012), especially in relation to migration law matters, stating: 'had we taken a position [on this matter] we would have been forced to close in 2009'. TUCUM's prognostic framing was thus set on protecting the collective agreements by combating informal work and exploitation of the undocumented, or as one of the core organisers stated:

> We always demand wages according to the collective agreement. [...] We will not participate in making deals that result in a person getting lower pay. [...] We will not be servants of the state nor the police. Rather, we will protect these people and make sure that they have confidence in us. [...] There shall not exist 'sending them home' – rather we will nail those that take advantage of them.

The UMS has furthermore firmly refrained from union-organisation of the undocumented (2012), arguing that in addition to being a fruitless enterprise, it would be counter-productive to legitimise their legal status quo. As a core activist explained:

> They want to show that undocumented migrants are workers, contrary to the police – [...] their job is to expel. [...] How would they organise? There's no logic. [...] There's no undocumented worker who can stand up against their employer to demand a collective agreement, or good salary, or better conditions. There is only one situation, where the undocumented come to you – when there is a conflict, when the employer doesn't want to pay. Then he can wag the finger at the employer without being afraid. [...] If we would reconcile with [the idea of] undocumented workers remaining undocumented in the Swedish system, we would then be accepting informal work. We cannot do that. [...] Why would it matter to be unionised if the UMW cannot be equal to a Swede. [...] It's not helping undocumented workers, it's helping the Swedish unions. [...] But of course, if we speak about opinion, [...] it matters a lot because the union can also strengthen the undocumented, [...] from an illegal to a legal status – they have chosen a new route. [...] The organisation [UMS] becomes more legal. That is why we are collaborating.

For some core UMS activists however, the trade-off of not earning support from the unions for legalisation, while at the same time being co-opted into the battle against informal work, was considered being against the interests of the UMS. Consequently, frame disputes within the UMS led one side to emphasise dependency on the existence of informal work as 'putting bread on the table', and that collaboration with the established unions had enticed the organisation away from its main objective of regularisation. The other side would attempt to pressure TUCUM union representatives by demanding that member unions give (equal) priority to cases on behalf of undocumented workers transferred to them. One UMS activist, after withdrawal from TUCUM, stated (2011):

> The unions have been a bit afraid of their members, [...] for carrying the cases to the courts [...] and with this fear, bureaucracy enters into the centre. [...] The unions have received massive criticism from their members who do not want union organisation [of undocumented workers].

The TUCUM (union)-representatives would acknowledge this problem, but would also underline the need to proceed with caution with this sensitive matter regarding 'perceived fellowship' (cf. Lindberg 2013). One TUCUM representative in 2011, expanded on the tensions in approaching TUCUM member-unions and the risks of escalating prognostic disputes:

> They are tiptoeing, [...] in all the unions, [...] – an expression of simply not daring to offend member groups. [...] As soon as a union sees that, well they [TUCUM] are not delivering what we think is reasonable and good, they will leave [TUCUM]. So all of this is a sensitive chapter. [...] It becomes an internal union matter if we would dedicate much time on someone who is not a member.

In a follow-up interview in 2015, the prognostic frame would however be amplified towards 'tiptoeing' among member unions:

> Well we have had some trickiness with unions that do not organise undocumented workers and additionally have a damn rigid approach to this that one has to be member in a union, a number of months, one, two or three before one does whatsoever. Well that is a breach to TUCUM statutes. [...] There are some unions that have reasoned that way – plainly idiotic. Well actually, they should be excluded from TUCUM.

A firmer line would however also be drawn between those deemed to be 'representable' and those 'non-representable' undocumented workers. The reasoning was as follows:

> If they have chosen to enter [become members], and they receive help, and they get their 5000€ or something, [...] and then they exit, then they come back when they are in trouble again, then we certainly [will] say no. [...] Of course, it would be different if they worked as a cleaner and then got work in the metal industry, and there they maybe don't even have a chance to become members. [...] But, [...] if they come back and have problems in the same agreement area and have left the union, [...] then they receive no help. Then what applies, is as for anybody else, you have to be in the union for three months, or one month or whatever rules one has. [...] Then we are harsh as hell. It's just... Well it's a demand [to be unionised].

To understand this reaction in 2015, it is necessary to go back to 2009 where the communication between unions and UMS was broken. Following the summer of 2012, after a series of weeks without visitors, TUCUM set about establishing new channels with the support organisation Crossroads[11], The Red Cross, *Stockholms Stadsmission*, The No One is Illegal Network and *Médecins du Monde*. These collaborations have, according to TUCUM representatives, been strengthened since 2012 and helped to restore visitor flow, not least through the periodical staffing of the Crossroad centre and venues for the project *Mötesplats för Papperslösa*[12].

---

11 Information and support centre for EU migrants living in poverty and homelessness.

12 'Meeting Place for Undocumented Migrants', a three year project run by The Red Cross and *Stockholms Stadsmission* with the purpose of 'contributing to a decrease in

However, since 2012 visits to the centre have increasingly come to comprise EU-migrants from Bulgaria and Romania, in 2015 composing about fifty percent of the total. One core organiser provides insights into how boundary framing has brought about revisions in terms of 'mutual self-interest' and 'perceived fellowship' within TUCUM when encountering this new group of workers:

> If one comes from such countries where there is some kind of union tradition that resembles our own, then we can say: 'you should know this'. But, those are often not the ones who are coming. Many have been from countries, from Romania and from Bulgaria, [...] and, they are as poor as hell many of them too. [...]It is really tricky. [...] Then we would probably to some degree, turn the blind eye. [...] It totally depends on how long [they have been here]. [...] Although, many of these EU-migrants, [...] they are not much better off than undocumented migrants. But, [...] we surely have to draw the line because otherwise it could happen that Norwegians come here [who work informally]. [...] We must draw the line somewhere, and we are actually called 'centre for undocumented', so it's no moral story. [...] That then an equally large, maybe even bigger group actually, of EU-migrants would arrive, that we could not imagine. [...] We have run a couple of cases for Roma people. [...] So, would we take care of 100 000 [internal] EU-migrants too, who most of them work under bloody dodgy circumstances? [...] It's not possible and the unions are not managing it either, unfortunately. There is nobody who can manage this. The EU cannot manage it, and nobody can [...]. It would possibly be if one closes the EU. Well, that the EU is shut, and one goes back to, well, the order that was before the EU. [...] We just make it simple for ourselves, from case to case. [...] Its cold, but that's the way it is. But, this damn exploitation, [...] certainly, this we never saw earlier, of course something is wrong when one has to live this way in 2015.

This interview illustrates that this 'something' wrong brings forward the frame extension through both emotional empathy and political understanding of the 'dodgy circumstances'. This theoretically, may ground for solidarity, but it also depends on the framing of political opportunities, i.e. when irregularity occurs, as well as the magnitude of the diagnosis and the protection of the labour rights of regular workers. Thus, undocumented and EU migrant workers who enter the informal labour market in Sweden and then seek union representation may be invited on the basis of their precarity, measured in terms of: access to formal employment, grievance of employer abuse, and risking expulsion. Roma people arriving from Bulgaria and Romania are said to fare just as bad as, or worse than, the undocumented, therefore fitting these requirements. Yet, as the 'line' must be drawn somewhere, they, as well as those coming from outside EU, may also come to meet the same 'coldness' as due to that being 'the way things are'.

---

the vulnerability undocumented migrants and other migrant groups are living in'. The project was terminated in 2015 (Red Cross 2015).

Concluding Discussion

Through the core activist and union organisers' experiences of engagements within two union renewal enterprises, this chapter has illuminated a set of challenges for extending solidarity. The previous paragraphs have illustrated that internal frame disputes regarding 'perceived fellowship' and differences in political opportunity frames within unions for the undocumented persist (cf. Lindberg 2013). In relation to a 'communal conduct', the organisers have raised the difficulty of retaining employment for undocumented migrant workers in conjunction with union representation in conflicts. The difficulties entailed were particularly evident in the case of the SAC, where members described themselves as the primary handlers of negotiations with employers. For the union organisers this meant their role was reduced to advocacy, which they had found increasingly contested through lack of support from larger base of union members. This lack of a 'communal conduct' was attributed to both old and undocumented members. Concerning the latter, this was understood as moving on with their lives after having received residence permits, or not wanting to risk expulsion while remaining undocumented. Regarding the old members, this was related to not expressing adequate fellowship by either not appearing at blockades, or in some instances, not displaying more than 'tolerance' towards the challenges this group of workers faced. In addition to this, internal framing disputes between local union offices have occurred in which the undocumented workers' organisers were blamed for offering support to non-members and contributing to informality. These factors have together limited prospects for extended solidarity.

Similar tendencies were found in the Trade Union Centre for Undocumented Migrants (TUCUM) through referrals of workers' cases by receiving unions. The representatives have expressed frustration with unions who, despite being members in the centre, had circumscribed the centre's promise to offer representation to the undocumented in conflicts. This was raised as a sensitive matter due to the centre's intermediate position between different unions. It has signalled an absence among union members regarding 'mutual self-interest' in protecting the interests of the undocumented. This framing dispute was also associated with the 2009 resignation of Undocumented Migrants Stockholm (UMS) from the TUCUM board. Although this provided TUCUM with additional challenges in reaching out to undocumented workers, following 2012 new collaborations with civil society organisations were established and some internal tensions eased as certain member unions successively expressed stronger commitment towards cases referred to them. With these changes, a greater expression of solidarity towards another precarious category of workers, namely EU-migrants, followed.

However, with this also a stricter appraisal rhetoric of undocumented workers' 'perceived fellowship' and 'communal conduct'.

Despite the generally gloomy outlook among unions to extend solidarity with undocumented migrant workers through a diagnostic and prognostic framing consensus, these latest developments have highlighted that forging solidarity indeed has transformative qualities on union political identity. This suggests that there is need to prioritise collaborations with support organisations as means to innovate additional forms, and ways to extend inclusion to informally employed EU – and new coming undocumented – migrants who share many of the same forms of gross exploitation. Furthermore, it might be that the presently insistent emergency situation can carry future options of a more negotiable and transformative character of solidarity.

Today, the role of trade unions in assisting the undocumented is steadily assuming urgent policy relevance. Swedish authorities (as of 2015) are struggling to manage the arrival of over one-hundred and sixty-thousand refugees and asylum-seekers. In response to public unease, burning asylums and growing support for right-wing xenophobic forces, the Swedish government has, in a spectacular *diplomatic* manoeuvre, promised to refuse asylum status to approximately half this number, adopting a policy of mass deportation for those deemed 'economic migrants' rather than 'genuine' asylum-seekers (Crouch 2016). Enforcing such a return process, by way of planned chartered aircraft flights to the countries of origin, will doubtlessly prove problematic. Rather, it is more likely that a considerable number of people will chose to evade detection and avoid expulsion, inevitably becoming submerged as undocumented migrants in the lowest stratums of the informal economy. For trade unions committed to assisting the undocumented migrant workers, this will indeed reinstate the dilemma in which perceived national and sectional interests, in a general socio-political climate increasingly unsympathetic to migrants, may yet decisively confront any wider impulse to solidarity.

References

Adler, L. H. and Cornfield, D. B. 2014. 'The United States: Tackling Inequality in Precarious Times'. In Adler, Lee H., Maite Tapia and Lowell Turner (eds.) *Mobilizing against Inequality: Unions, Immigrant Workers, and the Crisis of Capitalism*. Ithaca: Cornell University Press, 35–51.

Alberti, G., Holgate, J. and Turner, L. 2014. 'Opportunity and Choice for Unions Organizing Immigrant Workers: A Comparison across Countries and Industries.' In Adler, Lee H., Maite Tapia and Lowell Turner (eds.) *Mobilizing against*

Inequality: Unions, Immigrant Workers, and the Crisis of Capitalism. Ithaca: Cornell University Press, 109–130.

Balasubramanian, G. 2015. 'Union decline: A geography based assessment.' *Indian Journal of Industrial Relations* 50/3, 373–385.

Benford, R. D. 1993. 'Frame disputes within the nuclear disarmament movement.' *Social Forces* 71/3, 677–701.

Benford, R. D. and Snow, D. A. 2000. 'Framing processes and social movements: An overview and assessment.' *Annual Review of Sociology* 26, 611–639.

Blee, K. M. and Taylor, V. 2002. 'Semi-structured interviewing in social movement research.' In Klandermans, Bert and Suzanne Staggenborg (eds.) *Methods of Social Movement Research*. Minneapolis: University of Minnesota Press, 92–117.

Crouch, D. 2016. 'Sweden sends sharp signal with plan to expel up to 80,000 asylum seekers.' *The Guardian*, January 28. Accessed March 10, 2016. <http://www.theguardian.com/world/2016/jan/28/sweden-to-expel-up-to-80000-rejected-asylum-seekers>

Farber, H. 2015. 'Union organizing decisions in a deteriorating environment.' *Industrial and Labor Relations Review* 68/5, 1126–1156.

Featherstone, D. 2012. Solidarity: Hidden Histories and Geographies of Internationalism. London: Zed Books.

Fine, J. 2011. 'New forms to settle old scores: Updating the worker centre story in the United States.' *Relations Industrielles/Industrial Relations* 66/4, 604–630.

Frank, D. 2012. 'State, Union and Unauthorized Migrants.' *Nordic Journal of Migration Research* 2/4, 298–307.

Frege, C. M. and Kelly, J. 2003. 'Union revitalization strategies in comparative perspective.' *European Journal of Industrial Relations* 9/1, 7–24.

Gahan, P. and Pekarek, A. 2013. 'Social Movement Theory, Collective Action Frames and Union Theory: A Critique and Extension.' *British Journal of Industrial Relations* 51/4, 754–776.

Gamson, W. and Meyer, D. S. 1996. 'Framing political opportunity'. In McAdam, Doug, John D. McCarthy and Mayer N. Zald (eds.) *Comparative Perspectives on Social Movements: Political Opportunities, Mobilizing Structures, and Cultural Framings*. New York: Cambridge University Press, 275–90.

Gunnarson, G. 1965. *Arbetarrörelsens Genombrottsår i Dokument*. Stockholm: Prisma.

Hellgren, Z. 2014. 'Negotiating the boundaries of social membership: Undocumented migrant claims-making in Sweden and Spain.' *Journal of Ethnic and Migration Studies* 40/8, 1175–1191.

Holgersson, H. 2011. *Icke-medborgarskapets urbana geografi*. Göteborg: Glänta produktion.

Holmgren, A. 2007. *RITA: Rättvis Ingång till Arbete. En Rapport om Papperslösa i Städbranschen*. Fastighetsanställdas Förbund.

Inghammar, A. 2010. 'The employment contract revisited: Undocumented migrant workers and the intersection between international standards, immigration policy and employment law.' *European Journal of Migration and Law* 12/2, 193–214.

Karlsson, M. and Warlenius, R. 2012. '*Ett sekel av syndikalism: Sveriges Arbetares Centralorganisation 1910–2010*.' In Ighe, Ann, Kristina Boréus, Maria Karlsson and Rikard Warlenius (eds.) *Ett Sekel av Syndikalism: Sveriges Arbetares Centralorganisation 1910–2010*. Stockholm: Federativ, 10–94.

Khosravi, S. 2010. *'Illegal' Traveller: An Auto-Ethnography of Borders*. Basingstoke: Palgrave Macmillan.

Kjellberg, A. 2013. 'Kan fackets försvagning hejdas – facklig styrka och organisering i en globaliserad värld.' In Lindberg, Ingemar and Anders Neergaard (eds.) *Bortom Horisonten: Fackets Vägval i Globaliseringens Tid*. Stockholm: Premiss, 39–89.

Kjellberg, A. 2016. *Kollektivavtalens täckningsgrad samt organisationsgraden hos arbetsgivarförbund och fackförbund*. Research Report 2013:1 (Updated March 8, 2016). Department of Sociology, Studies in Social Policy, Industrial Relations, Working Life and Mobility, Lund University.

Lag och Avtal 2010. *Den hårdföre förhandlaren*. Accessed March 15, 2016. <http://www.lag-avtal.se/tidningen/article3036090.ece>

Lindberg, I. 2013. 'Solidaritet och egenintresse – om facket och det kollektiva handlandets dilemma.' In Lindberg, Ingemar and Anders Neergaard (eds.) *Bortom Horisonten: Fackets Vägval i Globaliseringens Tid*. Stockholm: Premiss, 90–118.

MacDonald, I. T. 2014. 'Towards neoliberal trade unionism: Decline, renewal and transformation in North American labour movements.' *British Journal of Industrial Relations* 52/4, 725–752.

Milkman, R. 2015. 'Immigrant workers and the labour movement in the USA.' In Schierup, Carl-Ulrik, Ronaldo Munck, Branka Likić-Brborić and Anders Neergaard (eds.) *Migration, Precarity, & Global Governance: Challenges and Opportunities for Labour*. Oxford: Oxford University Press, 160–176.

Milkman, R., Bloom, J. and Narro, V. 2010. *Working for Justice: The L.A. Model of Organizing and Advocacy*. Ithaca, NY: ILR Press/Cornell University Press.

Munck, R. 2015. 'Globalisation, trade unions and labour migration: A transformationalist approach.' In Schierup, Carl-Ulrik, Ronaldo Munck, Branka Likić-Brborić and Anders Neergaard (eds.) *Migration, Precarity, and Global*

Governance: Challenges and Opportunities for Labour. Oxford: Oxford University Press, 101–117.

Neergaard, A. 2015a. '"Det fackliga löftet": Solidaritet, fackföreningsrörelse och arbetskraftsinvandring.' In Calleman, Catharina and Petra Herzfeld Olsson (eds.) *Arbetskraft från Hela Världen. Hur blev det med 2008 års Reform?* Rapport no. 2015:9, Delmi (Delegationen för migrationsforskning), 200–243.

Neergaard, A. 2015b. 'Migration, racialisation and forms of unfree labour: The dilemma of trade union solidarity.' In Schierup, Carl-Ulrik, Ronaldo Munck, Branka Likić-Brborić and Anders Neergaard (eds.) *Migration, Precarity, and Global Governance: Challenges and Opportunities for Labour*. Oxford: Oxford University Press, 139–159.

Penninx, R. and Roosblad, J. 2000. *Trade Unions, Immigration, and Immigrants in Europe, 1960–1993: A Comparative Study of the Attitudes and Actions of Trade Unions in Seven West European Countries*. New York: Berghahn Books.

Red Cross 2015. *Röster från skuggsamhället – att leva som papperslös i Sverige*. Accessed August 6, 2016. <http://www.redcross.se/press-och-opinion2/rapporter/roster-fran-skuggsamhallet---att-leva-som-papperslos-i-sverige/>

SAC 2016. *Västerorts LS har uteslutits ur SAC*. Accessed March 15, 2016. <https://www.sac.se/Aktuellt/Nyheter/V%C3%A4sterorts-LS-har-uteslutits-ur-SAC>

Sager, M. 2011. 'Everyday Clandestinity: Experiences on the Margins of Citizenship and Migration Policies.' PhD. diss., Faculty of Social Sciences, Centre for Gender Studies, Lund University.

Sassen, S. 2006. *Territory, Authority, Rights: from Medieval to Global Assemblages*. Princeton, NJ: Princeton University Press.

Schiller, B. 1967. *Storstrejken 1909: Förhistoria och Orsaker*. Göteborg: Elander.

Selberg, N. 2014. 'The laws of "illegal" work and dilemmas in interest representation on segmented labor markets: À propos irregular migrants in Sweden.' *Comparative Labor Law and Policy Journal* 35/2, 247–288.

Selberg, N. 2015 'Om kriminaliseringen av papperslösas arbete och argumenten för att avskaffa den.' In Calleman, Catharina and Petra Herzfeld Olsson (eds.) *Arbetskraft från Hela Världen. Hur blev det med 2008 års Reform?* Rapport no. 2015:9, Delmi (Delegationen för migrationsforskning). 362–412.

Sigvardsdotter, E. 2012. 'Presenting the Absent: an account of undocumentedness in Sweden.' PhD diss., Kulturgeografiska institutionen, Uppsala University.

Snow, D. A. and Benford, R. D. 1988. 'Ideology, frame resonance, and participant mobilization.' In Klandermans, Bert, Hanspieter Kriesi and Sidney G. Tarrow (eds.) *From Structure to Action: Comparing Social Movement Research across Cultures*. Greenwich, Conn.: JAI Press, 197–217.

Snow, D. A., Rochford, E. B., Worden, S. K. and Benford, R. D. 1986. 'Frame alignment processes, micromobilization and movement participation.' *American Sociological Review* 51/4, 464–481.

Stahre, U. 2007. Den Globala Staden: Stockholms Nutida Statsomvandling och Sociala Rörelser. Stockholm: Bokförlaget Atlas.

Svensk författningssamling (SFS) 2013. *Lag om rätt till lön och annan ersättning för arbete utfört av en utlänning som inte har rätt att vistas i Sverige*. SFS 2013:644. Stockholm: Justitiedepartementet.

TUCUM 2016. *Fackligt center för papperslösa hjälper papperslösa*. Accessed March 10, 2016. <http://www.fcfp.se/?page_id=43>

Turner, L. 2005. 'From transformation to revitalization: A new research agenda for a contested global economy.' *Journal of Industrial Relations* 32/4, 383–399.

Carl-Ulrik Schierup, Aleksandra Ålund & Lisa Kings

13. Reading the Stockholm Riots – A Moment for Social Justice?

Abstract: This chapter discusses the 2013 riots in Stockholm in the perspective of a range of urban rebellions in disadvantaged metropolitan neighbourhoods of the North-Atlantic region over the past three decades of neoliberal transformation. The authors examine consequences of securitisation and police repression, institutional racism, the corrosion of citizenship and the structuring of inequality in Swedish cities and they ask whether the Stockholm uprising could possibly open space for new political voices.

What happens to a dream deferred? Does it dry up

like a raisin in the sun? Or fester like a sore? ... Or does it explode?

Langston Hughes, 1951

'Riots', 'Uprisings' or the Rebirth of Civil Society?

'I have a dream', declaimed Reverend King on his March on Washington fifty years ago. It was a vision of a truly inclusive American nation. Yet, King soon found himself pondering whether the dream was not turning into that very 'nightmare' that Malcolm X had insisted continued to be the reality of the American Dream for black citizens. 'I watched that dream turn into a nightmare', King admitted in his last Christmas sermon in 1967, 'as I moved through the ghettos of the nation and saw my black brothers and sisters perishing on a lonely island of poverty in the midst of a vast ocean of material prosperity, and saw the nation doing nothing'.[1] Two years earlier, tension in the ghettos had exploded in the Watts rebellion; subsequently, following years of repression of Black and Latino struggles, the Los Angeles uprising of 1992 struck the nation with awe. This was a sobering moment in American history (Gooding-Williams 1993); but the window of opportunity was lost in the euphoria over the fall of the 'Evil Empire', promises of 'The End of History' and seemingly limitless financial pyramid games, or Ponzi-style investment scams.

1 Available at: http://www.ecoflourish.com/Primers/education/Christmas_Sermon.html (Accessed May 5, 2016).

There was a 'Swedish Dream' as well. A dream of changing an ethnocentric 'People's Home'[2] into a cosmopolitan home of peoples, merging extended rights of citizenship with a political framework divorced from nativist obsession. In the booming reformist spirit of the mid-1970s, new policies were conceived in terms of 'Equality, Partnership and Freedom of Choice', boldly rephrasing the revolutionary 1789 trinity into the credo of a liberal multicultural welfare society (Ålund and Schierup 1991), a particular Swedish 'exceptionalism' (Schierup and Ålund 2011). It was for long a dream of hope shared by subaltern others, but, by the 2000s, a nightmare for many of the country's inhabitants, who are experiencing institutional racism, social disadvantage, securitisation and police repression.

Nevertheless, at the time of the rebellion of *les exclues* in French suburbia, in 2005, Sweden was, on paper, still depicted as a positive liberal multicultural welfare state. But just four years later, in the late summer of 2009, Sweden was to experience its own urban rebellions in suburban districts on fire in the cities of Malmö, Gothenburg and Uppsala. In the spirit of the official denunciation of 'multiculturalism' by leading European politicians like Merkel, Sarkozy and Cameron, these Swedish riots were largely read by government and media as an expression of cultural deviancy, deficient socialisation of youngsters of migrant and, in particular, Muslim, background, and as a provocation to the European heritage and its 'liberal core values' (Schierup and Ålund 2011). Internationally, the 2009 Swedish riots passed relatively unnoticed. Domestically, they were already sinking into public oblivion when, on 14 May 2013, the killing of a 69-year-old man by the police in Husby, a socially disadvantaged Stockholm suburban neighbourhood of 12,000 inhabitants, sparked, from 19 May, five days of rage among young rioters. Cars, schools, youth centres, local shops, a kindergarten and a police station were set on fire. There were, as well, five days of clashes between rioters and police across the suburban neighbourhoods of the north-western and southern metropolis, and minor incidents in other Swedish cities. According to the acid judgment of one journalist, 'violence and racism within the police organisation was exposed as clearly as a skeleton on an x-ray slide' (Langhorst 2013). Although hardly more violent than the 2009 events, but taking place in the capital and more widespread in urban areas, these riots were widely interpreted in the international press as revealing a deep crisis in the 'Swedish model', which had mutated into a hazardous neoliberal experiment. It was a crisis 'more about economics than immigration' commented the *Financial Times*; and more about social inequality than culture (Financial Times 2013). Another difference between 2009 and

2 Social democratic idiom for the welfare state, stemming from the 1930s.

2013 is the role that politically articulate new urban movements of young Swedes (predominantly from migrant backgrounds) have played in producing alternative readings of the riots in terms of their claims for social justice.

If the riots of 2009 were a Swedish Watts, Stockholm 2013 could be read as its LA-92 – a 'dream exploded', a crisis of neoliberal politics, a sobering moment of truth. But will it be more than a window of opportunity closing? This is the question we focus on in this article. Our title alludes to *Reading Rodney King* (Gooding-Williams 1993); a classic work on race, urban segregation and the structure of cultural, political and economic power in the United States. But we also using the term 'reading the riots' – a title used by the *Guardian* and the London School of Economics for their study into the UK riots –hint at similarities between the London 2011 riots and Stockholm 2013 (The Guardian 2013). Both countries have recent histories of neighbourhood gentrification, welfare retrenchment and the proliferation of privately organised social services and education institutions taking place over three decades of neoliberal politics. It is an art which Sweden first learnt from Thatcherism and Tony Blair's 'Third Way', but in which it now, in some respects, excels to such a degree that it has (depending on your point of view) become the example to follow or, alternatively, a dire warning. Thus, behind the dramatic clashes of May 2013 lay another drama just as shattering – as a local Stockholm politician commented, 'long before Swedish media or the political elite had any idea of the existence of Husby and of what kind of area it is. [It is] a drama of discrimination, poverty, stigmatisation and deep social as well as political cleavages. About a city and a society getting torn apart'.[3]

We therefore see Stockholm 2013 as one of a series of instances of urban unrest across disadvantaged metropolitan neighbourhoods in the North Atlantic region over the past decades of neoliberal transformation; a development we shall relate, with a focus on urban policing, to the corrosion of citizenship and the structuring of inequality in Swedish society and its larger cities. Our point of departure is an understanding of contemporary riots as uprisings that are claiming social justice. We see them as 'unarticulated' urban justice movements (Dikeç 2007). For, behind the smokescreen of conspicuous violence, the contemporary Swedish scene also reveals the emergence of an autonomous, non-violent, 'articulated' and organisationally embedded justice movement contesting urban degradation and reclaiming Sweden in terms of an inclusive citizenship, social welfare and democracy. With this backdrop, we attempt to question here whether Stockholm

3 Social Democratic health politician, Jonas Sjölander on his personal blog (Sjölander 2013).

2013 could be read, not as signifying the irrevocable passing of a Swedish dream, but as a high point in the creation of a new movement among young people – a movement with a vision that looks beyond the threat of a 'state of exception', with government arrogating ever more unchecked power to itself. We illustrate in the following section how local activist movements – and in particular The Megaphone, situated in Husby – relate to the Stockholm riots, and suggest the emergence of new, urban, justice movements.

A State of Exception

Urban rebellions, like Brixton 1981, Los Angeles 1992, Paris 2005, Tottenham 2011 and Stockholm 2013, all appear to be sparked by alleged police brutality and the excessive use of force, when general tension – built up through systematic surveillance and daily humiliation – bursts. In each case, this combines with a perceived lack of official democratic channels for a just investigation of these 'police incidents'. And the common sense representation of events, at the end of the day, pushes the blame for fatal police action on to the victims or their communities. This may be mediated through racial phantasmagoria, as in the court case following the brutal roadside beating of citizen Rodney King, which provoked the Los Angeles uprising (Gooding-Williams 1993), or through post-colonial exoticism as in the case of the police killing in Husby, Stockholm. Read how the local community organisation, *The Megaphone*, reported on the media coverage of the police's inexplicable action in storming a flat and shooting an elderly man in the head:

> […] in all dailies […] [there are] pictures of the balcony where he waves a knife. The 'machete man' […] this is a label created so that we the readers shall think: 'oh, he sounds crazy, just as well that the police shot him […] [W]e make him a monster. Then he is not worth shit […] [M]achete sounds jungle. Sounds non-Swedish. Even better.[4]

For the locally based movement for social justice, the killing was experienced as an instance of the excessive use of force that carried a strong disciplinary message to the inhabitants of a stigmatised neighbourhood:

> How can a team of SWAT-police break into a flat against a sixty-nine year old man and kill him?? […] If this had happened against Karl-Erik,[5] sixty-nine years, in Kungsholmen[6] it would have been a scandal. Now it will become another story about a mad man in the

4 Blog (Megafonen 2013b).
5 Typical traditional Swedish name with 'white' connotation.
6 A predominantly 'white' high income area in the capital.

> hood [...] [L]isten. This is neither the first nor the last time. The police does not exist to serve common people, the workers, the community, the kids [...] the police is present to protect the political and economic elite: terrify us, discipline us [...] The police teach us in practice what the school teaches us theoretically: as a poor working man and non-white you are worth less, in Sweden and in the entire world.[7]

A neighbour has been murdered: a view reinforced by the fact that the police initially delivered patently false information about the circumstances surrounding the death. This led to the calling of peaceful protests in the local community and, later, demands for a public explanation from the police and for an independent investigation (outside the purview of the Swedish police force).[8] Six days later, the first reports emerged of a violent uprising in Husby. The tragic death and suspicion of the unnecessary police violence were identified, in retrospect, as the sparks that lit the flames. The morning after the riots began, The Megaphone invited the media to a press conference that was broadcast on national television (Arborén and Magnusson 2013). In a statement that was read by one of its representatives and supported by two eyewitnesses, the organisation condemned the police's brutality and their racist comments in their encounters with the youth. But, allegedly, no dialogue with the police or representatives of the government ensued; a fatal closing down of democratic avenues for the expression of legitimate grievances. According to a BlogSpot on The Megaphone homepage:

> What the police and the large media will brand as general chaos [...] this, what is always written about suburbia and its people is, in reality, a protest against the murder on Monday [...] [It is] definitely not a coincidence, an isolated riot. This remains the only way of expressing frustration when other democratic avenues are closed. Here is organisation, peaceful demonstrations have taken place, but initiatives for dialogue have been left unanswered. The police investigate their own people and will say that no mistake has been made...[9]

The feelings of injustice and lack of dialogue were hardly repaired when prime minister, Fredrik Reinfeldt blamed the riots (at a press-conference on 21 May, two days after the start of the riots) on 'angry young men' who needed to overcome 'cultural barriers' and come to terms with the rules in a democratic society for expressing dissatisfaction and making claims. He spoke of the government's persistent efforts to support the development of disadvantaged urban areas and the important role of the local suburban community itself in reinstating order.

---

7 Blog (Megafonen 2013b).

8 Chaaban and Ekstrand (2013). Incidents like the killing in Husby are investigated by a special unit within the police.

9 Blog (Megafonen 2013c).

In response Jimmie Åkesson, the chairman of the nationalist-populist party, the Swedish Democrats, compared premier Reinfeldt, in a Stockholm on fire, with the Emperor Nero fiddling as Rome burned[10] and demanded stronger security measures against young hooligans. But critical voices from the Left blamed the premier for neglecting 'angry young men's' cries for respect and help; for avoiding any government responsibility for the social problems underlying the suburban crisis (Wikström 2013); for pushing responsibility for solving the crisis on to local communities themselves; and for closing his eyes to the deeply problematic Americanisation of Swedish society (Kielos 2013).

In an account in the daily *Aftonbladet*, the Panthers, a community-based justice organisation in Gothenburg, acting in solidarity with The Megaphone (their sisters and brothers in 'the eye of the storm'), described the premier's initial statement as alienating disadvantaged citizens in that it delegitimised their place in the nation.

> Here we stand together. The Panthers and The Megaphone. If we did not exist, who should have taken the responsibility of trying to understand the shadows moving in our streets with stones in their hands? These shadows born in Swedish hospitals, registered with Swedish tax-authorities, who went to Swedish schools, spent their time hanging out in Swedish youth centres, and who wish to work in this country, to pay taxes and to die, but whom our prime minister still manages to fabricate into 'foreigners', depicting their action as the result of 'cultural barriers' [...] angry young men who need to overcome some cultural barriers and become part of society (Badpa and Solmaz 2013).

This pinpoints the 'irregularisation' of citizenship (Nyers 2010), through official and popular discourses, through legislation, as well as through the everyday practices of security personnel, including the police, military and bureaucrats. We see this as linked to a 'state of exception' (Agamben 2005), understood as the extension of state power through which the rights pertaining to citizenship can be reduced, overridden or denied by governments; in the process, the boundaries between the status of citizen and noncitizen become increasingly blurred. More specifically, while the processes of irregularising citizenship may formerly have been part of how a politics of exception operated, such processes can now be observed as part and parcel of the 'normal' working of most states (Nyers 2006).

Like other North-Atlantic societies, Sweden has, during the last decade, taken essential steps towards a state of exception, in particular in its so-called 'urban

10 Parliamentary debate on May 23, 2013.

development areas'[11] which are poor, suburban neighbourhoods in larger cities with a high proportion of citizens from Africa and the Middle East. In other words, visible minorities are being stigmatised in terms of 'race', 'national origin' or 'immigrant background'. These neighbourhoods have become security hot-spots with their inhabitants under continuous police surveillance (Peterson and Åkerström 2008), and subject to multiple identity checks and stop-and-search raids. The surveillance was ramped up in 2008 by the REVA-project (*Rättssäkert och effektivt verkställighetsarbete*, i.e. Legal Certainty and Effective Enforcement). This collaboration between the police, the migration service and the Swedish prison service, partly financed by the European Refugee Fund, aimed to combat irregular migration through increased identity checks and deportations. As REVA broadened its regional impact to Stockholm in 2013, it was criticised by anti-racist activists as a step towards the setting up of a 'police state'. Racial profiling, in connection with identity checks taking place at transport hubs (e.g., Metro stations), has been criticised for targeting not just the 'undocumented', but numerous Swedish citizens of colour. It represents, in effect, a fusion of capillary migration control with surveillance of the stigmatised 'accidental citizen' (Nyers 2006).

In the social media, young activists describe Husby and similar neighbourhoods in Swedish suburbia as forgotten reservations of joblessness, poverty and lack of a future, in which the police act as a counterinsurgency force rather than as protectors of the local population:

> I think about Husby [...] Black and Blue policemen with gold embroidered crowns come when the state is under threat, not when people die. The police come when people without a passport try to survive; the police come when resistance has passed into desperation. And then we talk about the 'security of the police'. Exclusion from the social security system, deportations and violence [...] What to do when you never become a part of non-surburbia. Of non-invisibility.[12]

From the police's perspective, they view Husby and the Stockholm suburbs as perilous no-go zones 'where the next murder of a policeman will happen', rather than being inclined to talk about the Husby police killing on 14 May (Johansson

---

11 Regeringskansliet 2013. *Urbana utvecklingsområden: en statistisk uppföljning utifrån sju indikatorer.* Available at: <http://www.regeringen.se/rapporter/2013/11/urbana-utvecklingsomraden-2013---statistisk-uppfoljning-utifran-7-indikatorer/> (Accessed May 5, 3016).

12 'Jag tänker på Husby', thewhoryspirit blog (20 May 2013). (Link accessed 10 July, 2013 and quoted in Schierup, Ålund and Kings, 2014: 7. Our translation of the quote. Access to link no longer possible). <http://thewhoryspirit.wordpress.com/2013/05/20/jag-tanker-pa-husby/>

2013). In line with this view, a major study of 'discriminatory policing' in Sweden[13] concludes that the suburbs are described by the police as potentially threatening places, inhabited by youth of 'other ethnic backgrounds', with a low trust in the authorities. Ethnic minorities are the focus for a growing apparatus of surveillance and securitisation; socially marginalised places have become stigmatised and criminalised and it is enough to live in or to be present in a certain area to be subject to control.

In effect, the idea of 'policing the crisis' is as relevant as ever (Hall et al. 1978). A permanent tension between the police and young people has built up across the disadvantaged Swedish suburbs. This perhaps explains the silence of the police when faced with demands to explain their behaviour and debate with the community following the Husby 'incident'. What results is fertile ground for rebellion (Peterson and Åkerström 2008). Changing the meaning and quality of police work appears then to be a prerequisite for any political reform. The police are not in themselves the deepest source of the conflict, nor its solution. But the 'bluejackets' are the symbol of a society perceived as racist; they are the most visible targets of resentment and hatred as the praetorians guarding speculative financialisation, welfare retrenchment, the seizing of public land and assets and the segregative processes of urban transformation. Such practices are producing new geographies of inequality and undermining trust in the promises of a nation that still represents itself as the custodian of liberal democracy, prosperity and equal opportunity.

In 2009, thirty youngsters stood on a Backa square in Gothenburg holding up a handmade placard on which they had written, on a flattened card-board box, the reasons they were throwing stones at the police. It sums up how the young dispossessed still feel:

> We stand here every day. Poseidon, the tenants' association, the police, the authorities, see us standing here, but do not care about the matter. Jobs or some effort from the municipality or the social welfare service is needed. The authorities have seen us growing up and standing here for five or six years, but nothing is done [...] [T]his is our only way to be seen ... (Göteborgs-Posten 2009)

Economic Restructuring, Welfare Retrenchment and Urban Transformation

The post-second world war 'Swedish model' enjoyed an international reputation for combining a dynamic economy and an active labour-market policy geared

13 Peterson and Åkerström 2008.

towards occupational upgrading and free access to education.[14] Its extended, tax-financed public service sector aimed at the abolition of poverty, the forging of social mobility for the working class and, not least, stimulating female labour-market participation and gender equality. In effect, this resulted, from the 1950s to 1970s, in a seemingly stable trend towards diminishing social inequality, making Sweden one of the most equal societies in the OECD area (OECD 2011). Since the mid-1970s, this reputation has been merged with the fame of harbouring one of Europe's most successful policies for integrating immigrants, appearing to promise a development of what has been laid out as the ideal model of a multicultural welfare society (Rex 1985; Castles 1994). It involved an easy access to naturalisation, unconditional access to full social rights and equality concerning employment based on residence (Sainsbury 2012), fast access to political participation and the recognition of claims in terms of ethnic and cultural identity. To this was added Europe's most welcoming policy of asylum. In some ways, for immigrants and new ethnic minorities, the promises of the model were not actually realised. Most significantly the dogma that a strong welfare state and an active labour-market policy would *as such* guarantee equal treatment and equal opportunities in the labour market – a stance long argued by unions and employers – meant the absence of sturdy anti-discrimination legislation. Nevertheless, prevailing institutional practices did guarantee even the most disadvantaged a basic social security (Schierup and Ålund 2011; Ålund and Schierup 1991).

However, from the beginning of the 1990s, both the political playing field and basic social conditions have changed substantially. A recession at the threshold of the '90s was followed by austerity policies. A new 'Third Way' social democratic regime favoured neoliberal monetarism over Keynesianism and full employment. Unemployment rose to levels unknown since the great depression of the 1930s; from 1.5 percent in 1989 to 8.1 per cent in 1993, but among the 'foreign born' from 3.5 per cent to a stunning 24 per cent during the same period, and with disproportions in the *level of unemployment* particularly striking for those born in Africa, Asia, and European countries outside the EU, and their Swedish-born children (Schierup, Hansen and Castles 2006, Chapter 8). This condition essentially still prevails today, with an unemployment that is, in particular, concentrated among youth. A parallel reorientation of Swedish labour-market policies along the lines of US- or UK-style workfare regimes and more restrictive access to supplementary welfare benefits and (with the rise to power from 2006 of centre-right governments) stringent limits to public health cover, has contributed to the production

14 Including all higher education.

of a marginalised reserve army of labour. It is exposed to the market discipline of precarious low-wage niches, and, pushed from the centre to the periphery of the welfare system, into a casualised secondary labour market and a degraded informal sector (Schierup and Scarpa 2016 [Forthcoming]).

The burden of this change was felt disproportionately in disadvantaged suburban neighbourhoods in large cities, officially designated as 'urban development areas,[15] which had a large proportion of new immigrants and citizens with ethnic backgrounds from outside the pre-2004 EU-15. Participation in the formal labour market is significantly lower in these areas than the Swedish average, or the average in large cities, and the average income among those who do have work is significantly lower (Andersson, Magnusson and Holmqvist 2010). In Husby, for example, the employment rate is close to 24 per cent lower than in the greater Stockholm region, and most of those who work hold low-income jobs.[16] What has caused most worries among politicians and social workers is, however, the large number of young people who neither hold any type of formal employment, nor are involved in education.[17] Whereas the national average is 20 per cent among youth between 20 and 25 years of age, in urban development areas the average of young people neither in work or education is double, with rates close to 50 or 60 per cent in certain disadvantaged areas. The child poverty rate in these areas varies between 28 and 62 per cent (Salonen 2012). Added to this, a sweeping deregulation of the public school system (launched from the early 1990s with the explicit rationale of stimulating 'diversity' and civil society initiatives) has created an open field for speculative risk capital and insider deals (Further in Chapter 7). This has caused a widening gap in educational opportunities and school results, between high-income and deprived suburban areas (Kornhall 2013).

For some, the brighter side of this rapid transformation was the stunning rise in corporate profits from the mid-1990s. Together with a marked redistribution of income, it was to bestow on Sweden the dishonourable position it has held to this day as the OECD member state with the fastest growing index of inequality (OECD 2011);[18] a trend exacerbated by consecutive tax reductions introduced by centre-right governments from 2006 onwards. This, and Sweden's coming out of the 2008 recession in better shape than most of its fellow travellers in a crisis-ridden European Union, has been a favourite theme of the international business

15 See Regeringskansliet 2013.

16 See Regeringskansliet 2013.

17 See Regeringskansliet 2013.

18 Albeit starting out from a remarkably low level compared to countries like the UK or the US. See also <http://www.oecd.org/social/inequality.htm> (Accessed May 5, 2016).

media. As late as February 2013, the *Economist* referred to Sweden as 'The next supermodel' in terms of reduced public spending, the cutting of marginal and corporate taxes and introducing publicly financed, but privately organised, social services across a broad range (The Economist 2013a). Yet, the 2013 riots appear to have tarnished Sweden's glorious reputation in the corporate world. While the *Economist* found the riots 'A blazing surprise' (The Economist 2013b) disrupting the Scandinavian 'idyll' by 'arson and unrest', and wondered whether the 'integration of immigrants' was failing, the *Financial Times* (2013) pondered that it was time for Sweden to question the range of privatisation and market-driven development. Sweden went too far, from a social democratic display window to a neoliberal experiment, and needs to find a balance. The Husby riots were a symptom. Politicians must understand and address the causes for a galloping inequality, both in terms of income distribution and deregulation of public services, with the consequences of school reform for deprived suburban neighbourhoods being seen as particularly worrying (Financial Times 2013). The *Wall Street Journal* found that the riots spotlighted a growing socioeconomic rift, 'dealing Sweden's reputation for equality and tolerance a severe black eye' (Ledel and Stoll 2013).

Thus the Stockholm riots set the international focus on the geography of urban inequality, most conspicuously in larger cities like Malmö, Gothenburg and Stockholm. Increasing social polarisation is a general contemporary trend in cities across the world, though with an immense variety of configurations. In the United States and the United Kingdom the term 'suburbia' denotes, for example, urban decongestion, lower residential density and private home ownership. In Sweden and France, in contrast, 'suburbia' (the Swedish *förorten* and the French *banlieue*) has come to signify deprived municipal housing areas inhabited by a majority of poor immigrants and their offspring, together with members of other disadvantaged groups.

In effect, it is essential to relate Swedish urban development to the historical contexts and the origins of segregation. In the late 1960s and the early 1970s, the ambitious suburban municipal housing programme 'The One Million Dwellings Programme' (*Miljonprogrammet*) was targeted at raising the general standard of living and providing affordable housing. Newly built suburban neighbourhoods, including Husby, were meant to symbolise the 'pinnacle of Swedish modernity', but soon came to represent the shortcomings of modern social engineering. Particularly since the 1990s, several of these suburban areas have been transformed from 'mixed neighbourhoods' to low-income areas where the majority are from 'migrant backgrounds' (Ericsson, Molina and Ristilammi 2002).

From this perspective, the riots of 2009, followed by those of 2013, signify a disastrous set-back to decades of Swedish urban policy, including the national large-scale 'Metropolitan Policy' *Storstadspolitiken* adopted by parliament in 1998 (Regeringskansliet 1998:165). The Metropolitan Policy was marked by significant flaws, including the omission of a focus on racism and discrimination, linked to the wider political economy and structure of power in the larger cities (e.g. Tedros 2008). More conclusively, grand plans for urban restructuring and moves to combat growing urban segregation and social inequality have largely been quashed by the major policy trends of the 2000s – from 'welfare' to 'workfare' and from public sector and civil society partnerships to market-driven projects. Under these forces, the understanding of marginality has been displaced from institutional and structural causality to a focus on individualised problems and solutions (Schierup, Hansen and Castles 2006). This has taken place in tandem with the emergent politics of securitisation and the representation of suburbia as the breeding ground for religious fundamentalism and a threat to democracy and liberal 'core values' (Schierup, Hansen and Castles 2006). Reflecting on this shift in the contemporary Swedish cityscape, Ove Sernhede, professor of social work, argues that what were earlier seen as problems to be addressed through social policy, today tend to become matters for police intervention (Sernhede 2010).

Police violence is indeed referred to by youth as a continuous pattern that triggered the riots – but there is, too, the backdrop of a structurally contingent urban geography of inequality, expressed in ethno-racial terms. Nor is it just the concentration of poverty and unemployment that is the background to youth unrest, but feelings of neglect and injustice, as here summarised in a video message by Emory Douglas, former minister of culture in the Black Panthers, sent to its present-day sister organisation, the Panthers of Gothenburg:

> [A] valid request turned into a nightmare and ignited the many decades of frustrations and neglect that imploded into the destruction of the community [...] frustration borne from a long train of abuses and neglect from an unjust system which has never shown equal respect for all of it citizens. You must join together to correct injustice, heal the community, and educate the young people to the real power they have because they are the future right now.[19]

Advanced Marginality and its Contestation: From 'Noise' to 'Voice'

A new, vigorous trans-ethnic mobilisation of suburban youth is emerging out of the changing Swedish cityscapes of the third millennium. Movements of young suburbanites spell out, in word and deed, their anger over their ghettoisation,

19 Megafonen 2013d.

their concerns about social inequality, racism and the need for justice. This can be designated as an *urban justice movement*. Their distinguishing mark is that place is the basis for mobilisation. The notion of 'suburbia' (*förorten*), imagined and lived, is used as a collective identity to raise consciousness about processes of marginality and to mobilise to influence politics through accepted as well as unconventional modes of action.

From this perspective, we see the contemporary city as constituting a strategic terrain for conflict and contestation, with 'advanced marginality' (Wacquant 1996) as the starting point for exploring the causes and implications of contemporary urban geographies of poverty and the making of the precariat. Mustafa Dikeç (2007) significantly deepens the meaning of 'advanced marginality', in emphasising that deprived neighbourhoods may be actually teeming with collective grassroots activism. Reflecting on French urban policy, Dikeç argues that space and place cannot be considered as given, but are produced by multiple practices and discourses. Suburban multiethnic districts are, on the one hand, increasingly constituted as 'badlands' in public discourse and, related to this, exposed to repressive forms of state intervention. But they are also potential or actual sites of political mobilisation driven by democratic ideals. He sees contemporary youth rebellions in France, but also in European cities in general 'not merely as intrinsic acts of violence' (Dikeç 2007: 138), but as responses to structurally embedded processes of segregation, unemployment, ethnic discrimination and the restructuring of welfare. Urban revolts are, he argues, 'justice movements'; that is movements questioning spatially and socially pronounced injustices, embedded in wider political contexts. Dikeç emphasises the importance of recognising activist groups as a public 'voice' – articulate movements aiming for deliberative dialogue – often rendered inaudible in public discourse, because of the attention paid to the 'noise' of spectacular revolts.

Swedish cities exhibit a variety of orientations and forms of organisation among new urban justice movements in Sweden. They range from strictly local initiatives and spectacular cultural events to the long-term building of activist platforms with local, national and international ramifications. FORIX (*Förorternas Riksdag*, the Suburban Parliament) was among the more spectacular initiatives. It functioned as a forum for critical debate, a scene for alternative suburban cultural expression and a rallying point for urban justice movements across the country. In the wake of FORIX's ambition to gather organisations, activists and network under a single umbrella, a new think-tank, *För Orten* (For the Local)[20], was launched in 2013. *Miljardprogrammet* (the Billion Programme) is another broad suburban

20 Available at: http://forix.se/?page_id=23 (Accessed May 5, 2016).

initiative, which attempts to build a national network for grassroots mobilisation among inhabitants of the One Million Dwelling Programme aimed at neighbourhood renewal.

Among numerous, new, locally-based community initiatives and activist networks, the Megaphone and the Panthers (referred to earlier) stand out as the most organised, politically articulate and influential. The Megaphone (*Megafonen*) originally started its activities in Husby, Stockholm, where the 2013 riots took off. It uses the slogan inspired by past Latin American anti-imperialist struggles; 'A united suburb can never be defeated'. The Panthers took off in the deprived neighbourhood of Biskopsgården in Gothenburg. While deriving their name from and linking their identity to past Black struggles in the United States, living legends like Bobbie Seal and Emory Douglas are also contemporary sources of inspiration in their work.

Both The Megaphone and the Panthers combine local rootedness with national and international networking. They forge alliances with other civil society actors, and articulate goals and visions in broad public contexts. During the past five years, both have expanded geographically and in terms of numbers of supporters, activists and participants. The Megaphone has spread its activist network to wider areas in suburban Stockholm and The Panthers have extended their activities to Malmö, connecting to similar urban initiatives in Copenhagen. Education through individual assistance, study-groups, movie seminars and discussion meetings – directed towards both local youth and adults – are basic to their work. Both The Megaphone and The Panthers provide critical voices in the media, and are present at public demonstrations and take part in conferences on urban issues. They act as watchdogs and pressure groups concerned with political and administrative decisions at local, city and national level. For them autonomy from party politics, other civil society organisations and the state is seen as essential, both in terms of legitimacy and their actual capacity to carve out independent agendas.

For the purposes of this article, The Megaphone is of particular interest, due to its location in Husby, Stockholm, and as an example that exposes the interconnection of place-based livelihoods, emergent modes of civic agency and their wider structural contexts, not least in connection with the 2013 riots. It was formed during winter 2008/9 as a community reaction to the reporting on the fatal assault on and death of a Husby resident, Ahmed Ibrahim Ali, nicknamed 'Romário'. Romário was a well-known football player in the area, but because of the way the media reported the murder, deploying stereotypical imagery about young suburban males, he was portrayed as a criminal and a gang-member. At the same time, another spectacular assault caused the death of a young man,

Riccardo Campogiani, in central Stockholm. Media reporting on this murder, where victim and perpetrator came from better-off backgrounds and lived in a more prosperous area, conveyed completely different messages. It resulted in a public outcry and a demonstration against street violence by over 10,000 people. It was out of frustration over what was perceived in the Husby youth community as a discriminatory representation of the murder of Romário compared to that of Campogiani, that the Megaphone took off as the voice of Husby, challenging the dominant media's stigmatising stereotypes of suburbia – a new 'megaphone' for voices seldom heard.

Defining itself as part of Sweden's 'new popular movement' (*den nya folkrörelsen*), The Megaphone formulates its objectives as: 'working for social justice in Sweden through organising young people in the suburbs in a society where everyone has equal opportunities and are included in all important political decisions; a society with collectively owned municipal services as opposed to a massive clearance sale of public property; the making of a society for all free from racism, sexism and class oppression' through 'mobilising the power that repression in suburbia gives birth to' (Megafonen n.d.).

This awareness of being a 'new popular movement' was also reported by the Swedish journalist Karin Elfving (2012), focusing on the attraction of The Megaphone for suburban youth in relation to symbolic power and identity formation. She concludes that belonging and identity have different meanings for youth in Husby than for their immigrant parents. This is exemplified in quotes taken from her dialogue with young people in the community. 'What am I – Kurd, Swede or Eritrean? This we have all gone through and this is what unites us', explains Ailin Moaf, a young activist from Husby. 'I do not, as my parents do, feel at home in the Persian association, and many more wouldn't in the Somalian or the Kurdish. I guess The Megaphone is what we feel as a home for us'. She goes on to explain that it is the very experience of injustice and a common interest in Husby that forges a strong sense of community and belonging focused on The Megaphone, together with the feeling of the power to effect change. Elfving goes on to quote another Megaphone activist, Basar Gerecci, who finds that what he experiences as the forging of deepening socioeconomic rifts between people and between urban neighbourhoods, may summon up similar movements of contestation elsewhere. But for a movement to succeed, it needs an organisational platform and serious work, as well as people prepared to commit themselves.

The popular educational programme Harakat, run by the Megaphone in collaboration with the Red Cross in Stockholm, is a case in point. Support from established organisations, as well as participation by prominent researchers and politicians, have lent it legitimacy. Moreover, The Megaphone's activities include demonstrations against the closing down or the subcontracting of public health and care services in the suburbs of Stockholm to corporate entrepreneurs, interventions in arguments over redevelopment and privatisation of municipal housing (Hatherley 2013), along with debates with politicians on urban renewal – often against heavy odds. Currently, its activities have broadened from local community issues to engagement in national campaigns to support asylum seekers and irregular migrants, which involves a solidarity network against the REVA police action against the undocumented.[21]

Altogether, in spite of a controversial public image, the development of The Megaphone demonstrates basic elements in the making of a social movement: an organisational platform, continuity, collective identity and legitimacy. Its public profile was significantly enhanced in connection with the Stockholm 2013 uprising where The Megaphone took a major step into the national and international mediascape. Its members managed to capture noticeable space in the national media, stubbornly working to make the public and politicians look beyond the burning cars to see the reality of unequal citizenship and the structural issues to explain what was taking place.[22] The day after the killing on 14 May, The Megaphone issued a critique of the bias in media reporting of the incident, organised a peaceful public demonstration, and invited the police for talks with the local community. After calling a press-conference the day after the riots began, the organisation became recognised as the tribune of suburbia.

The Megaphone stresses its mission is democratic and non-violent:[23] 'We in the Megaphone together with others from the area have […] taken advantage of our democratic rights in order to gain a hearing and making the police answer for their action.' And 'We claim social justice, but they answer with batons and dogs'. A detailed report from the homepage reads:

> As a fusty smell of poisonous smoke spread across the neighbourhood many of us went into the streets of Husby to find out what had happened. There we were met by masked police in armour with dogs and batons. The police went on the attack against local people who had gathered on the square. Defenceless people were beaten by batons and chased from their domiciles. We simply did not have any right to be there […] outside of our own homes. We also did not have a right to question the methods of the police as their response was to run after us again from different directions with their dogs and batons. Indiscriminately, the police went on to beat young people, parents who had gathered on the

21 See Megafonen 2013a.

22 See Strand 2013.

23 See Megafonen 2013c.

> spot and social service field-workers from the community. People who had chosen to discuss, argue and demonstrate against police violence now had batons hurled against them. Then it became obvious that the violence of the police was directed against all in Husby.[24]

A public statement from the police force over the killing of the 69-year-old man in Husby on 14 May came only on 7 August, after the police investigation had closed. The verdict on the incident was that it was an act of 'self-defence' on the part of the police officer who had pulled the trigger. Currently, the director of the public prosecution authority, who officially closed down the investigation, has been reported to the Ombudsmen for Justice over what is described as a flawed investigation.

From 'Exceptionalism' towards a 'State of Exception'?

Sweden's handling of its urban question, though criticised for being 'Americanised', still looks a far cry from the mass incarceration invested in the transformation of America's 'hyper-ghettos' into the 'surrogate ghetto' (Wacquant 2000) of its huge prison-industrial complex. And compared with the United Kingdom, the legal aftermath to the Stockholm riots appears restrained. In Sweden, about 90 per cent of the reported incidents that, according to the Swedish police, were related to the riots of 2013, have been dropped. Only a handful of suspects have, at the time of writing, been brought to court and have received comparatively mild sentences.[25] This is compared to 2,700 persons brought to court across England after the 2011 riots, many of whom received long prison sentences (Bridges 2012). It is a difference in scale that is hardly explainable by the larger extent of the London riots, nor by the fact that the Stockholm riots did not involve looting as in the UK. While in the UK the dominant political reaction following the riots pointed to more and tougher policing, this has not been the case in Sweden. Violence as a means of expressing social grievance was certainly universally denounced as 'completely unacceptable' by speakers across the entire Swedish political spectrum. But, apart from the populist Sweden Democrats demanding tougher police action, the political debate on the riots has not been dominated by arguments for solving the urban crisis through police repression or criminalising the young. Finally, the official line on Sweden 2013 is hardly on a par with the UK's branding of the London 2011 riots: 'blaming the breakdown of families and lack of character in the young, rather than structural issues' (Bridges 2012: 1).

---

24 See Megafonen 2013c.

25 See Bizzozero 2013.

The dominant political understanding of the 2013 uprising does appear to signal a sobering moment of self examination. The tone was set by, among others, the chairman of Sweden's powerful social democratic party, Stefan Löfven.[26] Commenting on Facebook on the first night of the Stockholm riots, he saw them as a reminder of a 'responsibility resting heavily on all of us, who are working politically', implying that the discussion of the riots should focus on finding 'concrete solutions to the real problems' – getting to grips with youth unemployment, providing educational opportunities for all and creating sustainable housing and urban milieus. Although the Right and the Left differ in terms of their concrete policies for redressing poverty and urban marginality, this is the general position that has resonated across the political left-right divide, even permeating a major debate on the riots in parliament, held on 31 May 2013.[27] Moreover, in contrast to the political reception of the Swedish 2009 riots, in 2013 there was, with some exceptions, an absence of references to the 'problem of immigration'. There was also an absence of interest in 'deviant cultures' and 'deficient socialisation'. This made premier Reinfeldt, talking the talk of 'cultural barriers' in his initial comment on the riots, appear beyond the pale. The rioters were read, across the political spectrum, as 'youngsters' or 'young men' rather than 'immigrant', 'ethnic minority' or 'Muslim' youth. Rather than further fuelling the existing stigma of 'suburbia', there was a general political re-appraisal of an engaged local civil society in Husby and other Stockholm suburbs for its important role in resisting violence.

Despite this apparent shift in Swedish political discourse at the time, what seemed to have escaped notice is the detrimental impact of existing structural racism and institutional discrimination on Swedish suburbia and on the legitimate rights of its residents; the widening polarisation between metropolitan livelihoods in centre and periphery; and the way that the most disadvantaged are losing faith in democracy and state-delivered social justice. The deafening silence across much of the mainstream political spectrum that was the reply to The Megaphone's outspoken demand for an independent investigation into the Husby killing, boded ill. The closing of the investigation on this 'police incident' by 7 August, with the total exoneration of the policeman who shot 'the man with the knife' in the head at close range on 14 May, indicated that Sweden has some way to go before recognising its impending 'state of exception'.

---

26 See <https://www.facebook.com/stefanlofven/posts/571823579525207> (Accessed May 5, 2016).

27 See Sveriges Riksdag (2013).

Unrest in Stockholm's suburbia has calmed down, but beneath the surface bubbles a constant frustration. We argue that the root causes of rebellion lie not in city districts like Husby or in the fact of segregation in cities such as Stockholm, Malmö and Gothenburg per se, but in social polarisation – where conflicts over space, race, income and power intersect. There is a need now to contextualise community activism and relate it to the social forces in which it is embedded. It demands that we look at ethnic and residential segregation, the marginalisation and social exclusion of racialised minorities, the polarisation of income distribution related to neoliberal restructuring and welfare retrenchment, the securitisation of the police and the force's increasing brutality. Given all these factors, there is an obvious lack of democratic space in which the 'alternative voices'[28] of suburbia can be promoted. For it is the voices of the excluded and marginalised that, in Sweden as in other EU countries, challenge the mainstream and call into question the 'flattering and valorising picture of superior European values and a democratic, open and tolerant way of life' (Fekete, Bouteldja and Mühe 2010).

The Megaphone of suburbia, despite being muffled by or stigmatised in the national media, has, nonetheless become a symbol of resistance, of popular will and of belonging. Civil society activism, such as that exemplified in The Megaphone, has become a source of identity, solidarity and resistance, particularly among youth in multiethnic suburbia. By creating numerous links to sister organisations, the short history of The Megaphone indicates the birth of a new networked popular movement (*folkrörelse)* or justice movement. Thus, we have argued these new autonomous actors within civil society are demanding their place among Swedish popular movements. Through their focus on urban social justice, their active presence as critical public voices in the mass media, and through knowledge production and public demonstrations, they have proved themselves to be a new political subject, different from established civil society actors. In the process, emergent youth justice movements have created new agendas for reclaiming the city as well as rights of citizenship.

In conclusion, Stefan Jonsson's reading of the Stockholm riots[29] enunciates the radical challenge that uprisings now present to us all:

> That we live in an age of riots would thus mean that we do no longer – or still do not – live in an age of democracy. Therefore it hardly makes sense to combat or to crush rebellions.

28 The 'Alternative Voices on Integration' project was created in 2009 by Liz Fekete at the Institute of Race Relations, to draw attention to innovative European community-based initiatives that challenge racism, break down stereotypes and effect change.

29 Jonsson (2014), with reference to Alain Bertho (2009).

Better, then, to provide space for them in politics, so that the silence and the noise can be converted into words.

Acknowledgements

This chapter was first published as 'Reading the Stockholm riots – a moment for social justice?' in *Race and Class* 55/1, 2014, pp. 1–21. We are deeply grateful to Liz Fekete, Jenny Bourne and Hazel Waters at the Institute of Race Relations for their qualified and meticulous editing of the manuscript.

Acknowledgement of Funding

We appreciate generous funding by FORTE, the Swedish Research Council for Health, Working Life and Welfare [grant number 2006–1524].

References

Agamben, G. 2005. *State of Exception.* Chicago & London: The University of Chicago Press.

Andersson, R., Magnusson, L. and Holmqvist, E. 2010. *Contextualising ethnic residential segregation in Sweden: welfare, housing and immigration-related politices.* Country Report for Sweden, NORFACE's Research Programme on Migration. Helsinki: Helsinki University.

Arborén, H. and Magnusson, Ö. 2013. '"En protest mot dödsskjutningen".' *Svt*, May 20. Accessed August 8, 2016. <http://www.svt.se/nyheter/lokalt/stockholm/megafonen-det-var-en-protest-mot-dodsskjutningen>

Ålund, A. and Schierup, C.-U. 1991. *Paradoxes of Multiculturalism. Essays on Swedish Society.* Aldershot: Avebury. Republished 2009 as E-Book on the REMESO home-page, Linköpings University as: <http://liu.diva-portal.org/smash/record.jsf?pid=diva2:213706>

Badpa, H. and Solmaz, M. 2013. 'Skrivgruppen Pantrarna: Till en nation som brinner.' *Aftonbladet*, June 23. Accessed March 29, 2016. <http://www.aftonbladet.se/kultur/article16832905.ab>

Bertho, A. 2009. *Le temps des émeutes.* Paris: Fayard.

Bizzozero, D. 2013. 'Få domar kopplade till Husbyupploppen.' *POLITICO*, July 29. Accessed August 8, 2016. <http://www.politico.se/artikel/6534/f%C3%A5-domar-kopplade-till-husbyupploppen/>

Bridges, L. 2012. 'Four days in August: the UK riots.' *Race & Class* 54/1, 1–12.

Castles, S. 1994. 'Democracy and multicultural citizenship: Australian debates and their relevance for Western Europe.' In Bauböck, Rainer (ed.) *From Aliens to Citizens: Redefining the Status of Immigrants in Europe*. Aldershot: Avebury, 3–28.

Chaaban, S. and Ekstrand, P. 2013. 'Megafonen: Poliser kan inte utreda poliser.' *Metro*, May 21. Accessed March 29, 2016. <http://www.metro.se/stockholm/megafonen-poliser-kan-inte-utreda-poliser/EVHmet!4gdgisUvWJgg/>

Dikeç, M. 2007. Badlands of the republic. Space, politics and urban policy. Oxford: Blackwell.

The Economist 2013a. 'The next supermodel.' *Economist*, February 2. Accessed July 30, 2016. <http://www.economist.com/news/leaders/21571136-politicians-both-right-and-left-could-learn-nordic-countries-next-supermodel>

The Economist 2013b. 'A blazing surprise.' *Economist*, June 1. Accessed July 30, 2016. <http://www.economist.com/news/europe/21578725-scandinavian-idyll-disrupted-arson-and-unrest-blazing-surprise>

Elfving, K. 2012. 'Inte bara snack i megafonen.' *Svenska Dagbladet*, October 24. Accessed March 29, 2016. <http://www.svd.se/inte-bara-snack-i-megafonen>

Ericsson, U., Molina, I. and Ristilammi, P.-M. 2002. *Miljonprogram och media. Föreställningar om människor och förorter*. Stockholm and Norrköping: Riksantikvarieämbetet and Integrationsverket.

Fekete, L., Bouteldja, N. and Mühe, N. 2010. Alternative Voices on Integration in Austria, France, Germany, the Netherlands and the UK. London: Institute of Race Relations, NEF and EPIM. Gooding-Williams, R. 1993. Reading Rodney King. Reading Urban Uprising. New York and London: Routledge.

Financial Times 2013. 'The challenges of the Swedish model.' *Financial Times*, May 26. Accessed March 29, 2016. <http://www.ft.com/intl/cms/s/0/ba2fb9ee-c47e-11e2-9ac0-00144feab7de.html>

Göteborgs-Posten 2009. 'Arbetslöshet och trakasserier.' *Göteborgs-Posten*, August 20. Accessed Auguset 6, 2016. <http://www.gp.se/nyheter/g%C3%B6teborg/arbetsl%C3%B6shet-och-trakasserier-1.1062806>

The Guardian 2013. 'Sweden: reading the riots.' *The Guardian*, May 26. Accessed March 29, 2016. <http://www.theguardian.com/commentisfree/2013/may/26/editorial-sweden-reading-the-riots>

Hall, S., Critcher, C., Jefferson, T., Clarke, J. and Roberts, B. 1978. *Policing the Crisis: Mugging, the State and Law and Order*. London: Macmillan.

Hatherley, O. 2013. 'How Sweden's innovative housing programme fell foul of privatisation.' *The Guardian*, June 16. Accessed March 29, 2016. <http://www.theguardian.com/commentisfree/2013/jun/16/sweden-housing-programme-privatisation>

Hughes, L. 1990 [1951]. 'Montage of a dream deferred' In *Selected Poems of Langston Hughes*. New York, NY: Random House Inc.

Johansson, A. 2013. 'Efter upploppen i Husby: "Här kommer nästa polismord att ske"'. *Aftonbladet*, May 20. Accessed March 29, 2016. <http://www.aftonbladet.se/nyheter/article16806656.ab>

Jonsson, S. 2014. 'Dangerous, Chaotic and Unpleasant: Crowd Theory Today.' *Lo Squaderno* 33, 9–12.

Kielos, K. 2013. 'Riots and the Reinfeldt syndrome.' *Policy Network*. Accessed March 29, 2016. <http://www.policy-network.net/pno_detail.aspx?ID=4433&title=Riots+and+the+Reinfeldt+syndrome+>

King, M.L. 1967. A Christmas Sermon on Peace. Sermon delivered at Ebenezer Baptist Church, December 24. Accessed August 6, 2016. <http://www.ecoflourish.com/Primers/education/Christmas_Sermon.html>

Kornhall, P. 2013. *Barnexperimentet. Svensk skola i fritt fall.* Stockholm: Leopard förlag.

Langhorst, J. 2013. 'Husby: polisen håller i nyckeln.' *Feministiskt Perspektiv*, May 21. Accessed August 6, 2016. <https://feministisktperspektiv.se/2013/05/21/husby-polisen-haller-i-nyckeln/>

Ledel, J. and Stoll, J.D. 2013. 'Sweden riots spotlight growing economic rift.' Wall Street Journal, May 26. Accessed July 30, 2016. <http://www.wsj.com/articles/SB10001424127887323855804578507212136735842>

Megafonen n.d. 'Megafonens Program.' *Megafonen*. Accessed August 6, 2016. <http://megafonen.com/om/politiskt-program/>

Megafonen 2013a 'Demonstration mot Reva!' *Megafonen Blog*, February 26. Accessed August 6, 2016. <http://megafonen.com/ai1ec_event/demonstration-mot-reva/?instance_id=>

Megafonen 2013b. 'AYNA: Varför dom finns + Lögnen om Husby-mordet igår.' *Megafonen Blog*, April 14. Accessed August 6, 2016. http://megafonen.com/ayna-varfor-dom-finns-lognen-om-husby-mordet-igar/

Megafonen 2013c. 'Husby belägrat av poliser. Gå hem? Det här ÄR vårt hem.' *Megafonen Blog*, May 20. Accessed August 8, 2016. <http://megafonen.com/husby-belagrat-av-poliser-ga-hem-det-har-ar-vart-hem/>

Megafonen 2013d. 'Emory Douglas, legend från Svarta Pantrarna, ger sin bild av förortsrevolten i Sverige.' *Megafonen Blog*, May 29. Accessed August 8, 2016. <http://megafonen.com/emory-douglas-legend-fran-svarta-pantrarna-ger-sin-bild-av-forortsrevolten-i-sverige/>

Nyers, P. 2006. 'The accidental citizen: acts of Sovereignty and (un) making citizenship.' *Economy and Society* 35/1, 22–41.

Nyers, P. 2010. 'Forms of irregular citizenship.' In Squire, Vicki (ed.) *The contested politics of mobility: Borderzones and irregularity*. London: Routledge, 35–49.

OECD 2011. *Divided We Stand: Why Inequality Keeps Rising*. Paris: OECD Publishing.

Peterson, A. and Åkerström, M. (eds.) 2008. Den sorterande ordningsmakten. Studier av etnicitet och polisiär kontrol. Lund: Bokbox.

Regeringskansliet 1998. *Utveckling och rättvisa. En politik för storstaden på 2000-talet*. Regeringens Proposition 1997/98:165. Stockholm: Regeringskansliet.

Regeringskansliet 2013. *Urbana utvecklingsområden 2013: Statistisk uppföljning utifrån sju indikatorer*. Stockholm: Arbetsmarknadsdepartementet, Regeringskansliet.

Rex, J. 1985. *The Concept of a Multicultural Society*. Warwick: Centre for Research in Ethnic Relations.

Sainsbury, D. 2012. Welfare states and immigrant rights: The politics of inclusion and exclusion. Oxford: Oxford University Press.

Salonen, T. 2012. *Barnfattigdomen i Sverige. Årsrapport 2012*. Stockholm: Rädda Barnen.

Schierup, C.-U., Hansen P. and Castles, S. 2006 *Migration, Citizenship and the European Welfare State. A European Dilemma*. Oxford: Oxford University Press.

Schierup, C.-U. and Scarpa, S. 2016 [Forthcoming]. 'How the Swedish Model was (almost) lost. Migration, welfare and the politics of solidarity'. In Ålund, Aleksandra, Carl-Ulrik Schierup and Anders Neergaard (eds.) *Reimagineering the Nation. Essays on Twenty First Century Sweden*. Political and Social Change. Berne: Peter Lang.

Schierup, C.-U. and Ålund, A. 2011. 'The End of Swedish Exceptionalism? Citizenship, neo-liberalism and politics of exclusion.' *Race & Class* 53/1, 45–64.

Sernhede, O. 2010. 'Curtailed citizenship, social pedagogic and informal learning processes in youth culture.' In Eriksson, Lisbeth and Thomas Wiman (eds.) *Learning to fly: social pedagogy in a contemporary society*. Gothenburg: Daidalos.

Sjölander, J. 2013. 'Vi kan inte blunda längre (om Husby).' *Sjölander Blog*, May 21. Accessed August 8, 2016. <http://johansjolander.blogspot.se/2013/05/vi-kan-inte-blunda-langre-om-husby.html>

Strand, D. 2013. 'Bränna bilar – enda protesten som finns kvar.' *Aftonbladet*, May 23. Accessed August 8, 2016. <http://www.aftonbladet.se/kultur/article16826717.ab>

Sveriges Riksdag 2013. 'Aktuell debatt.' Web-TV. May 31. Accessed August 8, 2016. <http://www.riksdagen.se/sv/webb-tv/video/aktuell-debatt/aktuell-debatt_H0C120130531ad>

Tedros, A. 2008. 'Utanför storstaden. Konkurrerande framställningar av förorten i svensk storstadspolitik.' PhD diss., Gothenburg University.

Wacquant, L. 1996. 'The rise of advanced marginality: notes on its nature and implications.' *Acta Sociologica* 39/2, 121–39.

Wacquant, L. 2000. 'The new "peculiar institution". On the prison as surrogate ghetto.' *Theoretical Criminology* 4/3, 377–89.

Wikström, G. 2013. 'Reinfeldt skjuter ifrån sig det egna ansvaret.' *Svenska Dagbladet*, May 23. Accessed May 29, 2016. <http://www.svd.se/reinfeldt-skjuter-ifran-sig-det-egna-ansvaret>

René León Rosales & Aleksandra Ålund

14. Renaissance from the Margins: Urban Youth Activism in Sweden

Abstract: Analysing the formation of a political subjectivity among Swedish urban justice activists the authors discuss resistance against cultural stigmatization and social exclusion. An emergent critical public voice confronts marginalization within the formalised context of 'invited spaces' for citizenship dialogues as activists create new 'invented spaces' for public participation, in order to promote democratic development.

A new political subjectivity has taken root among activists in Sweden's disadvantaged urban neighbourhoods. It has been borne along by a contentious urban movement following upon youth uprisings in Swedish cities in 2009 and 2013. It brings into focus citizens' claims for social justice; a response to social polarization of the urban space forcing racialized identities upon a range of multi-ethnic neighbourhoods within segregated geographies of social exclusion and cultural stigmatization. It is a multifarious movement coming out of Sweden's stigmatised and socially marginalised 'suburbia' (*förorten* in Swedish). 'Suburbia' – or *förorten* – is home to subaltern population groups, in particular migrants of multiple backgrounds and their descendants.[1] We see this new so-called 'suburban movement' (Swedish: *förortsrörelsen*[2]) as an 'urban justice movement' (Dikeç 2007). Sensing that they are a 'new popular movement' (*den nya folkrörelsen),* these new actors in civil society find themselves heirs to a tradition that once struggled to create the Swedish welfare state. As we will discuss, new and old popular movements seem currently to come closer to each other in confronting a looming crisis of democracy.

We contend that the activism of subaltern suburbia represents the emergence of a political subjectivity, connected to particular experiences of democratic deficit in urban governance as well as territorial and cultural stigmatization of suburbia

1 The term *subaltern* is derived from Antonio Gramsci's (1997) work on cultural hegemony, referring to groups that are excluded from a society's power structures of political representation and thus denied the means by which people have a voice.

2 See also e.g. Sernhede and Söderman 2013; Tahvilzadeh 2013.

and its residents.[3] We concur with Reginald Grünenberg's (2012) description of political subjectivity as 'the ability to reflect on public order', which, at the same time means the ability to go beyond the given order and to conceive different ones. This can thus be read as the ability to both conceive another order and to take action; that is, to create 'new sites and scales of struggle' (Isin 2008: 39) and find their 'own ways of political participation' (Mansouri and Mikola 2014: 30). These new ways are related to the creation of what we, following Faranak Miraftab (2004), refer to as *invented spaces* of citizen participation within the informal political arena; thus extending the notion of political to the informal politics of civil society activism. With that as the background, we focus our research on the interconnection between political subjectivity and agency.

In exploring this interconnection we will in the following discuss organizations that have played a central role in the shaping the public discourse on the Stockholm riots in 2013 (see Chapter Thirteen). We pay particular attention to the organization *Megafonen* (The Megaphone), which engages young people from the most stigmatized and economically deprived suburbs in Stockholm. On the basis of our ongoing study of *Megafonen* and other actors within Sweden's suburban movement, we argue that the resistance to patterns of discrimination and injustice are at the very core of the activism expressed within the suburban movement. Following Miraftab (2004: 1) we will exemplify this activism through expressions of two interacting and mutually constitutive concepts of *invented* and *invited* spaces of citizenship (Miraftab 2004). Confronting marginalization within invited spaces for citizen's participation, Megafonen has proceeded to invent its own spaces for activism, based on educational training, public lectures and interventions in mass media, seminars, and protests and campaigns in public space.

We will highlight a discursively politicized reception of Megafonen represented as either activism for a democratic renewal or criminalized youth. We scrutinise a gender profiling of riots in the media as one example of a reductionist dominant public narrative about what is at stake. We discuss how learning processes within the movement have functioned as a necessary knowledge base for empowerment aimed at raising emancipatory consciousness and ultimately their emergence as political voices for advancing democratic development in urban contexts. In conclusion we reflect on the possibilities for connections between these new and old/established civil society organisations and movements.

3 Since 2012 we have been gathering data from several avenues: participant observation, netnography, interviews, video recordings of meetings, and interventions in public media, such as articles in newspapers.

The New Suburban Movement

We see organizations like the Megafonen as a manifestation of a wider renaissance of urban activism among marginalized groups exposed to racism and discrimination in Swedish society. It is, among others, young people from some of the most socio-economically disadvantaged metropolitan neighbourhoods of Sweden who have started these new organizations. They live in neighbourhoods affected by welfare cuts, high levels of unemployment and poverty with a majority of residents from so called 'visible minorities'; that is to say migrants and post-migrant generations with backgrounds in Asian, African and Latin American countries (Socialstyrelsen 2010).[4] The urban segregation in Sweden is comparable to the patterns of urban ethnic segregation of African-American and Asians in Los Angeles (Östh, Clark and Malmberg 2015) and many other cities across the global north. It represents a development of racialized urban geographies that deeply affect how different neighbourhoods are perceived, as well as how identities are formed, not least among children and young people (Lundström 2007; León Rosales 2010).

Movements as Megafonen, or similar organizations such as *Pantrarna för upprustningen av förorten* (the Panthers for the regeneration of the suburb) in Gothenburg, organize and raise awareness among the youth in their neighbourhoods to counteract cultural stigmatization and the politically orchestrated dismantling of welfare services. Megafonen's web site has the following statement: 'Megafonen works for a just society. We organize young people in the suburbs to create a society where everyone has equal opportunities and where the people make political decisions, not the other way around'.[5]

These organizations have successfully managed to win struggles, including putting pressure on local authorities for the opening of youth centres in vulnerable areas and the organization of opposition to the privatization of public housing. They have also upheld a constant struggle against the stigmatization of their neighbourhoods. These struggles highlight growing unemployment and the emergence of a vulnerable urban precariat. This pertains in particular to migrants from non-western countries and their offspring who experience the negative effects of polarising, socio-economically profiled, residential segregation, and a discriminatory social exclusion within education and the labour-market

4 In this article we use the term *post-migrant*, following Kira Kosnick (2010), to refer to individuals born in Sweden whose parents were born abroad.

5 Megafonens homepage <www.megafonen.com> (Accessed May 27, 2015). Authors' translation.

(Schierup and Ålund 2011). It is a development that bears witness to the impact of a neoliberal 'accumulation through dispossession' (Harvey 2005) in a country that once epitomised the quintessence of the welfare state.

Activists in organizations like Megafonen and Pantrarna, being for the most children of migrants, express a kind of political subjectivity connected with the experience of, reflection on, and activism against the subordinated position of migrants and their descendants. They are part of a social movement constituted by a broad variety of different, youth-led organizations and networks springing from the socio-cultural contexts of 'new ethnicities' (Hall 1992) from marginalized urban areas. Thus, while Megafonen and Pantrarna may have been the most visible in the public debate, they are not alone. They have developed their activities by networking among activists from similar organizations: *Förorten i Centrum* (The suburb in the Centre), *Grammofonen, Hassela Ungdomsrörelse* (The Hassela Youth Movement), *Hayat, Orten i Fokus* (The Community in Focus), *Rådet av enade kreoler* (The Council of United Creoles), *Rörelsen Gatans Ansikte och Röst* (The Face and Voice of the Street), *StreetGäris* (Street Girls), just to mention a few.

The activism of these organisations vary in what is emphasised: social- and community work, identity work, empowering processes, gender issues, antiracism, articulation of a political agenda, etc. Other differences are related to frames of political governance within the city where they are located, including legitimacy and support in local contexts. While the city of Malmö has had a majority of left and green parties in the city council, and has been supportive of new local organizations, the situation in Stockholm and Gothenburg was/is less so. Stockholm had conservative parties and Gothenburg left-green political majorities in the city council, until 2014. During 2015 social democrats constituted a majority in alliance with green party and left and feminist party became the majority also in the Stockholm City Council.

However, these new youth-led locally based organisations seem to represent a movement beyond the formally political. Swedish urban justice organisations with Megafonen as one of the most important, can be seen as part of a new form of youth-led activism emerging across the globe (Mackay 2011; Mansuri and Mikola 2014; Gordon and Taft 2011).

Fethi Mansouri and Maša Mikola (2014) argue that these new forms of youth activism signal a need to see beyond formalized indicators of political participation, as voting and party politics, which are regarded among youth as marginalizing their own experience and issue priorities. Youth have the capacity to invent new forms of citizenship, contend Mansouri and Mikola (2014: 34), which enable them 'to become political agents, instead of being patronised, overlooked, and ultimately disempowered. If this agency is not recognized', they continue, 'the voice of migrant youth is not only subjugated; but their reality as political agents able to adjust, challenge and engender different layers of citizenship will not be recognized'.

Research has tended to focus on youth apathy, contend also Hava R. Gordon and Jessica K. Taft (2011), because it concentrates on political socialization within different adult-run institutions/organisations. Thus, '[n]ormalisation of the discourse on political apathy among youth produces a perspective on youth activism as exceptionalism' (Gordon and Taft 2011: 1507).

This highlights a need to 'see beyond a narrow focus on the "political" while also understanding young people as agents – already actively involved in claiming, resisting and negotiating a range of competing responsibilities and freedoms' (Thomson et al. 2004: 221). As Engin F. Isin (2009) argues, compared with the eighteenth and nineteenth centuries, the twentieth century figure of citizenship changed as 'activist citizen making claims to justice' became the 'defining figure of contemporary global politics' (Isin 2009: 384).The birth of new 'acts of citizenship', enacted through struggles for rights and justice among various groups, illustrates how acts produce subjects as authentic citizens through creating 'new sites of contestation' (Isin 2009: 371). Below, we will illustrate these 'new sites of contestation' with Megafonen as an example of activist citizens claiming justice and show how their activism promotes the emergence of political subjectivity.

Political Subjectivity in the Making

Our critical theoretical understanding of the relation between agency and power is focused on the concept of political subjectivity. It is informed by the work of Michel Foucault and later research inspired by Foucault. Individual subjectivities, and thereby political agency, are seen as contingent on historical and societal power-relationships. Foucault (1983) sees power as a relational force that circulates through social interactions, which helps us to understand the productive aspects of relations of power, i.e. how the exercise of power always creates individuals and groups as political subjects, through complex and contingent relations of dominance and resistance. As Michel Foucault explains: 'There are two meanings of the word "subject": subject to someone else by control and dependence; and tied to his own identity by a conscience or self-knowledge. Both meanings suggest a form of power which subjugates and makes subject to' (Foucault 1983: 212). This notion of duality opens up the options to analyse both identification and dis-identification as well as submission and resistance, in complex interlinked relations within the same processes of subjectification (Butler 1993: 219). It is through the more or less intentionally strategic choices that people make in their everyday lives, choices that continually link with each other in different ways, that power relations are constantly re-created, strengthened and challenged.

Discussing the making of political subjectivity as expressed by activists within the suburban movement, we will thus focus on how their struggles epitomise subjectification (as subordination, dis-identification, resistance), through the emergence of an emancipatory consciousness and activist practice. We will use the notion of *voice* as an idiom for the expression of the political as active positioning in public space. Voice is a powerful metaphor for strategies of representation related to resistance among marginalized groups; unrecognized or silenced through stereotypes in mainstream public debate, in politics and popular culture. Thus, the concept of voice illustrates our understanding of political subjectivity which we, with Grünenberg (2012), have defined as 'the ability to reflect on public order': and to conceive of another order. The essence of political subjectivity is accordingly that 'a political subject has cognitive access to the concept of the *option*.' And, consequently, in 'those cases where there is no such cognitive access, a *political* thought will never develop in a human being!' (Grünenberg 2012).

Following this theoretical line of thought, it is possible to see how the very birth of Megafonen as an organization in 2009 gave a voice to fundamental aspects of the political subjectivity of its members in their 'mediation of the world' (Shaull 2005: 32). As already described in Chapter Thirteen, a defamatory media representation of the violent death of Ahmed Ibrahim Ali, a local football player commonly known as Romario, alerted the young founders of the Megaphone to the need to 'talk back' against stigmatization of their neighbourhoods and their lives. It was fundamentally a reaction against processes of subjectification in society which impose subordinated, stereotypical identities and marginalized positions; reducing the visibility of these places and people to denigrating representations (Bredström 2002; Brune 2004).

The way that the press initially reported the death of Ibrahim Ali is obviously not the whole explanation of why Megafonen was founded. It was rather the straw that broke the camel's back. Other experiences, other situations, other understandings of what positions are conferred on them in society; all converged to make the originators feel predestined to marginality. Four years later, during a group interview, some of the founding members of the Megafonen were asked to describe what kind of society they were fighting for. Rami Al-Khamisi, a local activist answered:

> I think it's about, at least when it comes to the suburbs; it's about people feeling like … second class citizens…You don't feel included. There's something wrong with your

> religion, there's something wrong with how you talk, there's something wrong with the colour of your skin, there's something wrong with your neighbourhood. You grow up with the idea that you are a problem in society. If we can change this and take this away, make people feel respected and recognized as citizens in this country, then we will have come a long way. (Rami, group interview 2012).

Rami illustrates here how feelings of marginalization, experienced by people 'in the suburbs', are related to how their faith, skin-color, ways of talking and neighbourhoods are regarded as 'problems'. He stresses also, in a Fanonian sense, how being 'a problem' in and to 'society' may be internalized by people as they grow up. It may, in consequence, produce a subjectification of self as the infinitely 'subordinated', as being a 'second class citizen', not conforming to the norm prescribing who represents the undeniably Swedish citizen. This is, for Rami, also connected to social class, to the internalization of oppression, to the erection of a 'mental barrier':

> Of course it is also about reducing the economic gap between social classes, about working against racism and all that, but on a personal level, if we live in a society where we are mentally entrapped and limited, something you can see both in the children growing up here and in our parents that never quite feel at home… […] This… [is the] mental barrier, that makes this neighbourhood so oppressed. (Rami, group interview, 27 July 2012)

This statement can also be seen as an illustration of how the personal is always political, especially for people in subordinate and marginal positions. It highlights effectively how the neoliberal turn affects migrant families and youth (cf. Ålund 2014). This connection between the private, between experienced situations, thoughts and feelings, and societal economic and political structures was expressed by other members of the Megaphone. Melody Farshin, for instance, participating in a discussion panel on the revolt in Husby that was held in the art gallery of Tensta (*Tensta Konsthall*) in June 2013, reminded the public of the basic connections between the Stockholm youth uprising and a shocking experience of police brutality in the neighbourhood (see also Chapter Thirteen):

> We had a 69 year old man who was shot dead in his apartment earlier that week and it's no coincidence that at the end of the week cars started to be burnt. In between we had a peaceful demonstration against police violence… The frustration is still there… It is still there, and then this takes place [the uprising], something that makes the whole body of scandal mongering journalists hyperventilate with joy. Husby was occupied by journalists overnight because of the material losses [referring to burning cars]. But the head and the mind and the soul have burned for a long, long time. Otherwise Megafonen would never have been founded in Husby. We would never have had people helping kids out with their homework in Husby, people who are not even trained educators, but they struggle with what they have. We would never have, even though we become worn out, having five additional jobs, sat there and tried to teach our young how to do

> this math homework that I myself am not sure that I [can] master. But we are there, and this organization exists. Husby has been very, very quiet for a long time, a lot thanks to Megafonen, because we took the time to deal with this frustration. (Recording from panel discussion, 15 June 2013)

In this emotionally charged intervention in the debate, Melody made clear the basic connection between the activism of the members of Megafonen and the poor social and economic conditions prevailing in Husby. She highlighted their work as one of the main reasons why there had not been riots in the neighbourhood earlier. This connection between the realities of lived life and informed education, highlights the meaning of how 'Learning from the Ground up' (paraphrasing Choundry and Kapoor 2010: 2) connects knowledge production with activist praxis; how 'informal learning and education work in the everyday worlds of social activism' and may bring into the open 'tensions over whose knowledge and voice(s) are heard'. One of the points Melody makes is that members of the Megafonen have for a long time been dealing with the widely spread sense of frustration in the area. Her statement can also be seen as an example of how central frustration is as a feeling when members of the Megafonen explain their engagement. Following sociologist Manuel Castells (2012), we can here see how social movements can also be seen as, 'movements of emotions'. Shared experiences, feelings of not belonging *or* belonging to segregated spheres of society can create fear, frustration, mistrust, alienation and despair. These feelings are often perceived as individual and not linked to a larger social structure. The new justice movements offer opportunities for transforming individual feelings of anger, outrage into collective feelings of injustice, and thus build a common ground for hope, empowerment through organization and learning processes enabling their members to become a joint public voice through collective action and claims.

This is brought out clearly in the political programme of Megafonen (2015). The organization makes several demands that: people of suburbia be provided with opportunities to influence political decisions which shape their everyday lives; security and surveillance measures be replaced by social programs; investments in public welfare services be enhanced to provide community meeting places, and space for leisure and active citizenship. In addition the organization demands a just educational system offering youth opportunities and knowledge for coping with secondary education; job opportunities and decent work for all; an end to housing privatisation and a policy that recognizes the right to affordable public housing.

These claims can be read as testimonies of injustices related to fundamental aspects of everyday life, such as housing, school, work and actual opportunities which have influenced people's lives. By articulating these claims, they are becoming activist citizens. This understanding is, translated into our theoretical discourse, in accord with Isin's essential argument on political subjectivity as being or becoming – through acts of citizenship – inherently political:

> Citizenship understood as political subjectivity shifts our attention from fixed categories by which we have come to understand or inherit citizenship to the struggles through which these categories themselves have become stakes. It also shifts our attention from already defined actors to the acts that constitute them. Rather than asking 'who is the citizen?' the question becomes 'what makes the citizen'? (Isin 2009: 383)

Stressing that acts precede actions, Isin (2009: 379) claims further that 'we must focus on rupture rather than order'. In a similar vein we understand the urban activism of the Megafonen as an expression of activist citizenship (Isin 2009). A new identity/identification emerged through the creation of a shared political subjectivity and where citizenship is learned through practices with a critical perspective on relations of power. It is, as the Megafonen illustrates, about practices of representation in public space targeted at changing an unjust distribution of material and symbolic resources, as will be discussed below.

Becoming a Public Voice

A range of activities has been initiated by Megafonen with the aim of strengthening local communities. Celebrating the optimism of the oppressed in *Chile,* expressed in the popular parole '*A people united will never be defeated*', they signal on their homepage, under the headline '*A united suburb can never be defeated*'[6], a will to mobilise marginalized neighbourhoods in a common struggle.[7] Day by day this *place struggle* has been about coping with education, homework support of pupils, workshops, festivals etc. Megafonen has also invited researchers, politicians and other activists to give lectures and participate in discussions with people from the neighbourhood, an exchange of knowledge organised within what was named Harakat – i.e. the movement in Arabic – raising issues on discrimination, segregation, gentrification, gender and education.

For the marginalised, the importance of developing a narrative of their own is also related to the recognition that actual openings in the public media and political sphere do indeed offer new space for their voices. This can be seen as yet another fundamental aspect of political subjectivity: the need to be heard. It

6 Swedish: 'En enad förort kan aldrig besägras.' Available at: <http://megafonen.com/>. Accessed July 30, 2016.

7 Available at: <http://megafonen.com/> Accessed July 30, 2016.

requires learning how to become a public voice. As Emma Dominguez, an activist in Megafonen, puts it:

> We have said that we should train new members and those who want to become more active by learning how to take space on a stage; to go on stage in public debates. It is important to be able to take one's place… [Y]ou grow a lot through being involved in public debates. (Interview with Emma, 21 January 2014)

Counteracting mainstream media discourse, including a stigmatizing reporting of subaltern activism in the daily press, television, etc., is central in learning to talk back. In *Talking back – Thinking Feminist, Thinking Black,* bell hooks (2015: 28) has pointed this out:

> We are rooted in our language, wedded, have our being in the words. Language is also a place of struggle. The oppressed struggle in language to recover ourselves – to rewrite, to reconcile, to renew. Our words are not without meaning. They are an action – a resistance. Language is also a place of struggle.

This extract brings the importance of 'language' to the fore when discussing oppressed peoples' struggles for overcoming stifling conditions of domination. Emma, in the interview excerpted above, stresses the need for the suburban disadvantaged to learn politically effective Swedish and present their own genuine experiences in public space. 'The knowledge they already have, has a thousand times more value than what they can learn in the books', she argues, and continues that '…it is quite important to get people to understand that they possess the knowledge, the right knowledge from the street, the knowledge of living in these places. Seeing this is so valuable.'

The emphasis in creating space for their own empowerment, to give value to their own knowledge and to nurture the confidence of talking in public has to be seen as a fundamental step towards the development of their political subjectivity and to the ways it challenges the lack of space for democratic participation.

A Dialogue that Ended Up as a Monologue

Megafonen succeeded in becoming a public voice through taking part in public debates relating to conditions and the fate of its neighbourhood and through being critical, in a major newspaper, of the conduct of local authorities.

The first major intervention in a public debate took place in 2012, when the young people in Husby were invited by the district administration to present young people's views and ideas on the local urban development program called *Järvalyftet*, which was also their first experience of participation within such an *invited space* for 'citizens dialogue' (Swedish: *medborgardialog*). Järvalyftet was launched in

2007 by the conservative majority in the Stockholm City Hall. The purpose of the program was to stimulate growth of the segregated area Järvafältet and promote its closer integration into the development of the Stockholm city region as a whole.

The area of *Järvafältet* includes several multi-ethnic suburbs of northwestern metropolitan Stockholm (e.g., Husby, Akalla, Tensta, Rinkeby), which were and are characterized by high unemployment, low voter turnout and poor school performance among the young. But the overall goal of development programs for *Järvafältet*, including *Järvalyftet*, to create a regional growth engine and develop a part of Stockholm to which people from the central city would want to move, has not materialized. Unemployment is still twice as high as in the city as a whole. 'Open' unemployment has increased since *Järvalyftet* started in 2007 and school results have deteriorated. As early as 2008 the *Järvalyftet* development program was questioned by local inhabitants and opposition political parties (Social democrats and the left) for its lack of information and its actual lack of democratic participation in the planning process. Its initial focus was on physical restoration. This included demolition of housing originating in the 1960s and the concomitant ejection of inhabitants from their apartments. It led to widespread popular dissatisfaction which in turn fuelled a protest campaign, gathering people from, among other places, Husby, and including Megafonen.

This public manifestation was locally perceived as 'struggles of the area's inhabitants for their right to participate in the planning of the new Järva', writes Rami Al-Khamisi (2015: 159), in a retrospective view under the heading of 'A dialogue that ended up as a monologue'. An actual dialogue with local inhabitants' which followed from 2009 'was a direct consequence of this campaign', he argues (Al-Khamisi, 2015: 159). To restore lost confidence, the Swedish municipal-owned housing company, *Svenska Bostäder,* which was responsible for the physical restoration within the programme, together with the local municipality, initiated meetings with the residents of the Järva area, where the residents' opinions were gathered. The response was tremendous, Al-Khamisi writes. After the first citizens' meeting, Megafonen suggested to the local politicians and civil servants that they ought actively to involve youth in order to offer them genuine opportunities to participate in the planning process and to contribute to it from their particular perspective. Megafonen was then invited by *Svenska Bostäder* to poll opinions among youth. It resulted in the commissioned report *To be young in Husby* (Megafonen 2010) based on a survey among local youth. The proposals provided by this report focused, in particular, on the importance of measures such as investment in education, employment and welfare services rather than physical renewal, which was not considered to be a priority. The report had seemingly no impact on the planning process. This generated, among activists in Megafonen, a lack of trust in the intentions of the citizens' dialogue. Furthermore, commenting on the engagement of 'decision makers', Rami Al-Khamisi (2015: 164) points to a general lack of information, even among local politicians, and criticises the actual decision-making process within Järvalyftet for being 'closed in character and centrally monitored'.

This kind of criticism brought out by Al-Khamisi in 2015 had already been voiced by Megafonen during the initial planning, when it was involved in Järva dialogues. These had actively involved young people, encouraged them to think about, comment on and influence the development of their local community. In their articles in the Swedish daily press commenting on their experience, members of Megafonen argued that the authorities are unwilling to listen to local people. The organisation's initial engagement in the planning process is described by Rami Al-Khamisi and Basar Gerecci (2012) as follows:[8]

> During this period we worked intensively and in close connection with the administrators and politicians responsible for the dialogue. They maintained that Järvalyftet was meant to bring about both small and big dreams, which motivated us to meet as many young people as possible and gather their constructive ideas [...] During the same three-year period *Järvalyftet* spoke in grandiose terms about Järva's future. We as citizens experienced a completely different process. We have seen a development of our areas, with health centres, tax offices, schools, banks and post offices being sold off and disappearing [...] Not even the simplest and most feasible changes, such as increased resources for recreation or regeneration of sports facilities, have been implemented. When we communicated our dissatisfaction to our local political representatives they seemed to be as abject as us, and even they referred to closed decision-making processes in the Stockholm City Council.

Al-Khamisi and Gerecci bring attention to broken promises from politicians which were likely to discourage further dialogue between policy-makers and residents:

> Democratic responsibility has been betrayed in the most nonchalant manner. When the citizenship dialogues were first held in Husby several thousand comments were gathered. It is these dialogues and input from inhabitants that the leaders of the city market proudly as a democratic miracle. That there was good attendance on these days is true. But what is a dialogue worth without action and actual measures? How can democracy be reduced to a numbers game, instead of being an issue of citizens' influence on actual policy? (Al-Khamisi and Gerecci 2012)

Al-Khamisi and Gerecci (2012) conclude that there is a need for the renewal of democratic institutions which could ensure that Järva's citizens are guaranteed their full democratic rights to influence political decisions. This is a necessary path for

8 Authors' translation from Swedish.

people's action in the suburbs of Järvafältet. Basar Gerecci, Rami Al-Khamisi and Amir Kekya (2012) continue in a following article to call attention to 'the failure of democracy' and state that the project, Järvalyftet, 'has since the beginning been dogged by protests against its undemocratic approach'. They stress the problem of segregation in terms of unequal power relationship: 'Segregation is not primarily a matter of geography – it is a question of power, and the gap between those who have and those who do not have it' (Gerecci, Al-Khamisi and Kekya 2012).

The core of the demands from the members of Megafonen, the right to be listened to and to influence local processes, can be seen as a call for 'citizen dialogues' that really deepen local democratic processes. They thus argue for 'creating new democratic structures that ensure local residents' direct influence in Järvalyftet', emphasising at the same time the need for the project to be continuously explained to all residents; something 'which has been completely absent', they conclude (Gerecci, Al-Khamisi and Kekya 2012).

Summarising retrospectively problems of social degradation and democratic deficit in the Järva area, Al-Khamisi states (2015: 167) that social movements, emerging in these disadvantaged areas, 'see it as their responsibility to struggle against urban degradation that takes place as a consequence of adverse political and economic decisions They demand inclusion in the democratic process and raise claims for the social regeneration of the area'.

Thus, while already giving voice to subaltern suburbia before the uprising in 2013, and continuously thereafter focusing on fundamental structural-institutional and democratic problems, Megafonen has consolidated its presence in public debate. This illustrates how invented spaces for influence can come about.

Resisting Gendered Dichotomization and Criminalization

Swedish justice claiming organisations that mediated alternative knowledge of the urban rebellion in Stockholm 2013 – stressing the accumulated impact of structural causality related to social exclusion, discrimination, racism and the stigmatisation of the 'suburb' – provide an example of how new spaces of resistance can provide access to the public domain. Their dissemination of an understanding of social injustice to a wider Swedish community illustrates how an opportunity (invented space) for citizen participation can be engineered within a broader public context and promote a counter-narrative to the dominant/official narrative. Yet, in many instances the mainstream media discourse on the Stockholm riots has accused Megafonen of criminal intent, blaming it for 'not condemning violence' or for outright complicity in violence (Kjöller 2013; Horn 2013). Megafonen members have, in parts of the media coverage, through 'guilt by association' logic, come to be compared to young *men* with a 'deviant culture' and criminal behaviour.

This framing of a defaming and criminalizing media dramaturgy and its stealthy link to the politics of securitization is critically exposed in the following excerpt from an interview with Emma Dominguez. She is a community leader and activist, who in 2013 – the year of the riots – was on the forefront of an extended campaign organised by Megafonen. It contested the sale and privatization of public housing in the Stockholm suburb of Alby, which it argued would have seriously adverse consequences for the most disadvantaged citizens of the neighbourhood:

> And then we started to believe it was a strategy to discredit the movement, because it becomes so much easier to dismiss us as criminals. And it's so simple, you know, to tar this image of us that already exists … here we are demonstrating and its lots of police cars. … [T]he outside[r] …can see that they are demonstrating, a lot of police officers, so, we are criminals, and then … it dismisses all our criticism and … the political act in itself. At the same time it had the opposite effect, I think, because it made us even angrier as well, and made us want to do even more, and refute them as well.' (Interview with Emma Dominquez, 21 January 2014)

Through the campaign *Alby is not for sale,* activists urged (unsuccessfully) the organization of a local referendum regarding the decision of the local municipality to sell 1,300 publicly owned apartments in Alby to a venture capitalist. Like the mixed reception of the Megafonen in the representation of the 2013 riots, the representation of the *Alby is not for Sale* campaign became an important learning experience for the Swedish suburban movement. It demonstrated a need for consolidating an alternative public narrative and it strengthened horizontal and vertical alliances of the subaltern. 'We believed that they didn't listen to the people (although we gathered over 6,500 names for the referendum) because they were mostly youths, mostly working class, and mostly immigrants' comments activist, Nabila Abdul Fattah (2015), one of the leading campaigners in *Alby is not for Sale.* However the fact that this stems from an interview concerning the promotion of Abdul Fattah as master of ceremonies at the Swedish Forum for Human Rights in November 2015 (from which she later abstained), perhaps better than anything, illustrates the true ambivalence with which the suburban movement has been represented, and in consequence that there is indeed a struggle over the politics of truth, throughout the Swedish polity at large, relating to the legitimacy and mission of the suburban movement.

We expound in the following – with respect to an ongoing discussion of Megafonen's positioning itself in relation to 'riots' – that this struggle over the politics of truth needs to be read through an intersectional lens with the aim of recording an intricate crisscrossing of race, class and gender.

One year after the riots different articles are still being published in the Swedish national press and social media referring to what actually happened in Husby and Alby during 2013.

In May 2014 a program on Swedish TV – *Uppdrag Granskning* ('Mission Scrutiny' – further on UG) – discussed the riots in Husby. The program's dramaturgy exposes a scenario of fear; threatening dark shadows of young men moving in the twilight of suburban evening: A vision of threat becomes mediatized. It replicated, in effect, a common sense discourse prevalent in Sweden as well as in the Nordic countries in general, in which stereotypically 'violent' young men and 'passive' young women are juxtaposed (e.g., Ålund 2003; Ålund and Alinia 2011; cf. Honkasalo 2013), thus portraying young women as victims of tradition, while their agency is rendered invisible.

This representation did not, however, pass unchallenged, with the program in question being criticised as an example of speculative and questionable journalism (see for example Dawod 2014; Mansur 2014).

Megafonen and its members themselves had in advance refused to participate in the UG program, but they published on their home page (Megafonen 2013) a statement about different accusations which had featured in the public media.

> Megafonen's role in suburban revolts is twofold. To be in place to monitor so that no more police brutality occurs and to convey a balanced picture of what is happening in our communities. We cannot represent everyone and everything but we try to balance out the distorted media images. The Megaphone did not start fires. We believe that these are not the right methods for long-term change. But we know that it is a response to deficiencies in the community. Unemployment, inadequate schools and structural racism are the underlying causes of what is happening today.[9]

Members of Megafonen (Farshin, de la Cerda and Dominguez 2014) also made an important contribution to an ongoing public debate through their article in the daily *Aftonbladet*, questioning the UG program.

> We in the Megaphone tried to give Husby an alternative voice to frame the story of this revolt that otherwise policemen and politicians have the authority to provide. A year later and the media thirst is apparent again, and SVT's 'Mission Scrutiny' (UG) is no exception. We have chosen to opt out of participation and distance ourselves from the program that was shown. The editor's mission is to uncover maladministration and abuse of power, but for lack of a better UG has instead chosen to reflect a biased view of events, speculating freely over the possible underlying factors and casually point at scapegoats.[10]

9 Authors' translation from Swedish.
10 Authors' translation from Swedish.

They conclude that '[t]he program is clearly trying to set good against evil, ordinary citizens against non-citizens. It is a dramaturgy that we choose not to join.' Consequently, they accused UG of forging a rhetoric that conjures up an essential difference between 'ordinary citizens' and 'criminal youth' and for presenting Husby's frustrated youth as 'non-citizens' in a fashion no less exclusive than the dehumanising social power structure that fanned the fire in the first place'.

A media intervention as in UG contributed intrinsically to a polarized discourse depicting society as split between 'good' and 'bad forces' and to the translation of resistance to the normal order of things in urban politics as a threat to society and by extension, criminal acts and potentially terrorism. A more explicitly gendered version of this narrative was propelled in another media drive, polarising images of the feminine network *StreetGäris* and Megafonen.

The StreetGäris network was formed in Husby in March 2013 through an initiative of a former member of Megafonen who felt the need for a place where young women could meet and support each other. They entered the public arena with a march and a party that they organized to address the riots in Husby. The journalist Lena Sundström (2014) praised the network for its action in terms of eventually providing 'something positive to rally around on Saturday night, to show a different picture of what their suburb is'. They offered viewing of the Champions League Final match outdoors in the community centre. 'The whole evening had been a party with dreams and football'. However, in our interviews with StreetGäris members in 2014[11], they voiced their frustration about being represented as warm-hearted young women in contrast to the, putatively, violent boys belonging to Megafonen.

Members of the network feel that the attention to their manifestation was misused, as the following excerpts from interviews show:

> Vanja: I think that the media have set StreetGäris against Megafonen, in a way that somehow represents us like loving and soft…the media has used it in an unjust way… setting Streetgäris and Megafonen against each other… it becomes a conflict situation that we do not recognize.
>
> Linda: Megafonen is bad and StreetGäris are good … they like to portray Megafonen as insurgents, those who support setting cars on fire.
>
> Maria: And it became like contrasts. Oh, we are on the right side in the society-

---

11 Interview with 3 representatives for StreetGäris, June 11, 2014: René León-Rosales, Sanna Berman and Aleksandra Ålund. *Linda* and *Maria* are anonymised names.

Vanja: And I think that this judgment highlights Streetgäris so that it gives the impression that journalists do not reject all of the suburb's initiative … while we … Streetgäris have been seen as a force to be reckoned with … they might have seen us as harmless … Megafonen has put more political demands on its agenda. We have not got there yet and we do not know if we will get there …. They had become very uncomfortable, and I do not think we were at that point particularly uncomfortable.

Linda: Typically, a typical gendered perspective, like male and female differences. Megafonen is often seen as a bunch of suburban guys that are kind of annoying… (Interview with three members of Streetgäris, 6 November 2014)

The StreetGäris members who were interviewed perceived that they were misused for purposes of dividing suburban actors by opposing images of peaceful-female-loving activities against male violent unrest. At the same time, in a panel discussion about Megafonen held in 2013 at the art museum in Tensta, a neighbourhood close to Husby, two female activists from Megafonen, Lucia Ramírez Tuesta and Melody Farshin, commented on the presence of young women from the organization in the streets of Husby during the 'riots' in the following way:

Lucia: It's very interesting that journalists often mention the guys, me and Valentina were there when it was burning. And then this chronicle talking about angry guys … just the boys' behaviour was published… but then there were many girls who saw it, and all were very, very angry and very upset, because they said that this is not just a boys' thing, we are here just as much as them! We girls are forgotten in this, for it is guys who burn, guys who are angry. We are also angry… We are just as angry about everything that happens.

Melody: If anything, I might add, we have more women than men in Megafonen. I myself am from Husby, raised in Husby, it is clear that it hurts my heart when I see my community on fire. But I fully understand what is happening. I was there from the first evening, and I can say that many members of Megafonen were here every night for a whole week, wandering in our spare time in order to contribute to calming down the area, talking to people and trying to hold a dialogue with people …

We find, in conclusion, that the critical reflections on the effects of mass media dramaturgy which dismiss the 'political' in the Stockholm 2013 rebellion and define the activists as criminals, have in effect strengthened the suburban movement's will to resist and created a platform for the emergence of wider activism. Through 'talking back' as a key strategy for participation in public political discourse, through questioning dominant narratives, they convey a connection between empowering work and political subjectivity.

Options Ahead?

A public event at a conference in Stockholm May 2015, organized by a number of civil society organisations concerning the issue of the crises of democracy illustrates this development. The aim of the conference reads as follows (Rädda Barnen 2015):

> The Swedish social model has grown out of engagement in civil society. Swedish citizens created organizations that have contributed to the development of society, socially, culturally and politically. These popular movements have formed the backbone of Swedish democracy by being the voice of the people in relation to public institutions and private interests. In recent decades, Sweden has undergone major changes. One of the clearest changes is that the composition of the population has changed fundamentally due to the migration of people from other parts of the world. The traditional Swedish civil society has in far too small an extent managed to incorporate this part of the population in the democratic process. It weakens civil society and the Swedish democracy. This we want to change.[12]

Established civil society organizations like Save the Children, The workers' educational association (ABF), People's Community Centres and Parks (*Folkets hus och parker*), the association for study promotion (*Studiefrämjandet*), Hassela Helpline (*Hasselarörelsen*) and The National Council of Swedish Youth Organisations (LSU), which sponsored the conference, had earlier organized a network meeting for what was described as the 'new movements from suburbia' such as Megafonen, Pantrarna, Movement Street Voice and Face (*Gatans röst och ansikte*) and others. The idea was to bring these groups together so that activists could exchange experiences and knowledge. According to the advertisement, the purpose of these meetings was to 'create pathways into our organizations for those who are outside, and we want to support the emergence of new organizations that can meet new needs of our society.' Obviously, these 'new needs' are rooted in the democratic deficit, the problem of representation of new movements and their voices in different contexts of society, both within civil society organizations and beyond.

In this gathering the issue of 'voice' was a dominant theme focused on representation and identity. Having a 'voice' is pivotal for strategies of representation (Hall 1992) – in established civil society organisations, in cultural politics and social practices, as expressions of citizen participation – through deliberative engagement in local and national political and institutional contexts.

---

12 See <http://www.mynewsdesk.com/se/radda_barnen/documents/demokratins-kris-aer-vaar-vad-goer-vi-aat-den-45358> (Accessed March 5, 2016). Authors' translation from Swedish.

The aforesaid conference on the crisis of democracy appears to demonstrate new possibilities for collaboration already in the making. Members of Megafonen are presently active or employed within several established civil society organisations, networking with each other and working strategically on promoting education and democracy, locally and nationally. This involvement can result in renewing the ideological scope of, what was once known as, civil society. The one time cradle of Swedish democracy which today has become rather 'tame' with and professionalized institutions bearing out the truth of Mary Kaldor's argument that '[b]ecoming 'tamed' means that you become the respectable opposition—the partner in negotiations' (Kaldor 2003: 589). Nevertheless, new movements of suburbia might become – through this cooperation – the springboard for civil society's renewal in the spreading of new democratic visions through practice.

Reimagining Democracy from the Margins

Suburban areas of large Swedish cities have been hit by growing poverty, long-term unemployment, stigmatization, the deterioration of the quality of schools but also by securitization and police surveillance. These processes have been driving forces for youth activism as justice movements, and their perception of the need to counteract dominant political, public and mass media discourses. Without perceived real opportunities for influencing decision making in local urban development, new forms of activism have developed through *invented spaces,* in terms of public manifestations, knowledge production through local study groups, mass media interventions, and active promotion of a critical voice in social media, including their own homepages.

Taking their place as a critical voice within the public space has become a constitutive element in the making of a political subjectivity. It has come about through learning processes within the movement related to often abortive campaigns and engagements in development 'partnerships' and 'dialogues', seen with hindsight as deluding mirages. The criminalizing representation of Ahmed Ibrahim Ali ignited the push to found the organization. Since then Megafonen has continuously challenged the mass media's role in establishing 'truths' in the mainstream public narrative and thus creating a space for their own voices.

We have demonstrated how gendering the riots and a polarization of *good* and *bad* forces shape the dominant narrative's reductionist perspective on what is at stake. We have discussed the case of *Järvalyftet* to show how young people's efforts springing from the urban fringe represent a battle for democracy. Discussing the lack of democratic influence within invited spaces for citizenship participation in local governance we have highlighted the importance of invented spaces and opportunities as well as challenges concerning the reception of contentious acts of citizenship in the wider public domain. Transforming personal experiences of oppression into awareness and collective practices has taken place through internal learning processes and the emergence of expanding networks across and beyond suburbia aimed at anchoring young subaltern voices in the wider public, articulating need for deepening democracy and social justice.

And it is here that new forms of activist citizenship are finding sources for advancing their own political subjectivity and possibly contribute to a renewal of democracy.

Let us, against this background, finally reflect on possible roads ahead which can help make sense of post-riot development in the short history of the new Swedish urban justice organisations and movements. The overall question that stands out is whether these new spaces of activism will develop a substantial version of institutionalised, Swedish 'popular movements' (*folkrörelser*) and become one facet among others in a civil society operating entirely within the confines of an authorised framework of governance?

We see today an increasing representation of formerly vilified youthful rebels across established and institutionalised civil society organisations and NGOs, and in influential positions in public services. Many embark on careers within education and the media. Is the fact that many contentious activists have lately been employed by established civil society organizations and municipalities a threat or an opportunity for the new suburban movement?

One scenario would be that the vitality of the movement will be weakened, since many of members of Megafonen and similar organisations are now engaged in more established organizations. This may lead to a strengthening of these organizations and their ability to include and work with the local communities in Sweden's most marginalized urban areas. However, it could at the same time mean that the organizations like Megafonen will in the long run fade out if they do not manage constantly to renew their leadership or to build up organizations that can manage to finance some of their more vital functions.

Another scenario is related to what Castells (1996: 498) depicted as a 'counter power of places'. Such a vision would demand an extension of urban justice activism beyond local 'place struggles' to develop a wider identity capable of transcending the local. It could, Castells contends, take place through the formation of a network among activists trans-locally and transnationally. And there are indeed initiatives for international networking, as well as identification and solidarity, beyond the local, with sister movements across the world. As it was formulated in the recently released essay *Kreol* (Tasin and Landehag 2015: 36), which discussed the issue of identity formation and hybridization among suburban youth: 'We should make contact with urban movements in Paris, London and Berlin ...and organize together – we share the same struggle'.

These scenarios face us with challenges in terms of theory and empirical research. What is in the making? Co-optation and disciplinary governmentality? Do we see a new transformative strategy in the making as activists forge networks and new alliances across a broader civil society? Will they, through transcending the corridors of power, make contradictions, conflicts and hidden alternatives visible?

Viewed from a present – marked by networking, engagement in established leftist think tanks and media and the building of alliances across civil society and the state – we can conclude that Megafonen is not an isolated case. It has become a role model for sister organizations that see themselves as Sweden's new people's movements – heirs to the contentious and transformative people's movements that once struggled for the establishment of the Swedish welfare state. We see a new movement contesting urban degradation and reclaiming Sweden in terms of an inclusive citizenship, social welfare and democracy. Through their engagement in education and consciousness-raising among youth they are re-connecting with the original meaning of Swedish folk-movements as schools of democracy. Thus, we see the suburban movement as carrying seeds of democratic renewal that has sprouted in many versions. It presents a vision of society and a version of activist citizenship which may in the long run play an important part in institutional transformation, deepening democracy and the work of truly reimagineering Sweden.

Acknowledgement of Funding

The work has taken place within a collaboration of research projects funded by the Swedish research councils: Vetenskapsrådet [Grant number 2013-7277-102936-14], Vetenskapsrådet [Grant number 721-2013-885] and FORMAS [Grant number 250-2013-1547].

References

Abdul Fattah, N. 2015. 'Introducing the Master of Ceremonies at the Swedish Forum for Human Rights.' Interview in *Human Rights Events,* July 30, 2015. Accessed March 5, 2016. <http://rwi.lu.se>

Al-Khamisi, R. 2015. 'Dialogen som blev en monolog.' In Lindholm, Theresa, Sandra Oliveira e Costa and Sofia Wiberg (eds.) *Medborgardialog – demokrati eller dekoration*? Arkus skrift no 72. Klippan: Ljungbergs tryckeri, 159–169.

Al-Khamisi, R. and Gerecci, B. 2012. 'Järvas medborgare måste få påverka.' *Dagens Nyheter,* March 31. Accessed March 5, 2016. <http://www.dn.se/debatt/stockholmsdebatt/jarvas-medborgare-maste-fa-paverka/>

Ålund, A. 2003. 'Social subordination, cultural resistance, transethnic identities.' In Brochmann, Grete (ed.) *The Multicultural Challenge, Volume 22.* Oxford: JAI, Elsevier Science Ltd, 245–261.

Ålund A. 2014. 'Politics of Belonging: A Narrative on Activism in Sweden.' *NORA* 22/4, 330–337.

Ålund, A. and Alinia, M. 2011. 'I skuggan av etno-kulturella stereotypier; Perspektiv på forskning om genus, jämställdhet och etniska relationer i Sverige.' *Sociologisk forskning* 2, 43–64.

Bredström, A. 2002. 'Maskulinitet och kamp om nationella arenor: reflektioner kring bilden av "invandrarkillar"' i svenska media.' In de los Reyes, Paulina, Irene Molina and Diana Mulinari (eds.) *Maktens (o)lika förklädnader: kön, klass & etnicitet i det postkoloniala Sverige: en festskrift till Wuokko Knocke.* Atlas, 182–206.

Brune, Y. 2004. 'Nyheter från gränsen – Tre studier i journalistik om 'invandrare', flyktingar och rasistiskt våld.' PhD diss., Department of Journalism, Media and Communication, University of Gothenburg.

Butler, J. 1993. *Bodies That Matter.* New York/London: Routledge.

Castells, M. 1996. 'The reconstruction of social meaning in the space of Flows.' In LeGates, Richard T. and Frederic Stout (eds.). *The City Reader.* London: Routledge, 493–499.

Castells, M. 2012. *Networks of Outrage and Hope: Social Movements in the Age of the Internet.* Cambridge: Polity.

Choundry, A. and Kapoor, D. (eds.) 2010. *Learning from the Ground Up.* New York: Palgrave Macmillan.

Dawod, N. 2014. 'De får skulden för upploppen i Husby.' *Aftonbladet,* May 14. Accessed March 5, 2016. <http://www.aftonbladet.se>

Dikeç, M. 2007. *Badlands of the Republic: Space, Politics and Urban Policy.* Wiley-Blackwell.

Farshin, M., De La Cerda, M. and Dominguez, E. 2014. 'Husbys unga är också vanliga medborgare.' *Aftonbladet,* May 14. Accessed March 5, 2016. <http://www.aftonbladet.se>

Foucault, M. 1983. 'The Subject and Power'. In Dreyfus, Hubert L. and Paul Rabinow (eds.) *Michel Foucault: Beyond Structuralism and Hermeneutics.* 2nd edition. Chicago: The University of Chicago Press, 208–226.

Gerecci, B., Al-Khamisi, R. and Kekya, A. 2012. 'Järvalyftet är ingen bra förebild.' *Svenska Dagbladet,* May 4. Accessed March 5, 2016. <http://www.svd.se/jarvalyftet-ar-ingen-bra-forebild>

Gordon, H. R. and. Taft, J. K. 2011. 'Rethinking Youth Political Socialization: Teenage Activists Talk Back.' *Youth & Society* 2011/43, 1499–1527.

Gramsci, A. 1997. *Selections from the Prison Notebooks: Antonio Gramsci.* Edited by Quinton Hoare and Geoffrey Nowell Smith. New York: International Publishers.

Grünenberg, R. 2012. 'What is a Democrat? An Attempt to Define the Democratic Personality.' *Fikrun wa Fann.* Accessed March 5, 2016. <http://www.goethe.de>

Hall, S. 1992. 'New ethnicities.' In James, Donald and Ali Rattansi (eds.) '*Race*', *Culture and Difference.* London: Sage, 252–260.

Harvey, D. 2005. *A brief history of Neoliberalism.* New York: Oxford University Press.

Honkasalo, V. 2013. 'Save the Girls! Gender Equality and Multiculturalism in Finnish Youth Work Contexts.' *Girlhood Studies* 6/2, 47–64.

hooks, b. 2015 [1989]. *Talking back: Thinking Feminist Thinking black.* New York: Routledge.

Horn, J. 2013. 'Dra in skattebidragen till Megafonen.' *Aftonbladet,* May 23. Accessed March 5, 2016. <http://www.aftonbladet.se/debatt/article16828442.ab>

Isin, E. F. 2008. 'Theorizing acts of citizenship.' In Isin, Engin F. and Greg M. Nielsen (eds.) *Acts of Citizenship.* London & New York: Zed Books, 15–43.

Isin, E. F. 2009. 'Citizenship in flux: The figure of the activist citizen.' *Subjectivity* 29, 367–388.

Kaldor, M. 2003. 'The idea of global civil society'. *International Affairs* 79/3, 583–593.

Kjöller, H. 2013. 'Megafon med oklar röst.' *Dagens Nyheter,* June 4. Accessed March 5, 2016.

Kosnick, K. 2010. 'Migrant Publics: Mass Media and Stranger-Relationality in Urban Space.' *Revue Européene des Migrations Internationales* 26/1, 37–55.

Lundström, C. 2007. *Svenska latinas – Ras, klass och kön i svenskhetens geografi.* PhD thesis. Uppsala University. Göteborg/Stockholm: Makadam Förlag.

Mackay, F. 2011. 'A movement of their own: voices of young feminist activists in the London Feminist Network.' *Interface: a journal for and about social movements* 3/2, 152–179.

Mansouri, F. and Mikola, M. 2014. 'Crossing Boundaries: Acts of Citizenship among Migrant Youth in Melbourne.' *Social Inclusion* 2/2, 28–37.

Mansur, T. 2014. 'Uppdrag Granskning svartmålar Megafonen.' *Dagens Arena,* May 15. Accessed March 5, 2016. <http://www.dagensarena.se>

Megafonen 2010. 'Att vara ung i Husby – Åsikter och synpunkter från 18–25 åringar.' Accessed March 5, 2016. <http://jarvadialogen.episerverhosting.com>

Megafonen 2013. 'Uttalande om Megafonens roll under förortsrevolterna.' Accessed March 5, 2016. <http://megafonen.com/uttalande-om-megafonens-roll-under-forortsrevolterna/>

Megafonen 2015. 'Megafonens program.' *Megafonen.* Accessed March 5, 2016. <http://megafonen.com/om/politiskt-program/>

Miraftab, F. 2004. 'Invited and Invented Spaces of Participation: Neoliberal Citizenship and Feminists' Expanded Notion of Politics.' *Wagadu* 1, 1–7.

Östh, J., Clark, A.V.W. and Malmberg, B. 2015. 'Measuring the Scale of Segregation Using K-nearest Neighbor Aggregates.' *Geographical Analysis* 47, 34–49.

Rosales, R. L. 2010. *Vid framtidens hitersta gräns – om maskulina elevpositioner i en multietnisk skola.* PhD thesis. Södertörns University/Stockholms University. Tumba: Mångkulturellt Centrum.

Rädda Barnen 2015. *Demokratins kris är vår – Vad gör vi åt den?* Accessed March 5, 2016. <http://www.mynewsdesk.com/se/radda_barnen/documents/demokratins-kris-aer-vaar-vad-goer-vi-aat-den-45358>

Schierup, C.-U. and Ålund, A. 2011. 'The End of Swedish Exceptionalism? Citizenship, neo-liberalism and politics of exclusion.' *Race and Class* 53/1, 45–64.

Sernhede, O. and Söderman, J. 2013. 'Kur mot kravaller.' *Sydsvenskan,* May 24. Accessed March 5, 2016. <www.sydsvenskan.se>

Shaull, R. 2005. 'Foreword.' In Freire, Paulo (ed.) *Pedagogy of the Oppressed. 30th anniversary edition.* Translated by Myra Bergman. New York and London: Ramos, 29–35.

Socialstyrelsen 2010. *Social rapport 2010.* Stockholm: Socialstyrelsen.

Sundström, L. 2014. 'Husbykravallerna från fem perspektiv.' *DN,* May 18. Accessed March 5, 2016. <http://www.dn.se>

Tahvilzadeh, N. 2013. 'Förortsrörelsen: antirasistisk klasskamp som platskamp.' *Mana,* February 3. Accessed March 5, 2016. <http://tidskriftenmana.se>

Tasin, L. and Landehag. A. 2015. *Kreol: Ett spoke går runt i orten.* Stockholm: Arena idé.

Thomson, R., Holland, J., McGrellis, S., Bell, R., Henderson, S. and Sharpe, S. 2004. 'Inventing adulthoods: a Biographical approach to understanding youth citizenship.' *The Sociological Review* 52, 218–239.

Political and Social Change

Edited by Martin Bak Jørgensen and Óscar García Agustín

Volume 1 Martin Bak Jørgensen / Óscar García Agustín (eds.): Politics of Dissent. 2015.

Volume 2 Laura Bang Lindegaard: Congestion. Rationalising Automobility in the Face of Climate Change. 2015.

Volume 3 Ben Dorfman (ed.): Dissent! Refracted. Histories, Aesthetics and Cultures of Dissent. 2016.

Volume 4 Aleksandra Ålund / Carl-Ulrik Schierup / Anders Neergaard (eds.): Reimagineering the Nation. Essays on Twenty-First-Century Sweden. 2017.

www.peterlang.com

www.ingramcontent.com/pod-product-compliance
Ingram Content Group UK Ltd.
Pitfield, Milton Keynes, MK11 3LW, UK
UKHW020032121026
15625UKWH00043B/324